The United States and Iraq Since 1990

The United States and Iraq Since 1990

A Brief History with Documents

Edited by Robert K. Brigham

A John Wiley & Sons, Ltd., Publication

This edition first published 2014
Editorial material and organization © 2014 Robert K. Brigham

Blackwell Publishing was acquired by John Wiley & Sons in February 2007.
Blackwell's publishing program has been merged with Wiley's global Scientific,
Technical, and Medical business to form Wiley-Blackwell.

Registered Office
John Wiley & Sons Ltd, The Atrium, Southern Gate, Chichester, West Sussex,
PO19 8SQ, UK

Editorial Offices
350 Main Street, Malden, MA 02148-5020, USA
9600 Garsington Road, Oxford, OX4 2DQ, UK
The Atrium, Southern Gate, Chichester, West Sussex, PO19 8SQ, UK

For details of our global editorial offices, for customer services, and for
information about how to apply for permission to reuse the copyright material in
this book please see our website at www.wiley.com/wiley-blackwell.

The right of Robert K. Brigham to be identified as the author of the editorial
material in this work has been asserted in accordance with the UK Copyright,
Designs and Patents Act 1988.

Wiley also publishes its books in a variety of electronic formats. Some content
that appears in print may not be available in electronic books.

Designations used by companies to distinguish their products are often claimed as
trademarks. All brand names and product names used in this book are trade
names, service marks, trademarks or registered trademarks of their respective
owners. The publisher is not associated with any product or vendor mentioned in
this book. This publication is designed to provide accurate and authoritative
information in regard to the subject matter covered. It is sold on the
understanding that the publisher is not engaged in rendering professional services.
If professional advice or other expert assistance is required, the services of a
competent professional should be sought.

Library of Congress Cataloging-in-Publication Data is available for this title
HB: 9781405198981
PB: 9781405198998

A catalogue record for this book is available from the British Library.

Cover image: U.S. Army 101st Airborne division soldiers walk past dust thrown
up by a helicopter. Near Mosul, Iraq © Misha Japaridze / AP / Press Association
Images
Cover design by Simon Levy

Set in 10/12 pt Sabon by Toppan Best-set Premedia Limited
Printed in Singapore by Ho Printing Singapore Pte Ltd

1 2014

To the memory of my sister

Contents

Preface

"My belief is we will, in fact, be greeted as liberators," Vice President Dick Cheney told a nationwide television audience shortly before the March 2003 U.S. invasion of Iraq. How could the vice president have been so wrong? American forces were bogged down in Iraq for another eight years, and after the U.S. troop withdrawal in December 2011, Iraq seemed no closer to national political reconciliation. The meaning and the history of the American wars for Iraq, therefore, remain as perplexing and confusing as they were when Cheney spoke those words so long ago. Why did the United States make such a vast commitment to a country that it had virtually ignored for so long? What did the United States hope to accomplish in its nearly two decades of war and hostilities in Iraq? Why, despite an enormous investment in Iraq, did the United States fail to transform the country? What have been the consequences of America's involvement in Iraq? This book seeks to place American intervention in Iraq in historical perspective and to answer these vital questions.

This book is the first study of American foreign policy toward Iraq that weaves national security documents and analysis of them into a single, comprehensive narrative. It traces the long and complicated history of U.S. policy toward Iraq from the Eisenhower administration's support for King Faisal's conservative regime in the 1950s to the Obama administration's ongoing commitment to the American-backed al-Maliki government in Baghdad today. One of the key themes of this book is the inability of U.S. policymakers to alter Iraqi outlook and policies despite an enormous American commitment to changing Iraq. It helps explain why, in the face of such failures, U.S. officials continued to overstate their potential influence in Iraq. Another major theme of this book is the lack of a political corollary to America's overwhelming military power in Iraq. Military intervention did not fundamentally shape the character and the nature of the Iraqi government and its actions, despite some claims to the contrary. The dogged pursuit of U.S.

policy objectives in Iraq came at an enormous price to ordinary Iraqis, as did the destructive policies of Saddam Hussein. Therefore, the human rights landscape in Iraq provides an overall backdrop to the story being told in this book, as does the public response to nearly two decades of war.

This book provides students, scholars, and general readers with a concise overview of America's wars for Iraq, using a broad range of U.S. and Iraqi government documents, UN reports, and public statements. These documents are included at the end of each chapter along with a useful timeline, suggestions for further readings, and some questions to consider. This format was developed specifically with the classroom in mind, and I have used my thirty years of college teaching experience to design a text that students and faculty will find balanced and thought-provoking. I hope that graduate students and scholars will also find this concise history useful as they seek answers to complicated problems concerning U.S. foreign policy. Studying U.S. policy toward Iraq has never been easy, for it was a complicated relationship that underwent many phases and transformations. But if the task of coming to terms with America's wars for Iraq is difficult, it is also essential. Like the Vietnam War, the wars for Iraq have raised important issues, such as the credibility of American leaders, their ability to understand a distant society and culture, the impact of public opinion on the formulation and implementation of U.S. foreign policy, the role of the United Nations in international relations, the role of human rights in the modern world, and the limits of American power.

The narrative of the wars for Iraq presented here does not ignore the role of U.S. policymakers and the ways in which the end of the Cold War and the global war on terror shaped dimensions of the conflict. There is considerable focus on international relations, the conduct of diplomacy, and the application of U.S. military power. I have attempted to consider American decision-making in the broader context of the nation's global outlook and policies. But there is also an emphasis on and appreciation of the impact of U.S. policy on the government in Baghdad and the stresses and strains of this alliance on ordinary Iraqis. The focus here is on high policy, but also on the very real human suffering that took place over two decades of war. I wrote this book because I perceived that there was a growing gap between the official narrative of success in Iraq and what the documents revealed. I have tried to treat U.S. policy toward Iraq with as much detachment as possible, allowing the documents to form the core of the narrative. Democrats and Republicans in Washington shared the burden of decision-making and neither party was particularly insightful. Four successive U.S. presidential administrations tried to develop policies to contain the government in Baghdad and change the political landscape in Iraq. None were particularly successful. This is the story of that effort told from the documentary evidence available today.

Acknowledgments

In writing this book I have incurred many debts, both personal and intellectual. First on any list must be my outstanding research assistants Debbie Sharnak, Selby Brown, Joy Backer, Sarah Craig, Meg Mielke, Hannah VanDemark, and Tom Enering. Many friends and colleagues gave generously of their time and expertise. Richard Aldous, Mark Bradley, Mel Leffler, Tony Badger, Andrew Preston, Jeremi Suri, Kyle Longley, Ann Heiss, Liz Borgwardt, Steven Jay Bourke, Lien-Hang Nguyen, Fred Logevall, Jim Hershberg, Andy Rotter, Richard Immerman, David Ryan, Tom Paterson, Robert McMahon, Scott Lucas, Beven Sewell, Garry Clifford, Michael Donoghue, Kenneth Hagan, and Michaela Hoenicke Moore offered invaluable suggestions. Colonels Gian Gentile and Greg Daddis of West Point provided sound advice and friendship, as did Major Jason Warren. George C. Herring, Frank Costigliola, and Owen S. Ireland continue to be mentors and friends. Marilyn Young, Lloyd Gardner, and Charles Neu were supportive and encouraging every step of the way.

I owe thanks to Cappy Hill, Jon Chenette, Cathy Baer, and John Mihaly at Vassar College, and to Bennett Boskey for his generous support of Vassar and me. Melissa Lape Naitza, Veronica Peccia, and Patricia Maio were especially helpful. My friends and colleagues at University College Dublin, my home away from Vassar, were very supportive. I especially want to thank Maurice Bric, Liam Kennedy, Sandra Scanlon, Kate Breslin, and Catherine Carey.

I am grateful to my colleagues in the History Department at Vassar College, who have provided such a supportive environment. Special thanks to Jim Merrell, Leslie Offutt, Miriam Cohen, Hiraku Shimoda, Miki Pohl, Julie Hughes, Paulina Bren, Michael Hanagan, Maria Hoehn, Nancy Bisaha, Quincy Mills, Rebecca Edwards, Lydia Murdoch, Josh Schreier, Mita Choudhury, Ismail Rashid, Tony Wohl, David Schalk, and Michelle Whalen. Steve Rock and Andy Davison of Vassar read various drafts of the manuscript and offered solid criticisms and valuable suggestions. Tom Blanton, Malcolm Byrne, and Robert Wampler at the National Security Archives were extremely helpful.

This book has gained much from the feedback of audiences at Duke University, Cambridge University, the University of Iowa, University College Cork, Birmingham University, New York University, Rutgers University, University College Dublin, and the University of Wisconsin. My research and writing were aided by a Fulbright year at University College Dublin as the Mary Ball Washington Professor of American History.

I am especially indebted to Peter Coveney and Deirdre Ilkson at Wiley-Blackwell for their vision and faith in me. Their equanimity and good humor have sustained me in many ways. Their good sense and keen minds have made this a better book.

From the beginning to the end of this project, my wife, Monica Church, and our daughter Taylor, have shared with me its frustrations and satisfactions. I thank them for their patience.

Dramatis Personae

General John Abizaid, commander, U.S. Central Command, July 2003–March 2007.

Mahmoud Abouhalima, member of terrorist cell that carried out the 1993 bombing of the World Trade Center in New York.

Ahmed Ajaj, member of terrorist cell that carried out the 1993 bombing of the World Trade Center in New York.

Madeleine Albright, U.S. ambassador to the United Nations, January 1993–January 1997; U.S. secretary of state for Bill Clinton, January 1997–January 2001.

Ali A. Allawi, Iraq's minister of trade and finance, 2003–2006.

Ayad Allawi, president of the Governing Council of Iraq, 2003; interim prime minister of Iraq, 2004–2005; head of Iraqiya political bloc in national Iraqi government, 2010–present.

Kofi Annan, secretary general of the United Nations, January 1997–December 2006.

Mohammed Atta, September 11 terrorist.

Nidal Ayyad, member of terrorist cell that carried out the 1993 bombing of the World Trade Center in New York.

Tariq Aziz, Iraq's foreign minister, 1983–1991.

James Baker, chief of staff for President Ronald Reagan, 1981–1985; secretary of the treasury for Ronald Reagan, 1985–1988; secretary of state for President George H.W. Bush, 1989–1992; chief of staff for President George H.W. Bush, 1992–1993.

Fayez Banihammad, September 11 terrorist.

Farzad Bazoft, Iranian-born journalist executed in Iraq on March 15, 1990.

Joseph Biden, former U.S. senator (D-Delaware) and vice president of the United States, January 2009–present.

Osama bin Laden, founder of al-Qaeda, killed in Pakistan, May 2, 2011.

Tony Blair, British prime minister, May 1997–June 2007.

Hans Blix, director of the United Nations Monitoring, Verification, and Inspection Commission, March 2000–June 2003.

L. Paul Bremer, administrator of the Coalition Provisional Authority, May 2003–June 2004.

George H.W. Bush, president of the United States, January 1989–January 1993.

George W. Bush, president of the United States, January 2001–January 2009.

Richard Butler, director of the United Nations Special Commission on Iraq, 1997–1999.

General George Casey, U.S. commander, coalition ground forces in Iraq, June 2004–February 2007.

Richard Cheney, secretary of defense for President George H.W. Bush, January 1989–January 1993, and vice president of the United States under George W. Bush, January 2001–January 2009.

Richard Clarke, chairman of the Counter-Terrorism Study Group, 1992–2003.

Bill Clinton, president of the United States, January 1993–January 2001.

Hillary Clinton, former U.S. senator (D-New York) and U.S. secretary of state, January 2009–December 2012.

General James Conway, U.S. commanding general of the 1st Marine Division and the I Marine Expeditionary Force, taking part in 2003 invasion of Iraq and the First Battle of Fallujah.

Conrad Crane, director of the U.S. Army Military History Institute and coordinator of the FM 3–24 field manual on counterinsurgency.

Ryan Crocker, U.S. ambassador to Iraq, 2007–2009, and U.S. ambassador to Afghanistan, 2011–present.

Charles Duelfer, deputy executive chairman of the United Nations Special Commission on Iraq, 1993–2000, and deputy head of the United Nations weapons inspection team, 2003–January 23, 2005.

Rolf Ekeus, director of the United Nations Special Commission on Iraq, 1991–1997.

Peter Feaver, U.S. special advisor for strategic planning and institutional reform, National Security Council, 2005–2007.

General Tommy Franks, commander, U.S. Central Command, July 2000–July 2003.

General Jay Garner, U.S. director of the Office for Reconstruction and Humanitarian Assistance for Iraq, 2003.

Robert Gates, U.S. secretary of defense, 2006–2011.

Colonel Gian Gentile, West Point history professor and former executive officer of combat brigade in Tikrit, Iraq, 2003, and commander, RSTA Squadron, 8–10 Cavalry, in Iraq in 2006.

Ahmed al-Ghmadi, September 11 terrorist.

Hamza al-Ghmadi, September 11 terrorist.

Saeed al-Ghmadi, September 11 terrorist.

April Glaspie, U.S. ambassador to Iraq, 1988–1990.

Mikhail Gorbachev, general secretary of the Communist Party of the Soviet Union, 1985–1991.

Richard Haass, director, U.S. State Department Policy Planning Staff, 2001–2003.

Hani Hanjour, September 11 terrorist.

Nawaf al-Hazmi, September 11 terrorist.

Salem al-Hazmi, September 11 terrorist.

Ahmad al-Haznawi, September 11 terrorist.

Saddam Hussein, fifth president of Iraq, 1979–2003, executed on December 30, 2006.

Eyad Ismoil, member of terrorist cell that carried out the 1993 bombing of the World Trade Center in New York.

Ibrahim Jaafri, former Iraqi prime minister.

Ziad Jarrah, September 11 terrorist.

Fred Kagan, senior fellow at the American Enterprise Institute and an architect of the surge.

Hussein Kamel, Iraq's minister of military industries, 1987–1995.

General Jack Keane, retired U.S. Army general and an architect of the surge.

John Kerry, U.S. senator (D-Massachusetts) and 2004 U.S. presidential candidate.

General Mark Kimmitt, U.S. deputy director for operations, Combined Joint Task Force-7, Iraq, 2003–2004.

Harold Koh, assistant secretary of state for democracy, human rights, and labor, 1998–2001, and legal advisor to the U.S. State Department, 2009–present.

Anthony Lake, U.S. national security advisor for President Bill Clinton, 1993–1997.

John McCain, U.S. senator (R-Arizona) and presidential candidate in 2008.

General Stanley McChrystal, U.S. commander, Joint Special Operations Command, 2003–2008.

Nouri al-Maliki, prime minister of Iraq, May 2006–present.

Khalid al-Mihdhar, September 11 terrorist.

Khalid Shaikh Mohammed, member of al-Qaeda and principal architect of the 9/11 attacks.

Majed Moqed, September 11 terrorist.

Robert Mueller, U.S. director of the Federal Bureau of Investigation, 2001–present.

Ahmed al-Nami, September 11 terrorist.

John Negroponte, U.S. ambassador to the United Nations, 2001–2004; U.S. ambassador to Iraq, 2004–2005; U.S. director of national intelligence for President George W. Bush, 2005–2007; U.S. deputy secretary of state for President George W. Bush, 2007–2009.

Barack Obama, former U.S. senator (D-Illinois) and president of the United States, January 2009–present.

General Ray Odierno, U.S. commander, coalition ground forces in Iraq, 2008–2010, and U.S. Army chief of staff, 2010–present.

Abdulaziz al-Omari, September 11 terrorist.

Leon Panetta, U.S. secretary of defense for president Barack Obama, July 2011–present.

Nancy Pelosi, Speaker of the U.S. House of Representatives, 2007–2010, and member of Congress (D-California), 1987–present.

General David Petraeus, U.S. commander, coalition ground forces in Iraq, 2007–2008; commander, U.S. Central Command, 2008–2010; commander, U.S. forces in Afghanistan, 2010–2011; director, U.S. Central Intelligence Agency, September 2011–November 2012.

Thomas Pickering, U.S. ambassador to Israel, 1985–1988; U.S. ambassador to the United Nations, 1989–1992.

General Colin Powell, U.S. national security advisor for President Ronald Reagan, 1987–1989; chairman of the Joint Chiefs of Staff for Presidents George H.W. Bush and Bill Clinton, 1989–1993; secretary of state for President George W. Bush, 2001–2005.

Samantha Power, former professor, Kennedy School of Government, Harvard University, and U.S. senior director for multilateral affairs and human rights, U.S. National Security Council, January 2009–present.

Ronald Reagan, president of the United States, January 1981–January 1989.

Harry Reid, U.S. senator (D-Nevada) and Senate majority leader.

Condoleezza Rice, U.S. national security advisor, January 2001–January 2005, and secretary of state, January 2005–January 2009, both for President George W. Bush.

Donald Rumsfeld, U.S. secretary of defense for President George W. Bush, January 2001–December 2008.

Muqtada al-Sadr, Shiite cleric and head of the Mahdi Army.

Mohammed Salameh, terrorist bomber in 1993 attack on World Trade Center, New York.

Jassim Mohammed Saleh, commander of the Iraqi army under Saddam Hussein, in charge of city of Fallujah following first battle.

Wafiq al-Samarrai, Iraq's director of military intelligence, 1991–1994.

General Ricardo Sanchez, U.S. commander, coalition ground forces in Iraq, June 2003–June 2004.

General Norman Schwarzkopf, commander of the U.S. Central Command, 1988–1991.

Brent Scowcroft, U.S. national security advisor for President Gerald R. Ford, November 1975–January 1997, and for President George H.W. Bush, January 1989–January 1993.

Marwan al-Shehhi, September 11 terrorist.

Mohand al-Shehri, September 11 terrorist.

Wail al-Shehri, September 11 terrorist.

Waleed al-Shehri, September 11 terrorist.

General Eric Shinseki, U.S. Army chief of staff, 1999–2003.

Satam al-Suqami, September 11 terrorist.

Jalal Talabani, Kurdish political leader and former president of Iraq.

Margaret Thatcher, British prime minister, May 1979–November 1990.

Max van der Stoel, special rapporteur for the United Nations Commission on Human Rights, 1991–2001.

John Warner, former U.S. senator from Virginia.

Paul Wolfowitz, U.S. deputy secretary of defense, January 2001–June 2005.

James Woolsey, U.S. director of the Central Intelligence Agency, 1993–1995.

John Yoo, U.S. deputy assistant attorney general in the Office of Legal Counsel at the U.S. Justice Department, 2001–2003.

Ramzi Yousef, member of terrorist cell that carried out the 1993 bombing of the World Trade Center in New York.

Abu Musab Zarqawi, Jordanian member of al-Qaeda.

Philip Zelikow, director of the 9/11 Commission and counselor of the U.S. Department of State, 2005–2007.

General Anthony Zinni, deputy commander, U.S. Central Command, 1996–1997; commander, U.S. Central Command, 1997–2000.

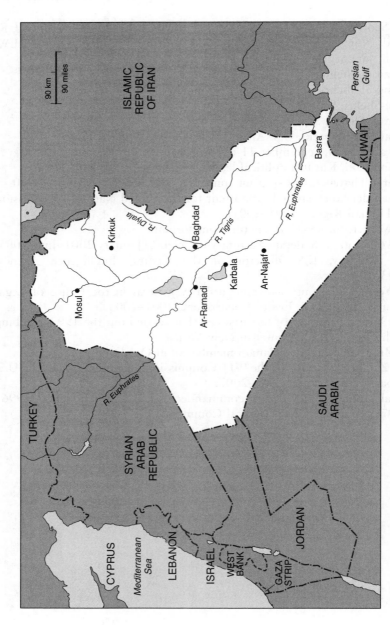

Map 1 Iraq and its six contiguous neighbors

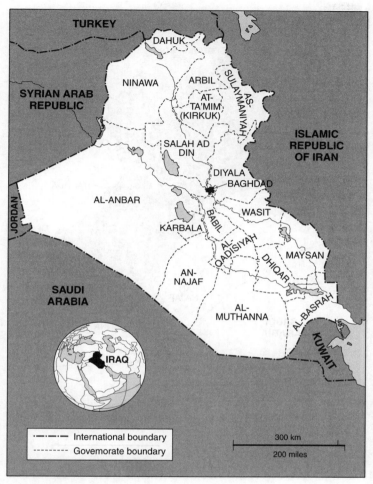

Map 2 Iraq's eighteen provinces

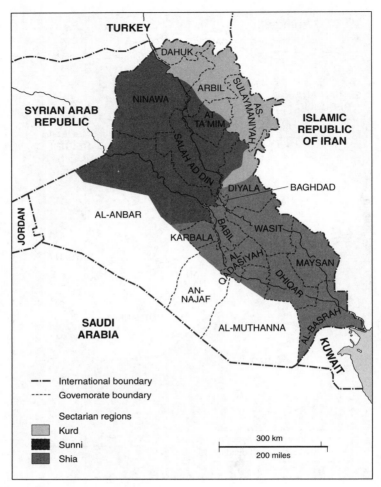

Map 3 Iraq's sectarian regions

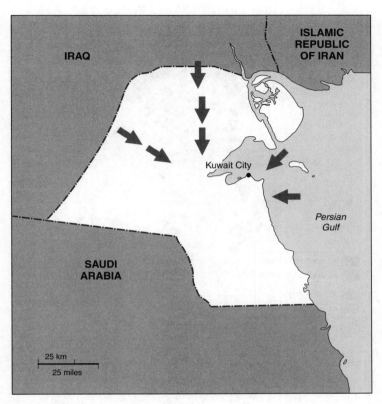

Map 4 Iraq's 1990 invasion of Kuwait

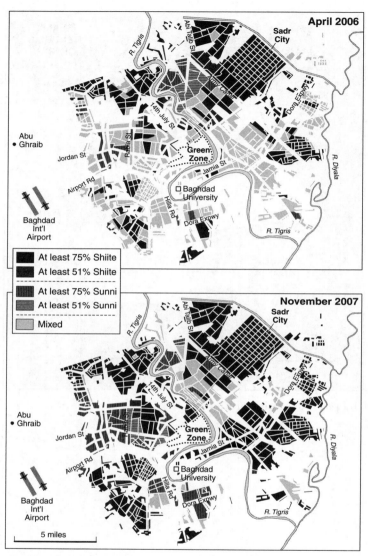

Map 5 The divided city: Iraq's sectarian neighborhoods

1

The First Gulf War, 1990–1991

Chronology

1957	Eisenhower Doctrine
1958	Military coup in Iraq against King Faisal II
1963	Baathist coup against General Abdul Karem Qassim
1968	Second Baathist coup led by General Ahmad Hasan al-Bakr
1979	Saddam Hussein seizes power in Iraq
1990	Iraq invades Kuwait
1991	The First Gulf War

"The Middle East has abruptly reached a new and critical stage in its long and important history," U.S. president Dwight Eisenhower explained to Congress in January 1957. "In past decades many of the countries in that area were not fully self-governing. Other nations exercised considerable authority in the area and the security of the region was largely built around

The United States and Iraq Since 1990: A Brief History with Documents,
First Edition. Edited by Robert K. Brigham.
© 2014 Robert K. Brigham. Published 2014 by Blackwell Publishing Ltd.

[handwritten: Why did Irq have inleost in Kwot]

their power. But since the First World War there has been a steady evolution toward self-government and independence. This development the United States has welcomed and has encouraged. Our country supports without reservation the full sovereignty and independence of each and every nation of the Middle East."[1] Eisenhower's commitment to an independent Middle East was the cornerstone of the Eisenhower Doctrine announced shortly after the 1956 Suez Crisis when Egypt's leader, Gamal Abdel Nasser, had seized and nationalized the Suez Canal. Britain, France, and Israel launched retaliatory strikes against Egypt, but Eisenhower did not support the raids. Instead, he warned old colonial powers that he would not allow them to maintain an imperial stance in the Middle East. More importantly, Eisenhower declared that the United States would not stand "idly by to see the southern flank of NATO completely collapse through Communist penetration and success in the Mid East."[2] Eisenhower believed that the Soviet Union's interest in the Middle East was "solely that of power politics. Considering her announced purpose of Communizing the world, it is easy to understand her hope of dominating the Middle East."[3]

Indeed, Eisenhower's deepest concern was that the United States might be losing ground to the Soviets in the Middle East. He feared that the loss of any country in the region to communism would so endanger American interests and those of its allies that the United States would be forced to alter its own political and economic systems. Eisenhower explained that the Middle East "contains about two thirds of the presently known oil deposits of the world and it normally supplies the petroleum needs of many nations of Europe, Asia and Africa." Even the United States, a net exporter of oil at the time, depended on cheap oil from the Middle East to maintain economic growth and production. If the Soviets captured the region or any part of it, Eisenhower worried that it would "have the most adverse, if not disastrous, effect upon our own nation's economic life and political prospects."[4] To counteract the Soviets, therefore, Eisenhower announced U.S. support for any nation feeling the communist threat. Specifically, the Eisenhower Doctrine pledged to "authorize the United States to cooperate with and assist any nation or group of nations in the general area of the Middle East in the development of economic strength dedicated to the maintenance of national independence." It would also approve "military assistance and cooperation with any nation or group of nations which desires such aid." Finally, it would commit "the employment of the armed forces of the United States to secure and protect the territorial integrity and political independence of such nations, requesting such aid, against overt armed aggression from any nation controlled by International Communism."[5] Congress, obviously moved by the president's speech, eventually approved Eisenhower's request for an additional $200,000,000 in discretionary funds in 1958 and 1959 to combat communism in the Middle East.

Much of Eisenhower's attention was devoted to Israel and her neighbors, but he was most worried about communist advances in what he called the "northern tier," Iraq, Iran, Turkey, and Pakistan. These vulnerable states were of significant geo-strategic importance, and Iraq and Iran held significant economic resources. Eisenhower bound them together in a mutual defense agreement known as the Baghdad Pact. Each of the four nations (with aid from Britain and the United States) pledged to support each other against communist advances. The Soviets called the Baghdad Pact "an appendage of NATO," proving to Eisenhower that the league was the right move. Eisenhower made other diplomatic moves to shore up the alliance. Early in his in presidency, Eisenhower had at least tacitly supported a coup against Iranian leader, Mohammed Mossadegh, returning the conservative shah to power in Iran. In Iraq, John Foster Dulles, Eisenhower's secretary of state, feared that the Soviets had turned more aggressive and that Baghdad leaders could feel "the hot breath of the Soviet Union on their necks." He urged Eisenhower to take a more aggressive stance in supporting the conservative monarchy led by King Faisal II and his deputy, Prime Minister Nuri al-Said. Eisenhower concurred, and the United States poured millions of dollars into Iraq to support the Baghdad government.

Thus was born America's commitment to Iraq and the beginning of the U.S. effort to influence and control politics in Baghdad. Like those that would follow it, Eisenhower's attempt to shore up the government in Baghdad against its many critics failed miserably. Within months of the passage of the Eisenhower Doctrine, on July 14, 1958, the conservative government was overthrown in a military coup. An unstable republic replaced the monarchy and ushered in a decade of rebellion. The new military government, led by General Abdul Karem Qassim, quickly abolished the monarchy, dissolved parliament, and officially recognized the Soviet Union and China. But Qassim's government also felt tremendous pressures that threatened to tear it apart. Kurds in northern Iraq launched an independence movement, and Qassim felt he was the target of constant coup plots instigated by Nasser in Egypt. Iraqi leaders were caught between their strong anti-Western feelings and the fear of U.S. intervention. In the summer of 1961, a dispute between Iraq and Britain over the right to Kuwaiti independence also threatened the Qassim government. Only a Soviet veto at the United Nations Security Council of a British resolution claiming Kuwait's full independence kept war at bay. The Arab League also played a pivotal role in the crisis, eventually inviting Kuwait to join its ranks, thus ensuring that Qassim's government would leave Kuwait alone. When President Kennedy officially received Kuwait's new ambassador to the United States in June 1962, Qassim withdrew Iraq's ambassador from Washington, downgraded its embassy in Washington to a consulate, and ordered the U.S. ambassador to leave Iraq.[6] Though he did not cut off all diplomatic relations completely, it was clear by 1962 that relations between Iraq and the United States were severely strained.

Diplomatic relations did not improve, even after Qassim was removed from power in another bloody coup. On February 8, 1963, Baathist army officers arrested Qassim and assassinated him, along with thousands of communists. There is some evidence, though not substantiated in documents, to suggest that U.S. intelligence officials aided the Baathists in their anti-communist raids.[7] The Baathists were predominantly Sunni, but were more secular than religious. They believed in Arab nationalism and pan-Arabism, a juggling act of national priorities and regional loyalties. They tended to be socialist, but had an almost allergic reaction to communism. The Baathists were also decidedly against Nasser's Egypt and its growing regional influence. The new Baghdad government was also a sworn enemy of Israel. The Baathists promised an Iraq free from old imperial ties and Western influence, but would come to depend on Western aid to support its government. For these reasons, U.S. policymakers trod lightly in Iraq.

In July 1968, a group of disaffected Baathist officers launched another coup and installed General Ahmad Hasan al-Bakr as leader of Iraq. These officers had grown increasingly despondent over the weak Iraqi economy and the failure of the previous Abdul Arif government to secure the northern regions of Iraq from Kurdish rebels. Shortly after taking power, al-Bakr secured complete authority by organizing a "select fraternity of political allies united by tribal and familial loyalties originating in common ancestry around the village of Tikrit."[8] At the heart of this group was an extended clan, the al-Bu Nasir. Among the young officers in this inner circle was Saddam Hussein, a relative of al-Bakr from the village of al-Auja, near Tikrit. Hussein was born in poverty on April 28, 1937. At age 10 he left his home for Baghdad, where he lived with an uncle and attended a local school. He joined the Baathist Party in 1957 and participated in anti-Qassim and anti-communist activity. He was a strong supporter of al-Bakr and had particular expertise in coopting or breaking tribal groups to extend the total control of the Baathists.[9] Though other Baathist leaders experimented with the forced collectivization of land ownership and nationalization of land, Hussein focused his energies on securing power. He coordinated the activities of the Republican Guard, an elite military unit, using them for internal policing and national security issues. He was not afraid to use the Guard to eliminate potential political rivals or to destroy the Communist Party within Iraq. For his efforts, al-Bakr made Saddam Hussein the second most powerful figure in the Iraqi government.

Hussein used this position to further consolidate Baathist power inside Iraq, but also to reposition Baghdad in the international system. Though a sworn enemy of communism, Hussein moved Iraq closer to the Soviet orbit in the 1970s by signing several agreements on oil development and allowing the Soviets to use Iraqi ports in exchange for military weapons. Still, relations between Moscow and Baghdad never developed beyond these preliminary agreements in the early 1970s, allowing U.S. policymakers to watch Iraq from a calculated distance. Initial U.S. support for Kurds in northern Iraq never amounted to much either, allowing Baghdad to talk tough against the Americans but little else. By the end of 1978, Iraq was a secondary concern for U.S. policymakers.

All of that changed in 1979. First, the Iranian revolution of that year, that had ushered radical Shiites into power in Tehran, threatened to engulf Iraq. The Shiite majority in Iraq had lived in fear of Baathist power since the 1963 coup, but took great solace in the Iranian revolution. Riots in the predominantly Shiite areas of Iraq, especially east Baghdad, led many Shiites to question al-Bakr's policies. Furthermore, there was talk in Baghdad of an alliance between Iraq and Syria that would move Saddam Hussein down the chain of command, replacing him with Syrian premier Hafez al-Assad. In a pattern that would become typical of his rule over the next twenty-five years, Hussein moved quickly against both groups. He ousted al-Bakr and declared himself president of the republic, chief of the army, and leader of the Baathist Party. He ordered the assassination of hundreds of political rivals, attacked Shiite radicals all over Iraq, and brutally suppressed the Kurdish independence movement in northern Iraq. By the end of the year, Saddam's control over Iraqi political life was complete.[10]

In the first months of his rule, Saddam Hussein came to suspect that a radical Iran was Iraq's greatest threat. Ironically, officials in Washington were beginning to believe that U.S. policy toward Iraq had to be altered significantly to deal with the new Iranian regime. The Reagan administration made a concerted effort to improve relations with Baghdad, even though Saddam had committed horrendous human rights violations against his own people. Reagan officials, narrowly focused on U.S. national security needs, feared that continued Iranian attacks against Iraqi oil facilities threatened U.S. interests. The Reagan White House was also concerned that "sustained Iranian pressure could . . . bring about Iraq's political collapse."[11] The last thing the Reagan administration wanted was Iranian revolutionary influence to spread in the region, and therefore it believed that Iraq could serve as a useful corrective to Iran's growing power and ambitions. There was also considerable support among western European allies for a new U.S. policy toward Iraq. France especially believed that Saddam Hussein was a moderate Arab in a radical region and the most secular nationalist in the Middle East. Reagan officials likewise held that the time was right to move Iraq away from its dependence on Soviet weapons. For nearly two decades Iraq had relied on Soviet arms shipments to shore up its military. By the mid-1980s, with the Soviets bogged down in Afghanistan, policymakers in Washington believed that the United States could drive a wedge between Moscow and Baghdad. Such thinking was predicated on the fact that the Iraqi government was making new overtures to the West based on its geo-strategic needs brought about in part by its war against Iran.

Iran and Iraq had been at war since 1980, after Iranian leaders rebuked Saddam's initial overtures of public support for the 1979 Iranian revolution. Iran's new revolutionary leaders, all Shiites, rejected the Sunni leadership in Iraq and encouraged Iraqi Shiites, a majority of the population, to rise up against their Sunni oppressors. Hussein responded by attacking Shiites inside Iraq, especially those belonging to the Dawa Party. The Baghdad government also verbally assailed Ayatollah Khomeini, leader of Iran's revolutionary movement. In April 1980 an Iranian-inspired assassination attempt against Saddam's closest Baghdad ally, Deputy Premier Tariq Aziz, led to further attacks against Iraq's Shiites and more harsh words for Iran. In a daring show of strength, Saddam Hussein ordered the execution of Ayatollah Mohammed Bakr al-Sadr, a popular Iraqi Shiite leader, who had been living under house arrest for months following the Iranian revolution. Baghdad also deported nearly 100,000 Shiites and closed off some of the holiest Shiite shrines inside Iraq. Finally, in September 1980, Saddam ordered limited attacks against key Arab regions inside Iran, especially in Shatt al-Arab and Khuzestan, hoping to destabilize the Shiite government in Tehran.

For two years Iraq held the upper hand. Slowly, however, as the revolutionary government solidified its hold on power in Tehran, Iran began a counteroffensive that would eventually push Iraqi troops back. For six years, in what it called the "Imposed War," Iran was on the offensive, often attacking and occupying territory inside Iraq. The United Nations finally brokered a ceasefire in July 1988, but not before hundreds of thousands of casualties and near-economic collapse for both nations. By the time of the ceasefire, it was clear that the Reagan administration had gone to great lengths to bring Iraq into the U.S. orbit. The Reagan White House had extended huge agricultural credits to Iraq during the war, and by 1987 those credits topped $1 billion, "the largest loan of its kind to any single country world wide."[12] Throughout the war the U.S. had also sent arms to Iraq against the protocols of several existing treaties and had even shared high-level intelligence cables and photographs of Iranian military movements with Baghdad.[13] There were several reports that supplies and material sent to Iraq under agricultural trade agreements were actually dual-purpose goods that Baghdad could, and did, use in the war against Iran.[14] The Department of Agriculture was famous for ignoring Saddam's abuses, and often stood in the way of economic sanctions against Baghdad for poor treatment of its Kurdish population and other human rights abuses inside Iraq.[15]

The ultimate expression of U.S. support for Iraq came in 1984, however, when the Reagan administration restored full ambassadorial relations with Baghdad. After U.S. support for Israel in the 1967 "Six Day War," the United States and Iraq had broken off formal diplomatic relations. As Baghdad moved closer to Moscow in the 1970s, it appeared as if relations between the United States and Iraq were damaged beyond repair. Reagan's gradual increase of support of Iraq in the mid-1980s reversed this course, however, and the full normalization of relations in 1984 helped Saddam's government ignore the fact that the Reagan administration had actually sent arms to Iran during its war against Iraq. In a desperate move to free American hostages in Lebanon, and to illegally fund the Contras in Nicaragua who were trying to overthrow the Sandinista government there, Reagan officials had agreed to secretly send Iran arms. Key White House officials believed that the revolutionary government in Iran had influence among the radicals in Lebanon and could work quietly for the release of the Americans being held against their will. The U.S. press quickly found out about the illegal exchange, and soon the Reagan administration had a full-blown scandal on its hands: The Iran-Contra Affair. Saddam Hussein was furious with Reagan for supporting Iran, and clearly believed that the United States was trying to support both sides to increase its influence in the region. Only intervention by Iraq's key allies in the region, particularly Saudi Arabia and, ironically, Kuwait, kept the Iran-Contra Affair from permanently damaging relations between Washington and Baghdad. In retrospect, the Iran-Contra Affair may have even given Saddam the upper hand in negotiations with Americans over his continued human rights abuses inside Iraq.

By the end of the Reagan years, despite Baghdad's continued attacks on Kurds and Shiites inside Iraq and its extended war against Iran, the National Security Council concluded that, "normal relations between the United States and Iraq would serve our longer term interests and promote stability in both the Gulf and the Middle East."[16] The Reagan administration had gradually shifted its weight to Saddam Hussein's Baathist government in Baghdad, though it never fully abandoned the idea of also influencing events in Iran. Normalization of relations with Iraq in 1984 ushered in an era of unusual cooperation between governments, and it appeared at the end of Reagan's eight years in office that the United States had reoriented its power and prestige in the Middle East by drastically changing course with some key nations, Iraq among them. As the end of the Soviet Union's ability to protect and support its allies became even more apparent by the end of the 1980s, the Reagan administration's policy of improving relations with Iraq seemed prescient.

George H.W. Bush and the New World Order

George H.W. Bush came to office in 1989, therefore, convinced that relations between Iraq and the United States would continue to improve. In his administration's first policy review of relations with Iraq, what became known as National Security Directive 26 (see DOCUMENT 1-A), President Bush and his national security team concluded that "The United States government should propose economic and political incentives for Iraq to moderate its behavior and to increase our influence with Iraq . . . We should pursue, and seek to facilitate, opportunities for U.S. firms to participate in the reconstruction of the Iraqi economy, particularly in the energy area, where they do not conflict with our non-proliferation and other significant objectives. Also, as a means of developing access to and influence with the Iraqi defense establishment, the United States should consider sales of non-lethal forms of military assistance. . . . "[17] The Bush administration also warned Iraq, however, that it would not tolerate any "illegal use of chemical and/or biological weapons," nor would it turn its back on human rights concerns inside Iraq.[18] Finally, White House officials concluded that Iraq had to "cease its meddling in external affairs . . . and be encouraged to play a constructive role in negotiating a settlement with Iran and cooperating with the Middle East peace process."[19]

Working through his newly appointed U.S. ambassador to Iraq, April Glaspie, the first woman to hold a senior embassy post in the Arab world, President Bush relayed his Iraqi policy to Saddam Hussein. The United States sought to "engage Iraq and direct it toward progressive and peaceful pursuits."[20] The Bush administration continued Reagan's policy of extending agricultural credits and new loans to Iraq, convincing Hussein that the United States needed Iraq as an ally in the region. He probably came to this conclusion because the Bush administration skillfully avoided attempts by several members of Congress, Senator Claiborne Pell of Rhode Island among them, to curtail U.S. support of Iraq on human rights grounds. Reports from Iraq indicated that the government had continued its persecution of Kurds and Shiites, but Saddam was hopeful that the Bush White House would look the other way and continue to support Iraq financially. When key allies agreed with Bush officials that Saddam looked like a voice of reason in the region, even modifying his stance on Israel somewhat, the new loans were granted and the Iraqi government spoke of a "warm and close" relationship with the United States and many of its Western allies.[21] As Americans celebrated the end of the 1980s, and an end to the Cold War, it appeared as if long-standing difficulties in the Middle East were also on a new course.

All of this changed, however, in the spring of 1990. U.S. officials had miscalculated Saddam Hussein's most important goal: political survival. In a move that was to be repeated throughout the next two decades, Hussein led a series of purges inside Iraq to bolster his hold on ultimate political power. Knowing all too well that his predecessor had been killed in office by disloyal officers, Saddam "was determined to use whatever means were required to avoid a similar fate."[22] He reportedly told a visitor to Baghdad that he knew "that there are scores of people trying to kill me . . . However, I am far cleverer than they are. I know they are conspiring to kill me long before they actually start planning to do so. This enables me to get them before they have the faintest chance of striking at me."[23] After several failed assassination attempts by his handpicked Republican Guard in 1989 and early 1990, Saddam launched a series of purges to regain control of his armed forces.

He also executed a journalist, Farzad Bazoft, on charges of espionage in March 1990, and this action began to undermine Iraq's new relationship with Western democracies. There is little evidence that Bazoft was a spy for Israel, as Saddam had claimed, but that did not stop the Baghdad government from convicting him of spying. Bazoft, in fact, had been sympathetic to Iraq's position in its war against his native Iran. He had been a severe critique of the Iranian revolution and the Ayatollah. Baghdad had invited him several times to report on the Iraq–Iran War from inside Iraq, largely because Saddam had found his criticism of Iran pleasing. During one visit, Bazoft learned that there was some physical evidence that Saddam might be engaged in a massive chemical or nuclear weapons program. Bazoft ventured outside of Baghdad to investigate the rumors. Upon his return to Baghdad, he was convinced that he had the news story of a lifetime. Several of his fellow journalists warned him to leave the country, which he tried to do at midnight on September 15, 1989. He was arrested at the airport, however, and brought to Baghdad for questioning by Saddam's notorious secret police, the Mukhbarat. After Bazoft had spent six weeks in detention, Saddam showed a tape of him confessing to his crimes. Despite sharp protest from several Western leaders, including British prime minister Margaret Thatcher, Bazoft was hanged in early March 1990. Alone, this action would not have led to a direct confrontation with the West, but taken together with the purges, the human rights violations, the continued rumors that Saddam was engaging in a massive chemical or nuclear weapons build up, and his increasingly harsh rhetoric against Israel, many in the Bush and Thatcher administrations began to doubt that Saddam had changed all that much.

The Israeli piece of Saddam's unraveling conciliatory policy toward the West is most confusing. After several public speeches in late 1988 and 1989 that suggested Iraq had backed away from its strident anti-Israel stance, Saddam went back to his usual bombastic rhetoric about war against Israel. He threatened that if Israel attacked Iraq, it would "be confronted by us with a precise reaction, using the means available to us according to the legitimate right to self-defense."[24] In April 1990, Saddam further boasted that "he who launches an aggression against Iraq or the Arab nation will now find someone to repel him. If we can strike him with a stone, we will. With a missile, we will . . . and with all the missiles, bombs, and other means at our disposal."[25] He must have known that the United States would not allow such rhetoric to spill over into reality. Israel, for that matter, would not allow Baghdad to have a weapons program progress to the point of providing an actual threat to its national security. Saddam must have feared that the Israelis were indeed planning a preemptive attack on his military installations and that he had to warn of regional war to stop them. It now seems clear that Hussein was over-invested in his weapons program. It provided the often paranoid leader with several kinds of security. First, knowledge of a weapons program had a domestic purpose. Control of such a dangerous and powerful arsenal was a warning to Saddam's many internal adversaries that he held all the power. Second, a weapons program told Iraq's Arab neighbors that Saddam was a leader to be reckoned with, a regional power that could not be ignored. Finally, it appears likely that Saddam thought a growing weapons program would actually act as a deterrent against an Israeli attack, despite the obvious and reverse perception in Jerusalem. Whatever Saddam's motivation, his weapons program was clearly seen as a direct threat to Israel, a threat that the Bush administration could not ignore.

Iraq Invades Kuwait

Still, there was hope in Washington that the improving relations with Iraq would provide the administration with enough leverage to "walk Saddam back" from the brink of war again. Hope was short-lived. In April 1990, Saddam demanded that the United States withdraw its forces from the region, including its navy patrolling international waters in the Persian Gulf. In addition, he declared that Iraq was now in possession of binary chemical weapons (CW), which would serve "as a deterrent sufficient to confront the Israeli nuclear program."[26] In late May 1990, at the annual meeting of the Arab League, ironically hosted by Baghdad, Saddam publicly accused the government of neighboring Kuwait of stealing Iraqi oil. He further demanded that Kuwait forgive Iraqi debts racked up in the war against Iran, a war Saddam claimed was fought on behalf of all Arab states against the hegemonic Iranians. Iran had twice launched attacks inside tiny Kuwait, attacks Saddam claimed that Iraq repelled because it was a good neighbor. Iraq had always had an uneasy relationship with Kuwait, laying claim to the small state the moment Baghdad gained its full independence from the British in 1961. The border had remained "a lingering source of dispute," but Saddam had never been so openly hostile to Kuwait as he was in the spring of 1990.[27] Iraq was financially stressed, and Saddam blamed Kuwait for much of it. Indeed, Iraq's indebtedness was occupying more and more of Saddam's time. One of the major causes of that economic distress, a fact that Saddam ignored, was that Iraq's military budget was unrealistic. In 1990, Iraq's military budget was $12.9 billion, or approximately $700 per citizen in a country where the average annual income was $1,950. By April 1990, Iraq had only enough cash reserves to cover governmental expenses for three more months and had a region-high inflation rate of 40 percent.[28] Hussein was clearly worried that the war with Iran had depleted Iraqi financial reserves at a time when oil prices were falling worldwide. The Iraqi treasury was in bad shape, and the last thing Saddam wanted was to turn to the International Monetary Fund for budget relief. He was also worried that his domestic political enemies would use Iraq's poor economic standing as a weapon against him.

In what seemed liked a desperate attempt to rescue Iraq from the brink of economic and political disaster, Saddam began to make plans for an invasion of Kuwait. The first volley of the attack was verbal. On July 18, 1990, Saddam warned Kuwait that, "War is fought with soldiers and much harm is done by explosions, killing and coup attempts – but it is also done by economic means. Therefore, we would ask our brothers who do not mean to wage war on Iraq: this is in fact a kind of war against Iraq."[29] He also accused Kuwait and the United Arab Emirates (UAE) of complicity with the United States to cheat on oil production quotas, thereby driving the price of oil down on the international market and costing Iraq billions of desperately needed dollars. There were also geo-strategic considerations in attacking Kuwait. The port of Shatt al-Arab had been closed to Iraqi shipping and oil depots because of debris left over from the Iraq–Iran War. This meant that Iraq now had only limited access to the vital Persian Gulf waters and that access to ports on the Khwar 'abd Allah – the waterway leading to the Persian Gulf – was crucial. Since Kuwait laid claim to the islands of Warbah and Bubiyan on the Khwar 'abd Allah, Iraq was in a difficult position. Attempts by other Arab states to mediate the conflict over the islands and Iraqi access to the Gulf failed in the summer of 1990, as the Iraqi deputy prime minister claimed that "no agreement has been reached on anything because we did not feel from the Kuwaitis any seriousness in dealing with the severe damage inflicted on Iraq as a result of their recent behavior and stands against Iraq's basic interests."[30] Kuwait quite reasonably had rejected all Iraqi demands for money and territory throughout 1990, but Kuwaiti leaders proposed instead a long-term loan and the sharing of revenue from the Ar-Rumaylah oilfield to help Iraq out of its current financial crisis. This further enraged Saddam, who thought the Kuwaitis were being paternalistic toward their more powerful northern neighbor.

One week after his first public challenge to Kuwait, on July 25, 1990, Saddam for the first time summoned U.S. Ambassador Glaspie to his Baghdad palace. He told her that many of his Arab neighbors had engaged in disappointing actions specifically aimed at Iraq and that he was going to have to take corrective measures. According to official Iraqi transcripts released shortly after her meeting with Saddam, Glaspie reportedly told the Iraqi leader that the Bush administration had nothing but friendly intentions toward his government and that the United States had no specific position on border disputes. "I have a direct instruction from the President to seek better relations with Iraq," she reported, according to the Iraqi source. "We have no opinion on the Arab–Arab conflicts, like your border disagreement with Kuwait."[31] Furthermore, the Baghdad source reported that Glaspie clearly stated that Secretary of State James Baker believed that the Iraq–Kuwait border issue "is not associated with America."[32] At the end of their meeting, Glaspie reportedly asked Saddam, "in the spirit of friendship – not in the spirit of confrontation," what his intentions were with regard to Kuwait. The Iraqi transcript did not reveal Saddam's response.

When news of this exchange reached the Bush administration, Ambassador Glaspie was called back to Washington to respond. She told the Senate Foreign Relations Committee that the Iraqi transcript of her conversation with Saddam Hussein had been "maliciously" edited "to the point of inaccuracy." She also claimed that she had warned Saddam not to attack Kuwait, telling him directly that the United States would not allow such a move to go unchallenged. She concluded her testimony by unequivocally stating that the United States did not give Saddam a "green light" to invade Kuwait and that Saddam must have been "stupid" to think otherwise.[33] The United States would support its clear and vital interests in the region, Glaspie told the Iraqi leader, and this included defending the territorial integrity of Kuwait.

A recently released National Security Council document seems to confirm Ambassador Glaspie's version of the conversation with Saddam (see Document 1-B). According to this internal memorandum dated July 25, the same day as the meeting in Baghdad, Saddam complained that the United States was trying to humiliate Iraq by working with Kuwait and the UAE to drive oil prices down. He also complained about reports of his government's human rights abuses in the American press, stating that he would not allow such transgressions. He also believed the ambassador when she stated that the president wanted to improve relations between the United States and

Iraq, but he warned that Iraq would not tolerate any U.S. "arm twisting" of Iraq to get its way. He believed that the upcoming visit of Israeli foreign policy leader Moshe Arens to Washington at "a time of crisis in the Gulf" was a clear sign that the United States favored Israel over peace in the Middle East. Saddam declared that Iraqis knew what war was, "wanted no more of it," but did not want the United States to "push us to it; do not make it the only option left with which we can protect our dignity."[34] In response, Ambassador Glaspie told Saddam that the United States had every reason to be concerned about Iraq's intentions toward Kuwait, especially when leaders in Baghdad "say publicly that Kuwaiti actions are the equivalent of military aggression." Furthermore, Glaspie argued, how was the United States supposed to respond when it learned that "many units of the Republican Guard have been sent to the border?"[35] Hussein assured the ambassador that he understood the Bush administration's position and duty as a superpower. Still, he asked, "how can we make them [Kuwait and the UAE] understand how deeply we are suffering?" Saddam hinted that the financial hardships facing Iraq made it impossible for the government to continue pensions for widows and orphans from the Iraq–Iran War, and that this was unacceptable.[36] At this point in the conversation, Glaspie reported, a notetaker and one of the interpreters "broke down and wept."[37] Glaspie ended the meeting with a hopeful comment about regional negotiations then being planned by Egypt's president Hosni Mubarak, and a warning that the United States would only support a peaceful resolution to the mounting crisis between Iraq and Kuwait.

Despite this apparent warning from Ambassador Glaspie, Saddam wasted no time in preparing for war. In mid-July, even before his meeting with Ambassador Glaspie, Saddam had deployed an entire armored division of the Republican Guard just north of the Iraqi border with Kuwait. There were reports circulating in the intelligence communities that as many as 3,000 military vehicles were on the road leading from Baghdad to Kuwait.[38] By August 1, 1990, there were eight Republican Guard divisions between Basra in southern Iraq and the Kuwaiti border. Because the deployment involved the careful coordination of nearly 140,000 Iraqi troops, over 1,500 Iraqi tanks, and massive amounts of heavy artillery, it was clear that Saddam had been planning the invasion for some time. Iraqi leaders had also fully mobilized its attack, fighter, and fighter-bomber aircraft to southern airbases in preparation for the invasion. Iraq's air force had become the envy of the region because of its size and diversity. It included many F-1, MiG 29, and Su-24 aircraft along with a modern air defense command-and-control system.[39] The air force had been a major reason why Iraq was able to resist total defeat in the Iraq–Iran War, and now it stood poised to attack its weaker southern neighbor, Kuwait, a nation with a very frail air defense system. Iraqi ground forces, now massed on Kuwait's border, were the largest in the Persian Gulf. They were well trained and well supported with heavy artillery. During the Iraq–Iran War, Saddam had insisted that Iraq build a modern transportation system inside Iraq to help resupply the Republican Guard. Now Saddam could use that road network to move men and supplies to the Kuwaiti border rapidly.

On August 2, 1990, Saddam's forces were in place and the invasion of Kuwait began. Three Republican Guard divisions attacked across the Kuwaiti frontier while an Iraqi mechanized division and an armored division launched a coordinated assault south into Kuwait along the Safwan Abdally axis, driving for the al-Jahra pass, the cut in the land on the eastern coast of Kuwait. By early afternoon, Iraqi forces had directly attacked key Kuwaiti government buildings in downtown Kuwait City. Special Republican Guard commando teams meanwhile raided the Kuwaiti amir's palace. The amir was able to escape to Saudi Arabia, but his brother, one of his closest allies in the government, was killed in the attack. By the evening of August 2, Iraqi forces had fully captured Kuwait City and were now on their way to secure blocking positions on the main routes from Saudi Arabia to Kuwait. Iraqi tanks moved south to capture key Kuwaiti ports on the coast. Kuwaiti forces were hopelessly outmatched and most of the fighting soon ended with Iraq in complete control of much of the country. Saddam was pleased with how quickly his invasion force had subdued Kuwait, and some analysts believe that he even eyed a bigger regional prize, Saudi Arabia. Although the evidence is still quite thin to support the idea of a larger Iraqi invasion, it is possible that Saddam had amassed much of his force in southern Kuwait in preparation for an attack against the oil-rich and more conservative state of Saudi Arabia, a close ally of the United States. Bush administration officials were rightfully fearful of what Iraq might gain by invading Saudi Arabia. "It would be very easy for him to control the world's oil," White House chief of staff John Sununu warned.[40] Sununu feared that the greatly outnumbered Saudi military would be no match for Saddam's troops, and therefore such an attack "would be heady for Saddam."[41] President Bush feared that Saddam would not only control the world's oil supply, but that he would also control the very military bases inside Saudi Arabia that the United States would need to launch an effective counterattack against Iraq.[42]

Despite some limited border raids inside Saudi Arabia, no full-force invasion ever materialized. Instead, Saddam now offered a justification and explanation for Iraq's invasion of Kuwait. In a brazen move that fooled no one, Saddam claimed that Iraq had invaded Kuwait because of populist Arab sentiments inside Kuwait that demanded freedom from the oppressive ruling al-Sabah family. A new "Free Kuwait Provisional Government" was now in charge in Kuwait, according to Saddam, and the Iraqis promised to withdraw "as soon as things settle and when the temporary free government asks us to do so."[43] No such Kuwaiti group ever existed, and it was clear to most that this was another of Saddam's attempts at regional deception. After about a week of this farce, Saddam simply signed an executive order annexing Kuwait, claiming it as Iraq's "province 19." He had long argued that Kuwait had belonged to Iraq before the British designated it a sovereign state, and now the world had been righted. In Baghdad, military leaders spoke of returning "the part and branch, Kuwait, to the whole and the Iraq of its origins."[44] The invasion and annexation of Kuwait had returned to Iraq something that was vital for the nation to be grand. And better access to the Gulf and the oil-rich Ar-Rumaylah fields assured Saddam a break from the grinding debt problems now plaguing Iraq. Of course, Saddam had seriously underestimated the international community's response to the invasion, and this would ultimately lead to his downfall and execution sixteen years later.

Building the Coalition against Saddam

The Bush administration wasted no time in responding to Iraq's invasion of Kuwait. The first action was to have President Bush sign an executive order freezing all Iraqi assets in the United States and those of the newly installed puppet government in Kuwait.[45] Next, the Bush administration went to the United Nations to secure a resolution condemning the Iraqi invasion. There was very little debate at the United Nations, as U.S. ambassador Thomas Pickering supervised the passage of UN Resolution 660 (see DOCUMENT 1-C), condemning the Iraqi invasion and demanding that "Iraq withdraw immediately and unconditionally all its forces to the positions which they were located on 1 August 1990." Finally, the UN resolution called upon Iraq and Kuwait to "begin immediately intensive negotiations for the resolution of their differences and supports all efforts in this regard, and especially those of the League of Arab States."[46] Four days later, the United Nations adopted Resolution 661, which reaffirmed the sentiments of Resolution 660, but which also prohibited all trade with Iraq and Kuwait and outlawed the transfer of any funds to the two countries as well. Only essential items were given a reprieve from the resolution, such as "supplies intended strictly for medical purposes, and, in humanitarian circumstances, foodstuffs."[47] Within days of Resolution 661, 90 percent of Iraq's imports and 97 percent of its exports were cut.[48] UN Resolution 662, issued on August 9, 1990, condemned Iraq's annexation of Kuwait and declared that the international community did not recognize Iraq's claims to Kuwait. Clearly, Saddam must have been alarmed by the speed with which the international community condemned Iraq's actions. Particularly surprising must have been the UN votes of Saddam's European allies, like France, that had staunchly supported Iraq during its war with Iran. Now, France stood with the international community in condemning Iraq's invasion of Kuwait. The United Nations would eventually pass ten more resolutions reproving Saddam's actions, authorizing military means to enforce economic sanctions, and ultimately approving a multi-national contingent to force an Iraqi withdrawal from Kuwait.

Alongside the UN resolutions, the Bush administration also launched what became known as Operation Desert Shield, a massive build-up of U.S. forces in and around Saudi Arabia to protect it from Saddam's Republican Guard now poised on the Saudi border. After obtaining King Fahd's approval, the Bush administration sent over 100,000 U.S. troops and airmen to Saudi Arabia to protect the kingdom, along with two squadrons of F-15 fighters and a brigade from the 82nd Airborne Division. President Bush also ordered U.S. naval ships stationed at Diego Garcia – a navy support facility that provides logistic support to operational forces forward-deployed to the Indian Ocean and Persian Gulf areas – directly into the Persian Gulf. This military operation became the largest American deployment since the Vietnam War. In addition to the navy ships from Diego Garcia, U.S. carriers in the Gulf of Oman and the Red Sea responded. Navy prepositioning ships rushed equipment and supplies for an entire marine brigade from Diego Garcia. One of the more interesting aspects of Operation Desert Storm was the use of deception cells to create the illusion that the United States was going to launch a unilateral attack against Iraqi-occupied Kuwait. U.S. forces established "Forward Operating Base Weasel," consisting of a phony network of camps manned by several dozen soldiers. According to an official Department of Defense source, U.S. troops used portable radio equipment cued by computers, and phony radio messages were passed between fictitious headquarters. In addition, smoke generators and loudspeakers playing tape-recorded tank and truck noises were used, as were inflatable Humvees and helicopters.[49] It was this full U.S. mobilization inside Saudi Arabia that Osama bin Laden later claimed was a violation of Islamic law, a move that led to his radicalization.

At the beginning of Operation Desert Shield, President Bush explained that the United States had no intention of invading Kuwait or Iraq. In a press conference on August 8, 1990, Bush made clear that U.S. troops were "in a defensive mode now, and therefore, that is not the mission to drive Iraqis out of Kuwait. We have economic sanctions that I hope will be effective to that end. And I don't know how long they will be there."[50] Furthermore, Bush concluded that the United States was "not at war." Instead, he explained, "We have sent forces to defend Saudi Arabia . . . my military objective is to see Saudi Arabia defended . . . our overall objective is to see Saddam Hussein get out and go back and have the rightful regime of Kuwait back in place."[51] Despite this public rhetoric, many in the Bush administration realized that Saddam was probably not going to leave Kuwait voluntarily and that U.S. armed forces would be needed to remove Iraqi troops. Secretary of Defense Richard Cheney moved the Pentagon into full-scale preparations for an invasion, even though General Colin Powell, the chairman of the Joint Chiefs of Staff, warned that removing Iraq from Kuwait by military force "would be the National Football League, not a scrimmage."[52] Cheney and President Bush chaffed at Powell's depiction of the Republican Guard, stating several times in national security meetings that Iraq had not performed that well against Iran in their recent war.

Before launching its attack against Iraq, the Bush administration worked tirelessly to build up a coalition of supportive allies in the region. Bush convinced most Arab states to support the UN resolutions and U.S. military action, should that become necessary. The Bush White House simultaneously convinced Syria to support the U.S. position on Iraq. Bush leaders persuaded Israel that cooperation between the United States and Arab states was, in effect, in Israel's national security interests. The pragmatic realism that dominated the Bush administration's worldview served the president well as he gathered support for the U.S. policy toward Iraq. In fact, after suffering several foreign policy setbacks, most notably the perception that the United States was doing nothing about human rights abuses in the Balkans and in China, the Bush team relished the feeling that it was in complete control of the narrative on Iraq and that the international community was quickly lining up behind U.S. policy.

Saddam had one last card to play, however, to destroy the international coalition gathering against him and preserve Iraq's annexation of Kuwait. Shortly before a long-scheduled superpower summit in Helsinki between Washington and Moscow, Saddam Hussein went on national television to encourage Soviet leader Mikhail Gorbachev to break relations with the United States and the enemies gathering against Iraq and chart an independent course with Iraq as a strong alley. Hussein even hinted that the only way the Soviet Union could remain a global power was to increase its number of friends in the Middle East. Saddam suggested that Iraq's foreign minister, Tariq Aziz, visit Moscow soon to discuss the possibilities of improving relations between Moscow and Baghdad. A defiant Gorbachev joined President Bush in Helsinki on September 9 for the summit, and, during one of their joint press conferences, the two world leaders issued a shared statement condemning Iraq's actions in Kuwait. The two agreed that "nothing short of a return to the pre-August 2 status of Kuwait can end Iraq's isolation" and that "nothing short of the complete implementation of the United Nations Security Council Resolutions is acceptable." They concluded that the United States and the Soviet Union were "determined to see this aggression end, and if the current steps fail to end it, we are prepared to consider additional ones consistent with the United Nations

Charter."[53] In a separate statement, an incensed Gorbachev left no doubt where the Soviet Union stood on the issue. He warned Saddam that the Soviet Union would not support his aggression in Kuwait and that Moscow stood behind the UN resolutions. Though he did not support the use of force to remove Iraq from Kuwait, he would not tolerate the violation of national sovereignty. He concluded, "what the present Iraqi leadership is doing is driving us to a dead end."[54] Gorbachev then declared that Tariq Aziz was not welcome in Moscow unless he was coming to share an Iraqi withdrawal plan with the Soviet Union.

Satisfied that he had done everything he could to make sure that Saddam understood that it was not "the United States against Iraq," but rather "Iraq against the world," Bush spent much of October focused on the congressional mid-term elections taking place in the United States.[55] Domestic economic problems had created some tension in the Republican ranks, and many of the president's own party members doubted his ability to provide them with coattails long enough to win their own individual races. Indeed, when the votes were counted, Republicans had lost one seat in the U.S. Senate and seven in the House of Representatives, giving Democrats clear majorities in both houses of Congress. Public opinion polls at the time suggested that most Americans wanted to see more vigorous action from the president, whether it was on policy toward China's human rights abuses, the growing conflict in the Balkans, the national economy, or Iraq's invasion of Kuwait. Bush was reluctant to move boldly on any of these issues, instead preferring to preserve the status quo and stability in the international system. A growing number of his political base began to question the president's commitment to promoting democracy abroad. Many of President Reagan's most loyal foreign policy supporters challenged President Bush publicly, suggesting that he was too tied to the traditional, isolationist wing of the Republican Party. Reagan Democrats and neoconservatives were especially critical of Bush. Neoconservative Norman Podhoretz, decrying what he considered Bush's ineffective policies in dealing with Moscow, Beijing, and Belgrade, noted, "The Bush problem is like *coitus interruptus*. Nothing is consummated."[56] A joke circulating in Washington at the time was that Bush would tell his national security team, "Don't do anything, just sit there!"[57]

Despite these criticisms and the growing feeling among many Republicans that Reagan would have handled foreign affairs more aggressively, Bush cautiously and prudently continued to support the United Nations process of issuing ever more specific resolutions against Iraq and quietly building up a coalition of allies to support multilateral military intervention if it was needed. At the end of November 1990 the United States spearheaded a resolution through the United Nations Security Council – Resolution 678 – which ordered Iraq to leave Kuwait by January 15, 1991 or face severe international consequences (see DOCUMENT 1-D). Specifically, Resolution 678 authorized UN member states to "use all necessary means . . . to restore international peace and security to the area."[58] Apparently fearing that the world was closing in, on the same day that Resolution 678 passed in the Security Council, Saddam released all hostages he had taken during the invasion of Kuwait, including many Americans. Sensing that the pressure may have produced a changing attitude in Baghdad, Bush invited Iraqi foreign minister Tariq Aziz to Washington to discuss to the crisis. Bush wanted Aziz to give a timetable for an Iraqi withdrawal from Kuwait that was consistent with UN Resolution 678. Baghdad refused to issue such an assurance, forcing the White House to speed up its military planning. Bush quickly gained military and financial commitments from twenty-eight nations, should a counterattack against Iraq be necessary. Still, the president was reluctant to commit to war against Iraq. During a November 8, 1990, press conference, one reporter suggested that British prime minister Margaret Thatcher did not share the president's caution. "Prime Minister Thatcher said yesterday that if, indeed, Saddam doesn't withdraw from Kuwait that you and the allies will use force. I haven't heard you say that before. You've talked about wanting to retain the option of war, but would you use force?" Bush answered, "I don't want to say what I will or will not do."[59]

What Bush was willing to do was exhaust every possible diplomatic effort to remove Iraq from Kuwait. On January 9, 1991, just six days before Resolution 678 required Iraq to withdrawal from Kuwait, President Bush sent Secretary of State James Baker to meet with Tariq Aziz in Geneva. A frustrated Baker concluded that Aziz was not interested in serious negotiations. In a communiqué to the president, Baker made it clear "that he discerned no evidence whatsoever that Iraq was willing to comply with the international community's demand to withdraw from Kuwait and comply with the United Nations resolutions."[60] Bush had given Baker a letter for Saddam, and hoped that Aziz would agree to take it to Baghdad. When Aziz refused, most inside the Bush administration knew that war was imminent. Some members of the coalition attempted to make contact with Saddam Hussein, including UN secretary general Pérez de Cuéllar, who traveled to Baghdad in January 1991, but with the same result. Against this backdrop, a reluctant President Bush went to Congress on January 12, 1991 to get authorization for the use of military force against Iraq. Congress complied, giving the Bush administration the authority to use the "United States Armed Forces pursuant to United Nations Security Council Resolution 678."[61] Two days later, Saddam and the Iraqi National Assembly called on the people of Iraq "to proceed toward holy jihad." Saddam warned President Bush that if he believed Iraqi forces could be quickly "neutralized," then "you are deluding yourself and this delusion will place you in great trouble."[62] On January 15, 1991, Resolution 678's deadline for an Iraqi withdrawal from Kuwait passed, Bush signed National Security Directive 54 (see DOCUMENT 1-E), an executive order to start hostilities against Iraq. When the military leadership at the Pentagon confirmed that U.S. armed forces were fully prepared for operations in Kuwait and Iraq, the war began like clockwork.

Operation Desert Storm

On January 16, 1991, at 3:35 in the afternoon, several B-52 bombers took off from their bases in Louisiana for the Persian Gulf. Each bomber was carrying conventionally armed air-launched cruise missiles. The target list included Iraq's air defense and command-and-control centers.[63] Though a host of other countries were involved, it was the U.S. command that supervised the four-phase "air, naval, and ground offensive" that took place throughout January.[64] The goal was to dismantle Iraq's air defense system, strike at the Iraqi leadership, and reduce the combat capacity of Iraqi armed forces. Even though Iraq's offensive air capabilities were extremely limited, Saddam decided to reserve them for use in the ground war he knew would follow the initial air campaign. He believed that his air defense systems could counter the coalition's air war just enough to allow him to extend the war into Israel and Saudi Arabia, primarily through SCUD missile attacks. Such attacks, according to Saddam, would destroy the international coalition, making it more difficult for Bush to wage war against Iraq. Saddam had spent the last five years building up Iraq's air defense systems, and the country had invested a disproportionate amount of its defense budget to ensure that the airbases could survive massive air attacks. Saddam built twenty-four very large and heavily fortified main operating bases and "a further thirty major dispersal airfields."[65] Some of these airbases, according to military historian Lawrence Freedman, were the size of London's Heathrow Airport.[66] Saddam had the most sophisticated anti-aircraft weaponry available in the region protecting these bases. He also possessed French Mirage F-1s, the latest surface-to-air missiles (SAMs), and a state-of-the-art anti-aircraft artillery system. His prized possession was SCUD missiles, which he launched against Israel beginning on January 18 and continuing for several days. Saddam had hoped this would draw Israel into the fight and break up the coalition that the Bush administration had worked so hard to create, including Arab states that might side with Iraq if Israel joined the effort against Saddam. According to Colin Powell, the Bush White House needed to keep Israel from responding to the SCUD attacks "if we were going to preserve the Arab end of the coalition."[67] Israel complied with a little push from Washington, and the air war continued.

Curiously, but predictably, Saddam had integrated his air defense system into a unified central command with control centers hidden in underground shelters in and around Baghdad. Saddam feared losing control of any aspect of his military structure to political rivals, so he always kept his command composition close at hand. This centralization meant that it was easy for coalition air attacks to disrupt the coordination of the national air defense network by simply destroying a few of these command centers. This was most evident in the use of Iraq's SAMs, which were ineffective after the first few days of combat because they could not be centrally controlled. Within days, coalition forces had severely limited Iraq's ability to counter allied air power, and this made all the difference. By the end of January 1991, coalition air forces had inflicted tremendous damage on Saddam's air defenses, his command structure, and his air force while suffering relatively few losses.

Of course, American policymakers had predicted as much. During the weeks before the air attacks began, Bush administration officials had made sure that the gradualist approach to the air war in Vietnam was not repeated. Most of the military planners had served in Vietnam, and, like Colin Powell, few were eager to follow the limited war strategy in Iraq. During the Vietnam War, the Johnson administration had used air power to send messages to Hanoi, trying to convince Ho Chi Minh that to continue to arm the southern revolution would come at too high a price. The goal was to bomb North Vietnam sufficiently to diminish Hanoi's willingness to continue the fight. A secondary goal was to use the bombings to lift morale in Saigon and assure South Vietnam's leaders that the United States was committed to their survival. The chief complaint about Operation Rolling Thunder, as the air attacks against North Vietnam were named, was that the incremental pressure allowed Hanoi to make adjustments, such as evacuating its major population bases and constructing hardened air defenses. Still, the Vietnamese suffered enormous casualties under U.S. bombs, no matter how gradual Bush administration officials claimed the bombing of North Vietnam had been. In any event, Bush officials worried that the predictability of the air strikes had also bought Hanoi time to consider options for survival, and this mistake would not be repeated. According to Lawrence Freedman, an expert on warfare, the "determination to avoid incrementalism of this sort was the starting point" for the Bush administration's air campaign against Saddam.[68] Accordingly, the air strikes against Iraq were code named "Instant Thunder."

From the initial planning stages, it was clear that to remove Saddam from Kuwait the coalition would also have to make a major commitment of ground forces. Colin Powell had insisted all along that air power was going to be no substitute for ground troops. After the First Gulf War, Powell recounted for a reporter the moment when he told President Bush that a sizeable ground force would be needed to meet coalition goals. Powell explained to Bush that "the secondary air campaign, the secondary attacks, the amphibious feints, and then finally the deep hook around the left side of the Iraqi forces," would require a "much larger force" than had been called for during Operation Desert Shield planning. And then Powell recalled, "I laid out the size of that force. There were some gasps. . . ." Powell reported that the president listened very carefully and then asked, "Now Colin, you and Norm [General Schwarzkopf] are really sure that air power alone can't do it?" Powell responded, "Mr. President, I wish to God that I could assure you that air power alone could do it but you can't take that chance. We've gotta take the initiative out of the enemy's hands if we're going to go to war. We've got to make sure that this is . . . there is no ordained conclusion and outcome, that there'll be no guessing as to, you know, we're going to be successful with this plan and this is the plan we recommend."[69] The president eventually agreed and gave General Norman Schwarzkopf, who would oversee the coalition forces in Iraq, the size of force Powell recommended, nearly 235,000 soldiers and marines.

Saddam Hussein had hoped that the United States would indeed commit its troops to a ground war against Iraq because he erroneously believed that a "second Vietnam" would ensue. Hussein told his top lieutenants that the American public had an adverse reaction to body bags, and that as soon as the full cost of a ground war against Iraq was known to the American people, they would force a U.S. withdrawal. He predicted that his army of 1 million men, the world's fourth largest, would be able to inflict enough damage on U.S. troops to produce the desired result. He developed a strategy to ensure this outcome. Saddam hoped to use extensive fortifications to push coalition forces into confined areas and then have his well-protected military kill them at will. He also went on a propaganda offensive that highlighted potential American casualties. In a speech on February 11, 1991 (DOCUMENT 1-F), Saddam warned:

> Iraqis, your enemy believed it was capable of achieving its goals and reversing the course of history, and when he failed, he resorted to direct armed aggression. Here we are in the fourth week of this aggression with the Iraqis becoming more firm in their faith, and shining out more in front of the whole world.
>
> The resistance of our heroes to the warplanes and rockets of aggression and shame is the strongest indication of the steadfastness, faith and light in the hearts of the Iraqis and their great readiness not to give up the role willed to them by God, the will to which they responded, faithfully and obediently.
>
> All the good people will be victorious as Iraq, and victory will restore to the Iraqis all the requirements for a free and honorable living that they will merit as a reward for their patience and steadfastness.[70]

Saddam's actions and words promised a long and costly war should the United States decide to intervene.

Even in the U.S., some national security analysts were predicting unusually high casualties for coalition troops given the experience, leadership, and numbers in the Iraqi army.[71] Public opinion polls backed up the dire predictions. According to a poll conducted just before the air campaign began, a majority of Americans did not support the war against Iraq if it meant sustaining 1,000 U.S. troop deaths.[72] Powell countered these observations by telling the president that he "did not do marginal economic analysis looking for crossover points. I go with enough to make sure . . . we're not operating on the margin."[73] Powell was also aware that the nature of the Vietnam War had conditioned the general mood of the American public. High causalities with little to show for it and a draft meant thousands of angry people in the streets during the war. He could counter this by going into Iraq and Kuwait with overwhelming force in support of very clear and limited political goals, and with an all-volunteer army. The UN resolution and the congressional authorization on the use of force provided the political guidelines needed for such a war. Powell, an initial skeptic on the war, was now convinced that the American public would support the coalition effort once the battle plan became a reality.

Powell's predictions now seem prescient, at least for the initial phases of the First Gulf War. On February 22, Bush issued an ultimatum to Saddam Hussein: Iraq must leave Kuwait within twenty-four hours or face the full brunt of coalition forces. Naturally, Saddam failed to comply with White House demands, so Bush ordered a full assault against Iraqi troops inside Kuwait. U.S. Marines led the invasion of Kuwait, while American troops backed by British and French forces outflanked Saddam by controlling southern Iraq. The much-vaunted Iraqi forces collapsed quickly. After two days of fighting, much of the Iraqi army inside Kuwait had been killed or captured, or had fled. Facing imminent defeat, Saddam ordered his troops to retreat from Kuwait under the cover of darkness. Soon, however, the main highway connecting Kuwait City with southern Iraq, Highway 6, was jammed with escaping vehicles. The sheer volume of traffic on the road led to slow progress, but it also enabled coalition aircraft to inflict severe damage on Saddam's escaping army. On the morning of February 26, several U.S. F-15 fighter jets bombed the Iraqi convoy "to trap its vehicles in the Multa Pass; they then flew south and attacked the rear of the convoy."[74] Most Iraqis abandoned the scene, but those that did not were instantly killed along what became known as the "Highway of Death."

On February 27, sensing that the goals of the UN resolutions had been met; President Bush ordered a temporary ceasefire. General Schwarzkopf boasted that the "gate is closed, there is no way out of here."[75] The general agreed that a ceasefire was in order and that the coalition had accomplished its goals. The United States agreed to end the ground war after a mere one hundred hours. According to Wafiq al-Samarrai, Saddam's director of military intelligence, however, no one in the Iraqi leadership expected the U.S. to honor the ceasefire. Samarrai claimed that Saddam was "close to tears" following the Iraqi ouster from Kuwait, but was overjoyed to learn of the ceasefire. Saddam was shocked that the coalition had permitted much of his Republican Guard forces to escape, "thus facilitating his retention of power."[76] The coalition military command also allowed Saddam to keep his helicopters, which he later used to crush his domestic opponents and make new threats against regional enemies. Most Bush administration officials believed that the destruction of a large part of Saddam's army in Kuwait and in southern Iraq would limit his capacity to inflict damage on others, but Iraq's quick retreat gave coalition forces little time to respond, and so the Republican Guard was not pursued as vigorously as necessary to cripple its offensive capabilities. Saddam understood immediately that he had been given a second chance. "Soon he was laughing and kidding and joking and talking about Bush," Samarrai claimed.[77] Within weeks, Saddam was back to his old tricks, broadcasting that the Iraqis "had demolished the aura of the United States, the empire of evil, terror and aggression."[78] Indeed, Saddam had his Republican Guard and he was still in power in Baghdad. A dejected President Bush noted that there was no symbolic Iraqi surrender, and in this way the First Gulf War was indeed like America's other modern wars in Korea and Vietnam. "It hasn't been a clean end," Bush concluded, "there is no battleship Missouri surrender."[79] Still, the president enjoyed enormous popularity at home and abroad, and with the demise of Soviet power the United States seemed positioned to create a new world order.

Bush's popularity was short-lived, however. The administration had made the calculated decision to end the war once Saddam's forces left Kuwait and not press on to Baghdad to remove the dictator. Regime change was never the administration's goal, Bush's national security advisor, Brent Scowcroft, reminded critics, it was simply a "hopeful byproduct."[80] Many neoconservatives argued, however, that Saddam was dangerous to global security as long as he stayed in power, and they were quite critical of the Bush administration for not going all the way to Baghdad. But the president decided to end the mission, stating "I firmly believe that we should not march into Baghdad. Our stated mission, as codified in UN resolutions, was a simple one – end the aggression, knock Iraq's forces out of Kuwait, and restore Kuwait's leaders."[81] Others on Bush's national security team agreed. Powell argued that the administration had made the right call. If coalition forces had marched to Baghdad, Powell warned, "we would be ruling Baghdad today – at unpardonable expense in terms of money, lives lost, and ruined regional relationships."[82] Scowcroft explained that "we might be worse off today" had the United States tried to march on Baghdad. "We had a crucial but limited objective in the Gulf War . . . the international coalition . . . was based on this carefully defined goal . . . If we had made Saddam's overthrow part of the objective, there would have been no international coalition: even during Desert Storm, our Arab allies stopped their troops at Iraq's border because they wanted no part of an attack on Iraqi territory." Scowcroft ironically concluded, "if we had succeeding in overthrowing Saddam, we would have confronted a choice between occupying Iraq with thousands of American troops for the indefinite future and creating a gaping power vacuum in the Persian Gulf for Iran to fill."[83] Secretary of State James Baker concurred, suggesting that the president had made the correct decision that was "enthusiastically endorsed by the military, our coalition partners, the Congress, and American public opinion."[84] Even the mercurial secretary of defense, Dick Cheney, did not support marching to Baghdad. "Once we cross over the line . . . it raises the very real specter of getting us involved in a quagmire figuring out who the hell is going to govern Iraq."[85] The pragmatic president and his national security experts all agreed that the mission had been accomplished.

To underscore this point, the Bush team went on the public relations offensive. "The ghosts of Vietnam have been laid to rest beneath the sands of the Arabian desert," Bush boasted.[86] Others applauded the efficacy of the all-volunteer army and the Powell Doctrine that had provided the strategy necessary for an overwhelming victory. Bush highlighted the close coordination of the coalition and declared a new world order, one in which responsible nations would maintain peace through collective security and enlightened U.S. leadership. General Schwarzkopf was hailed as a hero, and many cities held ticker tape parades to welcome returning soldiers.

As historian George Herring has noted, however, "war is seldom so neat."[87] Within months of the ceasefire, Saddam had rearmed his notorious Republican Guard and used them to crush his domestic opponents. Sensing that Saddam had been weakened, and encouraged by Bush administration officials, Kurds in the north and Shiites in the south launched uprisings against Saddam's oppressive rule and in retaliation for his vicious attacks on them in 1987. Hussein crushed them with brutal force, killing some 350,000 and displacing tens of thousands more. The Bush administration had hoped that Saddam's defeat in Kuwait would inspire a military coup inside Iraq, especially among disgruntled Sunni officers who the administration believed were frustrated by Saddam's arbitrary decision-making. The Kurdish rebellion was complicated by the fact that America's staunch ally, Turkey, did not support an independent Kurdish state on its border. Other White House officials feared that a popular uprising by Iraq's Shiite majority might lead to a pro-Iran policy from Baghdad, something the Bush administration had long feared. While Saddam slaughtered tens of thousands of his own people, the Bush administration struggled with geopolitics.

Some critics of the Bush administration suggested that the president's own words had led to the rebellions inside Iraq, and that it was now unconscionable to debate what to do about Saddam's brutal attacks. In a speech in mid-February 1991, Bush urged Iraqis "to take matters into their own hands, to force Saddam Hussein, the dictator, to step aside."[88] Baker hoped to instigate a rebellion among some Sunnis, including Saddam's own army officers, by making it "clear that we would shed no tears if Saddam were overthrown."[89] The plan backfired, and forced Bush into the unenviable position of watching acts of genocide develop inside Iraq. Saddam was not masterminding a plot to destroy all Kurds, but he used mass killings to eliminate the Kurdish insurgency. As human rights scholar and Obama official Samantha Power has noted, the Bush administration feared that this public relations disaster would "negate all the gains the Gulf War had brought the Bush White House."[90] Indeed, public opinion polls that had shown the president with the highest approval rating in history now dropped significantly.[91] Moved by the tragedy, the Bush White House announced "Operation Provide Comfort," the establishment of coalition-supported refugee camps for Kurds in the north. In addition, U.S., British, and French aircraft would patrol the northern Kurdish regions and eventually establish a no-fly zone for the Iraqi helicopters used in the raids. The containment of Saddam Hussein, then, was the policy inherited by Bill Clinton when he defeated George H.W. Bush in the 1992 election.

Notes

1 Eisenhower Doctrine, January 5, 1957, announced by the president in a special message to Congress. A full text of the speech is available at the Miller Center, University of Virginia.

2 "President Dwight D. Eisenhower to Secretary of State John Foster Dulles, December 12, 1956," Whitman File: Dulles-Herter Series, Box 6, Dwight D. Eisenhower Presidential Library.

3 Eisenhower Doctrine, January 5, 1957, announced by the president in a special message to Congress. A full text of the speech is available at the Miller Center, University of Virginia.

4 Ibid.

5 Ibid.

6 Peter Hahn, *Mission Accomplished? The United States and Iraq since World War I* (New York: Oxford University Press, 2012), 47.

7 Hanna Batatu, *The Old Social Classes and the Revolutionary Movements of Iraq: A Study of Iraq's Old Landed and Commercial Classes and of its Com-*

munists, Ba'athists, and Free Officers (Princeton: Princeton University Press, 1978), 985–986.

8 Hahn, *Mission Accomplished?*, 53.
9 Toby Dodge, *Inventing Iraq: The Failure of Nation Building and a History Denied* (New York: Columbia University Press, 2003), 162.
10 Judith Miller and Laurie Mylroie, *Saddam Hussein and the Crisis in the Gulf* (New York: Times Books, 1990), 42–56.
11 United States Department of State, "Iran–Iraq War: An Analysis of Possible Shift from Position of Strict Neutrality, October 7, 1983, To: Mr. Eagleburger, From: Nicholas Veliotes and Jonathan Howe."
12 Lawrence Freedman and Efraim Karsh, *The Gulf Conflict, 1990–1991: Diplomacy and War in the New World Order* (Princeton: Princeton University Press, 1993), 25.
13 State Department, "Bell Discusses Possible Helicopter Sale to Iraq," Document Number 55, Electronic Briefing Book #82, *Shaking Hands with Saddam Hussein: The U.S. Tilts Toward Iraq, 1980–1984*, National Security Archives, Washington, D.C.
14 State Department, "Notifying Congress of Truck Sale," Document Number 44, Electronic Briefing Book #82, *Shaking Hands with Saddam Hussein: The U.S. Tilts Toward Iraq, 1980–1984*, National Security Archives, Washington, D.C.
15 Lauren Holland, "The U.S. Decision to Launch Operation Desert Storm," *Armed Forces and Society* 25 (1999): 227.
16 National Security Directive 26, "U.S. Policy Toward the Persian Gulf," The White House, October 2, 1989.
17 Richard Haass, *War of Necessity, War of Choice: A Memoir of Two Iraq Wars* (New York: Simon & Schuster, 2009), 47.
18 Ibid.
19 Ibid.
20 Hahn, *Mission Accomplished?*, 87.
21 Freedman, *The Gulf Conflict*, 25–26.
22 Ibid., 29.
23 Ibid.
24 Baghdad Radio, January 5, 1990.
25 Department of Defense, "Conduct of the Persian Gulf War," April 1992, Report to Congress, 44.
26 Ibid.
27 Lawrence Freedman, *A Choice of Enemies: America Confronts the Middle East* (New York: PublicAffairs, 2008), 216.
28 Department of Defense, "Conduct of the Persian Gulf War," 44.
29 Baghdad Radio, July 18, 1990.
30 Department of Defense, "Conduct of the Persian Gulf War," 46.
31 Hahn, *Mission Accomplished?*, 88.
32 Ibid.
33 Ibid.
34 April Glaspie Memo, July 25, 1990.
35 Ibid.
36 Ibid.

37   Ibid.
38   Department of Defense, "Conduct of the Persian Gulf War," 46.
39   Ibid., 48.
40   George Bush and Brent Scowcroft, *A World Transformed* (New York: Alfred A. Knopf, 1998), 335.
41   Ibid.
42   Hahn, *Mission Accomplished?*, 95.
43   E. Lauterpacht. et al., *The Kuwaiti Crisis: Basic Documents* (New York: Cambridge University Press, 1991), 100.
44   As quoted in Freedman, *A Choice of Enemies*, 217.
45   Haass, *War of Necessity, War of Choice*, 60.
46   UN Resolution 660, August 2, 1990.
47   Freedman, *A Choice of Enemies*, 222.
48   Ibid.
49   The Department of Defense, "Conduct of the Persian Gulf War," 34.
50   The President's News Conference, August 8, 1990.
51   Ibid.
52   As quoted in Hahn, *Mission Accomplished?*, 96.
53   *Washington Post*, September 10, 1990.
54   Ibid.
55   As quoted in Hahn, *Mission Accomplished?*, 98.
56   As quoted in Derek Chollet and James Goldgeier, *America Between the Wars: From 11/9 to 9/11* (New York: PublicAffairs, 2008), 34.
57   This joke is told repeatedly in Washington, D.C.
58   UN Resolution 678, November 29, 1990.
59   The President's News Conference on the Persian Gulf Crisis, November 8, 1990.
60   The President's News Conference on the Persian Gulf Crisis, January 9, 1991.
61   H.J. Resolution 77, 102nd Congress, 1st session.
62   As quoted in Freedman, *The Gulf Conflict*, 282.
63   Department of Defense, "Conduct of the Persian Gulf War," 141.
64   As quoted in Freedman, *The Gulf Conflict*, 301.
65   Ibid., 302.
66   Ibid.
67   As quoted in Hahn, *Mission Accomplished?*, 101.
68   Freedman, *A Choice of Enemies*, 235.
69   Colin Powell interview on PBS Frontline, at http://www.pbs.org/wgbh/pages/frontline/gulf/oral/powell/1.html, accessed January 7, 2013.
70   Saddam Hussein, speech of February 11, 1991, Iraq News Agency-Baghdad Radio.
71   Freedman, *A Choice of Enemies*, 236.
72   Ibid.
73   As quoted in Bob Woodward, *The Commanders* (New York: Simon & Schuster, 2002), 319–320.
74   Freedman, *A Choice of Enemies*, 250.
75   Ibid.
76   Ibid., 251.

77   Ibid.
78   Ibid.
79   Ibid.
80   As quoted in George C. Herring, *From Colony to Superpower: U.S. Foreign Relations Since 1776* (New York: Oxford University Press, 2008), 910.
81   As quoted in Hahn, *Mission Accomplished?*, 106.
82   Colin Powell, "U.S. Forces: Challenges Ahead," *Foreign Affairs* (Winter 1992/1993).
83   Brent Scowcroft, "Why We Stopped the Gulf War," *Newsweek*, September 23, 1996.
84   As quoted in Hahn, *Mission Accomplished?*, 106.
85   As quoted in Herring, *From Colony to Superpower*, 911.
86   Arnold Isaacs, *Vietnam Shadows: The War, Its Ghosts, and its Legacy* (Baltimore: Johns Hopkins University Press, 1997), 65.
87   Herring, *From Colony to Superpower*, 910.
88   As quoted in Hahn, *Mission Accomplished?*, 107.
89   Ibid., 107–108.
90   Samantha Power, *A Problem From Hell: America and the Age of Genocide* (New York: Basic Books, 2002), 241.
91   *Gallup Poll Monthly*, August 1992.

DOCUMENTS

─────────── Document I-A ───────────

Excerpts from National Security Directive 26, "U.S. Policy Toward the Persian Gulf," October 2, 1989

Access to Persian Gulf oil and the security of key friendly states in the area are vital to U.S. national security. The United States remains committed to defend its vital interests in the region, if necessary and appropriate through the use of U.S. military force, against the Soviet Union or any other regional power with interests inimical to our own. The United States also remains committed to support the individual and collective self-defense of friendly countries in the area to enable them to play a more active role in their own defense and thereby reduce the necessity for unilateral U.S. military intervention. The United States also will encourage the effective support and participation of our western allies and Japan to promote our mutual interests in the Persian Gulf region.

. . . It is important for the United States to continue to nurture the mutually beneficial and enduring cooperative security relationships with the GCC states that grew our of the Iran/Iraq war. The Department of Defense should seek to maintain and, if possible, increase its peacetime and contingency access to cooperation through military exercises, prepositioning arrangements and contingency planning.

The United States will sell U.S. military equipment to help friendly regional states meet their legitimate defense requirements, so long as such sales do not present a security threat to Israel.

The Secretaries of State and Defense should develop a strategy for a long-term program of arms sales to Saudi Arabia and the other GCC states that serves our national interest but does not increase Israel's security burden. This strategy should focus on those sales likely to be requested that might be controversial, such as main battle tanks and advanced fighter aircraft, and outline actions for the Administration to undertake in order to obtain congressional and domestic support for such sales.

Normal relations between the United States and Iraq would serve our longer-term interests and promote stability in both the Gulf and the Middle East. The United States Government should propose economic and political incentives for Iraq to moderate its behavior and to increase our influence with Iraq. At the same time, the Iraqi leadership must understand that any illegal use of chemical and/or biological weapons will lead to economic and political sanctions, for which we would seek the broadest possible support from our allies and friends. Any breach by Iraq of IAEA safeguards in its nuclear program will result in a similar response. Human rights considerations should continue to be an important element in our policy toward Iraq. In addition, Iraq should be urged to cease its meddling in external affairs, such as in Lebanon, and be encouraged to play a constructive role in negotiating a settlement with Iran an cooperating in the Middle East peace process.

We should pursue, and seek to facilitate, opportunities for U.S. firms to participate in the reconstruction of the Iraqi economy, particularly in the energy area, where they do not conflict with our non-proliferation and other significant objectives. Also, as a means of developing access to and influence with the Iraqi defense establishment, the United States should consider sales of non-lethal forms of military assistance, e.g., training courses and medical exchanges, on a case by case basis.

The United States should continue to be prepared for a normal relationship with Iran on the basis of strict reciprocity. A process of normalization must begin with Iranian action to cease its support for international terrorism and help obtain the release of all American hostages, which will not be a matter for bargaining or blackmail. Other criteria Iran must meet before full normalization of U.S.-Iranian relations include halting its subversive activities and improving relations with its neighbors, making a good faith effort toward a peace treaty with Iraq, and improving its human rights practices . . .

QUESTIONS TO CONSIDER

1 Why did U.S. policymakers believe normalized relations with Iraq were important in 1989?
2 What steps did the United States need to take to improve relations with Iraq?
3 What were the key national security goals of U.S. policymakers toward the Persian Gulf region prior to the First Gulf War?

———————————— **Document 1-B** ————————————

Meeting between Saddam Hussein and U.S. Ambassador April Glaspie, excerpts from April Glaspie memorandum, July 25, 1990

Excerpts from "Secret Section 01 of 05 Baghdad 04237, E.O. 12356, DECL:OADR TAGS: SUBJECT: Saddam's Message of Friendship to President Bush."

SUMMARY: SADDAM TOLD THE AMBASSADOR JULY 25 THAT MUBARAK HAS ARRANGED FOR KUWAITI AND IRAQI DELEGATIONS TO MEET IN RIYADH, AND THEN ON JULY 28, 29 OR 30, THE KUWAITI CROWN PRINCE WILL COME TO BAGHDAD FOR SERIOUS NEGOTIATIONS. "NOTHING WILL HAPPEN" BEFORE THEN, SADDAM HAD PROMISED MUBARAK. – SADDAM WISHED TO CONVEY AN IMPORTANT MESSAGE TO PRESIDENT BUSH: IRAQ WANTS FRIENDSHIP, BUT DOES THE USG? IRAQ SUFFERED 100,000'S OF CASUALTIES AND IS NOW SO POOR THAT WAR ORPHAN PENSIONS WILL SOON BE CUT; YET RICH KUWAIT WILL NOT EVEN ACCEPT OPEC DISCIPLINE. IRAQ IS SICK OF WAR, BUT KUWAIT HAS IGNORED DIPLOMACY. USG MANEUVERS WITH THE UAE WILL ENCOURAGE THE UAE AND KUWAIT TO IGNORE CONVENTIONAL DIPLOMACY. IF IRAQ IS PUBLICLY HUMILIATED BY THE USG, IT WILL HAVE NO CHOICE BUT TO "RESPOND," HOWEVER ILLOGICAL AND SELF DESTRUCTIVE THAT WOULD PROVE. –ALTHOUGH NOT QUITE EXPLICIT, SADDAM'S MESSAGE TO US SEEMED TO BE THAT HE WILL MAKE A MAJOR PUSH TO COOPERATE WITH MUBARAK'S DIPLOMACY, BUT WE MUST TRY TO UNDERSTAND KUWAITI/UAE "SELFISHNESS" IS UNBEARABLE. AMBASSADOR MADE CLEAR THAT WE CAN NEVER EXCUSE SETTLEMENT OF DISPUTES BY OTHER THAN PEACEFUL MEANS. END SUMMARY . . .

. . . SADDAM SAID HE FULLY BELIEVES THE USG WANTS PEACE, AND THAT IS GOOD. BUT DO NOT, HE ASKED, USE METHODS WHICH YOU SAY YOU DO NOT LIKE, METHODS LIKE ARM-TWISTING– . . .

. . . SADDAM SAID THAT THE IRAQIS KNOW WHAT WAR IS, WANT NO MORE OF IT–"DO NOT PUSH US TO IT; DO NOT MAKE IT THE ONLY OPTION LEFT WITH WHICH WE CAN PROTECT OUR DIGNITY" . . .

. . . PRESIDENT BUSH, SADDAM SAID, HAS MADE NO MISTAKE IN HIS PRESIDENCY VIS-A-VIS THE ARABS. THE DECISION ON THE PLO DIALOGUE WAS "MISTAKEN," BUT IT WAS TAKEN UNDER "ZIONIST PRESSURE" AND, SADDAM SAID, IS PERHAPS A CLEVER TACTIC TO ABSORB THAT PRESSURE . . .

. . . AMBASSADOR SAID THERE WERE MANY ISSUES HE [Saddam] HAD RAISED SHE WOULD LIKE TO COMMENT ON, BUT SHE WISHED TO USE HER LIMITED TIME WITH THE PRESIDENT TO STRESS FIRST PRESIDENT BUSH'S DESIRE FOR FRIENDSHIP AND, SECOND, HIS STRONG DESIRE, SHARED WE ASSUME BY IRAQ, FOR PEACE AND STABILITY IN THE MID EAST. IS IT NOT REASONABLE FOR US TO BE CONCERNED WHEN THE PRESIDENT AND THE FOREIGN MINISTER BOTH SAY PUBLICLY THAT KUWAITI ACTIONS ARE THE EQUIVALENT OF MILITARY AGGRESSION, AND THEN WE LEARN THAT MANY UNITS OF THE REPUBLICAN GUARD HAVE BEEN SENT TO THE BORDER? IS IT NOT REASONABLE FOR US TO ASK, IN THE SPIRIT OF FRIENDSHIP, NOT CONFRONTATION, THE SIMPLE QUESTION: WHAT ARE YOUR INTENTIONS?

SADDAM SAID THAT WAS INDEED A REASONABLE QUESTION. HE ACKNOWLEDGED THAT WE SHOULD BE CONCERNED FOR REGIONAL PEACE, IN FACT IT IS OUR DUTY AS A SUPERPOWER. "BUT HOW CAN WE MAKE THEM (KUWAIT AND UAE) UNDERSTAND HOW DEEPLY WE ARE SUFFERING." THE FINANCIAL SITUATION IS SUCH THAT THE PENSIONS FOR WIDOWS AND ORPHANS WILL HAVE TO BE CUT. AT THIS POINT, THE INTERPRETER AND ONE OF THE NOTETAKERS BROKE DOWN AND WEPT . . .

. . . AT THIS POINT, SADDAM LEFT THE ROOM TO TAKE AN URGENT CALL FROM MUBARAK. AFTER HIS RETURN, THE AMBASSADOR ASKED IF HE COULD TELL HER IF THERE HAS ANY PROGRESS IN FINDING A PEACEFUL WAY TO DEFUSE THE DISPUTE. THIS WAS SOMETHING PRESIDENT BUSH WOULD BE KEENLY INTERESTED TO KNOW. SADDAM SAID THAT HE HAD JUST LEARNED FROM MUBARAK THE KUWAITIS HAVE AGREED TO NEGOTIATE. THE KUWAITI CROWN PRINCE/PRIME MINISTER WOULD MEET IN RIYADH WITH SADDAM'S NUMBER TWO, IZZAT IBRAHIM, AND THEN THE KUWAITI WOULD COME TO BAGHDAD ON SATURDAY, SUNDAY OR, AT THE LATEST, MONDAY, JULY 30.

"I TOLD MUBARAK," SADDAM SAID, THAT "NOTHING WILL HAPPEN UNTIL THE MEETING," AND NOTHING WILL HAPPEN DURING OR AFTER THE MEETING IF THE KUWAITIS WILL AT LAST "GIVE US SOME HOPE."

THE AMBASSADOR SAID SHE WAS DELIGHTED TO HEAR THIS GOOD NEWS. SADDAM THEN ASKED HER TO CONVEY HIS WARM GREETINGS TO PRESIDENT BUSH AND TO CONVEY HIS MESSAGE TO HIM . . .

. . . IT WAS PROGRESS TO HAVE SADDAM ADMIT THAT THE USG HAS A "RESPONSIBILITY" IN THE REGION, AND HAS EVERY RIGHT TO EXPECT AN ANSWER WHEN WE ASK IRAQ'S INTENTIONS. HIS RESPONSE IN EFFECT THAT HE TRIED VARIOUS DIPLOMATIC/CHANNELS BEFORE RESORTING TO UNADULTERATED INTIMIDATION HAS AT LEAST THE VIRTUE OF FRANKNESS. HIS EMPHASIS THAT HE WANTS PEACEFUL SET-TLEMENT IS SURELY SINCERE (IRAQIS ARE SICK OF WAR), BUT THE TERMS SOUND DIFFICULT TO ACHIEVE. SADDAM SEEMS TO WANT PLEDGES NOW ON OIL PRICES AND PRODUCTION TO COVER THE NEXT SEVERAL MONTHS. GLASPIE

QUESTIONS TO CONSIDER

1 According to Ambassador Glaspie, what were Saddam Hussein's regional goals?
2 How did Saddam Hussein characterize U.S. actions in the Middle East?
3 What did Ambassador Glaspie tell Saddam Hussein about U.S. relations with Iraq and the conflict with Kuwait?

──────────── **Document 1-C** ────────────

United Nations Resolution 660, August 2, 1990

The Security Council,
    Alarmed by the invasion of Kuwait on 2 August 190 by the military forces of Iraq.
    Determining that there exists a breach of international peace and security as regards the Iraqi invasion of Kuwait,
    Acting under Articles 39 and 40 of the Charter of the United Nations,

1. Condemns the Iraqi invasion of Kuwait;
2. Demands that Iraq withdraw immediately and unconditionally all its forces to the positions in which there were located on 1 August 1990;

3. Calls upon Iraq and Kuwait to begin immediately intensive negotiations for the resolution of their differences and supports all efforts in this regard, and especially those of the League of Arab States;
4. Decides to meet again as necessary to consider further steps to ensure compliance with the present resolution.

Adopted at the 2932nd meeting by 14 votes to none. One member (Yemen) did not participate in the vote.

QUESTIONS TO CONSIDER

1   What were the key provisions of UN Resolution 660?
2   What were member states empowered to do?

──────── **Document 1-D** ────────

United Nations Resolution 678, November 29, 1990

The Security Council,

Recalling and reaffirming its resolutions 660 (1990) of 2 August 1990, 661 (1990) of 6 August 1990, 662 (1990) of 9 August 1990, 664 (1990) of 18 August 1990, 665 (1990) of 25 August 1990, 666 (1990) of 13 September 1990, 667 (1990) of 16 September 1990, 669 (1990) of 24 September 1990, 670 (1990) of 25 September 1990, 674 (1990) of 29 October 1990 and 667 (1990) of 28 November 1990,

Noting that, despite all efforts by the United Nations, Iraq refuses to comply with its obligation to implement resolution 660 (1990) and the above-mentioned subsequent relevant resolutions, in flagrant contempt of the Security Council,

Mindful of its duties and responsibilities under the Charter of the United Nations for the maintenance and preservation of international peace and security,

Determined to secure full compliance with its decisions,

Acting under Chapter VII of the Charter,

1. Demands that Iraq comply fully with resolution 660 (1990) and all subsequent relevant resolutions, and decides, while maintaining all its decisions, to allow Iraq one final opportunity, as a pause of goodwill, to do so;
2. Authorizes member states co-operating with the Government of Kuwait, unless Iraq on or before January 15 1991 fully implements, as set forth in

paragraph 1 above, all the mentioned resolutions, to use all necessary means to uphold and implement resolution 660 (1990) and all subsequent relevant resolutions and to restore international peace and security in the area;

3. Requests all States to provide appropriate support for the actions undertaken in pursuance of paragraph 2 above;

4. Requests the States concerned to keep the Security Council regularly informed on the progress of actions undertaken in pursuant to paragraphs 2 and 3 above;

5. Decides to remain seized of the matter.

Adopted at the 2963rd meeting by 12 votes to 2 (Cuba and Yemen), with 1 abstention (China).

QUESTIONS TO CONSIDER

1 How did UN Resolution 678 differ from UN Resolution 660?
2 Did UN Resolution 678 provide the rationale and justification for a counterattack against Iraq?

Document 1-E

Excerpts from National Security Directive 54, January 15, 1991

. . . Iraq, by virtue of its unprovoked invasion of Kuwait on August 2, 1990, and its subsequent brutal occupation, is clearly a power with interests inimical to our own. Economic sanctions mandated by UN Security Council Resolution 661 have had a measurable impact upon Iraq's economy but have not accomplished the intended objective of ending Iraq's occupation of Kuwait. There is no persuasive evidence that they will do so in a timely manner. Moreover, prolonging the current situation would be detrimental to the United States in that it would increase the costs of eventual military action, threaten the political cohesion of the coalition of countries arrayed against Iraq, allow for continued brutalization of the Kuwaiti people and destruction of their country, and cause added damage to the U.S. and world economies. This directive sets forth guidelines for the defense of vital U.S. interests in the face of unacceptable Iraqi aggression and its consequences.

. . . I hereby authorize military actions designed to bring about Iraq's withdrawal from Kuwait. These actions are to be conducted against Iraq and Iraqi forces in Kuwait by U.S. air, sea and land conventional military forces, in coordination with the forces of our coalition partners, at a date and time I shall determine and communicate through National Command Authority channels. This is authorization is for the following purposes:

a. to effect the immediate, complete and unconditional withdrawal of all Iraqi forces from Kuwait;
b. to restore Kuwait's legitimate government;
c. to protect the lives of American citizens abroad; and
d. to promote the security and stability of the Persian Gulf

To achieve the above purposes, U.S. and coalition forces should seek to:

a. defend Saudi Arabia and the other GCC states against attack;
b. preclude Iraqi launch of ballistic missiles against neighboring states and friendly forces;
c. destroy Iraq's chemical, biological, and nuclear capabilities;
d. destroy Iraq's command, control, and communications capabilities;
e. eliminate the Republican Guard as an effective fighting force; and
f. conduct operations designed to drive Iraq's forces from Kuwait, break the will of Iraqi forces, discourage Iraqi use of chemical, biological, or nuclear weapons, encourage defection of Iraqi forces, and weaken Iraqi popular support for the current government.

...The United States shall seek the maximum participation of its coalition partners in all aspects of operations conducted in either Kuwait or Iraq.

The United States will encourage Iraq's neighbors Syria and Turkey to increase their forces along their borders with Iraq so as to draw off Iraqi forces from, and resources devoted to, the Kuwait theater of operations.

The United States will discourage the government of Israel from participating in military action. In particular, we will seek to discourage any preemptive actions by Israel. Should Israel be threatened with imminent attack or be attacked by Iraq, the United States will respond with force against Iraq and will discourage Israeli participation in hostilities.

The United States will discourage any participation in hostilities by Jordan. Similarly, the United States will discourage any Jordanian facilitation of, support for, Iraqi military efforts. The United States will also discourage violation of Jordanian territory or airspace.

The United States recognizes the territorial integrity of Iraq and will not support efforts to change its current boundaries.

Should Iraq resort to using chemical, biological, or nuclear weapons be found supporting terrorist acts against U.S. or coalition partners anywhere in the world, or destroy Kuwait's oil fields, it shall become an explicit objective of the United

States to replace the current leadership of Iraq. I also want to preserve the option of authorizing additional punitive actions against Iraq.

All appropriate U.S. government departments and agencies are to prepare and present to me for decision those measures necessary for stabilizing to the extent possible energy supplies and prices during hostilities.

Military operations will come to an end only when I have determined that the objectives set forth in paragraph 2 above have been met.

George H.W. Bush

QUESTIONS TO CONSIDER

1   What were the key foreign policy directives of NSC #54?
2   Was NSC #54 a declaration of war?
3   Was the scope of U.S. action against Iraq limited, or open-ended?

——————— **Document I-F** ———————

Excerpts from speech by Saddam Hussein, February 11, 1991, Iraqi News Agency-Baghdad Radio

Iraqis, your enemy believed it was capable of achieving its goals and reversing the course of history, and when he failed, he resorted to direct armed aggression. Here we are in the fourth week of this aggression with the Iraqis becoming more firm in their faith, and shining out more in front of the whole world.

The resistance of our heroes to the warplanes and rockets of aggression and shame is the strongest indication of the steadfastness, faith and light in the hearts of the Iraqis and their great readiness not to give up the role willed to them by God, the will to which they responded, faithfully and obediently.

All the good people will be victorious as Iraq, and victory will restore to the Iraqis all the requirements for a free and honorable living that they will merit as a reward for their patience and steadfastness.

Those who look for triumph should search for it not outside the great chapter of time that has elapsed, because it exists in each hour of the confrontation, in each day and week since the first hour of the siege, . . . since the first day of the armed confrontation until the last day and hour, God willing.

Those who question when and how aggression was defeated should see it in the first moment that the President of the so-called greatest country was forced – as he said – to take the decision of war after the decision of the embargo instead of dialogue, and to ally against us those whom he did bring together when America's power looked so small to him, or thus God willed it.

With this he lost his prestige and made America lose its prestige as the biggest, or greatest, nation, as he calls it.

Bush lost his prestige when he lost conviction and lost the ability to convince through dialogue in order to avoid the course of using arms.

He lost prestige when he brought in the arms which the West had intended against the Warsaw Pact, against one of the countries of the third world, which is an Arab country.

QUESTIONS TO CONSIDER

1   Why did Saddam Hussein think that Iraq would prevail in a war with the United States?
2   According to Saddam Hussein, what was Iraq's greatest asset in the coming struggle against the United States?
3   Why would the United States move to a war footing in Iraq, according to Saddam Hussein?

2

Clinton and Containment, 1992–2001

Chronology

November 1992	Bill Clinton elected U.S. president
February 1993	Bombing of World Trade Center in New York
February 1994	UN report warns of attacks against Kurds
March 1995	United Nations expands sanctions and no-fly zone in Iraq
August 1995	Defection of Hussein Kamel
June 1997	Project for a New American Century, Statement of Principles
October 1998	Iraq Liberation Act of 1998
December 1998	Operation Desert Fox

"Based on the evidence that we have, the people in Iraq would be better off if they had a different leader," claimed newly elected president, Bill Clinton, in January 1993. "But my job is not to pick their rulers for them. I always tell everybody that I am a Baptist. I believe in deathbed conversions.

The United States and Iraq Since 1990: A Brief History with Documents,
First Edition. Edited by Robert K. Brigham.
© 2014 Robert K. Brigham. Published 2014 by Blackwell Publishing Ltd.

If he [Saddam Hussein] wants a different relationship with the United States and with the United Nations, all he has to do is change his behavior."[1] Much of Saddam's behavior was being monitored by two large no-fly zones over Iraq, which limited Baghdad's capabilities to harm Kurds in northern Iraq and Shiites in the southern part of the nation. International weapons inspectors regularly toured Iraq, requesting access to sites that some suspected as potential plants for chemical, biological, or nuclear projects. In addition, there was an international sanctions regime in place that severely limited what Iraqis could import. Though Saddam Hussein remained in power, he was strictly contained. This was how the Bush administration had left affairs in Iraq, even though Bush himself could never capitalize on Saddam's confinement for his political gain. The messy end of the First Gulf War – no clear surrender, Saddam still in power and still in control of the Republican Guard – along with other cautious foreign policy acts, meant that Bush was vulnerable to political attacks during the 1992 presidential campaign.

Bill Clinton scored huge points in the presidential campaign by focusing on America's poor economic performance, but his attacks on Bush's foreign policy positions also helped secure his election. Clinton charged that Bush had time and again chosen the pragmatic path in dealing with the world's most pressing problems. From his famous unwillingness to use military force at the end of the Cold War to bury the Soviet Union on the dust heap of history, to his reluctance to march to Baghdad to take out Saddam Hussein once and for all, Bush was not an activist president in foreign affairs, claimed neoconservatives who demanded a more aggressive U.S. foreign policy. Clinton picked up on these charges, arguing that Bush offered no concrete vision of America's future international role after the Cold War, suggesting that Bush's national security team seemed perplexed by the lack of a bipolar framework for U.S. foreign policy.

In several key areas around the globe, Clinton maintained, the Bush team offered tough talk, but little else. For instance, the Bush administration offered only minor sanctions against the new military government in Haiti following a coup there in September 1991. Bush refused to intervene militarily to restore the popularly elected government of Jean-Bertrand Aristide. In Somalia, Bush agreed to send 35,000 U.S. troops to the region, but only in a limited capacity. The troops could transport UN peacekeeping forces, distribute food and medical aid, and provide technical expertise. They could not, however, engage in any military effort to stop the rampaging warlords. In the former Yugoslavia, the six republics of Marshal Tito's "socialist utopia" threatened each other with regularity. Slobodan Milosevic helped create the aura of ancient ethnic hatreds to construct a greater Serbia at the expense of other ethnic groups. In the summer of 1991 he launched attacks in Croatia, hoping to annex that territory. The following year he made a temporary alliance with Bosnian Serbs in an effort to exterminate Bosnia's Muslims. Despite the telltale signs of greater destruction to come, no one in the Bush administration forcefully advocated intervention to stop Milosevic. "Where is it written that the United States is the military policeman of the world?" asked State Department spokesperson Margaret Tutwiler.[2] Secretary of State James Baker concurred, concluding that the United States had "no dog in this fight."[3] Bush also took a cautious approach following the limited victory against Saddam Hussein, leaving a human rights and regional security crisis behind. As U.S. troops forced the Iraqi army out of Kuwait under a restricted mandate, Hussein was already targeting his Kurdish and Shiite enemies. Clinton claimed that the Bush White House had encouraged Kurds to rebel, but did nothing when Saddam unleashed his Republican Guard on them in revenge for their uprising.

Much like John F. Kennedy had portrayed the Eisenhower administration – and by extension Republican presidential hopeful Richard Nixon – as out of touch with a fast-changing and dangerous world in 1960, Clinton used Bush's pragmatism to score foreign policy points. In a speech at the World Affairs Council in Los Angeles just before the election, Clinton argued, "foreign and domestic policy are two sides of the same coin. If we can't compete in the global economy, we'll pay for it at home." Noting Bush's inability to keep pace with the changing world around him, Clinton continued his attack, "The same president who refused to make changes as American wages fell from first to thirteenth in the world was slow to recognize the changes in Eastern Europe and the former Soviet Union. The same administration that did nothing as ten million Americans lost their jobs due to tired, old economic policies also stood by as courageous Chinese students were attacked with tanks in Tiananmen Square."[4] This mixture of economics and foreign policy would come to shape Clinton's interest in globalization during the campaign. He believed that economic liberalization and the resulting expansion of democracy would make life intolerable for the world's totalitarian regimes, and that Bush was vulnerable on this issue. International relations had once been the sitting president's trump card against Clinton, especially following the Gulf War victory. But late in 1992 Clinton found his voice in foreign affairs and criticized the president routinely for his "ambivalence about supporting democracy." Clinton charged that Bush was eager to "befriend potentates and dictators" and that the president simply did not seem "at home in the mainstream prodemocracy tradition in American foreign policy."[5] Many Reagan Democrats and some neoconservatives supported Clinton over Bush because they believed that America had a duty to promote democracy around the globe through a more muscular foreign policy.

Clinton's effective campaigning brought him to the White House in January 1993 determined to take action where George H.W. Bush had refused to show initiative. But events around the globe quickly taught Clinton that humanitarian intervention and democracy promotion came with a price. This was especially true in Iraq, where Clinton immediately found himself pursuing many of the Bush administration's policies. Despite his campaign rhetoric, Clinton had no intention of using U.S. forces to topple Saddam Hussein, and he certainly did not want the responsibility for governing Iraq should there be a coup. The internal political dynamics suggested there would be a civil war should Saddam fall, and that would leave a political vacuum inside Iraq, one probably filled with sectarian violence that would be difficult to subdue. Clinton officials also worried that Saddam had created a state dependent on Baathist Party technocrats, and that if this state should fall, a long period of state-building would be necessary simply to take care of the most basic functions of government. Unlike many other nations where civil society programs and infrastructure mature along with government agencies, Iraq had not developed any of the trappings of nationhood outside of the Baathist Party. Given this complicated set of circumstances, Clinton seemed perfectly happy to ensure that Iraq comply with UN Resolution 687, issued in April 1991 (see DOCUMENT 2-A) as a way to contain Saddam Hussein's ambitions and provide greater regional security. Containment, then, became the cornerstone of the Clinton administration's policies toward Iraq.

The administration's dependence on the United Nations limited Clinton's options in Iraq, but the Security Council's willingness to tighten a global containment regime through Resolution 687 allowed Clinton to adjust his policies periodically. Known as the "mother of all resolutions," Resolution 687 was highly prohibitive. It required Iraq to accept Kuwait's national boundaries as recognized in a letter from the prime minister of Iraq to the king of Kuwait in 1932. Iraq was now also responsible for Kuwait's property losses suffered in the August 1990 invasion. This was especially painful for Saddam, but the United Nations only added to his misery by affirming that Iraq was indeed responsible for its international debt. A sanctions regime was also established that prohibited "the sale or supply to Iraq of commodities or products" that were not related to public health and humanitarian issues. Furthermore, the resolution required Saddam to confirm that he was following the Geneva Protocols for the production and use of poisonous gases and biological weapons. He had to identify the sites of production and storage, and then was required to "unconditionally accept the destruction, removal, or rendering harmless" of all nuclear, biological, chemical weapons (NBCs).[6] The United Nations also insisted that international inspectors be allowed to tour Iraq freely to determine if Saddam had destroyed these NBC programs.[7]

Since the end of the First Gulf War there had been a growing concern in Washington that Saddam was back at work on a massive weapons program.

Much of this fear stemmed from information suggesting American intelligence reports had grossly underestimated Saddam's development of weapons of mass destruction. According to a report prepared for the House Armed Services Committee in April 1992 (see DOCUMENT 2-B), "U.S. intelligence agencies did not know the entire picture" in Iraq when it came to NBC warfare capabilities.[8] The report concluded that U.S. military and civilian officials had "painted an overly optimistic picture of the extent of damage caused by the Coalition's strategic bombing offensive," and that U.S. intelligence agents were "totally unaware of more than 50 percent of all the major nuclear weapons installations in Iraq."[9] It also appeared likely that Saddam had evacuated his top scientists from NBC facilities during the First Gulf War, but now they were back at work. The report painted a grim picture of postwar Iraq, suggesting that Saddam was funneling money and technical resources into a massive weapons program in order to keep his domestic opponents from open rebellion and to threaten his neighbors. There was also a sense that Saddam had felt so humiliated by the outcome of the First Gulf War that he never wanted to be that vulnerable again. A relatively quick build up of his weapons program would allow Saddam to once again shape the international discussion on Iraqi debt and regional power.

The Clinton administration seemed right to be concerned about Iraq's weapons program. Inspectors from the United Nations and the International Atomic Energy Agency (IAEA) complained regularly that Saddam had not been cooperative in their postwar investigations. In what some critics called Saddam's strategy of "cheat and retreat," weapons inspectors were often presented with falsified or missing reports on past programs and intransigent Iraqi officials. When pressed to provide past documentation on Iraq's weapons program, Saddam would often say that all records had been destroyed during the First Gulf War. A few months later, he would produce a very limited document that showed virtually no weapons program at all. This would be followed by more documentation requests from the inspectors and then more denials from Baghdad.[10] This diplomatic dance was inevitably frustrating, but Saddam seemed to believe that he could maintain this uncooperative posture indefinitely. On this, and many other issues concerning the NBC programs, he was terribly wrong.

Because of Saddam's intransigence, the United Nations voted in March 1995 to continue its sanctions against Iraq and to expand the no-fly zones. More and more evidence surfaced that Saddam was lying about his weapons program, and this caused considerable consternation in the White House and at the United Nations. According to the Clinton administration, in early 1995, Iraq disingenuously claimed that "it has never had a biological weapons program."[11] UN inspectors had discovered about 17 tons of "biological growth media," which could be used to produce biological weapons, but Saddam denied knowing anything about the cache. More troubling were reports from IAEA inspectors who had interviewed a dissident Iraqi nuclear scientist who had defected. He claimed that Saddam had indeed restarted Iraq's nuclear weapons program and that it was much further along than the international community had predicted. Saddam continued to deny such reports, but took action inside Iraq to limit the inspectors' access to documents and sites. Iraq's refusal to cooperate with international inspections was enough to extend the sanctions against Baghdad, and it is surprising that Saddam was not more cooperative. One theory that has recently surfaced concerning Saddam's actions is that there was only a limited weapons program in postwar Iraq, mostly biological and chemical, but that Saddam himself spread the idea that he possessed a massive weapons program to keep domestic and regional rivals at bay. The lack of evidence inside Iraq of what were later called weapons of mass destruction following the 2003 invasion supports this theory. Saddam's refusal to cooperate with weapons inspectors takes on new meaning if we follow this reasoning. There were other issues inside postwar Iraq that were also a serious concern for Clinton and the international community.

One of the most pressing problems for Clinton personally was Saddam's treatment of the Kurds in northern Iraq. Clinton's national security advisor, Tony Lake, set the tone for the administration on this issue in a speech at the Johns Hopkins School of Advanced International Studies in Washington on September 21, 1993 (see DOCUMENT 2-C). Lake declared that the Clinton administration was not opposed to "using our military forces for humanitarian purposes . . . such missions will never be without risk, but as in all other aspects of our security policy, our military leadership is willing to accept reasonable risks in the service of our national objectives."[12] Lake specifically mentioned Saddam's ongoing treatment of the Kurds in northern Iraq, suggesting that Baghdad had continued to violate the no-fly zone created over northern Iraq at the end of the First Gulf War. The Bush administration had established the no-fly zone as part of Operation Provide Comfort, designed to protect Kurds from Saddam's vicious attacks. Early reports from the Clinton administration confirmed that Baghdad had resumed its harassment of the Kurds. Although Clinton was confident that the northern no-fly zone had deterred Saddam from "a major military offensive in the region," Baghdad still possessed other weapons against the Kurds.[13] In September 1994, the Iraqi regime cut electrical power to several northern districts. Over 1 million Kurds were without power, and more than 350,000 lacked sufficient water, sanitation, and hospital services. Saddam's troops had also moved into the largely Kurdish city of Mosul, Iraq's third-largest city located on the west bank of the Tigris River, approximately 400 kilometers from Baghdad. Clinton worried that Saddam was embarking on his own sanctions against the Kurds, refusing to send humanitarian aid and other essential items north. Instead, Saddam reserved aid relief for his favored supporters and the military.[14] There were also reports that Saddam had placed a bounty on international relief workers, offering a reward to anyone who killed an aid worker and thereby stopped humanitarian assistance from reaching the Kurds.[15] The UN special rapporteur for the Commission on Human Rights, Max van der Stoel, reported in February 1994 that Baghdad was "engaged in war crimes and crimes against humanity, and may have committed violations of the 1948 Genocide Convention" in its treatment of the Kurds.[16] Some at the United Nations worried that Saddam's actions in the north placed "survival of the Kurds in jeopardy."[17] Others in the Clinton White House suggested that "torture was widespread in Iraq and results from a system of state terror. . . ."[18] There is little doubt that Saddam had resumed his war against the Kurds during the Clinton years.

Shiites in southern Iraq did not fare much better. By 1995 it was clear that Saddam had engaged in one of the largest programs of ecocide in the region. His Republican Guard routinely shelled the villages that were home to those called "the marsh Arabs," hoping that destruction of their villages would cause depopulation in the predominantly Shiite areas. The destruction of nearly 70 percent of marsh villages made refugees of hundreds of thousands of people and destroyed a base of opposition to Saddam's rule. The forced displacement of Shiites caused an artificial urbanization of southern Shiites and disrupted even the most elementary sociopolitical patterns that had developed in southern villages since the mid-nineteenth century. As attacks against them escalated, thousands of Shiites fled for nearby Iran, or migrated to the Shiite slum areas in north Baghdad. Here, Saddam could keep an eye on them and control their movement. Baghdad, after all, was not part of the no-fly zone. Once these southern communities were destroyed, Saddam's secret police, the Mukhabarat, captured several important Shia clerics and held them prisoner without bringing formal charges.[19]

As Shiites and Kurds suffered under Saddam's cruel rule, Baghdad used their suffering to suggest that international sanctions were causing this grief. Saddam became quite skilled at allowing international reporters to see the suffering at first hand, but not allowing reporters to talk to those suffering most. He blamed the sanctions regime for starving Iraqi children, but in reality it was Saddam who had kept food and humanitarian aid from Kurds and Shiites. In 1994, the Clinton administration argued that Saddam was sitting on 1.6 million gallons of oil that had been authorized for sale by the UN Security Council to provide basic foodstuffs and medical attention to ordinary Iraqis.[20] Iraq refused to sell its oil because some of the proceeds would also have to be used to compensate Kuwait for property and other losses during the August 1990 invasion. So Saddam used the media to get his story out. In one unfortunate exchange, Clinton's ambassador to the United Nations, Madeleine Albright, unknowingly added to the controversy during an interview with a television reporter. The interviewer asked, "We have heard that half a million children have died. I mean that's more children than died during Hiroshima. And, you know, is the price worth it?" Albright suggested that "this is a very hard choice," but that "we think the price is worth it."[21] Later, a disappointed Albright reported that she should have "answered the question by reframing it and pointing out the inherent flaws in the premise behind it. Saddam Hussein could have prevented any child from suffering by simply meeting his obligations." Albright continued, "my reply had been a terrible mistake, hasty, clumsy and wrong. Nothing matters more than the lives of innocent people. I had fallen into a trap and said something that I simply do not mean."[22] Viewers were treated to images of starving Iraqi children and interviews with Iraqi officials who blamed the sanctions for their despair just before Albright's on-air comments, driving home the point Saddam was trying to make.

Yet there is also clear evidence that ordinary Iraqis suffered greatly under UN sanctions. In what some scholars have called "the cruelest sanctions in the history of international governance," millions of Iraqis lacked adequate health care, education, food, and water.[23] Saddam's refusal to use the Oil for Food Program effectively or to supply his people with needed services was part of the reason ordinary Iraqis suffered. But the "systematic impoverishment" of Iraq caused by the sanctions and the continued air strikes had a far greater impact on the lives of Iraq's citizens.[24] Throughout the sanctions regime, child mortality, waterborne diseases, and malnutrition increased dramatically. Even the UN Human Rights Commission eventually agreed that the sanctions against Iraq violated international human rights law.[25] Eventually, the Commission passed a resolution condemning the sanctions and resulting suffering as a human rights violation.[26] To underscore his anger over the impact of UN sanctions against Iraq, Denis Hallady, the UN humanitarian coordinator in Iraq in 1997–1998, resigned. Hallady claimed that he did so because, "above all, my innate sense of justice was and still is outraged by the violence that UN sanctions have brought upon, and continues to bring upon, the lives of children, families – the extended families, the loved ones of Iraq. There is no justification for killing the young people of Iraq, not the aged, not the sick, not the rich, not the poor."[27]

Global protests against the UN actions did not influence decision-making in New York, however, as the Security Council remained committed to the sanctions and to forcing Saddam to comply with UN demands. In early October 1994 an undeterred Saddam Hussein moved his Hammurabi Division of the Republican Guard toward its border with Kuwait. By October 8, Iraq's 15th Mechanized Brigade had been deployed to within 20 kilometers of the Kuwaiti border. Most of its heavy artillery was now pointed at targets inside Kuwait, and new troops from the Republican Guard's al-Nida Division arrived daily. By October 11 Iraqi troop strength near Kuwait was over 60,000 and there was clear evidence that "Iraq would be capable of launching an attack by October 13."[28] The United Nations was aware of Saddam's move and passed yet another resolution demanding that he "immediately withdraw all military units recently deployed to southern Iraq."[29] Clinton, for his part, ordered the immediate deployment of additional U.S. military forces to the Persian Gulf, including the USS *George Washington* carrier battle group and its accompanying cruise missile ships. Clinton sent in a new contingent of marines and two teams to operate Patriot missile batteries. Saddam eventually withdrew his troops from Kuwait, but he had gone on notice that he was not about to follow the dictates of Resolution 687, especially in regard to Kuwait.

The two biggest unresolved issues on Kuwait concerned prisoners of war and reparations. As he retreated from Kuwait in early 1991 Saddam had made sure that his army took plenty of human shields in the form of Kuwaiti prisoners. According to Resolution 687, Iraq was responsible for the full repatriation of those prisoners still alive and a full accounting of those killed. Iraq had also agreed to participate fully in a new committee formed by the International Committee of the Red Cross (ICRC) to resolve the prisoner issue. Beginning in 1992, however, Iraq boycotted those meetings and refused to provide Kuwait with any information concerning the condition of the prisoners. The ICRC held over fifty meetings on Kuwaiti prisoners, and when pressed Saddam simply replied that he "had no information."[30] After Saddam was ousted from power in 2003, the ICRC discovered mass graves of Kuwaiti prisoners and began the humanitarian process of "mortal remains exhumations and identifications."[31] DNA testing revealed the identity of 227 individuals out of the 605 missing prisoners. The tests also confirmed that Kuwaiti prisoners had been executed in 1990–1991.[32] (See DOCUMENT 2-D, REMARKS OF THE HONORABLE IBRAHIM M. AL-SHAHEEN, DEPUTY CHAIRMAN OF THE KUWAITI NATIONAL COMMITTEE FOR P.O.W.S IN IRAQ.)

Saddam was no less forthcoming with war reparations. According to UN Resolution 687, Iraq had to establish a fund "to pay compensation for claims" that resulted from its 1990 invasion of Kuwait. The United Nations Compensation Commission supervised this fund and UN Resolution 705, passed by the Security Council in August 1991, required that Iraq contribute up to 30 percent of its oil revenue to the special fund.[33] According to international law, Iraq was responsible for "any direct loss, damage, including environmental damage and the depletion of natural resources, or injury to foreign Governments, nationals and corporations," as a result of its "unlawful invasion and occupation of Kuwait."[34] Furthermore, the United Nations declared that "all Iraqi statements made since 2 August 1990 repudiating its foreign debt are null and void," and it demanded that Iraq "adhere scrupulously to all of its obligations concerning servicing and repayment of its foreign debt."[35] The special commission created five categories of claims. The lowest claim allowed was $2,500 for an individual forced to leave their work or residence. The largest legal claims filed were multi-billion-dollar demands by Kuwait's oil sector for loss of revenue and oil resources. In total there was $53 billion in claims, of which $37 billion was to go to Kuwait's oil sector which was government-owned. Naturally, Saddam refused to pay the government of Kuwait anything. His way around this obligation was simply to reduce his oil exports, or to falsify Iraq's reporting to the United Nations. The lack of revenue played into Saddam's plan to starve out Kurds in northern Iraq, however, so the United Nations allowed Iraq to sell $1 billion-worth of oil every three months for food. From these Iraqi oil sales sanctioned by the United Nations Oil for Food Program, a smaller percentage of the revenue went to the UN Compensation Commission.[36]

Like many postwar programs aimed at containing Saddam, the war reparations regime was not fully effective. Saddam claimed that he was a prisoner of British and American interests and that Westminster and Washington had used the UN Security Council to punish Iraq unnecessarily. He was willing to use the various sanctions against his government to improve his hold on power inside Iraq, however, offering kickbacks and special deals to many states if they supported some of Baghdad's nefarious activities. For example, it appears likely that France and Russia pressured the international community to lift sanctions against Iraq for their own financial gain and because they agreed with many human rights activists who claimed that sanctions had hurt the Kurds. According to an official report to Congress on the success of the Oil for Food Program in Iraq, it was clear that many states doubted the efficacy of sanctions and that "growing regional and international sympathy for the Iraqi people resulted in a pronounced relaxation of regional enforcement – or even open defiance – of the Iraq sanctions."[37] The Clinton administration argued that continued sanctions were critical to preventing Saddam from acquiring equipment that could be used to reconstitute banned weapons systems and simultaneously force him to repay Kuwait for its losses. Still, Iraq's borders remained porous, and millions of dollars worth of smuggled goods made their way to Saddam's supporters and friends. It also seems clear that Iraq's economy, though it had lost significant buying power since 1980, was able to sustain Saddam's aggressive regional ambitions.

The most serious problem remained Saddam's weapons program. In 1995 Saddam's son-in-law and minister of military industries, Hussein Kamel, defected to Jordan and was soon interrogated by American intelligence agents. Kamel reported that before the First Gulf War, Iraq had a much larger weapons program than the UN inspectors had thought. This was especially true for biological and nuclear weapons, Kamel claimed. He also suggested that Iraq still possessed hundreds of thousands of documents outlining the extent of its weapons program, though he confessed that Baghdad had destroyed all of its stocks of chemical and biological weapons following the First Gulf War. Reportedly, he also told Rolf Ekeus, head of the UN weapons inspection team, that Saddam was desperate to resume the program, but lacked the capability because of international scrutiny.[38] The UN inspectors used this information to force Saddam into a corner that they hoped would reverse public perceptions about the sanctions against Iraq and allow them greater access to alleged weapons sites inside the country. When confronted with this new information, members of Saddam's regime claimed that they were shocked, and they blamed Kamel for hiding information on the weapons program from them. In a desperate move, Saddam suggested that Kamel had been hiding all weapons program documents on his chicken farm in Iraq and he then invited UN inspectors to tour the farm. What they found was over a million pages of documents relating to Saddam's prewar weapons program.[39] After six months of living in Jordan, Kamel returned to Iraq, however, because he found life intolerable outside of his native land. Saddam forced his daughter to divorce Kamel, and shortly thereafter ordered Kamel's entire family – brothers, parents, nieces, and nephews – to be executed.

According to Rolf Ekeus, many critics of American policy toward Iraq have misinterpreted the Kamel story. Ekeus has suggested that the international community's fixation on "rusting drums and pieces of munitions containing low-quality chemicals" led many people to believe Kamel's insistence that Iraq destroyed its chemical and nuclear stockpiles following the First Gulf War, missing the point entirely. Ekeus wrote:

> During its war against Iran, Iraq found that chemical warfare agents, especially nerve agents such as sarin, soman, tabun and later VX, deteriorated after just a couple of weeks' storage in drums or in filled chemical warfare munitions. The reason was that the Iraqi chemists, lacking access to high-quality laboratory and production equipment, were unable to make the agents pure enough. (UNSCOM found in 1991 that the large quantities of nerve agents discovered in storage in Iraq had lost most of their lethal property and were not suitable for warfare.)
>
> Thus the Iraqi policy after the Gulf War was to halt all production of warfare agents and to focus on design and engineering, with the purpose of activating production and shipping of warfare agents and munitions directly to the battlefield in the event of war. Many hundreds of chemical engineers and production and process engineers worked to develop nerve agents, especially VX, with the primary task being to stabilize the warfare agents in order to optimize a lasting lethal property. Such work could be blended into

ordinary civilian production facilities and activities, e.g., for agricultural purposes, where batches of nerve agents could be produced during short interruptions of the production of ordinary chemicals.

This combination of researchers, engineers, know-how, precursors, batch production techniques and testing is what constituted Iraq's chemical threat – its chemical weapon.[40]

In other words, Ekeus believed Iraq did indeed possess a weapon's program, but it was not of the nature that most imagined.

Richard Butler, who replaced Ekeus as chief UN weapons inspector in Iraq in 1997, disagreed. He believed that Saddam did indeed have a hidden biological and nuclear weapons program and that Baghdad was simply lying to the international community. Under Butler, UN inspectors focused on gaining access to many sites inside Iraq that Saddam had claimed were presidential palaces. These numbered over 1,000 buildings in various locations. Baghdad refused, claiming that it would be inappropriate for foreign nationals to tour Iraqi presidential palaces. An incensed Butler found little support for his position at the United Nations. Kofi Annan, the UN secretary general, and Tariq Aziz, Iraq's foreign minister, agreed that "Iraq's sovereignty and territorial integrity" needed to be protected and that inspectors would treat the sites "with dignity."[41] Though they were given limited access to the presidential palaces, UN inspectors had to request permission to visit these sites, allowing Iraq to continue to avoid complete compliance with Resolution 687.

A dejected Bill Clinton reported to Congress that Saddam continued to "cheat and retreat" and that White House was growing increasingly frustrated by his refusal to cooperate with weapons inspectors.[42] Clinton also feared that the sanctions regime was showing signs of fatigue. The Multinational Interception Force (MIF) assembled in the Persian Gulf to restrict maritime smuggling into and out of Iraq had noticed a dramatic increase in the number of illegal operations since the beginning of 1996, and this development greatly troubled Clinton. In March and April of that year, over $1 million dollars worth of oil was intercepted as part of Iraq's illegal shipments.[43] Apparently, Iran had set up an illicit smuggling ring, demanding to be paid outrageous bribes for smuggling Iraqi oil to the covert international market. Some 40,000–65,000 metric tons of oil were transported illegally each month.[44] To counter this growing problem, Clinton increased the U.S. presence in the Gulf, but also called upon America's maritime allies to join the United States in a renewed effort to patrol the area. Despite some success, it was clear that the sanctions were not airtight, and that Saddam could still find money to support his weapons program. Clinton redoubled American efforts, but the UN weapons inspectors under Rolf Ekeus suggested Saddam was gaining ground.

In early 1997 Ekeus reported that he had at last uncovered evidence that Iraq maintained large numbers of operational SCUD missiles, "possibly with CBW [chemical and biological weapons] warheads."[45] Clinton wasted no time in pushing Ekeus to force Iraq to agree to an actual inspection of SCUD weapons or face dire consequences. An unusually compliant Saddam Hussein agreed, allowing the removal of 130 SCUD motors from Iraq for extensive testing in the United States. The UN Security Council took notice, passing Resolution 1051 which tightened sanctions against dual-use imports, that is products that had a civilian as well as military purpose.[46] This was especially important in the search for chemical and biological weapons because most items and research could easily be masked as for domestic purposes. But in the game of chicken that Saddam seemed most happy playing with weapons inspectors, Iraq refused to allow the United Nations to carry out its work inside Iraq. A furious Clinton urged the United Nations to do something about this latest development. On February 23, 1998, Kofi Annan and Iraq's foreign minister Tariq Aziz signed a Memorandum of Understanding agreeing that, "any further Iraqi violation of the relevant UNSC [United Nations Security Council] resolutions would result in the severest consequences for Iraq."[47] The United Nations confirmed this agreement by passing Resolution 1154 on March 2, 1998, and by sending the new UN chief weapons inspector, Richard Butler, to Iraq.

In his first reports back to the United Nations, Butler claimed that Saddam had once again seemed willing to cooperate, but that the new agreement on inspections was still being tested. The first test was Iraq's compliance in allowing weapons inspectors to tour the forbidden presidential palaces. These inspections began at the end of March 1998, and initial reports suggested that Saddam had only allowed a "baseline survey" of the eight main presidential palaces. Inspectors reported that at each site access to outbuildings was denied by locks and steel doors. Butler had all along maintained that these palaces were in fact large compounds used for weapons production. He also suspected that Saddam was moving much of his research material around the country, using each of these facilities as a holding station until UN inspectors left. Furthermore, Butler was still unable to verify "that all of Iraq's SCUD missiles warheads filled with biological agents . . . have been destroyed."[48] But Butler's reports no longer found a positive reception back at UN headquarters in New York.

Butler grew increasingly frustrated with the UN Security Council because it would not back a resolution to support the use of force to see its own resolutions enforced. The 1990s were a major turning point for the United Nations in the use of peacekeeping forces, yet many member states did not want the United Nations to violate national sovereignty. In 2005 the UN would adopt the "Right to Protect" principle, which allowed member states to intervene in the affairs of a sovereign state if that state could not, or refused to, provide basic services and human rights to its people. But, in 1998, after harrowing experiences in Rwanda and other African nations, the UN was reluctant to use force in Iraq. Butler declared that he had no alternative but to withdraw his inspectors, which he did in early December 1998 because Saddam continued to obstruct the UN's work.

While inspections ground to a halt at the end of 1998, human rights abuses inside Iraq continued to increase. The United Nations Human Rights Commission had determined that the Iraqi government had committed "massive and grave violations of human rights."[49] Fearing the worst, the Clinton administration evacuated all Americans in northern Iraq working for non-governmental organizations or U.S.-funded organizations because they too had become targets of Saddam's attacks. The House of Commons launched a campaign, called INDICT, to bring Saddam Hussein "before an international tribunal to face charges of war crimes, crimes against humanity, crimes against peace and the crime of genocide."[50] The U.S. Senate followed suit, passing its own resolution (Senate Resolution 179) in March 1998 to establish an international criminal tribunal for Iraq to examine Baghdad's treatment of the Kurds and marsh Arabs. At the time, international lawyers were gathering in Rome to consider the establishment of an international criminal court that would try such crimes and replace the UN's special tribunal system for the most heinous of crimes. The more pressure mounted against Saddam to stop his human rights abuses inside Iraq, the more he seemed to push the boundaries of acceptable behavior. In March 1998, Max van der Stoel reported that his ongoing investigations had revealed that hundreds of prisoners had been executed at the Abu Ghraib and Radwaniyah prisons inside Iraq and that most of these were people being held for political reasons.[51] The UN Commission on Human Rights passed a resolution in April condemning Iraq's actions.

Containment Plus

By mid-December 1998 the Clinton administration had decided containment alone was not enough to deter Saddam Hussein. Human rights abuses had continued to increase, Saddam had refused to pay full war reparations to Kuwait or account for its missing, Baghdad was still smuggling oil out of the country, periodically Iraq massed its troops along the Kuwaiti border, and Saddam continued to play cat and mouse with UN weapons inspectors. Clinton's new policy of dealing with Iraq meant keeping sanctions and the no-fly zones in tack, but also launching direct military attacks against Saddam's warmaking capabilities. On December 16, 1998, the United States Central Command (USCENTCOM) military forces launched cruise missile attacks against military targets inside Iraq in what is now known as Operation Desert Fox. In addition to the missile strikes, about 650 air sorties were flown, and around 600 bombs were dropped.[52] Most of the targets were of a military nature. The targets included "thirty missile and warhead development and manufacturing facilities, twenty-seven air defense sites, and six airfields."[53] In addition, Republican Guard units were targeted and two barracks were attacked, possibly killing as many as 1,600 troops.[54] At the United Nations, the other three permanent members of the Security Council – France, Russia, and China – protested against British and American air strikes. There were also demonstrations against the attacks throughout the Arab world. Clinton justified the attacks, arguing that Saddam had left him no choice, "Iraq has abused its final chance."[55] Britain's prime minister Tony Blair also defended the action, suggesting that "just because we can't get in the cage and strike him down, it doesn't mean we should leave the cage untouched and the bars too fragile to hold him. What we have done is put him back securely and firmly in the cage."[56]

The bombing raids did not stop Saddam Hussein from continuing his repugnant policies, but they did destroy the international coalition that had come together to support the First Gulf War. According to Charles Duelfer, the deputy chief UN weapons inspector from 1992 to 1998, the December 1998 air attacks against Iraq destroyed the postwar containment policy of Iraq. "Little of consequence was destroyed on the ground," Duelfer claimed, "but the bombing killed UNSCOM [the UN weapons inspection program] and the illusion that the Security Council could implement its objectives. The council was in turmoil. There had been a no vote authorizing force. Washington argued it wasn't necessary. The Russians, French, and Chinese felt otherwise and were furious."[57] Duelfer had always been a critic of the sanctions regime and especially the UN's weapons inspection program. "This was not arms control," he complained in an interview following the 1998 air strikes, "this was coercive disarmament, like the Treaty of Versailles imposed on Germany after World War I."[58] Ordinary citizens agreed. From London to Paris, from New York to San Francisco, thousands protested against the U.S. bombing raids.

Clinton and Blair remained steadfast, however, arguing that containing Iraq would continue to require "a strong military presence in the area" and that Britain and the United States would "remain ready to use it if Saddam tries to rebuild his weapons of mass destruction, strikes out at his neighbors, challenges allied aircraft, or moves against the Kurds."[59]

Some critics of Desert Fox worried that Saddam might take advantage of the situation by gaining a coalition of sympathetic allies that could help Iraq. Saddam had all along labeled the no-fly zones an imperial Western plot to "partition the region to seize control over its oil wealth."[60] Some evidence suggests that there was growing sympathy for this position inside Iraq among the Sunni minority whom Saddam had called "the swords of the state."[61] There must have been regional support for this view as well because illegal Iraqi oil exports increased dramatically from $250 million in 1998 at the time of Desert Fox to $2.6 billion in 2001. The three opposition states on the Security Council – France, Russia, and China – continued to protest against the sanctions, the Desert Fox attacks, and the Kuwaiti war reparations. The American public began to voice its displeasure with Clinton's containment policy in poll after poll. Some thought that the United States was not doing enough to remove Saddam from power, while others protested that UN sanctions and U.S. bombing raids were hurting civilians most. Many Americans thought that Saddam was winning the public relations war against the sanctions regime and few supported the UN weapons inspection program. Polls showed that most Americans were supportive of Desert Fox, but more still wanted to see the United States remove Saddam Hussein from power by force. Using force to support containment no longer appealed to the American public.[62] Furthermore, Saddam had been fighting back in the court of public opinion, skillfully using his ambassador to the United Nations, Mohammed al-Douri, to challenge American claims about Iraqi weapons (see DOCUMENT 2-E, LETTER DATED 5 MAY 2001 FROM THE PERMANENT REPRESENTATIVE OF IRAQ TO THE UNITED NATIONS). A dejected Bill Clinton acknowledged that Saddam had grown to be a thorn in his side. "I hate that son of a bitch," Clinton told his close friends.[63]

Regime Change

As public support for the containment of Iraq withered, Clinton faced political pressure to take more aggressive action against Baghdad. Clinton had come into office claiming that he supported the promotion of human rights and democracy abroad and believed that the United States at times had to use force to protect these ideals. Throughout his presidency Clinton was faced with serious questions about humanitarian intervention. He had long favored Teddy Roosevelt's words that "there are occasional crimes committed on so vast a scale and of such peculiar horror" that the United States had a duty to step in. "In extreme cases action may be justifiable and proper." Roosevelt had concluded that in a few cases, depending on the "degree of the atrocity and upon our power to remedy it . . . we could intervene by force of arms . . . to put a stop to intolerable conditions."[64] Clinton was also a Wilsonian in the sense that he believed in both a liberal internationalism that required the promotion of democracy abroad and in building "rules and institutions that advance collective security and cooperation among democracies."[65] Echoing Roosevelt and Wilson, Clinton warned, "Saddam Hussein reminds us of what we learned in the 20th century and warns us of what we must know about the 21st. In this century, we learned through harsh experience that the only answer to aggression and illegal behavior is firmness, determination, and when necessary action" (see DOCUMENT 2-F).[66] By 1999, Clinton was determined to see that Iraq was contained, but for the first time he considered the use of force to be a viable substitute for the sanctions regime and international weapons inspection.

Many who had supported him in the 1992 presidential election welcomed the change. This group of neoconservative activists had abandoned Clinton during his 1996 re-election campaign precisely because they believed his actions on the promotion of democracy and human rights had not matched his rhetoric. He had not pushed the Russians hard enough on either of these issues, and some critics charged that Clinton had signed trade deals with China without requiring that Beijing amend its human rights practices and be more democratic. As for Iraq, many former supporters believed Clinton had waited too long to take action, and that this had allowed Saddam Hussein to build up his arsenal and continue his attacks on his domestic opponents and regional rivals. Clinton heard these criticisms, and by 1998 had moved the United States to a more aggressive stance in world affairs.

This new approach to foreign policy had two main components. Clinton would build up U.S. military capabilities that had atrophied because of recent budget cuts, and he would support the creation of a judicial deterrent to war crimes, crimes against humanity, and genocide. He combined both with more aggressive action in hot spots around the globe. Clinton's new secretary of state, Madeleine Albright, supported this development. She had long chided Colin Powell, chairman of the Joint Chiefs of Staff, that he was too cautious with his military. "What is the point of having this superb military you're always talking about if we can't use it?"[67] While others in the administration were handcuffed by memories of Vietnam, Albright claimed she was a child of Munich, and did not suffer from the Vietnam syndrome. She had significant backing from a growing group of liberal intellectuals who also supported humanitarian intervention. Though critical of Clinton for failing to act in Rwanda and being slow to respond in the Balkans, this group of liberal internationalists hoped the administration was moving toward the day when it would commit U.S. troops early in a conflict to protect human rights and promote democracy. Though they disagreed with neoconservatives on many points, the liberal internationalists did support the notion that American ideals were universal and that the United States had to stand up for these values, especially in the face of tyrants like Saddam Hussein. Many feared, however, that Clinton was not ready to take action in Iraq, and that he played politics with American values. As David Rieff, a liberal intellectual and a critic of Clinton's foreign policy wrote,

"To say that one is guided by moral principles, and then make it plain that these moral principles will only be binding situationally is to risk losing moral as well as operational coherence."[68]

Following Desert Fox, Clinton was determined to prove these critics wrong. He was also determined to stop Saddam Hussein from threatening U.S. interests around the globe. Accordingly, Clinton made a clear commitment to enhancing America's military capabilities after Desert Fox. He used budget surpluses created in part by his cost-cutting measures and the dividends produced by globalization to increase military spending substantially. In 1999, for example, Clinton proposed a $112 billion increase in military spending over the next six years.[69] By the time Clinton left office in 2001 his administration had revamped the American military through massive budget increases. The United States was now spending 22 percent more on military operations and maintenance than it did when Clinton took over the White House. The military technology budget for 2001, where most new weapons systems were housed, exceeded that of the rest of the world entirely. Enlistments in the armed forces were up considerably from just a decade before, and the United States had preponderant naval and air power. Clinton, once hesitant in his use of force, would launch eighty-four U.S. military operations in his eight years in office.

Still, many of Clinton's political opponents did not believe he was prepared to use force to remove Saddam Hussein from power. A group of neoconservatives organized a campaign aimed at embarrassing Clinton politically, but also forcing him to take more aggressive action. Known as the Project for a New American Century, this group wrote several open letters to Clinton and editorials in the major daily newspapers in the United States arguing that the time had come to implement "a strategy for removing Saddam's regime from power."[70] They reasoned that diplomacy "is clearly failing," and that the policy of containment "has been steadily eroding over the past several months."[71]

Unlike liberal internationalists and Woodrow Wilson, they had no penchant at all for creating a rule-based international order with supporting institutions. Instead, they argued that the American project was all about the spread of freedom and democracy – a goal to be pursued by the force of arms when necessary. To accomplish this goal in the Middle East, many neoconservatives envisioned a series of military actions across the region with the permanent establishment of U.S. military outposts stretching across the entire zone. They believed U.S. troops would be like antibodies, attracting would-be terrorist attackers toward them and not Israel and the United States. Many in this group had been liberal Democrats and early supporters of John F. Kennedy's soaring rhetoric that America needed to bear any burden and pay any price to protect freedom around the globe. In the 1970s, they disagreed strenuously with Henry Kissinger's view of the world, claiming that détente was surrendering too much power to the Soviets. They believed that U.S. intelligence assessments of the Soviets were inaccurate, and called for a more vigilant policy to counteract Moscow's aggression. Most became Reagan Democrats in the 1980s, and believed that George H.W. Bush and Clinton had abandoned all the gains made in the Reagan years. In their Statement of Principles of June 1997 (see DOCUMENT 2-G), they said: "We seem to have forgotten the essential elements of the Reagan Administration's success: a military that is strong and ready to meet both present and future challenges; a foreign policy that boldly and purposefully promotes American principles abroad; and national leadership that accepts the United States' global responsibilities."[72]

One of the administration's most severe critics was Paul Wolfowitz, who had served in the Reagan administration and was a long-time supporter of a more muscular U.S. foreign policy. Wolfowitz argued that "the Clinton administration has been reluctant to declare Saddam's removal a goal of U.S. policy and as a result has failed to develop a serious strategy for achieving that goal. Some of the erosion of the anti-Saddam coalition can be attributed to fatigue and the effects of time, but much is also related to the fact that our partners do not see U.S. policy leading anywhere."[73] Wolfowitz had a growing number of supporters in Congress who passed a supplemental spending bill in May 1998 that included $5 million "for assistance to the Iraqi democratic opposition for such activities as organization, training, communication and dissemination of information, developing and implementing agreements among opposition groups, compiling information to support the indictment of Iraqi officials for war crimes. . . ."[74] Congress went further in August 1998, passing Public Law 105-235, which enumerated Saddam Hussein's violations of UN resolutions and resolved that "the Government of Iraq is in material and unacceptable breach of its international obligations, and therefore the President is urged to take appropriate action, in accordance with the Constitution and relevant laws of the United States, to bring Iraq into compliance with its international obligations."[75]

At the end of October 1998, one week before the U.S. congressional mid-term elections, Congress demanded that the Clinton administration openly pursue regime change in Iraq. This was an unprecedented request and highlighted how far ideology had come in the formulation and implementation of U.S. foreign policy. In the "Iraq Liberation Act of 1998," Congress declared that "it should be the policy of the United States to support efforts to remove the regime headed by Saddam Hussein from power in Iraq and to promote the emergence of a democratic government to replace that regime."[76] The president was now authorized to give Iraqi opposition groups funds to promote a coup, including military aid. Though Clinton publicly supported this measure and signed it into law, he had grave reservations about what would follow in Iraq following Saddam's removal from power. He was not alone in these concerns. Many of George H.W. Bush's former officials voiced concern that this more aggressive stance toward Iraq did not take into account the full realm of strategic necessities. They feared that the removal of Saddam by force would lead to an extended period of armed nation-building with no guarantee of success. Furthermore, they argued, that such responsibility could commit the United States to a long-term occupation of Iraq, something the Bush administration had tried desperately to avoid. It was clear that the United States had the power to remove Saddam, but success in operational objectives was not the same thing as carrying out America's policy objectives. Was it really in America's long-term interests to occupy Iraq for a decade or more?, wondered several policymakers.

One of the most outspoken critics of regime change was U.S. Marine Corps general, Anthony Zinni, who was also the chief of CENTCOM when it launched Operation Desert Fox. Zinni argued that the December 1998 air strikes had fulfilled the president's policy objectives by leading to the further containment of Saddam Hussein. The dictator was "contained," according to General Zinni. "It was a pain in the ass, but he was contained. He had a deteriorated military. He wasn't a threat to the region." Zinni also warned that regime change in Iraq could produce chaos in the region. "I think a weakened, fragmented, chaotic Iraq, which could happen if this isn't done carefully, is more dangerous in the long run than a contained Saddam is now."[77] Clinton shared Zinni's concern, and though he spoke openly about regime change in Iraq, his actions were far more pragmatic. In the first months of 1999, Clinton ordered renewed air strikes against Saddam's key military targets, but did not launch an all-out ground invasion of Iraq. Clinton's critics suggested that "toppling Saddam is the only outcome that can satisfy the vital U.S. interest in a stable and secure Gulf region," yet the president resisted that last step.[78] Instead, he planned to continue containment plus, fearing that to do more would lead to strategic and policy confusion. Clinton the Wilsonian was balancing his desire to promote democracy and freedom abroad – his policy objectives – with the means and costs to carry out these objectives. He concluded that it was in America's best long-term interest to continue containment plus, and he simultaneously pursued the creation of a cooperative and rule-based international order. For example, Clinton took a leadership role in the Rome meetings on the creation of an international criminal court to try war crimes, crimes against humanity, and genocide. This combination of Wilsonian ideals – democracy promotion through graduated military pressure and containment and the creation of a new liberal world order – seemed well suited to Clinton.

Such policies, however, created a growing ideological rift between many of Clinton's early activist supporters and the administration. This gulf widened after Americans became targets of international terrorists attacks. The first coordinated assault on U.S. soil by a terrorist group in years was the 1993 World Trade Center bombing. In February 1993, seven international terrorists belonging to Osama bin Laden's Islamic extremist group, al-Qaeda, planted a bomb in the parking garage of the World Trade Center. The bomb created a 100-foot crater "several stories deep and several more high," and it killed six people. FBI investigators joined the New York City Joint Terrorism Task Force to find the killers. They had been tracking Islamic fundamentalists in the region for months and believed that they were close to discovering a terrorist operational ring when the attacks occurred. Following the attack, 700 FBI agents launched a worldwide investigation. They turned up a vehicle identification number for the van used in the bombings, and arrested Mohammed Salameh when he returned to the rental agency weeks later to collect his $400 deposit on the rented vehicle. Three more suspects – Nidal Ayyad, Mahmoud Abouhalima, and Ahmed Ajaj – were also arrested following leads available at the crime scene. FBI agents also found the apartment where the bomb had been produced, and there was evidence that more attacks were in the making. Eventually, investigators concluded that Ramzi Yousef was the mastermind behind the attacks, leading to his arrest in Pakistan in 1995. The driver of the van, Eyad Ismoil, was also arrested with Yousef.

With six of seven suspected terrorists now in the United States pending trial, the FBI continued to piece together the picture of an international terrorist organization. Yousef, it turned out, was the nephew of Khalid Shaikh Mohammed, al-Qaeda's chief propaganda operative, who would later mastermind the September 11 attacks on the World Trade Center towers. The FBI eventually built up a case against al-Qaeda for a host of terrorist activities around the globe, including the October 1993 killing of U.S. soldiers in Somalia, the 1996 truck bombing at Khobar Towers barracks in Dharan, Saudi Arabia, the 1998 bombing of U.S. embassies in Kenya and Tanzania, and the bombing attack against the USS *Cole* in port in Yemen in October 2000. More than 275 people had been killed in these attacks and hundreds more were wounded. Clinton responded to these terrorist attacks by increasing the scope of the work of his chief counterterrorism expert, Richard Clarke. Clarke suggested in retrospect that Clinton "declared a war on terror before the term became fashionable."[79] He understood that international terrorism was the post-Cold War era's new threat, and that it needed to be dealt with at the highest levels of the government. Clarke had access to all senior-level cabinet officials in the Clinton years, and this helped him advise the president on how the terrorists were operating. Working closely with Clarke's group of experts, Clinton launched successful preemptive strikes against al-Qaeda efforts to establish a militant Islamist base in Bosnia, and against terrorist camps inside Afghanistan and Sudan.

Two millennium bombings were thwarted when intelligence investigators uncovered an al-Qaeda plot to disrupt New Year celebrations.

Some critics claim that Clinton did not use the CIA and other agencies effectively in his counterterrorism plan, however, and this created the impression among several administration opponents that he was not doing enough to stop al-Qaeda. One detractor, journalist Laurie Mylroie, claimed that Clinton allowed al-Qaeda to operate freely because he did little to disrupt its relationship with Saddam Hussein.[80] Admiral James Woolsey, who directed the CIA from 1993 to 1995, later supported her views. The Iraqi–al-Qaeda connection soon became a rallying point for those who thought that Clinton's containment plus and his counterterror program were not vigorous enough. Although there is some evidence to suggest that Osama bin Laden met with a senior Iraqi official in Khartoum in 1994 or 1995 to ask for permission to use Iraqi territory as an international training ground, the 9/11 Commission which investigated the terrorist attacks on September 11, 2001 concluded that there was no link between the 1993 bombing of the World Trade Center and Iraq.[81] It was an al-Qaeda operation from start to finish. Furthermore, it appears likely that Saddam never would have allowed al-Qaeda access to his political base among Iraqi Sunnis, a political calculation borne out by events following the 2003 U.S. invasion of Iraq.

Clinton faced his last days in office with a growing concern about al-Qaeda and a policy of containing Saddam Hussein by increasing sanctions, monitoring his weapons program, launching periodic air strikes at Iraqi military installations, enforcing the two no-fly zones, implementing UN resolutions, and joining a growing international movement for a judicial deterrent against the greatest human rights abusers. He also had concluded that containment plus had worked. Saddam was still in power, but he was greatly weakened. He could no longer threaten his neighbors because his military capabilities had been greatly reduced through limited air strikes. Although he continued to punish Kurds and Shiites inside Iraq by denying them food, medical care, and access to national politics, he had not been capable of launching any new military attacks against them. UN inspectors were no longer operating inside Iraq, but it seemed clear that at best Saddam's weapons program was uncoordinated and dysfunctional. Still, Clinton had not engaged fully in regime change, and this created ideological opposition to his policies. Furthermore, many of his sharpest critics suggested that containment plus was no strategy at all, just as George H.W. Bush's status quo plus at the end of the Cold War had not defined America's policies sharply enough. Clinton's international supporters had also abandoned the president. Once part of an international coalition to squeeze Saddam Hussein, Russia, France, and China backed away from long-term commitments in Iraq. Instead, they favored lifting the sanctions against Iraq and allowing more trade.

In hindsight, there is some speculation that Clinton's containment plus could have continued indefinitely. Supporters suggest that Saddam was contained and was no longer a threat to the region. The United States could have continued containment plus for years at acceptable costs and risks. Democratic presidential candidate Al Gore, Clinton's vice president, wanted to continue containment plus as the best policy for dealing with Saddam Hussein's Iraq. His defeat by George W. Bush ushered in instead an administration committed to regime change in Iraq. The Bush administration also suspected that there was more to the Iraq–al-Qaeda relationship than Clinton was willing to admit. Events of September 11, 2001 created the opportunity, then, for a bold shift in U.S. policy.

Notes

1 As quoted in Richard Haass, *War of Necessity, War of Choice: A Memoir of Two Iraq Wars* (New York: Simon & Schuster, 2009), 155.
2 As quoted in George C. Herring, *From Colony to Superpower: U.S. Foreign Relations since 1776* (New York: Oxford University Press, 2008), 924.
3 As quoted in Derek Chollet and James Goldgeier, *America Between the Wars: From 11/9 to 9/11* (New York: PublicAffairs, 2008),126.
4 Text of Clinton speech on foreign affairs, Los Angeles, World Affairs Council, U.S. Newswire, August 13, 1992.
5 As quoted in Chollet and Goldgeier, *America Between the Wars*, 42.
6 UN Resolution 687, April 3, 1991.
7 Ibid.
8 "Intelligence Successes and Failures in Operations Desert Shield/Desert Storm," U.S. House of Representatives, Committee on Armed Services, 103rd Congress, 1st Session, August 1993, 35.
9 Ibid., 35–36.
10 "Status on Iraq, Communication from the President of the United States, October 27, 1994," Transmitting a Report on the Status of Efforts to Obtain Iraq's Compliance with the Resolutions Adopted by the UN Security Council (Washington, D.C.: U.S. Government Printing Office, 1994), 3–4.
11 "Status on Iraq, Communication from the President of the United States, May 17, 1995," Transmitting a Report on the Status of Efforts to Obtain Iraq's Compliance with the Resolutions Adopted by the UN Security Council (Washington, D.C.: U.S. Government Printing Office, 1995), 1.
12 "From Containment to Enlargement," Anthony Lake, assistant to the president for national security affairs, Johns Hopkins University, School of Advanced International Studies, Washington, D.C., September 21, 1993.
13 "Status on Iraq, Communication from the President of the United States, December 30, 1994," Transmitting a Report on the Status of Efforts to Obtain Iraq's Compliance with the Resolutions Adopted by the UN Security Council (Washington, D.C.: U.S. Government Printing Office, 1994), 4.

14   Ibid.
15   Ibid.
16   "Status on Iraq, Communication from the President of the United States, October 27, 1994," 4–5.
17   Ibid.
18   Ibid.
19   Ibid.
20   Ibid.
21   As quoted in Lawrence Freedman, *A Choice of Enemies: America Confronts the Middle East* (New York: PublicAffairs, 2008), 294–295.
22   Madeleine Albright, *Madam Secretary: A Memoir* (New York: Miramax Books, 2003), 174–175.
23   Joy Gordon, *Invisible War: The United States and the Iraq Sanctions* (Cambridge, MA: Harvard University Press, 2010), 1.
24   Ibid.
25   United Nations Commission on Human Rights, "The Adverse Consequences of Economic Sanctions on the Enjoyment of Human Rights: Working Paper Prepared by Marc Bossuyt" (June 21, 2000).
26   United Nations, Sub-commission on Human Rights, "Humanitarian Situation of the Iraqi Population, Sub-commission on Human Rights Decision 2000/112," August 18, 2000.
27   Denis Halladay, acceptance speech, 2003 Gandhi International Peace Award.
28   "Status on Iraq, Communication from the President of the United States, October 27, 1994," 4–5.
29   UN Resolution 949, October 15, 1994.
30   "The Iraqi Documents: A Glimpse into the Regime of Saddam Hussein," U.S. House of Representatives, Subcommittee on Oversight and Investigations, Committee on International Relations, 109th Congress, 2nd Session, April 6, 2006 (Washington, D.C.: Government Printing Office, 2006), 9.
31   Ibid.
32   Ibid.
33   UN Resolution 705, August 15, 1991.
34   UN Resolution 687.
35   Ibid.
36   UN Resolution 986, April 14, 1995.
37   Kenneth Katzman, "Iraq: Oil-for-Food Program, International Sanctions, and Illicit Trade," updated April 16, 2003, Foreign Affairs, Defense, and Trade Division, Congressional Research Service.
38   *Frontline* online at http://www.pbs.org/wgbh/pages/frontline/shows/unscom/experts/defectors.html, accessed January 10 2013.
39   Ibid.
40   *Washington Post*, June 29, 2003.
41   Freedman, *A Choice of Enemies*, 296.
42   "Status on Iraq, Communication from the President of the United States, October 23, 1995," Transmitting a Report on the Status of Efforts to Obtain Iraq's Compliance with the Resolutions Adopted by the UN Security Council (Washington, D.C.: U.S. Government Printing Office, 1995), 1–3.

43 "Status on Iraq, Communication from the President of the United States, May 4, 1996" Transmitting a Report on the Status of Efforts to Obtain Iraq's Compliance with the Resolutions Adopted by the UN Security Council (Washington, D.C.: U.S. Government Printing Office, 1996), 2.

44 "Status on Iraq, Communication from the President of the United States, March 7, 1997," Transmitting a Report on the Status of Efforts to Obtain Iraq's Compliance with the Resolutions Adopted by the UN Security Council (Washington, D.C.: U.S. Government Printing Office, 1997), 3.

45 Ibid., 2

46 UN Resolution 1051, March 27, 1996.

47 "Status on Iraq, Communication from the President of the United States, April 3, 1998," Transmitting a Report on the Status of Efforts to Obtain Iraq's Compliance with the Resolutions Adopted by the UN Security Council (Washington, D.C.: U.S. Government Printing Office, 1998), 1.

48 "Status on Iraq, Communication from the President of the United States, June 24, 1998," Transmitting a Report on the Status of Efforts to Obtain Iraq's Compliance with the Resolutions Adopted by the UN Security Council (Washington, D.C.: U.S. Government Printing Office, 1998), 4.

49 "Status on Iraq, Communication from the President of the United States, May 4, 1996," 1.

50 "INDICT the Butcher of Baghdad," American Kurdish Information Network, January 15, 1997.

51 "Status on Iraq, Communication from the President of the United States, April 3, 1998," 6.

52 Freeman, *A Choice of Enemies*, 296.

53 Ibid., 297.

54 Ibid.

55 As quoted in Peter Hahn, *Mission Accomplished?: The United States and Iraq since World War I* (New York: Oxford University Press, 2012), 125.

56 As quoted in Freedman, *A Choice of Enemies*, 297.

57 Charles Duelfer, *Hide and Seek: The Search for Truth in Iraq* (New York: PublicAffairs, 2009), 161–170.

58 Ibid., 68–72.

59 As quoted in Freedman, *A Choice of Enemies*, 297.

60 As quoted in Hahn, *Mission Accomplished?*, 125.

61 Ibid.

62 Freedman, *A Choice of Enemies*, 297.

63 As quoted in Taylor Branch, *The Clinton Tapes: Conversations with a President* (New York: Simon & Schuster, 2003), 516–517.

64 As quoted in Gary J. Bass, *Freedom's Battle: The Origins of Humanitarian Intervention* (New York: Vintage, 2009), 3.

65 G. John Ikenberry, Thomas J. Knock, Anne-Marie Slaughter, and Tony Smith, *The Crisis of American Foreign Policy: Wilsonianism in the Twenty-first Century* (Princeton: Princeton University Press, 2009), 2.

66 Text of President Clinton's address to the Joint Chiefs of Staff and Pentagon staff, February 17, 1998.

67 Herring, *From Colony to Superpower*, 932.

68   As quoted in John Dumbrell, *Clinton's Foreign Policy: Between the Bushes, 1992–2000* (London: Routledge, 2009), 80. Rieff has since reversed himself on this position.

69   Ibid., 142.

70   Project for the New American Century, "Letter to President Clinton, January 26, 1998."

71   Ibid.

72   Project for the New American Century, "Statement of Principles, June 3, 1997."

73   Paul Wolfowitz, Op-ed, *Washington Post*, November 9, 1997.

74   As quoted in Hahn, *Mission Accomplished?*, 129.

75   Ibid.

76   H.R. 4655, "Iraq Liberation Act of 1998 (Enrolled Bill, Sent to the President), Bill Summary and Status for the 105th Congress, Public Law 105-338, October 31, 1998, Sponsor, Representative Gilman, Related Bill S.2525, 6.

77   Hahn, *Mission Accomplished?*, 130.

78   Tom Ricks, *Fiasco: The American Military Adventure in Iraq* (New York: Penguin, 2006), 22–23.

79   Richard Clarke, *Against All Enemies: Inside America's War on Terror* (New York: Free Press, 2004), 129.

80   Hahn, *Mission Accomplished?*, 128.

81   *The 9/11 Commission Report, with Related Documents* (Boston: Bedford/St. Martin's, 2007), 88–91, 104–107.

DOCUMENTS

Document 2-A

Excerpts from United Nations Resolution 687, April 6, 1991

RESOLUTION 687 (1991)

Adopted by the Security Council at its 2981st meeting, on 3 April 1991
  The Security Council,
  Recalling its resolutions 660 (1990) of 2 August 1990, 661 (1990) of 6 August 1990, 662 (1990) of 9 August 1990, 664 (1990) of 18 August 1990, 665 (1990) of 25 August 1990, 666 (1990) of 13 September 1990, 667 (1990) of 16 September 1990, 669 (1990) of 24 September 1990, 670 (1990) of 25 September 1990, 674 (1990) of 29 October 1990, 677 (1990) of 28 November 1990, 678 (1990) of 29 November 1990 and 686 (1991) of 2 March 1991,
  Welcoming the restoration to Kuwait of its sovereignty, independence and territorial integrity and the return of its legitimate Government,

Affirming the commitment of all Member States to the sovereignty, territorial integrity and political independence of Kuwait and Iraq, and noting the intention expressed by the Member States cooperating with Kuwait under paragraph 2 of resolution 678 (1990) to bring their military presence in Iraq to an end as soon as possible consistent with paragraph 8 of resolution 686 (1991),

Reaffirming the need to be assured of Iraq's peaceful intentions in the light of its unlawful invasion and occupation of Kuwait,

Taking note of the letter sent by the Minister for Foreign Affairs of Iraq on 27 February 1991 and those sent pursuant to resolution 686 (1991),

Noting that Iraq and Kuwait, as independent sovereign States, signed at Baghdad on 4 October 1963 "Agreed Minutes Between the State of Kuwait and the Republic of Iraq Regarding the Restoration of Friendly Relations, Recognition and Related Matters", thereby recognizing formally the boundary between Iraq and Kuwait and the allocation of islands, which were registered with the United Nations in accordance with Article 102 of the Charter of the United Nations and in which Iraq recognized the independence and complete sovereignty of the State of Kuwait within its borders as specified and accepted in the letter of the Prime Minister of Iraq dated 21 July 1932, and as accepted by the Ruler of Kuwait in his letter dated 10 August 1932,

Conscious of the need for demarcation of the said boundary,

Conscious also of the statements by Iraq threatening to use weapons in violation of its obligations under the Geneva Protocol for the Prohibition of the Use in War of Asphyxiating, Poisonous or Other Gases, and of Bacteriological Methods of Warfare, signed at Geneva on 17 June 1925, and of its prior use of chemical weapons and affirming that grave consequences would follow any further use by Iraq of such weapons,

Recalling that Iraq has subscribed to the Declaration adopted by all States participating in the Conference of States Parties to the 1925 Geneva Protocol and Other Interested States, held in Paris from 7 to 11 January 1989, establishing the objective of universal elimination of chemical and biological weapons,

Recalling also that Iraq has signed the Convention on the Prohibition of the Development, Production and Stockpiling of Bacteriological (Biological) and Toxin Weapons and on Their Destruction, of 10 April 1972,

Noting the importance of Iraq ratifying this Convention,

Noting moreover the importance of all States adhering to this Convention and encouraging its forthcoming Review Conference to reinforce the authority, efficiency and universal scope of the convention,

Stressing the importance of an early conclusion by the Conference on Disarmament of its work on a Convention on the Universal Prohibition of Chemical Weapons and of universal adherence thereto,

Aware of the use by Iraq of ballistic missiles in unprovoked attacks and therefore of the need to take specific measures in regard to such missiles located in Iraq,

Concerned by the reports in the hands of Member States that Iraq has attempted to acquire materials for a nuclear-weapons programme contrary to its obligations under the Treaty on the Non-Proliferation of Nuclear Weapons of 1 July 1968,

Recalling the objective of the establishment of a nuclear-weapons-free zone in the region of the Middle East,

Conscious of the threat that all weapons of mass destruction pose to peace and security in the area and of the need to work towards the establishment in the Middle East of a zone free of such weapons,

Conscious also of the objective of achieving balanced and comprehensive control of armaments in the region,

Conscious further of the importance of achieving the objectives noted above using all available means, including a dialogue among the States of the region,

Noting that resolution 686 (1991) marked the lifting of the measures imposed by resolution 661 (1990) in so far as they applied to Kuwait,

Noting that despite the progress being made in fulfilling the obligations of resolution 686 (1991), many Kuwaiti and third country nationals are still not accounted for and property remains unreturned,

Recalling the International Convention against the Taking of Hostages, opened for signature at New York on 18 December 1979, which categorizes all acts of taking hostages as manifestations of international terrorism,

Deploring threats made by Iraq during the recent conflict to make use of terrorism against targets outside Iraq and the taking of hostages by Iraq,

Taking note with grave concern of the reports of the Secretary-General of 20 March 1991 and 28 March 1991, and conscious of the necessity to meet urgently the humanitarian needs in Kuwait and Iraq,

Bearing in mind its objective of restoring international peace and security in the area as set out in recent resolutions of the Security Council,

Conscious of the need to take the following measures acting under Chapter VII of the Charter,

1. Affirms all thirteen resolutions noted above, except as expressly changed below to achieve the goals of this resolution, including a formal cease-fire;

A

2. Demands that Iraq and Kuwait respect the inviolability of the international boundary and the allocation of islands set out in the "Agreed Minutes Between the State of Kuwait and the Republic of Iraq Regarding the Restoration of Friendly Relations, Recognition and Related Matters", signed by them in the exercise of their sovereignty at Baghdad on 4 October 1963 and registered with the United Nations and published by the United Nations in document 7063, United Nations, Treaty Series, 1964;

3. Calls upon the Secretary-General to lend his assistance to make arrangements with Iraq and Kuwait to demarcate the boundary between Iraq and Kuwait, drawing on appropriate material, including the map transmitted by Security Council document S/22412 and to report back to the Security Council within one month;

4. Decides to guarantee the inviolability of the above-mentioned international boundary and to take as appropriate all necessary measures to that end in accordance with the Charter of the United Nations;

B

5. Requests the Secretary-General, after consulting with Iraq and Kuwait, to submit within three days to the Security Council for its approval a plan for the immediate deployment of a United Nations observer unit to monitor the Khor Abdullah and a demilitarized zone, which is hereby established, extending ten kilometres into Iraq and five kilometres into Kuwait from the boundary referred to in the "Agreed Minutes Between the State of Kuwait and the Republic of Iraq Regarding the Restoration of Friendly Relations, Recognition and Related Matters" of 4 October 1963; to deter violations of the boundary through its presence in and surveillance of the demilitarized zone; to observe any hostile or potentially hostile action mounted from the territory of one State to the other; and for the Secretary-General to report regularly to the Security Council on the operations of the unit, and immediately if there are serious violations of the zone or potential threats to peace;

6. Notes that as soon as the Secretary-General notifies the Security Council of the completion of the deployment of the United Nations observer unit, the conditions will be established for the Member States cooperating with Kuwait in accordance with resolution 678 (1990) to bring their military presence in Iraq to an end consistent with resolution 686 (1991);

C

7. Invites Iraq to reaffirm unconditionally its obligations under the Geneva Protocol for the Prohibition of the Use in War of Asphyxiating, Poisonous or Other Gases, and of Bacteriological Methods of Warfare, signed at Geneva on 17 June 1925, and to ratify the Convention on the Prohibition of the Development, Production and Stockpiling of Bacteriological (Biological) and Toxin Weapons and on Their Destruction, of 10 April 1972;

8. Decides that Iraq shall unconditionally accept the destruction, removal, or rendering harmless, under international supervision, of:
   (a) All chemical and biological weapons and all stocks of agents and all related subsystems and components and all research, development, support and manufacturing facilities;
   (b) All ballistic missiles with a range greater than 150 kilometres and related major parts, and repair and production facilities;

9. Decides, for the implementation of paragraph 8 above, the following:
    (a) Iraq shall submit to the Secretary-General, within fifteen days of the adoption of the present resolution, a declaration of the locations, amounts and types of all items specified in paragraph 8 and agree to urgent, on-site inspection as specified below;
    (b) The Secretary-General, in consultation with the appropriate Governments and, where appropriate, with the Director-General of the World Health Organization, within forty-five days of the passage of the present resolution, shall develop, and submit to the Council for approval, a plan calling for the completion of the following acts within forty-five days of such approval:
        (i)   The forming of a Special Commission, which shall carry out immediate on-site inspection of Iraq's biological, chemical and missile capabilities, based on Iraq's declarations and the designation of any additional locations by the Special Commission itself;
        (ii) The yielding by Iraq of possession to the Special Commission for destruction, removal or rendering harmless, taking into account the requirements of public safety, of all items specified under paragraph 8 (a) above, including items at the additional locations designated by the Special Commission under paragraph 9 (b) (i) above and the destruction by Iraq, under the supervision of the Special Commission, of all its missile capabilities, including launchers, as specified under paragraph 8 (b) above;
        (iii) The provision by the Special Commission of the assistance and cooperation to the Director-General of the International Atomic Energy Agency required in paragraphs 12 and 13 below;
10. Decides that Iraq shall unconditionally undertake not to use, develop, construct or acquire any of the items specified in paragraphs 8 and 9 above and requests the Secretary-General, in consultation with the Special Commission, to develop a plan for the future ongoing monitoring and verification of Iraq's compliance with this paragraph, to be submitted to the Security Council for approval within one hundred and twenty days of the passage of this resolution;
11. Invites Iraq to reaffirm unconditionally its obligations under the Treaty on the Non-Proliferation of Nuclear Weapons of 1 July 1968;
12. Decides that Iraq shall unconditionally agree not to acquire or develop nuclear weapons or nuclear-weapons-usable material or any subsystems or components or any research, development, support or manufacturing facilities related to the above; to submit to the Secretary-General and the Director-General of the International Atomic Energy Agency within fifteen days of the adoption of the present resolution a declaration of the locations, amounts, and types of all items specified above; to place all of its nuclear-weapons-usable materials under the exclusive control, for custody and

removal, of the International Atomic Energy Agency, with the assistance and cooperation of the Special Commission as provided for in the plan of the Secretary-General discussed in paragraph 9 (b) above; to accept, in accordance with the arrangements provided for in paragraph 13 below, urgent on-site inspection and the destruction, removal or rendering harmless as appropriate of all items specified above; and to accept the plan discussed in paragraph 13 below for the future ongoing monitoring and verification of its compliance with these undertakings;

13. Requests the Director-General of the International Atomic Energy Agency, through the Secretary-General, with the assistance and cooperation of the Special Commission as provided for in the plan of the Secretary-General in paragraph 9 (b) above, to carry out immediate on-site inspection of Iraq's nuclear capabilities based on Iraq's declarations and the designation of any additional locations by the Special Commission; to develop a plan for submission to the Security Council within forty-five days calling for the destruction, removal, or rendering harmless as appropriate of all items listed in paragraph 12 above; to carry out the plan within forty-five days following approval by the Security Council; and to develop a plan, taking into account the rights and obligations of Iraq under the Treaty on the Non-Proliferation of Nuclear Weapons of 1 July 1968, for the future ongoing monitoring and verification of Iraq's compliance with paragraph 12 above, including an inventory of all nuclear material in Iraq subject to the Agency's verification and inspections to confirm that Agency safeguards cover all relevant nuclear activities in Iraq, to be submitted to the Security Council for approval within one hundred and twenty days of the passage of the present resolution;

14. Takes note that the actions to be taken by Iraq in paragraphs 8, 9, 10, 11, 12 and 13 of the present resolution represent steps towards the goal of establishing in the Middle East a zone free from weapons of mass destruction and all missiles for their delivery and the objective of a global ban on chemical weapons;

D

15. Requests the Secretary-General to report to the Security Council on the steps taken to facilitate the return of all Kuwaiti property seized by Iraq, including a list of any property that Kuwait claims has not been returned or which has not been returned intact;

E

16. Reaffirms that Iraq, without prejudice to the debts and obligations of Iraq arising prior to 2 August 1990, which will be addressed through the normal mechanisms, is liable under international law for any direct loss, damage, including environmental damage and the depletion of natural resources, or injury to foreign Governments, nationals and corporations, as a result of Iraq's unlawful invasion and occupation of Kuwait;

17. Decides that all Iraqi statements made since 2 August 1990 repudiating its foreign debt are null and void, and demands that Iraq adhere scrupulously to all of its obligations concerning servicing and repayment of its foreign debt;

18. Decides also to create a fund to pay compensation for claims that fall within paragraph 16 above and to establish a Commission that will administer the fund;

19. Directs the Secretary-General to develop and present to the Security Council for decision, no later than thirty days following the adoption of the present resolution, recommendations for the fund to meet the requirement for the payment of claims established in accordance with paragraph 18 above and for a programme to implement the decisions in paragraphs 16, 17 and 18 above, including: administration of the fund; mechanisms for determining the appropriate level of Iraq's contribution to the fund based on a percentage of the value of the exports of petroleum and petroleum products from Iraq not to exceed a figure to be suggested to the Council by the Secretary-General, taking into account the requirements of the people of Iraq, Iraq's payment capacity as assessed in conjunction with the international financial institutions taking into consideration external debt service, and the needs of the Iraqi economy; arrangements for ensuring that payments are made to the fund; the process by which funds will be allocated and claims paid; appropriate procedures for evaluating losses, listing claims and verifying their validity and resolving disputed claims in respect of Iraq's liability as specified in paragraph 16 above; and the composition of the Commission designated above;

F

20. Decides, effective immediately, that the prohibitions against the sale or supply to Iraq of commodities or products, other than medicine and health supplies, and prohibitions against financial transactions related thereto contained in resolution 661 (1990) shall not apply to foodstuffs notified to the Security Council Committee established by resolution 661 (1990) concerning the situation between Iraq and Kuwait or, with the approval of that Committee, under the simplified and accelerated "no-objection" procedure, to materials and supplies for essential civilian needs as identified in the report of the Secretary-General dated 20 March 1991, and in any further findings of humanitarian need by the Committee;

21. Decides that the Security Council shall review the provisions of paragraph 20 above every sixty days in the light of the policies and practices of the Government of Iraq, including the implementation of all relevant resolutions of the Security Council, for the purpose of determining whether to reduce or lift the prohibitions referred to therein;

22. Decides that upon the approval by the Security Council of the programme called for in paragraph 19 above and upon Council agreement that Iraq has completed all actions contemplated in paragraphs 8, 9, 10, 11, 12 and 13

above, the prohibitions against the import of commodities and products originating in Iraq and the prohibitions against financial transactions related thereto
contained in resolution 661 (1990) shall have no further force or effect;

23. Decides that, pending action by the Security Council under paragraph 22
above, the Security Council Committee established by resolution 661
(1990) shall be empowered to approve, when required to assure adequate
financial resources on the part of Iraq to carry out the activities under
paragraph 20 above, exceptions to the prohibition against the import of
commodities and products originating in Iraq;

24. Decides that, in accordance with resolution 661 (1990) and subsequent
related resolutions and until a further decision is taken by the Security
Council, all States shall continue to prevent the sale or supply, or the promotion or facilitation of such sale or supply, to Iraq by their nationals, or
from their territories or using their flag vessels or aircraft, of:
    (a) Arms and related materiel of all types, specifically including the sale or
        transfer through other means of all forms of conventional military
        equipment, including for paramilitary forces, and spare parts and com-
        ponents and their means of production, for such equipment;
    (b) Items specified and defined in paragraphs 8 and 12 above not other-
        wise covered above;
    (c) Technology under licensing or other transfer arrangements used in
        the production, utilization or stockpiling of items specified in subpara-
        graphs (a) and (b) above;
    (d) Personnel or materials for training or technical support services relat-
        ing to the design, development, manufacture, use, maintenance or
        support of items specified in subparagraphs (a) and (b) above;

25. Calls upon all States and international organizations to act strictly in accordance with paragraph 24 above, notwithstanding the existence of any
contracts, agreements, licences or any other arrangements;

26. Requests the Secretary-General, in consultation with appropriate Governments, to develop within sixty days, for the approval of the Security Council,
guidelines to facilitate full international implementation of paragraphs 24 and
25 above and paragraph 27 below, and to make them available to all States and
to establish a procedure for updating these guidelines periodically;

27. Calls upon all States to maintain such national controls and procedures and
to take such other actions consistent with the guidelines to be established
by the Security Council under paragraph 26 above as may be necessary to
ensure compliance with the terms of paragraph 24 above, and calls upon
international organizations to take all appropriate steps to assist in ensuring
such full compliance;

28. Agrees to review its decisions in paragraphs 22, 23, 24 and 25 above, except
for the items specified and defined in paragraphs 8 and 12 above, on a regular
basis and in any case one hundred and twenty days following passage of the

present resolution, taking into account Iraq's compliance with the resolution and general progress towards the control of armaments in the region;

29. Decides that all States, including Iraq, shall take the necessary measures to ensure that no claim shall lie at the instance of the Government of Iraq, or of any person or body in Iraq, or of any person claiming through or for the benefit of any such person or body, in connection with any contract or other transaction where its performance was affected by reason of the measures taken by the Security Council in resolution 661 (1990) and related resolutions;

G

30. Decides that, in furtherance of its commitment to facilitate the repatriation of all Kuwaiti and third country nationals, Iraq shall extend all necessary cooperation to the International Committee of the Red Cross, providing lists of such persons, facilitating the access of the International Committee of the Red Cross to all such persons wherever located or detained and facilitating the search by the International Committee of the Red Cross for those Kuwaiti and third country nationals still unaccounted for;

31. Invites the International Committee of the Red Cross to keep the Secretary-General apprised as appropriate of all activities undertaken in connection with facilitating the repatriation or return of all Kuwaiti and third country nationals or their remains present in Iraq on or after 2 August 1990;

H

32. Requires Iraq to inform the Security Council that it will not commit or support any act of international terrorism or allow any organization directed towards commission of such acts to operate within its territory and to condemn unequivocally and renounce all acts, methods and practices of terrorism;

I

33. Declares that, upon official notification by Iraq to the Secretary-General and to the Security Council of its acceptance of the provisions above, a formal cease-fire is effective between Iraq and Kuwait and the Member States cooperating with Kuwait in accordance with resolution 678 (1990);

34. Decides to remain seized of the matter and to take such further steps as may be required for the implementation of the present resolution and to secure peace and security in the area.

QUESTIONS TO CONSIDER

1   What specific actions does UN Resolution 687 endorse?
2   How will UN Resolution 687 be enforced? Who will enforce it?
3   How have past UN resolutions shaped UN Resolution 687?
4   Do you think UN resolutions are effective?

———————— **Document 2-B** ————————

Excerpts from "Intelligence Successes and Failures in Operations Desert Shield/Desert Storm," U.S. House of Representatives, Committee on Armed Services, 103rd Congress, 1st session, August 1993

"...The intelligence community had a good handle on Iraq's chemical capabilities, but a poor knowledge of its nuclear capabilities.... One of the clearest examples of an intelligence failure during Operations Desert Shield/Desert Storm was the inability to provide intelligence quickly and reliably to warfighters throughout the theater of operations."

". . . The U.S. intelligence agencies had been closely watching Iraq's nuclear, biological and chemical capabilities for many years before Kuwait was invaded. This had nothing to do with political relations with Baghdad. A major target of U.S. intelligence has long been NBC capabilities, whether they be in friendly or hostile nations.

Although NBC has long been a major focus of all U.S. intelligence agencies, it is clear from the postwar revelations extracted by the United Nations that U.S. intelligence agencies did not know the entire picture. Based on what is known now, the U.S. intelligence community:

- Had good intelligence on Iraqi chemical capabilities.
- Had poorer intelligence on Iraq's nuclear capabilities, in fact, based on data gleaned from defectors and other sources since the end of the war, it is now known that we were totally unaware of more than 50 percent of all the major nuclear weapons installations in Iraq.
- Had an indeterminate record on Iraq's biological capabilities, given that the U.N. has extracted very little additional information on Iraqi biological capabilities, there is no new data base against which to judge the performance of the U.S. intelligence agencies against Iraqi biological weapons before the war.

There was clearly inadequate data on Iraq's nuclear operations. However, it is only fair to point out that before Operation Desert Storm, the U.S. intelligence agencies knew full well that they had inadequate information. Estimates from individual analysis of the time it would take Baghdad to build a nuclear device ranged from six months to 10 years, reflecting the sizable holes the analysts knew made Swiss cheese of their data base.

Unfortunately during the war, U.S. military and civilian officials painted an overly optimistic picture of the extent of the damage caused by the Coalition's strategic bombing offensive."

QUESTIONS TO CONSIDER

1   What lessons can be learned from intelligence operations in Iraq during Desert Shield/Desert Storm?
2   Should policymakers act on limited information?
3   How do you plan for the unexpected contingencies that naturally exist during international conflict?

Document 2-C

Excerpts from the remarks of Anthony Lake, assistant to the president for national security affairs, "From Containment to Enlargement," Johns Hopkins University, School of Advanced International Studies, Washington, D.C., September 21, 1993

". . . In the eight months since he took office, President Clinton has pursued those goals vigorously. We have completed a sweeping review of our military strategy and forces. We have led a global effort to support the historic reforms in Russia and the other new states. We have helped defend democracy in Haiti and Guatemala and secured important side agreements that pave the way for enactment of the North American Free Trade Agreement. We have facilitated major advances in the Mideast peace process, working with our Arab partners while strengthening our bonds with Israel. We have pursued steps with our G-7 partners to stimulate world economic growth. We have placed our relations with Japan on a new foundation and set a vision of a New Pacific Community. We are putting in place practical policies to preserve the environment and to limit the spread of weapons of mass destruction. We have proceeded with sweeping reductions in nuclear arms and declared a moratorium on testing as we move toward a comprehensive test ban. We have struggled with the complex tragedy in Bosnia. And we have worked to complete our mission or ensuring lasting relief from starvation in Somalia.

But engagement itself is not enough. We also need to communicate anew why that engagement is essential. If we do not, our government's reactions to foreign events can seem disconnected; individual setbacks may appear to define the whole; public support for our engagement likely would wane; and America could be harmed by a rise in protectionism, unwise cuts to our military force structure or readiness, a loss of the resources necessary for our diplomacy – and thus the erosion of US influence abroad.

Stating our purpose is neither academic nor rhetorical. What we do outside our borders has immediate and lasting consequences for all Americans. As the President often notes, the line between foreign and domestic policy has evaporated. Our choices about America's foreign policy will help determine whether Americans' real incomes double every 26 years, as they did in the 1960s, or every 36 years, as they did during the late '70s and '80s. Whether the 25 nations with weapons or mass destruction grow in number or decline. Whether the next quarter century will see terrorism, which injured or killed more than 2000 Americans during the last quarter century, expand or recede as a threat. Whether the nations or the world will be more able or less able to address regional disputes, humanitarian needs and the threat of environmental degradation."

"... In such a world, our interests and ideals compel us not only to be engaged, but to lead. And in a real-time world of change and information, it is all the more important that our leadership be steadied around our central purpose.

That purpose can be found in the underlying rationale for our engagement throughout this century. As we fought aggressors and contained communism, our engagement abroad was animated both by calculations of power and by this belief: to the extent democracy and market economics hold sway in other nations, our own nation will be more secure, prosperous and influential, while the broader world will be more humane and peaceful.

The expansion of market-based economics abroad helps expand our exports and create American jobs, while it also improves living conditions and fuels demands for political liberalization abroad. The addition of new democracies makes us more secure because democracies tend not to wage war on each other or sponsor terrorism. They are more trustworthy in diplomacy and do a better job of respecting the human rights of their people.

These dynamics lay at the heart of Woodrow Wilson's most profound insights; although his moralism sometimes weakened his argument, he understood that our own security is shaped by the character of foreign regimes. Indeed, most Presidents who followed, Republicans and Democrats alike, understood we must promote democracy and market economics in the world – because it protects our interests and security; and because it reflects values that are both American and universal.

Throughout the Cold War, we contained a global threat to market democracies; now we should seek to enlarge their reach, particularly in places of special significance to us.

The successor to a doctrine of containment must be a strategy of enlargement – enlargement of the world's free community of market democracies.

During the Cold War, even children understood America's security mission; as they looked at those maps on their schoolroom walls, they knew we were trying to contain the creeping expansion of that big, red blob. Today, at great risk of oversimplification, we might visualize our security mission as promoting the enlargement of the "blue areas" of market democracies. The difference, of course, is that we do not seek to expand the reach of our institutions by force, subversion or repression.

We must not allow this overarching goal to drive us into overreaching actions. To be successful, a strategy of enlargement must provide distinctions and set priorities. It must combine our broad goals of fostering democracy and markets with our more traditional geostrategic interests. And it must suggest how best to expend our large but nonetheless limited national security resources: financial, diplomatic and military.

In recent years, discussions about when to use force have turned on a set of vital questions, such as whether our forces match our objectives; whether we can fight and win in a time that is acceptable; whether we have a reasonable exit if we do not; whether there is public and congressional support. But we have overlooked a prior, strategic question – the question of 'where' – which sets the context for such military judgments.

I see four components to a strategy of enlargement.

First, we should strengthen the community of major market democracies - including our own – which constitutes the core from which enlargement is proceeding.

Second, we should help foster and consolidate new democracies and market economies, where possible, especially in states of special significance and opportunity.

Third, we must counter the aggression – and support the liberalization – of states hostile to democracy and markets.

Fourth, we need to pursue our humanitarian agenda not only by providing aid, but also by working to help democracy and market economics take root in regions of greatest humanitarian concern.

A host of caveats must accompany a strategy of enlargement. For one, we must be patient. As scholars observe waves of democratic advance are often followed by reverse waves of democratic setback. We must be ready for uneven progress, even outright reversals.

Our strategy must be pragmatic. Our interests in democracy and markets do not stand alone. Other American interests at times will require us to befriend and even defend non-democratic states for mutually beneficial reasons.

Our strategy must view democracy broadly – it must envision a system that includes not only elections but also such features as an independent judiciary and protections of human rights.

Our strategy must also respect diversity. Democracy and markets can come in many legitimate variants. Freedom has many faces."

"...The third element of our strategy of enlargement should be to minimize the ability of states outside the circle of democracy and markets to threaten it.

Democracy and market economics have always been subversive ideas to those who rule without consent. These ideas remain subversive today. Every dictator, theocrat, kleptocrat or central planner in an unelected regime has reason to fear their subjects will suddenly demand the freedom to make their own decisions.

We should expect the advance of democracy and markets to trigger forceful reactions from those whose power is not popularly derived. The rise of Burma's democracy movement led to the jailing of its most vocal proponent, Aung San Suu Kyi. Russia's reforms have aroused the resistance of the nomenklatura.

Centralized power defends itself. It not only wields tools of state power such as military force, political imprisonment and torture, but also exploits the intolerant energies of racism, ethnic prejudice, religious persecution, xenophobia, and irredentism. Those whose power is threatened by the spread of democracy and markets will always have a personal stake in resisting those practices with passionate intensity.

When such leaders sit atop regional powers, such as Iran and Iraq, they may engage in violence and lawlessness that threatens the United States and other democracies. Such reactionary, 'backlash' states are more likely to sponsor terrorism and traffic in weapons of mass destruction and ballistic missile technologies. They are more likely to suppress their own people, foment ethnic rivalries and threaten their neighbors.

In this world of multiplying democracies, expanding markets and accelerating commerce, the rulers or backlash states face an unpleasant choice. They can seek to isolate their people from these liberating forces. If they do, however, they cut themselves off from the very forces that create wealth and social dynamism. Such states tend to rot from within both economically and spiritually. But as they grow weaker, they also may become more desperate and dangerous.

Our policy toward such states, so long as they act as they do, must seek to isolate them diplomatically, militarily, economically, and technologically. It must stress intelligence, counterterrorism, and multilateral export controls. It also must apply global norms regarding weapons of mass destruction and ensure their enforcement. While some of these efforts will be unilateral, international rules are necessary and may be particularly effective in enforcing sanctions, transparency and export controls, as the work of the IAEA in Iraq demonstrates.

When the actions of such states directly threaten our people, our forces, or our vital interests, we clearly must be prepared to strike back decisively and unilaterally, as we did when Iraq tried to assassinate former President Bush. We must always maintain the military power necessary to deter, or if necessary defeat, aggression by these regimes. Because the source of such threats will be diverse and unpredictable, we must seek to ensure that our forces are increasingly ready, mobile, flexible and smart, as the President and Secretary Aspin have stressed.

Let me take a moment to illustrate what America's armed forces are doing, right now as we meet: In South Korea, some 37,000 U.S. troops are on guard against aggression from the North. In the Persian Gulf, the 'Abraham Lincoln' carrier battle group and other forces remain stationed as a follow up to Operation Desert Storm. And as we move toward new Middle East peace agreements, some 1000 soldiers continue to help keep the peace in the Sinai peninsula. Such forces cost money. Some people may regret our 'Bottom up Review' did not suggest a substantially smaller or cheaper force. But the fact is: these forces, the world's very best, are part of the necessary price of security and leadership in the world.

While some backlash states may seek to wall themselves off from outside influence, other anti-democratic states will opt to pursue greater wealth by liberalizing their economic rules. Sooner or later, however, these states confront the need to liberalize the flow of information into and within their nation, and to tolerate the rise of an entrepreneurial middle-class. Both developments weaken despotic rule and lead over time to rising demands for democracy. Chile's experience under General Pinochet proves market economies can thrive for a time without democracy. But both our instinct and recent history in Chile, South Korea and elsewhere tell us they cannot do so forever.

We cannot impose democracy on regimes that appear to be opting for liberalization, but we may be able to help steer some of them down that path while providing penalties that raise the costs of repression and aggressive behavior. These efforts have special meaning for our relations with China. That relationship is one of the most important in the world, for China will increasingly be a major world power, and along with our ties to Japan and Korea, our relationship with China will strongly shape both our security and economic interests in Asia. It is in the interest of both our nations for China to continue its economic liberalization while respecting the human rights of its people and international norms regarding weapons sales. That is why we conditionally extended China's trading advantages, sanctioned its missile exports and proposed creation of a new Radio Free Asia. We seek a stronger relationship with China that reflects both our values and our interests.

Our policies toward the Islamic world prove another example. Let me emphasize this point: our nation respects the many contributions Islam has made to the world over the past 1300 years, and we appreciate the close bonds of values and history between Islam and the Judeo-Christian beliefs of most Americans. We will extend every expression of friendship to those of the Islamic faith who abide in peace and tolerance. But we will provide every resistance to militants who distort Islamic doctrines and seek to expand their influence by force.

* * *

The Humanitarian Agenda

The fourth part of a strategy of enlargement involves our humanitarian goals, which play an important supporting role in our efforts to expand democracy and markets. Our humanitarian actions nurture the American public's support for our engagement abroad. Our humanitarian efforts also can stimulate democratic and market development in many areas of the world. Ultimately, the world trusts our leadership in that broader effort in part because it witnesses our humanitarian deeds: it knows that our responses to hunger and suffering, from Bangladesh to Somalia to Chernobyl, are an expression of who we are as a nation. Our humanitarian efforts must continue to include a broad array of programs – economic and military assistance, disaster relief, and projects to assist education, nutrition and health. Over the coming months we plan to work with Congress to reform this array of aid programs – to focus them more strategically and efficiently on the promotion of democracy and markets, environmentally sustainable development and early responses to social and economic chaos.

We face great challenges to our humanitarian instincts in this era, and far fewer barriers to action than there were during the period of superpower competition. Public pressure for our humanitarian engagement increasingly may be driven by televised images, which can depend in turn on such considerations as where CNN sends its camera crews. But we must bring other considerations to bear as well: cost; feasibility; the permanence of the improvement our assistance will bring; the willingness of regional and international bodies to do their part; and the likelihood that our actions will generate broader security benefits for the people and the region in question.

While there will be increasing calls on us to help stem bloodshed and suffering in ethnic conflicts, and while we will always bring our diplomacy to bear, these criteria suggest there will be relatively few intra-national ethnic conflicts that justify our military intervention. Ultimately, on these and other humanitarian needs, we will have to pick and choose.

Where we can make a difference, as in Somalia and Northern Iraq, we should not oppose using our military forces for humanitarian purposes simply because these missions do not resemble major wars for control of territory. Such missions will never be without risk, but as in all other aspects of our security policy, our military leadership is willing to accept reasonable risks in the service of our national objectives. . . ."

QUESTIONS TO CONSIDER

1 According to Tony Lake, what were the Clinton administration's major foreign policy objectives and how was the United States going to achieve them?

2 What does Lake think the administration's position on humanitarian intervention should be?

3 How will the United States deal with terrorists?

4 What are the major foreign policy crises facing the United States?

—————— **Document 2-D** ——————

Remarks of the Honorable Ibrahim M. Al-Shaheen, deputy chairman of the Kuwaiti National Committee for P.O.W.s in Iraq, August 6, 2006, U.S. House Committee on International Relations, Subcommittee on Oversight and Investigations

May I briefly introduce a summary of this humanitarian tragedy:

On the Second of August 1990, Iraqi armed forces invaded Kuwait in an act of aggression that was universally condemned. The Iraqi forces remained in Kuwait for seven months, during which they committed all sorts of atrocities against the Kuwaiti people. Such as, cruel executions of innocent individuals in front of their families, random and mass arrests of citizens, detained in various locations before transferring them forcefully to prisons in Iraq. A crime against humanity and a violation of human rights.

During the years that followed the liberation of Kuwait, every conceivable effort was exerted in vain, to convince the former Iraqi regime [Saddam Hussein] to account for the fate of the prisoners. A humanitarian committee chaired by the International Committee of the Red Cross was set up to resolve this issue. Iraq signed its commitment to actively participates [sic] in the meetings. But the former regime boycotted the meetings in 1992 until 1994, and then again boycotted them from 1998 until 2003. All along, Kuwait insisted on the humanitarian nature of the issue, expressing the importance for families to know the fate of their loved ones, whether they were alive and held prisoner, or deceased. Over 50 meetings were held before the fall of Saddam regime [*sic*], during which Iraq's answers to Kuwait's requests to identify the fate of the prisoners was the claim that it had no information. It was only after the fall of Saddam's regime that the search process picked up steam, breaking free from all deadlock criminally imposed by that regime for such a long period. Key information that had been insistently requested and persistently denied, suddenly became available. It was possible to locate the first mass graves and to start up with the process of mortal remains exhumations and identifications.

Mr. Chairman, Members of the Committee, results achieved to date, confirmed through DNA tests, the identification of 227 individuals out of the 650 prisoners. The tests also confirmed the [*sic*] they were executed in 1990–91.

Hence, it is ascertained that the former Iraqi regime intentionally violating all its obligations on this tragic humanitarian issue.

It is appalling to realize just how much mental distress has been needlessly imposed on POW's families by such immoral behavior extended over such a long period of time, and perhaps for years to come, until all individual cases are definitely resolved. Family members of disappeared persons are certainly considered to be victims as well, and subject to the worse psychological torments.

All possible hints and bits of information leading to identity, the final fate and burial site of the prisoners are most valuable. We appreciate the kindness and assistance of our friends in the U.S. in sharing such information. We are aware of the presence of a huge amount of documents alleged to belong to the former Iraqi regime. Certainly many of them are useful in resolving several issues. But we have to caution that some of them might be forged. We, in Kuwait have been offered several of such documents. But it is important and most useful to follow all leads, by seriously investigating all available documents and information, so that bits and pieces can by [sic] used to solve the many puzzles left by Saddam. Even though that this particular document had discrepancies, other documents could be useful.

To conclude, I extend our thanks to the U.S. Congress, Government and Military, for the support we have been receiving.

QUESTIONS TO CONSIDER

1 Did Iraq violate signed agreements on the treatment of POWs?
2 What does international humanitarian law say about the treatment of POWs?

Document 2-E

Letter dated May 5, 2001, from the permanent representative of Iraq to the United Nations addressed to the secretary general, United Nations, New York

On instructions from my Government, I should like to inform you that on 29 April 2001 *The New York Times*, the mouthpiece of world Zionism, published a report that in 1987 Iraq had tested a radiological bomb. It regarded this as "moral barbarism", and it reported the concern of American experts at the possibility that Iraq was importing the materials necessary to make such a bomb. United States officials seized on this false report, and on 1 May 2001 a spokesman for the Department of State expressed the concern of his Government at the possibility of Iraq acquiring radiological weapons. He made use of this false report as a prelude to promoting his Government's policy of urging that the embargo against the people of Iraq should be strengthened and that the aggression against it should be continued. In order to refute these fabrications, we should like to place before you the facts set forth hereunder.

1. In 1987, at the height of the people of Iraq's glorious defence of its land against the Iranian invasion and against the use by Iran of weapons of mass destruction, an Iraqi technician conceived the idea of making a defensive radiological bomb. Iraqi specialists explored the technical and practical aspects of this idea, and they ascertained that it was not feasible. They abandoned it on the grounds that it was not efficacious and would cause soil contamination that it would be difficult to clean up after the expulsion of the invaders. The idea died, and no radiological bombs were manufactured and none were tested.

2. In 1995, in the context of the complete transparency of its dealings with the International Atomic Energy Agency (IAEA) and the former Special Commission with a view to closing the files on the nuclear and other issues, Iraq informed IAEA and the former Special Commission of all minor details, research projects and ideas, including the idea of the Iraqi technician for a defensive radiological bomb. IAEA was persuaded by the clarifications provided by the Iraqi side that the idea had not been feasible. It was also stated in the former Special Commission's report of 11 April 1996 that "Iraq declared that no order to produce radiological weapons was given and the project was abandoned" (S/1996/258, para. 91).

    Since 1995, the reports of IAEA have stated that it has obtained from the Iraqi side a complete picture of its former programmes. The Agency's report of 9 April 1998 (S/1998/312, para. 35) states that:

    "The Iraqi counterpart has fulfilled its obligation to produce a document containing a summary of the technical achievements of its clandestine nuclear programme. The summary is regarded by IAEA to be consistent with the technically coherent picture of Iraq's clandestine nuclear programme developed by IAEA in the course of its activities in Iraq."

    In its report of 27 July 1998 (S/1998/694, para. 35), the Agency States that:

    "As previously recorded, there are no indications of Iraq having retained any physical capability for the indigenous production of weapon-usable nuclear material in amounts of any practical significance, nor any indication Iraq has acquired or produced weapon-usable nuclear material other than the nuclear material verified by IAEA and removed from Iraq in accordance with paragraph 13 of resolution 687 (1991)."

3. Following the United States-British aggression against Iraq of 16 December 1998, IAEA continued its activities in Iraq under the Safeguards Agreement concluded by Iraq and the Agency in accordance with the Treaty on the Non-Proliferation of Nuclear Weapons. The Agency's inspection teams continued to visit Iraq and to verify that there were no activities that were contrary to Iraq's undertakings under the Non-Proliferation Treaty. The most recent Agency inspection team visited Iraq between 21 and 23 January 2001, and in his letter dated 6 April 2001 addressed to the President of the Security

Council (S/2001/337, enclosure), the Director General of the Agency stated the following concerning the visit.

"... the Agency carried out, in January 2001, a physical inventory verification of the declared nuclear material in Iraq, pursuant to the Safeguards Agreement concluded between Iraq and the Agency in accordance with the Treaty on the Non-Proliferation of Nuclear Weapons. With the cooperation of the Iraqi authorities, Agency inspectors were able to verify the presence of the nuclear material remaining in Iraq that is subject to safeguards."

The above information confirms that the suspicions of the United States are misplaced and lack any rationale and that there is no indication that they are credible. Indeed, the article itself reports that non-American nuclear experts are saying that Iraq has neither programmes to develop radiological weapons nor the reactors needed to make radioactive materials for them.

4. The article in *The New York Times* states that the newspaper obtained the information concerning the radiological bomb from a private institution that, in turn, acquired it from United Nations officials. This acknowledgement once again confirms that the former Special Commission had the habit of leaking and distorting the information it obtained from its work in Iraq and of using it for the purposes of the United States-Zionist policy of aggression against Iraq. This admission can be added to the former Special Commission's black record of using the mechanisms of the United Nations to spy on Iraq and fabricate crises with it in order to justify the unilateral use of force against it by the United States and its abject dependency the United Kingdom. It ought to be said in this connection that the American Deputy Executive Chairman of the former Special Commission, Charles A. Duelfer, published an article in *The Los Angeles Times* on 22 April 2001 in which he accused Iraq of endeavouring to spread foot-and-mouth disease in the world. This false charge illustrates the tendentious approach of Special Commission officials, and especially of the "Anglo-Saxons" among them, when dealing with Iraq.

5. The timing of the resuscitation of this defunct subject and of its inflation in such a distorted manner are to be seen in the context of the anti-Iraq campaign being waged by the United States for the purpose of maintaining the embargo and promoting so-called smart sanctions. This also distracts attention from the crimes the United States has been committing against the people of Iraq, including as they do: the ongoing daily aggression in the unlawful no-flight zones; the maintenance of the comprehensive sanctions that have taken the lives of nearly 2 million Iraqis, most of them children and women; and the use of depleted uranium, which constitutes the crime of the epoch and "moral barbarism" in its most manifest form. This is to say nothing of the American moral barbarism that found expression in the use of nuclear

weapons against Japanese civilians at Hiroshima and Nagasaki, in the use of chemical weapons against the people of Viet Nam and biological weapons against the people of Cuba and in other crimes in all parts of the world. In raising this storm of mendacity the United States is also trying to affect the official and civic support and sympathy in all parts of the world for Iraq and for its just cause and the demand for the lifting of the unjust embargo against Iraq and for a halt to the ongoing aggression against it.

I should be grateful if you would have this letter circulated as a document of the Security Council.

Signed Mohammed A. Al-Douri
Ambassador
Permanent Representative

QUESTIONS TO CONSIDER

1 Did Iraq think about making a radiological bomb? Was the project completed, according to this document?
2 Were orders given in the 1990s for Iraqi scientists to pursue a radiological bomb?
3 Did the Iraqi government under Saddam Hussein think it had cooperated with UN weapons inspectors?

--------------- **Document 2-F** ---------------

Text of President Clinton's address to the Joint Chiefs of Staff and Pentagon staff, Washington, D.C., February 17, 1998

Thank you very much, Mr. Vice President, for your remarks and your leadership. Thank you, Secretary Cohen, for the superb job you have done here at the Pentagon and on this most recent very difficult problem. Thank you, General Shelton, for being the right person at the right time.

Thank you, General Ralston, and the members of the joint chiefs, General Zinni, Secretary Albright, Secretary Slater, DCIA Tenet, Mr. Bowles, Mr. Berger, Senator Robb thank you for being here and Congressman Skelton. Thank you very much, and for your years of service to America and your passionate patriotism both of you. And to the members of our armed forces and others who work here to protect our national security.

I have just received a very fine briefing from our military leadership on the status of our forces in the Persian Gulf. Before I left the Pentagon, I wanted to talk to you and all those whom you represent the men and women of our military. You, your friends and your colleagues are on the front lines of this crisis in Iraq.

I want you, and I want the American people, to hear directly from me what is at stake for America in the Persian Gulf, what we are doing to protect the peace, the security, the freedom we cherish, why we have taken the position we have taken.

I was thinking as I sat up here on the platform, of the slogan that the first lady gave me for her project on the millennium, which was, remembering the past and imagining the future.

Now, for that project, that means preserving the Star Spangled Banner and the Declaration of Independence and the Constitution and the Bill of Rights, and it means making an unprecedented commitment to medical research and to get the best of the new technology. But that's not a bad slogan for us when we deal with more sober, more difficult, more dangerous matters.

Those who have questioned the United States in this moment, I would argue, are living only in the moment. They have neither remembered the past nor imagined the future.

So first, let's just take a step back and consider why meeting the threat posed by Saddam Hussein is important to our security in the new era we are entering.

This is a time of tremendous promise for America. The superpower confrontation has ended; on every continent democracy is securing for more and more people the basic freedoms we Americans have come to take for granted. Bit by bit the information age is chipping away at the barriers economic, political and social that once kept people locked in and freedom and prosperity locked out.

But for all our promise, all our opportunity, people in this room know very well that this is not a time free from peril, especially as a result of reckless acts of outlaw nations and an unholy axis of terrorists, drug traffickers and organized international criminals.

We have to defend our future from these predators of the 21st century. They feed on the free flow of information and technology. They actually take advantage of the freer movement of people, information and ideas.

And they will be all the more lethal if we allow them to build arsenals of nuclear, chemical and biological weapons and the missiles to deliver them. We simply cannot allow that to happen.

There is no more clear example of this threat than Saddam Hussein's Iraq. His regime threatens the safety of his people, the stability of his region and the security of all the rest of us.

I want the American people to understand first the past, how did this crisis come about?

And I want them to understand what we must do to protect the national interest, and indeed the interest of all freedom-loving people in the world.

Remember, as a condition of the cease-fire after the Gulf War, the United Nations demanded not the United States the United Nations demanded, and Saddam Hussein agreed to declare within 15 days this is way back in 1991 within 15 days his nuclear, chemical and biological weapons and the missiles to deliver them, to make a total declaration. That's what he promised to do.

The United Nations set up a special commission of highly trained international experts called UNSCOM, to make sure that Iraq made good on that commitment. We had every good reason to insist that Iraq disarm. Saddam had built up a terrible arsenal, and he had used it not once, but many times, in a decade-long war with Iran, he used chemical weapons, against combatants, against civilians, against a foreign adversary, and even against his own people.

And during the Gulf War, Saddam launched Scuds against Saudi Arabia, Israel and Bahrain.

Now, instead of playing by the very rules he agreed to at the end of the Gulf War, Saddam has spent the better part of the past decade trying to cheat on this solemn commitment. Consider just some of the facts:

Iraq repeatedly made false declarations about the weapons that it had left in its possession after the Gulf War. When UNSCOM would then uncover evidence that gave lie to those declarations, Iraq would simply amend the reports.

For example, Iraq revised its nuclear declarations four times within just 14 months and it has submitted six different biological warfare declarations, each of which has been rejected by UNSCOM.

In 1995, Hussein Kamal, Saddam's son-in-law, and the chief organizer of Iraq's weapons of mass destruction program, defected to Jordan. He revealed that Iraq was continuing to conceal weapons and missiles and the capacity to build many more.

Then and only then did Iraq admit to developing numbers of weapons in significant quantities and weapon stocks. Previously, it had vehemently denied the very thing it just simply admitted once Saddam Hussein's son-in-law defected to Jordan and told the truth. Now listen to this, what did it admit?

It admitted, among other things, an offensive biological warfare capability notably 5,000 gallons of botulinum, which causes botulism; 2,000 gallons of anthrax; 25 biological-filled Scud warheads; and 157 aerial bombs.

And I might say UNSCOM inspectors believe that Iraq has actually greatly understated its production.

As if we needed further confirmation, you all know what happened to his son-in-law when he made the untimely decision to go back to Iraq.

Next, throughout this entire process, Iraqi agents have undermined and undercut UNSCOM. They've harassed the inspectors, lied to them, disabled monitoring cameras, literally spirited evidence out of the back doors of suspect facilities as inspectors walked through the front door. And our people were there observing it and had the pictures to prove it.

Despite Iraq's deceptions, UNSCOM has nevertheless done a remarkable job. Its inspectors the eyes and ears of the civilized world have uncovered and destroyed more weapons of mass destruction capacity than was destroyed during the Gulf War. This includes nearly 40,000 chemical weapons, more than 100,000 gallons of chemical weapons agents, 48 operational missiles, 30 warheads specifically fitted for chemical and biological weapons, and a massive biological weapons facility at Al Hakam equipped to produce anthrax and other deadly agents.

Over the past few months, as they have come closer and closer to rooting out Iraq's remaining nuclear capacity, Saddam has undertaken yet another gambit to thwart their ambitions.

By imposing debilitating conditions on the inspectors and declaring key sites which have still not been inspected off limits, including, I might add, one palace in Baghdad more than 2,600 acres large by comparison, when you hear all this business about presidential sites reflect our sovereignty, why do you want to come into a residence, the White House complex is 18 acres. So you'll have some feel for this.

One of these presidential sites is about the size of Washington, D.C. That's about how many acres did you tell me it was? 40,000 acres. We're not talking about a few rooms here with delicate personal matters involved.

It is obvious that there is an attempt here, based on the whole history of this operation since 1991, to protect whatever remains of his capacity to produce weapons of mass destruction, the missiles to deliver them, and the feed stocks necessary to produce them.

The UNSCOM inspectors believe that Iraq still has stockpiles of chemical and biological munitions, a small force of Scud-type missiles, and the capacity to restart quickly its production program and build many, many more weapons.

Now, against that background, let us remember the past here. It is against that background that we have repeatedly and unambiguously made clear our preference for a diplomatic solution.

The inspection system works. The inspection system has worked in the face of lies, stonewalling, obstacle after obstacle after obstacle. The people who have done that work deserve the thanks of civilized people throughout the world.

It has worked. That is all we want. And if we can find a diplomatic way to do what has to be done, to do what he promised to do at the end of the Gulf War, to do what should have been done within 15 days within 15 days of the agreement at the end of the Gulf War, if we can find a diplomatic way to do that, that is by far our preference.

But to be a genuine solution, and not simply one that glosses over the remaining problem, a diplomatic solution must include or meet a clear, immutable, reasonable, simple standard.

Iraq must agree and soon, to free, full, unfettered access to these sites anywhere in the country. There can be no dilution or diminishment of the integrity of the inspection system that UNSCOM has put in place.

Now those terms are nothing more or less than the essence of what he agreed to at the end of the Gulf War. The Security Council, many times since, has reiterated this standard. If he accepts them, force will not be necessary. If he refuses or continues to evade his obligations through more tactics of delay and deception, he and he alone will be to blame for the consequences.

I ask all of you to remember the record here what he promised to do within 15 days of the end of the Gulf War, what he repeatedly refused to do, what we found out in 1995, what the inspectors have done against all odds. We have no business agreeing to any resolution of this that does not include free, unfettered access to the remaining sites by people who have integrity and proven confidence in the inspection business. That should be our standard. That's what UNSCOM has done, and that's why I have been fighting for it so hard. And that's why the United States should insist upon it.

Now, let's imagine the future. What if he fails to comply, and we fail to act, or we take some ambiguous third route which gives him yet more opportunities to develop this program of weapons of mass destruction and continue to press for the release of the sanctions and continue to ignore the solemn commitments that he made?

Well, he will conclude that the international community has lost its will. He will then conclude that he can go right on and do more to rebuild an arsenal of devastating destruction.

And some day, some way, I guarantee you, he'll use the arsenal. And I think every one of you who's really worked on this for any length of time believes that, too.

Now we have spent several weeks building up our forces in the Gulf, and building a coalition of like-minded nations. Our force posture would not be possible without the support of Saudi Arabia, Kuwait, Bahrain, the GCC states and Turkey. Other friends and allies have agreed to provide forces, bases or logistical support, including the United Kingdom, Germany, Spain and Portugal, Denmark and the Netherlands, Hungary and Poland and the Czech Republic, Argentina, Iceland, Australia and New Zealand and our friends and neighbors in Canada.

That list is growing, not because anyone wants military action, but because there are people in this world who believe the United Nations resolutions should mean something, because they understand what UNSCOM has achieved, because they remember the past, and because they can imagine what the future will be depending on what we do now.

If Saddam rejects peace and we have to use force, our purpose is clear. We want to seriously diminish the threat posed by Iraq's weapons of mass destruction program. We want to seriously reduce his capacity to threaten his neighbors.

I am quite confident, from the briefing I have just received from our military leaders, that we can achieve the objective and secure our vital strategic interests.

Let me be clear: A military operation cannot destroy all the weapons of mass destruction capacity. But it can and will leave him significantly worse off than he is now in terms of the ability to threaten the world with these weapons or to attack his neighbors.

And he will know that the international community continues to have a will to act if and when he threatens again. Following any strike, we will carefully monitor Iraq's activities with all the means at our disposal. If he seeks to rebuild his weapons of mass destruction, we will be prepared to strike him again.

The economic sanctions will remain in place until Saddam complies fully with all U.N. resolutions. Consider this already these sanctions have denied him $110 billion. Imagine how much stronger his armed forces would be today, how many more weapons of mass destruction operations he would have hidden around the country if he had been able to spend even a small fraction of that amount for a military rebuilding.

We will continue to enforce a no-fly zone from the southern suburbs of Baghdad to the Kuwait border and in northern Iraq, making it more difficult for Iraq to walk over Kuwait again or threaten the Kurds in the north.

Now, let me say to all of you here as all of you know the weightiest decision any president ever has to make is to send our troops into harm's way. And force can never be the first answer. But sometimes, it's the only answer.

You are the best prepared, best equipped, best trained fighting force in the world. And should it prove necessary for me to exercise the option of force, your commanders will do everything they can to protect the safety of all the men and women under their command.

No military action, however, is risk-free. I know that the people we may call upon in uniform are ready. The American people have to be ready as well.

Dealing with Saddam Hussein requires constant vigilance. We have seen that constant vigilance pays off. But it requires constant vigilance. Since the Gulf War, we have pushed back every time Saddam has posed a threat.

When Baghdad plotted to assassinate former President Bush, we struck hard at Iraq's intelligence headquarters.

When Saddam threatened another invasion by amassing his troops in Kuwait along the Kuwaiti border in 1994, we immediately deployed our troops, our ships, our planes, and Saddam backed down.

When Saddam forcefully occupied Irbil in northern Iraq, we broadened our control over Iraq's skies by extending the no-fly zone.

But there is no better example, again I say, than the U.N. weapons inspection system itself. Yes, he has tried to thwart it in every conceivable way, but the discipline, determination, year-in-year-out effort of these weapons inspectors is doing the job. And we seek to finish the job. Let there be no doubt, we are prepared to act.

But Saddam Hussein could end this crisis tomorrow simply by letting the weapons inspectors complete their mission. He made a solemn commitment to the international community to do that and to give up his weapons of mass destruction a long time ago now. One way or the other, we are determined to see that he makes good on his own promise.

Saddam Hussein's Iraq reminds us of what we learned in the 20th century and warns us of what we must know about the 21st. In this century, we learned through harsh experience that the only answer to aggression and illegal behavior is firmness, determination, and when necessary action.

In the next century, the community of nations may see more and more the very kind of threat Iraq poses now a rogue state with weapons of mass destruction ready to use them or provide them to terrorists, drug traffickers or organized criminals who travel the world among us unnoticed.

If we fail to respond today, Saddam and all those who would follow in his footsteps will be emboldened tomorrow by the knowledge that they can act with impunity, even in the face of a clear message from the United Nations Security Council and clear evidence of a weapons of mass destruction program.

But if we act as one, we can safeguard our interests and send a clear message to every would-be tyrant and terrorist that the international community does have the wisdom and the will and the way to protect peace and security in a new era. That is the future I ask you all to imagine. That is the future I ask our allies to imagine.

If we look at the past and imagine that future, we will act as one together. And we still have, God willing, a chance to find a diplomatic resolution to this, and if not, God willing, the chance to do the right thing for our children and grandchildren.

Thank you very much.

QUESTIONS TO CONSIDER

1   What was President Clinton's rationale for Operation Desert Fox? Was it justified?
2   President Clinton states that UN sanctions have denied Saddam Hussein $110 billion in revenues that he could have put towards a weapons program. Do you think this policy was justified?

——————— **Document 2-G** ———————

Project for a New American Century, Statement of Principles, June 3, 1997

American foreign and defense policy is adrift. Conservatives have criticized the incoherent policies of the Clinton Administration. They have also resisted isolationist impulses from within their own ranks. But conservatives have not confidently advanced a strategic vision of America's role in the world. They have not set forth guiding principles for American foreign policy. They have allowed differences over tactics to obscure potential agreement on strategic objectives. And they have not fought for a defense budget that would maintain American security and advance American interests in the new century.

We aim to change this. We aim to make the case and rally support for American global leadership.

As the 20th century draws to a close, the United States stands as the world's preeminent power. Having led the West to victory in the Cold War, America faces an opportunity and a challenge: Does the United States have the vision to build upon the achievements of past decades? Does the United States have the resolve to shape a new century favorable to American principles and interests?

We are in danger of squandering the opportunity and failing the challenge. We are living off the capital – both the military investments and the foreign policy achievements – built up by past administrations. Cuts in foreign affairs and defense spending, inattention to the tools of statecraft, and inconstant leadership are making it increasingly difficult to sustain American influence around the world. And the promise of short-term commercial benefits threatens to override strategic considerations. As a consequence, we are jeopardizing the nation's ability to meet present threats and to deal with potentially greater challenges that lie ahead.

We seem to have forgotten the essential elements of the Reagan Administration's success: a military that is strong and ready to meet both present and future challenges; a foreign policy that boldly and purposefully promotes American principles abroad; and national leadership that accepts the United States' global responsibilities.

Of course, the United States must be prudent in how it exercises its power. But we cannot safely avoid the responsibilities of global leadership or the costs that are associated with its exercise. America has a vital role in maintaining peace and security in Europe, Asia, and the Middle East. If we shirk our responsibilities, we invite challenges to our fundamental interests. The history of the 20th century should have taught us that it is important to shape circumstances before crises emerge, and to meet threats before they become dire. The history of this century should have taught us to embrace the cause of American leadership.

Our aim is to remind Americans of these lessons and to draw their consequences for today. Here are four consequences:

- we need to increase defense spending significantly if we are to carry out our global responsibilities today and modernize our armed forces for the future;
- we need to strengthen our ties to democratic allies and to challenge regimes hostile to our interests and values;

- we need to promote the cause of political and economic freedom abroad;
- we need to accept responsibility for America's unique role in preserving and extending an international order friendly to our security, our prosperity, and our principles.

Such a Reaganite policy of military strength and moral clarity may not be fashionable today. But it is necessary if the United States is to build on the successes of this past century and to ensure our security and our greatness in the next.

Elliott Abrams, Gary Bauer, William J. Bennett, Jeb Bush, Dick Cheney, Eliot A. Cohen, Midge Decter, Paula Dobriansky, Steve Forbes, Aaron Friedberg, Francis Fukuyama, Frank Gaffney, Fred C. Ikle, Donald Kagan, Zalmay Khalilzad, I. Lewis Libby, Norman Podhoretz, Dan Quayle, Peter W. Rodman, Stephen P. Rosen, Henry S. Rowen, Donald Rumsfeld, Vin Weber, George Weigel, and Paul Wolfowitz

---

QUESTIONS TO CONSIDER

1   What priorities does the Project for a New American Century set?
2   Are they realistic?
3   How will they be accomplished? Is this a good use of American resources?
4   Are there limits to American power?

3

The Invasion of Iraq, 2003

Chronology

September 11, 2001	Terrorist attacks on World Trade Center and Pentagon
October 2001	Coalition attacks on Taliban and al-Qaeda
June 2002	President announces Bush Doctrine at West Point
October 2002	Congress authorizes use of armed force in Iraq
February 2003	Colin Powell's speech before the United Nations
February 15, 2003	Global protests against pending invasion of Iraq
March 20, 2003	Invasion of Iraq begins

The United States and Iraq Since 1990: A Brief History with Documents,
First Edition. Edited by Robert K. Brigham.
© 2014 Robert K. Brigham. Published 2014 by Blackwell Publishing Ltd.

It was a beautiful Tuesday morning, September 11, 2001, when Mohammed Atta and Abdulaziz al-Omari boarded a flight from Portland, Maine, to Boston's Logan International Airport. Once in Boston, Atta and Omari joined Satam al-Suqami, Wail al-Shehri, and Waleed al-Shehri on American Airlines Flight 11, bound for Los Angeles. In another part of Logan, five other Arabs – Marwan al-Shehhi, Fayez Banihammad, Mohand al-Shehri, Ahmed al-Ghmadi, and Hamza al-Ghmadi – boarded United Airlines Flight 175, also bound for Los Angeles. All ten had passed through metal detectors and answered security questions at the departure gate. None of them aroused suspicion at the airport. Down the eastern corridor, in Washington, D.C., five more men tried to board a domestic flight, American Airlines Flight 77, to Los Angeles. At Dulles International Airport's main terminal, Khalid al-Mihdhar and Majed Moqed set off the metal detectors with their carry-on baggage. Mihdhar was sent through a second metal detector, and this time no alarm sounded. He was waved through to the departure gate. Moqed set off the second alarm too, but was given a personal wand inspection and was allowed to proceed to the gate. Mihdhar and Moqed waited patiently at their departure gate for three more members of their group, Hani Hanjour, Nawaf al-Hazmi, and his brother, Salem al-Hazmi. Hanjour and Salem al-Hazmi cleared the first security checkpoint with no problem. Nawaf al-Hazmi set off the alarms at both the first and second metal detectors, but again airport security conducted a personal wand inspection and cleared him for entry to the departure area. In Newark, New Jersey, four more men, Saeed al-Ghmadi, Ahmed al-Nami, Ahmad al-Haznawi, and Ziad Jarrah boarded United Airlines Flight 93, going to Los Angeles, without incident.

By 8:00 a.m. on the morning of September 11, nineteen men, most of them in their early twenties, had boarded four transcontinental flights at three different international airports, avoiding detection despite setting off security alarms and paying for their first-class or business-class tickets with cash. Fifteen of the nineteen were from Saudi Arabia, one was from Lebanon, one from Egypt, and two were from the UAE. None was from Iraq. The men aboard American Airlines Flight 11 from Boston moved into action first, stabbing several passengers and gaining access to the cockpit. The flight crew called airline headquarters to warn that the plane had been hijacked and was now flying erratically. At 8:46 a.m., at precisely the time when United Airlines Flight 175 left Boston, American Airlines Flight 11 smashed into the North Tower of the World Trade Center in Manhattan, killing all on board instantly and causing severe damage on impact. Once United Airlines 175 was in the air, the airline crew issued a similar distress call. At 9:03 a.m., the plane hit the South Tower of the World Trade Center, setting off a series of events that would lead to the ultimate collapse of both towers.

In Washington, another American Airlines flight, 77, prepared for departure. Unaware that two planes had just hit the towers in New York, air traffic control at Dulles International Airport cleared the pilots for takeoff. At 9:37 a.m., the plane hit the Pentagon, home to the U.S. Defense Department, at over 530 miles per hour, killing hundreds instantly. By this time, airline management knew something was wrong and accordingly ordered all American Airlines flights on the east coast suspended. The last plane, United Airlines Flight 93 from Newark to San Francisco, had already departed by the time the other three planes had hit their targets. Passengers were now aware of what had happened in New York and Washington and determined that they were not going to allow a similar fate befall Flight 93. Passengers rushed the cockpit, but were stymied when one of the hijackers flew the plane violently to disrupt the passengers' forward momentum. It now seems clear that the passengers saved the plane from hitting the U.S. Capitol or the White House. Instead, at 10:02 a.m. on September 11, Flight 93 had a crash landing in a field near Shanksville, Pennsylvania. All passengers were killed instantly upon impact.

At the time of the attacks, George W. Bush was in Sarasota, Florida, visiting an elementary school to promote his new administration's education policy. Told first that a twin-engine plane had hit the North Tower in New York, the president assumed pilot error had created the disaster. At 9:05 a.m., just minutes after the first two planes had hit the Twin Towers, Andrew Card, the chief of staff, whispered to president, "A second plane hit the second tower. America is under attack."[1] The Secret Service rushed Bush to the airport, not sure if it was safe for him to return to Washington. President Bush had taken calls from Vice President Richard Cheney, New York governor George Pataki, and FBI director Robert Mueller to gain a better sense of what was happening. During a return call to Cheney, the president warned, "Sounds like we have a minor war going on here. I heard about the Pentagon. We're at war . . . somebody's going to pay."[2] By 3:15pm on the afternoon of September 11, the president's view had many supporters. Rushed to Offutt Air Force Base in Nebraska for safety, Bush met with his national security team through a secure video teleconference. During this conversation, all agreed that al-Qaeda, a terrorist organization with cells around the globe, was most likely responsible for the attacks. At 8:30 that evening, following a return to Washington, the president addressed the nation: "We will make no distinction between the terrorists who committed these acts and those who harbor them."[3]

Indeed, within weeks of the September 11 attacks, the United States, Britain, and the Northern Alliance (Afghani resistance fighters) launched air raids and ground assaults against the Taliban and al-Qaeda in Afghanistan. The Bush administration correctly summarized that the Taliban leadership in Kabul had supported al-Qaeda, allowing the terrorist group to use

Afghanistan as a training base and sanctuary. The military response was swift, focused, and deadly. Within two months, the Taliban had been driven from power and had taken refuge with al-Qaeda leaders in the mountainous border region with Pakistan. The American public overwhelmingly supported the attacks, as did the U.S. Congress. By mid-2002, several senior Bush administration officials believed that the war had been won in Afghanistan and that it was now time to focus on other terrorist threats, most notably Iraq. They shifted intelligence resources from Afghanistan to Iraq, and prepared for a larger struggle against global terrorism. Some critics have suggested that this decision paved the way for a long and costly war in Afghanistan because the Taliban simply regrouped, and by 2005 were launching attacks against Kabul once again. In retrospect, the Bush administration may have focused on the wrong enemy at the wrong time. It now seems clear that Iraq occupied a special place in the Bush administration's war on terror, and that events in Baghdad may have overwhelmed other considerations.

Connecting Terrorists to Iraq

At the time of the September 11 attacks, few could have predicted a renewed American war in Iraq, but from those early days following the attacks until the March 2003 invasion the Bush administration made a strong connection between the hated Saddam Hussein and the September 11 hijackers. Secretary of Defense Donald Rumsfeld agreed with the president that the United States should not limit its reprisal attacks to just the al-Qaeda terrorist network, but should also include those states that supported and harbored terrorists, including Iraq, Afghanistan, Libya, Sudan, and Iran. Paul Wolfowitz, the deputy secretary of defense, picked up this theme shortly after the September 11 attacks, telling one television interviewer that "most regimes that support terrorism against us support terrorism against their own people basically. They rule by terror. And one of our greatest allies against them, whether it's in Iraq or in any other part of the world is going to be defeat by their own people. And as we develop strategies, our target is not the people. Our target is the regimes and the people are very often going to be our ally."[4] It is interesting to note that the only country suspected of harboring terrorists Wolfowitz specifically mentioned by name was Iraq. It now seems clear that the Bush administration had come into power in January 2001 with the idea of launching preemptive attacks against Iraq because key members of the national security team saw Saddam Hussein and his followers as a primary threat to American interests and regional stability.

At the very first national security meeting held by the new Bush administration, several key players suggested getting rid of Saddam Hussein.[5] Secretary of State Colin Powell was the lone voice of opposition, favoring instead smart sanctions against Iraq and continued weapons inspections. Powell suspected that Saddam might have rekindled his interest in the further development of weapons of mass destruction, but that the United States could coordinate a program to contain him. But many others in the administration, especially Wolfowitz and Richard Perle, the chairman of the Defense Policy Board, which advises the Pentagon, rejected the idea of smart sanctions and instead supported efforts to overthrow Saddam. President Bush decided to pursue both strategies in the spring of 2001, ordering the various parties to make the best case for each option. Powell's job of selling smart sanctions was complicated, however, because there was little international support for such a measure and, without that support, new sanctions were impossible. The neoconservatives who made up the core of the group favoring regime change in Iraq had momentum in their favor. This group of policymakers had come to the Bush administration after being frustrated with Democrats like Bill Clinton who had publicly supported the promotion of democracy around the globe but who had not used American military power to encourage it. For nearly three decades, the neoconservatives had been arguing for a more muscular foreign policy, and the early days of the Bush administration saw this view prosper as Powell floundered.

Modern neoconservatism was born in the late 1930s among a small group of intellectuals who believed in social progress and the universality of rights but feared that communism under Stalin had grown excessive. By the late 1940s their ideas had cemented around the belief that all totalitarian regimes would crumble if pushed hard enough. In 1989 and 1991, the neoconservatives celebrated the end of the Cold War and the collapse of the Soviet Union. In their book *Present Dangers*, two leading neoconservatives, William Kristol and Robert Kagan, argued that victory over the Soviets and the eastern European bloc could be repeated if the United States was willing to add muscle to its foreign policy. They wrote, "To many the idea of America using its power to promote change of regimes in nations ruled by dictators rings of utopianism. But in fact, it is eminently realistic. There is something perverse in declaring the impossibility of promoting democratic change abroad in light of the record of the past three decades."[6]

Wolfowitz, Bush's new deputy secretary of defense, became the administration's most outspoken proponent of regime change in Iraq. He had had a long and distinguished career in government before joining the Bush administration, first working for U.S. senator Henry "Scoop" Jackson (D-Washington) as an aide and later with Fred Ikle, the director of the U.S.

Arms Control and Disarmament Agency. In the latter post, Wolfowitz had become one of the most important members of "Team B," a committee designed to offer a counter-assessment of the Soviet threat. Team B challenged many of Henry Kissinger's beliefs about Soviet intentions and capabilities, suggesting that the U.S. policy of détente had distracted American policymakers from Moscow's "darker side."[7] During the Carter years Wolfowitz moved to the Pentagon, where he would return after a Clinton-era sabbatical as the dean of the Paul Nitze School at Johns Hopkins University and ambassador to Indonesia. Following neoconservative precepts, Wolfowitz believed regime change was possible in Iraq. He also supported the idea that there was a universal hunger for liberty in all people and that they would rise up to support democratic challenges to most dictatorial regimes. During his confirmation hearing before the Senate Armed Services Committee, Wolfowitz established his view that if a realistic option to overthrow Saddam Hussein presented itself, "I would certainly think it was worthwhile."[8]

The decision to link the terrorist attacks with Iraq was first made, however, by Secretary of Defense Donald Rumsfeld, during the initial national security team meeting following the September 11 attacks. Rumsfeld believed that the administration should focus its efforts more broadly than just the terrorist group al-Qaeda, believing that Iraq and other nations had supported the radicals. At a secret meeting at Camp David on September 14, 2001, Rumsfeld and Wolfowitz argued again that the United States should also target Iraq for its role in the September 11 attacks. And it now seems clear from retrospective statements from Vice President Richard Cheney and National Security Advisor Condoleezza Rice that many of Bush's top national security advisors favored adding Saddam Hussein to the target list. "Unless you were there, in a position of responsibility after September 11," Rice reported in April 2009, "you cannot possibly imagine the dilemmas that you faced in trying to protect Americans." Rice was responding to a student at Stanford University, where Rice had taught for decades, who openly questioned the link between Iraq and the September 11 attacks during a question-and-answer period with the former national security advisor and secretary of state. Likewise, Dick Cheney defended the administration's decision to attack Iraq following the terrorist attacks on U.S. soil because "part of our responsibility, as we saw it, was not to forget the terrible harm that had been done to America."[9]

Yet there is little evidence connecting Saddam Hussein and the September 11 attacks, and several members of the Bush administration's national security team made this clear at the time. Richard Clarke, the Bush administration's coordinator for security and counterterrorism, has argued that the linkage of the terrorist attacks and Saddam was "not appropriate." Clarke has also suggested that high-level U.S. officials wanted to torture

Iraqi prisoners of war to get forced confessions to link Baghdad and the terrorist attacks against New York and Washington. According to Clarke, the Bush administration was embarrassed that it had ignored scores of warnings before September 11 from the Central Intelligence Agency and some analysts at the National Security Council "that urgent action was needed to preempt a major al-Qaeda attack."[10] Several top-level State Department officials in the Bush administration agree with Clarke's characterization. Richard Haass, who then was the director of policy planning at the State Department, reported at the time that there were no links between Saddam Hussein and the September 11 terrorists. According to Haass, it was well known in the State Department that the idea that Saddam was involved in the attacks was "far fetched," primarily because of the dictator's "mistrust of independent terrorist organizations" and his belief that continued sanctions did not have international support.[11] Still, by early 2002 even Colin Powell supported regime change in Baghdad.

At a congressional hearing on February 6, 2002, Powell told members of Congress that the president was exploring a full range of options in Iraq, including "regime change." Powell insisted that Saddam Hussein harbored terrorists and that "it has long been . . . a policy of the United States government that regime change would be in the best interests of the region."[12] Powell's initial pessimism on regime change in Iraq had given way to substantial public support, primarily because the president wanted it that way. Following the September 11 attacks, Bush had moved further and further into the camp that believed that "terrorist supporting countries were forging networks parallel to the process of globalization" and that there existed a strong connection between Iraq and the terrorist attacks. Any lingering doubt about the Bush administration's plans for Iraq vanished on January 29, with President Bush's 2002 State of the Union Address (see DOCUMENT 3-A). Bush told the nation and the world that the terrorists who attacked the United States on September 11 were like "ticking time bombs" set to go off without warning and fully supported by "outlaw regimes." The primary foreign policy objective of the United States in the post-September 11 world was clear, the president warned, "to prevent regimes that sponsor terror from threatening America or our friends and allies with weapons of mass destruction." This comment seemed particularly aimed at Saddam Hussein, whose own weapons program had been the subject of continued controversy since the First Gulf War. It also shifted the focus of the war on terror from the ongoing battles against the Taliban in Afghanistan to several other states, states that President Bush labeled the "axis of evil." These states, according to Bush, "pose a grave and growing danger. They could provide . . . arms to terrorists, giving them the means to match their hatred. They could attack our allies or attempt to blackmail the United States."[13] Bush made it clear that Saddam Hussein was a marked man.

To underscore the president's statements and outline the administration's new policy of regime change in Iraq, Vice President Dick Cheney went on a tour of the Middle East, shoring up support among America's allies for a potential invasion of Iraq. In a major speech delivered to the Council on Foreign Relations just before his departure, Cheney demanded that there should be "aggressive action" against Saddam Hussein, insisting that the dictator "harbored terrorists" and that the United Sates would never allow "terror states" or their "terrorist allies" to threaten its interests with weapons of mass destruction.[14] Cheney's chief of staff, I. Lewis "Scooter" Libby, worked closely with Douglas Feith, the undersecretary of defense for policy, in connecting the terrorists to Saddam Hussein and in spelling out a larger war on terror. Convincing the president that the United States needed to do more than simply retaliate against the September 11 plotters was "a real breakthrough," reported Feith, and it led to the creation of the Office of Special Plans (OSP), charged primarily with reviewing intelligence on Iraq's own weapons program and its link to terrorists.[15]

During his review, Feith concluded that the CIA under George Tenet had failed to see the clear connections between the terrorists and Saddam Hussein's government. Feith was especially incensed at the CIA's refusal to consider that a secret meeting took place in April 2001 in Prague between Mohammed Atta, one of the September 11 hijackers, and an Iraqi intelligence agent. The FBI had seen the same evidence Feith now considered proof of the connection, but had discounted it for several reasons. First, photographs of the person Feith suspected of being Atta in Prague revealed that it was not Atta. Second, the clear records of Atta's travels show that he was in the United States at the time. Third, Atta was filmed cashing at check at a bank in Virginia Beach, Virginia, just days before he was said to have been in Prague. Finally, Atta's cell phone shows he was making phone calls from his new apartment in Coral Springs, Florida, during the time he was supposed to be in Prague. Feith and Wolfowitz were undeterred. In a meeting the with the FBI's counterterrorism expert, Pasquale D'Amuro, Wolfowitz asked if it was impossible for Atta to have slipped out of the country after cashing the check in Virginia Beach and have someone else use his cell phone as a cover while he secretly met with an Iraqi intelligence agent in Prague. D'Amuro answered that it was possible, but not probable. Wolfowitz took this as confirmation of the connection between Saddam Hussein and the September 11 terrorists.[16]

The Bush Doctrine

Perhaps even more telling of the administration's efforts to link weapons of mass destruction, terrorists, and Saddam Hussein were the origins and development of what became known as the "Bush Doctrine." Originally outlined in a graduation speech before the cadets at West Point in June 2002, the Bush Doctrine was formally charted in the president's report on "The National Security of the United States of America" (NSS), released September 17, 2002 (see DOCUMENT 3-B).[17] In this document, the Bush administration spelled out its ambitious grand strategy based on its reading of the terrorist threat: "We will defend the peace by fighting terrorists and tyrants. We will preserve the peace by building good relations among the great powers. We will extend the peace by encouraging free and open societies on every continent."[18] The Bush Doctrine also pledged that the United States "will identify and eliminate terrorists wherever they are, together with the regimes that sustain them."[19] Bush pledged to launch preemptive strikes against the enemy, in this case Saddam Hussein, before he could attack the United States. The implication was that the terrorists had attacked the United States without the resources of a state, and that Saddam had motive to do even more damage than the sub-national al-Qaeda. Furthermore, the Bush administration argued that, in the absence of a tyrant like Saddam Hussein, democracy could flourish in Iraq and throughout the Middle East. Bush and his closest advisors believed that the United States needed to promote democracy in the Middle East because it was the lack of representative institutions within these states that drove terrorists to desperate measures. Those who supported tyranny, Bush reasoned, supported the terrorists, and therefore the United States needed to plant the seeds of democracy and watch them grow. For Bush, and much of his administration, democracy itself was a transformative power, and its expansion in the Middle East promised to make the United States more secure. With new democratic institutions, the middle class would take ownership of the political process alongside the traditional royal families and authoritarian regimes. Shared power through a more democratic state, Bush believed, could transform the Middle East from an unpredictable and potentially dangerous region into a stable and peaceful one. The Bush administration believed in Woodrow Wilson's old adage that the United States must make the world safe for democracy. The president believed firmly that history was on the side of the democratic states and that he had an obligation to use America's considerable power to bring about democratic change.

There were some in Iraq who also favored the talk of more participatory democracy. Throughout 2001 and 2002, a group of leading Shia intellectuals and professionals met in London to discuss the problems of Iraq, namely that Saddam Hussein had suppressed the Shia majority for far too long and the time had come to begin a pro-democracy movement in Iraq. Encouraged by George W. Bush's election, these moderate Shiites declared that "Dictatorship has been one of the main factors that have buttressed the structures of official sectarian and ethnic discrimination, and constitutional democracy, operating through vital and effective institutions, is the necessary cure for this virulent ailment" (see DOCUMENT 3-C, "DECLARATION OF THE SHIA"). They also called for a federal system in Iraq that granted more political and economic power to local entities:

> One of the key elements of the Iraqi conundrum is the near exclusive concentration of powers in the capital, Baghdad, in a manner that has robbed the outlying regions of any opportunity to address their local concerns, needs and special conditions and particularities. The solution has to be in the devolution of powers and authorities to these areas within a framework of broad administrative decentralisation.
>
> Federalism as a system would be designed to negotiate between the need to have a central authority with effective but not hegemonic powers, and regions that enjoy a high order of decentralised powers, all within a framework of careful delineation of rights and responsibilities as between the centre and the regions. Ideally, a federal system would also legislate for the maintenance of Iraq's unitary nature, but recognises the need to fully accommodate Iraq's diversity.
>
> Iraq's federal structure would not be based on a sectarian division but rather on administrative and demographic criteria. This would avoid the formation of sectarian-based entities that could be the prelude for partition or separation.
>
> The proposed federal system would grant considerable powers to the regions, including legislative, fiscal, judicial and executive powers, thereby removing the possibility of the centre falling under the control of a dominant group which would extend its hegemony over the entire country. Iraq's federalist structures would benefit greatly from the experience of countries that have adopted this system of government successfully.[20]

The Bush administration welcomed these moderate calls for more democracy and even supported some elements of federalism. Furthermore, the administration was pleased that Iraqis themselves were making the case against Saddam Hussein.

Not wanting to leave anything to chance, the administration also engaged Congress on the viability of preemptive strikes against Iraq. In September 2002 the president sent a letter to Congress, outlining in more detail his plans for Iraq. He suggested that Congress needed to be a partner in the goal of "disarming an outlaw regime." Bush argued that Saddam Hussein had been a constant threat to peace since 1990, when George Bush Senior was forced to launch attacks against Iraq to move Saddam's troops out of Kuwait. Since the First Gulf War, the president warned, Saddam had refused to cooperate with UN weapons inspectors and had engaged in gross human rights violations. According to the president, Baghdad had defied at least sixteen UN resolutions on weapons inspection, and it was likely that

Saddam Hussein was hiding something. The CIA had just submitted a report to Congress that suggested as much (see DOCUMENT 3-D). The most telling passage from the CIA's latest report removed all doubt about Saddam's ambitions: "most analysts assessed that Iraq had reconstituted its nuclear program."[21] At the president's request, Congress agreed to hold hearings on preemptive strikes against Iraq in anticipation that the Bush administration would eventually ask for a war resolution.

During the congressional hearings in September and October 2002, the Bush national security team spoke with one voice. They concluded that Saddam Hussein had weapons of mass destruction and close ties to international terrorism. The combination was volatile and required immediate action. Proof of Baghdad's intentions was the fact that Saddam had used lethal chemical weapons against his own people and that the latest report from the UN weapons inspection team had indicated that satellite photos showed new construction on buildings that could house nuclear weapons. The Bush team suggested that many human rights activists and scholars had been severely critical of Saddam's brutality against Kurds in Iraq's northern regions following the First Gulf War and that the UN weapons team knew Iraq best.[22] The veracity of the Bush administration's claims went unchallenged. Most in Congress took the testimony at face value. The most damning was Rumsfeld's testimony before the Senate Armed Services Committee. After covering certain "facts" about Iraq, Rumsfeld concluded that Saddam was "determined to acquire the means to strike the United States, its friends and allies, with weapons of mass destruction."[23]

Outside the halls of Congress, Vice President Dick Cheney went on the offensive. In a major speech in Nashville before the Veterans of Foreign Wars, Cheney concluded that Saddam had been much closer to obtaining nuclear weapons when he was driven out of Kuwait and the first weapons inspectors entered Iraq in 1991 than anyone had previously thought. This sworn enemy of the United States was building up his nuclear capabilities, Cheney warned, and he would "acquire nuclear weapons fairly soon."[24] The problem with the UN weapons inspections, Cheney suggested, was that "intelligence" was an uncertain business. The United States had "often learned more as a result of defections than we learned from inspection of the regime itself," Cheney concluded, suggesting that sending UN inspectors back to Iraq was a waste of valuable time.[25] The vice president then made his strongest pitch for an American invasion of Iraq leading to regime change, arguing that the United States would be seen as a liberator as the streets of Baghdad were sure "to erupt in joy in the same way the throngs in Kabul greeted the Americans." He concluded, "Extremists in the region would have to rethink their strategy of jihad. Moderates throughout the region would take heart. And our ability to advance the Israeli-Palestinian peace process would be enhanced, just as it was following the liberation of Kuwait."[26]

The president followed Cheney's remarks with a speech of his own at the United Nations on September 12, designed to convince the UN Security Council that history was on the side of the United States and to fulfill a promise that the president had made to British prime minister Tony Blair. Before throwing Britain's support behind regime change in Iraq, Blair had asked the president to seek UN support before invading Iraq. It was clear from his remarks that Bush was fully prepared to go ahead with the invasion, with or without the Security Council's support. Bush began his speech with a warning to member states of the United Nations: "We must choose between a world of fear and a world of progress. We cannot stand by while dangers gather." He then added that the conduct of the Iraqi government "is a threat to the authority of the United Nations, and a threat to peace." Bush promised to work with the Security Council for "the necessary resolutions," but it now seems clear that the president was perfectly willing to attack Iraq without a UN resolution authorizing the United States to do so.[27]

Simultaneously, the Bush administration released a White Paper, "A Decade of Deception and Defiance," designed to make its strongest case to date against Saddam Hussein. "This document provides specific examples of how Iraqi President Saddam Hussein has systematically and continually violated 16 United Nations Security Council resolutions over the past decade," the report said in its preface.[28] Though much of the report is unsubstantiated, one source caught the public's attention. According to the report, the *New York Times* reported that an Iraqi defector, Adnan Ihsan Saeed al-Haideri, claimed he had visited over twenty secret facilities inside Iraq for making chemical, biological, and nuclear weapons. The *Times* reported that al-Haideri supported his claims with government documents. Even if al-Haideri's reports were genuine, we now know that Saddam probably planted the documents as he tried to convince his own people that he had a weapons program.[29] Following the First Gulf War, there were insurgent operations by Shiites in several key regions of Iraq, including the strategically important cities of Karbala and Najaf. Saddam ordered Sarin nerve gas to be dropped on the insurgents, but a malfunction kept the operation grounded and the international community in the dark about Saddam's own insecurities. It now seems clear that the evidence to support the idea that Saddam held weapons of mass destruction came from Saddam himself as a way to frighten his domestic enemies and their supporters in Iran. Also cited in the report was the work of Max van der Stoel, a former UN human rights special rapporteur, who claimed that Iraq had executed at least 1,500 people during the previous year for political reasons, and that Iraq had over 16,000 disappearances or persons unaccounted for, the world's highest number.[30] For Saddam, the perception that he held weapons of mass destruction clearly had domestic political consequences. Although the Bush administration had no idea at the time that Saddam was behind the evidence to support the case of weapons of mass destruction, it used this evidence to support its invasion plan.

The full court press by the Bush administration produced the desired result. With little debate, the U.S. Congress gave the president the war resolution he had been seeking. On October 9, 2002, both houses of Congress passed H.J. 114 (see DOCUMENT 3-E), authorizing the president to "use the Armed Forces of the United States as he determines to be necessary and appropriate in order to defend the national security of the United States against the continued threat posed by Iraq" and to "enforce all relevant United Nations Security Council resolutions regarding Iraq."[31] Careful not to give the president a blank check as Congress had done with the Lyndon Johnson Gulf of Tonkin resolution in 1964, Congress did place limits on the administration's actions. The resolution required the president to consult Congress within forty-eight hours of taking direct military action in Iraq and to report on the war's progress to the appropriate congressional committees every sixty days.[32] There was significant bipartisan support for the resolution as key Democrats voted in favor. Most members of Congress believed, as Senator John McCain (R-Arizona) did, that the president's team had made "a convincing case" against Iraq. Tom DeLay, Republican majority leader of the House, concluded during the congressional debate that "military action is inevitable."[33]

A small minority in Congress opposed the resolution. Senator Robert Byrd (D-West Virginia) argued that it gave the president "unchecked authority." Senator Edward Kennedy (D-Massachusetts) concluded that only Congress could declare war. Few of the protests concerned the efficacy of the invasion itself. Most of those who opposed the resolution did so on constitutional grounds. Richard Gephardt, one of the authors of the resolution, had once been a Democratic presidential hopeful. By fall 2002 he was helping a Republican president gain broad war powers from Congress. Senate minority leader Tom Daschle (D-South Dakota), a Vietnam veteran and usually an outspoken critic of the Bush administration, also supported the motion.[34] In the end, the Senate passed the House version of the resolution without changing a single word. Just for safe measure, John Yoo, the deputy assistant attorney general, provided the Bush administration all the constitutional justification it needed to wage war against Saddam Hussein. Following the passage of H.J. 114, Yoo wrote that the Office of Legal Counsel had "no constitutional objection to Congress expressing its support of the use of military force against Iraq," but that the resolution was "legally unnecessary" since the "President has authority, without specific statutory authorization, to introduce troops into hostilities in a substantial range of circumstances."[35] This was the first of Yoo's many controversial rulings.

With the support of Congress, Bush then went to the American people to gain their support for the Iraqi invasion. In his most important speech to date on Iraq, his State of the Union address on January 28, 2003, President Bush followed up "A Decade of Deception and Defiance" with more hard evidence that Saddam had weapons of mass destruction and intended to use them. In what is now referred to as the "infamous 16 words," Bush declared, "The British government had learned that Saddam Hussein recently sought significant quantities of uranium from Africa."[36] Furthermore, Bush repeated allegations that Saddam had imported aluminum tubes to use in gas centrifuges, an essential item in the enrichment of uranium. Though both statements would later prove to be false, they played a tremendous role in the public discourse over the potential invasion of Iraq. Public opinion polls clearly showed that the president's allegations about Iraq's weapons of mass destruction had touched a nerve. A growing number of Americans believed that Saddam Hussein had developed nuclear capabilities, or was about to, and that he was motivated to use these weapons against the United States and its allies, particularly Israel.[37] Furthermore, polling suggested that most Americans believed that there was a connection between Baghdad and the September 11 terrorists and that Saddam Hussein was likely to share his nuclear bounty with them.[38] Reports from Britain only seemed to confirm the president's statements about Iraq's possession of weapons of mass destruction, especially what became known as the "Downing Street Memo" (see DOCUMENT 3-F), which were eventually leaked to the press in 2005 and clearly showed the White House effort to tie Saddam Hussein with al-Qaeda and a nuclear program despite no hard evidence of either.[39]

This "evidence" surfaced again during Secretary of State Colin Powell's February 2003 speech before the UN Security Council (see DOCUMENT 3-G). Powell was sent to the United Nations to secure a resolution that would back the U.S. invasion plan, but few in the Bush White House believed the UN would openly support regime change in Iraq. Instead, the president seemed perfectly willing to create a coalition of supporters himself, with ally Tony Blair in close support. Nonetheless, Powell, the good soldier, went to the United Nations to argue the president's case against Saddam Hussein. Powell began his presentation by reminding the Security Council that Iraq was already in clear violation of Security Council Resolution 1441, which had passed the Council by unanimous vote in November 2002. The resolution was designed to "disarm Iraq of its weapons of mass destruction."[40] Powell argued that the Security Council had given Iraq every opportunity to comply with the resolution, but that Baghdad had refused to allow UN weapons inspectors to tour highly sensitive installations. Powell quoted liberally from the most recent testimony of the chief UN weapons inspector Hans Blix, who had concluded that "Iraq appears not to have come to a genuine acceptance . . . of the disarmament which was demanded of it." He said that the United States supported the statements made by Dr. Blix and his colleague, Dr. Mohammed El-Baradei, and that Washington had new information – the African connection and the tubes – that highlighted even further the gross violations of Resolution 1441. Powell played several taped conversations between two senior Iraqi officers that proved that Iraq was violating 1441 knowingly. He then recited the list of American evidence against Saddam Hussein, including Iraq's "covert attempts to acquire high-specification aluminum tubes" necessary for enriching uranium.[41] Powell concluded his remarks with a stark warning: "Our concern is not just about these illicit weapons. It's the way that these illicit weapons can be connected to terrorists and terrorist organizations that have no compunction about using such devices against innocent people around the world."[42] He showed pictures of terrorist training camps and tried to make the connection between Iraq and Abu Musab Zarqawi, Osama bin Laden's chief lieutenant. Ultimately, Powell asked the Security Council to enforce 1441, even if that meant supporting military strikes against Iraq.

Powell had no idea that he had been sent to the United Nations by an over-eager Bush administration without all the facts. Years later, the Senate Select Committee on Intelligence reviewed the Bush administration's pre-war messages and concluded that Powell, among others, had used information that was "overstated, misleading, or incorrect."[43] Since most of Powell's speech was cleared by the CIA, the secretary of state was notably annoyed. After he resigned from the Bush White House, Powell criticized the CIA for the inaccuracies in their reporting. Powell claimed that "the intelligence community let us all down."[44] Powell did not criticize the president, however, or those in the White House who supported regime change. Nor did the secretary of state challenge the vice president or Rumsfeld at Defense when both continued to make the connection between Saddam Hussein and weapons of mass destruction, even though the evidence was called into question.

Still, Powell's presentation at the UN Security Council was highly effective in convincing the American public that the United States had to launch preemptive strikes against Iraq, even if it did not convince member states. Powell's comments also placed a tremendous burden on America's Atlantic alliance. It was clear from the beginning of the session that France, a permanent member of the Security Council, would never support using military force to compel Iraq to abandon its nuclear program. President Bush warned that this was not acceptable, and that he would push this issue. He claimed that the Security Council "shares our assessment of the danger, but not our resolve to meet it."[45] He then vowed to create a coalition of the willing "to act against this threat to peace." Bush ended his speech with a stinging indictment of the United Nations. He claimed that "the United Nations Security Council has not lived up to its responsibilities, so we will rise to ours."[46] Still, the Security Council did not bring the issue up for a vote, forcing the Bush administration to build its own coalition for an Iraqi invasion. The president warmed to this task, and within a few short weeks he had secured commitments from Britain, Spain, Russia, Chile, Cameroon, Angola, and Guinea, as well as partial acceptance from a variety of other states. An impatient Bush warned his close ally, Spain's prime minister Jose Maria Aznar, that he would wait until the middle of March 2003 before launching the invasion, but no longer.

As Bush waited, protestors took to the streets angered by the looming invasion. On February 15, 2003, the largest coordinated global protests in history took place. Millions of anti-war protestors marched in the United States, Great Britain, Ireland, Spain, Russia, South Africa, Japan, South Korea, India, and Germany, and there was even one small protest at McMurdo Research Station in Antarctica. Demonstrators shut down several government buildings in the United States and Great Britain, and in some cities blocked traffic with their bodies, carrying banners that read, "No Business as Usual." In London, nearly a million people gathered in Hyde Park to hear the Reverend Jesse Jackson and London mayor Ken Livingstone criticize the coming war. *New York Times* reporter Patrick Tyler claimed that the protests had shown that "there were two super powers on the planet, the United States and worldwide public opinion."[47] Even as the protests mounted in the spring of 2003, the Bush administration pressed for war in Iraq convinced that a quick victory would silence all critics.

The last hurdle the Bush administration needed to overcome to launch a preemptive attack against Iraq was a report by UN weapons inspector Hans Blix on March 7, 2003. Some Bush advisors feared that Blix would report progress on talks with Saddam Hussein over weapons inspection. Others, such as National Security Advisor Condoleezza Rice, argued that Blix would report mixed results and that his report would not stand in the way of an American invasion. In fact, much to the Bush administration's confusion and consternation, Blix told the United Nations that considerable progress had been made on several key points. "Initial difficulties raised by the Iraqi side about helicopters and aerial surveillance planes operating in the no-fly zone were overcome. That is not to say that the operation of inspections is free from frictions, but at this juncture we are able to perform professional no-notice inspections all over Iraq and to increase aerial surveillance."[48] Rice pressed Blix not to be overly positive in his assessment of Iraq's latest gambit because the United States was now going to determine what Baghdad had to do to comply with Resolution 1441. According to Rumsfeld, after "old Europe" refused to cooperate in the UN Security Council, the game had changed. No longer would Iraq be in compliance with the spirit of the resolution by simply allowing weapons inspectors back into the country. Once the United States was committed to an invasion, the rules would be different. From that moment on the burden of proof was no longer with the UN weapons inspection team or even the United States to prove that Iraq had weapons of mass destruction; the burden of proof was now on Iraq to prove that they did not. An angry Hans Blix declared that the United States wanted to see the United Nations sink into the East River.[49]

The Legal Debate

As the Bush administration moved closer to an invasion, the debate over just cause intensified. Many legal scholars questioned the Bush administration's legal rationale, claiming that violation of successive Security Council resolutions would not suffice unless there was a specific UN resolution providing the explanation and justification for an invasion of Iraq. Indeed, the Bush administration's argument seemed to contain several legal holes. Just before the invasion, U.S. ambassador to the United Nations, John Negroponte, offered the legal reasoning in a letter to the president of the Security Council (see DOCUMENT 3-H). He claimed that Iraq had failed to comply with the UN weapons inspectors since the end of the First Gulf War and that no further justification was needed.[50] The State Department's legal advisor, William Howard Taft IV, made a similar statement in late March 2003, claiming that, "Iraq's failure to comply with three council orders nearly 13 years apart was the principal legal justification for war."[51] Not to be outdone, John Bellinger at the National Security Council published a position paper for the White House, arguing that "the United States has clear authority under international law to use force against Iraq under present circumstances," including the notion that "in the modern age in which terrorism and the proliferation of WMDs [weapons of mass destruction] pose grave risks to global security, states cannot be required to wait for an attack before they can lawfully use force to defend themselves against forces that present a clear and present danger of attack."[52]

Yet many legal scholars, including Harold Koh who taught international law at Yale University and who served as Bill Clinton's undersecretary of state for democracy, human rights, and labor, and served in the Obama administration, claim that the "invasion of Iraq was illegal under international law."[53] For Koh, the rules for using force following the Cold War were clear: a state could lawfully breach "another's territorial sovereignty only if one or more of three conditions obtained: response to aggression, self-defense, or an explicit UN Security Council resolution."[54] The First Gulf War met two of the three requirements. The United States led an international coalition to oust Iraq from Kuwait, a clear sign of aggression from Saddam Hussein and his army. The UN Security Council passed a resolution granting authority for a military force to restore sovereignty to Kuwait. On these points, the legal defense of American military action seems clear. What is less clear is how UN resolutions not authorizing an invasion of Iraq could be used to justify an invasion of Iraq. The Bush administration's argument was circular, according to Koh. It claimed that an earlier UN resolution, number 678, which authorized the use of force to eject Iraq from Kuwait in 1991 and had been suspended following Saddam's retreat, could be "revived" in 2003. In other words, the justification for military intervention in Iraq in 2003 was granted in 1991. This was a dubious claim for many legal scholars. Without a new Security Council resolution authorizing the use of force in 2003, many international lawyers argued that the Bush administration's legal justification was suspect.

Equally troubling was the Bush administration's claims that it had the authority to launch preemptive strikes against Iraq because Baghdad threatened the United States. Following the First Gulf War there was considerable debate about the legality of the use of force over human rights violations and preemptive strikes for self-defense. When could a state intervene in the affairs of another state to stop mass atrocities from taking place, and when could a state launch preemptive attacks against a sovereign state it suspected of planning mischief? United States legal scholars explored the legal contours of humanitarian intervention throughout the 1990s. Gross human rights abuses in Somalia, Bosnia, Kosovo, Rwanda, Sierra Leone, East Timor, and Haiti challenged American foreign policy leaders. Clinton administration officials stumbled through the 1990s, never developing a comprehensive legal or security answer to these questions. The result was a haphazard foreign policy that led to intervention in some cases (Kosovo) and not in others (Rwanda). Few in the Clinton White House favored preemptive strikes against America's potential adversaries, so the foreign policy establishment in Washington delayed consideration of such actions. But following the September 11 attacks, the two issues – humanitarian intervention and preemptive strikes – were fused. The Bush White House asserted that it had a customary legal right of preemptive self-defense to protect the United States from threats posed by other countries, especially those harboring terrorists.[55] Customary law, in this context, is the traditional common rule or practice that has become an intrinsic part of the accepted and expected conduct in war. The Bush team argued that the United States had already been the victim of human rights violations and offensive military action in the September 11 terrorist attacks, and therefore it had a right to stop future attacks. Since Saddam Hussein had provided a safe haven for terrorists and encouraged their activities, he was now a direct threat to the United States. The dictator's efforts to secure weapons of mass destruction gave this reasoning a sense of urgency.

It now seems clear that the Bush team simply went through the motions at the United Nations, believing that it already had the legal and ethical right to invade Iraq. Only four months after 1441's passage, President Bush publicly stated that the United States did not need another UN resolution to make an invasion of Iraq legal. Perhaps the Bush White House went to the UN just before the invasion because Tony Blair, the British prime minister, had insisted upon it. But once Bush went public with his intent to invade Iraq, Blair quickly dropped his opposition to a non-UN-sanctioned military action. Some legal scholars and policymakers have long argued that the Bush administration could have disarmed Iraq without unilateral military intervention through "a multilateral strategy of disarmament plus enhanced containment plus more aggressive human rights intervention," a policy pursued by President Clinton, Bush's predecessor. That strategy, Harold Koh claims, would have "supported the continuation of the initial Bush approach of diplomacy backed by threat of force: restoring effective UN weapons inspections, disarming and destroying Iraqi weapons of mass destruction, and cutting off the flow of weapons and weapons-related goods into Iraq." Furthermore, Koh and his supporters believe that such a containment policy could have been developed alongside a more aggressive human rights platform that inserted human rights monitors into Iraq who had the potential to drive Saddam Hussein and his top lieutenants into exile and potentially to bring them "to justice before an appropriate international tribunal."[56] Instead, the Bush administration chose to go to war in Iraq because it believed that the United States had the legal right and responsibility to do so.

The War Plan

The military plans for the invasion had begun in earnest in the late fall of 2002. At the Pentagon, Rumsfeld worked closely with U.S. Army general Tommy Franks, the CENTCOM commander, who had been charged with drawing up the plans for the Iraqi invasion. From the earliest stages of the planning it was clear that Rumsfeld wanted a small force that acted quickly to defeat Saddam Hussein, control the Iraqi population of 24 million, and secure "a nation the size of California with porous borders."[57] Rumsfeld rejected the army's long-held assumptions about force structure and force-level requirements, insisting that Franks accomplish the many tasks charged to him with fewer resources than existing plans had called for and in a shorter time period. Casting aside the military's own strategic planning for conflict in Iraq, Desert Crossing, Rumsfeld argued that the army was not being sensible. He had a running battle with its command over the size and scope of the modern army, a conflict that led many civilians at the Pentagon and in the White House to suggest that the army was out of touch with current security requirements and did not properly understand the changing face of war. Rumsfeld had even suggested a significant downsizing of the army just before the September 11 attacks. Particularly troubling now was the administration's treatment of the officers who had significant experience in the region.

When the early war plans began to circulate among former military commanders, including Marine Corps general Anthony Zinni, and former U.S. Army general Norman Schwarzkopf, the commander of CENTCOM during the First Gulf War, they received sharp criticism. Zinni thought that the more ideological members of the Bush administration had not thought out the invasion thoroughly enough. "The more I saw, the more I thought that this was the product of the neocons who didn't understand the region and were going to create havoc there. These dilettantes from Washington think tanks never had an idea that worked on the ground."[58] Zinni, a veteran of Vietnam, looking at the prewar plans for Iraq claimed that he had "seen this movie before. It was called Vietnam."[59] Schwarzkopf, too, was skeptical of the administration's planning. He also feared that the civilians in charge of planning knew little of what would face them in Iraq, but were reluctant to reach out to those who did. "There are guys at the Pentagon who have been involved in operational planning for their entire lives," Schwarzkopf suggested, "and for this wisdom, acquired during many operations, wars, schools, for that just to be ignored, and in its place have somebody who doesn't have any of that training, is of concern."[60]

Most of the criticism focused on the size of the invasion force and the number of troops needed to provide security in post-Saddam Iraq. The administration believed that an invasion force of around 100,000 troops was adequate and that that force could be drawn down quickly to about 30,000 once the Baghdad regime collapsed. General Franks had been busy drawing up a war plan based on the administration's numbers. Paul Wolfowitz, the deputy secretary of defense, was insistent that the job could be done with few U.S. troops. He was particularly critical of General Eric Shinseki's (U.S. Army chief of staff) estimate that it would take several hundred thousand U.S. troops to secure Iraq. Wolfowitz told Congress that "There has been a good deal of comment – some of it quite outlandish – about what our postwar requirements might be in Iraq. Some of the higher end predictions that we have been hearing recently, such as the notion that it will take several hundred thousand U.S. troops to provide stability in post-Saddam Iraq, are wildly off the mark."[61] Rumsfeld supported his deputy, suggesting that it was "ludicrous to think that it would take more forces to secure the peace than win the war."[62]

But, other generals supported Shinseki's estimates and criticized the administration for not listening to their advice. Retired major general

William Nash stated publicly that it would indeed take at least 200,000 U.S. troops to secure post-Saddam Iraq and that it was impossible to predict the variables when it came to rebuilding the country. Retired air force colonel John Warden, long considered a strategic genius by national security experts, argued that the invasion plan was incomplete and carried a "very high risk from the strategic side with years of difficult and very expensive occupation."[63] The Bush administration countered, claiming that the entire occupation, no matter how long it took, would cost American taxpayers under $2 billion.[64] Yet there was severe criticism of the Bush administration's claim that entire divisions of the current Iraqi armed forces would join the United States once Saddam Hussein was overthrown. From the very beginning of war planning in Washington, Rumsfeld and other civilians at the Pentagon and the CIA argued that Iraqi troops could be counted upon to secure the country's borders, freeing American troops for other tasks. This was a rash prediction that did not come to pass. Still, the Bush administration, and Rumsfeld in particular, was committed to a small, united force that moved forward rapidly and overthrew Saddam Hussein quickly. Rebuilding the country would require far less troops and, from the Bush administration's vantage point, little planning.

Troop strength was not the only controversial aspect of the Bush administration's war plan. Before the invasion began, leading theorists who had been privy to the planning spoke with the press and described what was about to happen in Iraq. Among the more interesting interviews was that with Harlan Ullman, a military analyst at the Center for Strategic and International Studies, who had long been an advocate of U.S. airpower. Ullman depicted the Bush administration's initial strategy as "shock and awe." He described a complicated and disorienting show of force that might make the debate about ground troops inconsequential. "You'll see simultaneous attacks of hundreds of warheads, maybe thousands, so that very suddenly the Iraqi senior leadership, or much of it, will be eviscerated. At the same time, you'll see forces put into Iraq," to set up forward bases to protect oilfields and secure the borders, that "make the situation look virtually hopeless for Saddam Hussein and the leadership. The pressure will continue until we run out of targets."[65] Ullman and Rumsfeld shared a view that modern war could be managed in a way that focused on the enemy's "will, perception, and understanding." The goal was to use American power "with such compellance that even the strongest of wills will be awed."[66] Unlike the First Gulf War, where the United States amassed overwhelming troop strength, the goal this time around in Iraq would be a "concentrated series of strikes at many different kinds of targets," causing the Iraq regime to be "shocked" and "awed" into surrender.[67] According to U.S. Army major general Stanley McChrystal, then the vice director of operations at the Pentagon, this new way of making war was an "effects-based campaign." The goal was to make it apparent from the very beginning of military operations that there was no alternative to defeat for Saddam Hussein. "We are running an effects-based campaign that is partially kinetic, partially non-kinetic, partially information operations," General McChrystal reported. The success of effects-based bombing is "not just whether there is a hole in the room of a building but whether or not the function that the element did before ceases to be effective . . . In an effects-based campaign, we can achieve much shock and awe by hitting critical points."[68]

General McChrystal's optimistic predictions were matched by those who would be most responsible for overseeing the post-Saddam period of transition in Iraq. Once that planning had been moved to the Pentagon, few inside the Bush administration gave nation-building much attention. Those that did offered a rather benign view of what would follow an American invasion. Wendy Chamberlin, a senior official with the United States Agency for International Development (USAID), told the last meeting of the State Department's Iraq Working Group that the postwar period would be "very quick." She continued, "we are going to meet their immediate needs. We're going to turn it over to the Iraqis. And we're going to be out within the year."[69]

The War Begins

Reportedly, at the final meeting at CENTCOM in Qatar before the invasion began, General Franks showed his top commanders the opening scenes of the movie *The Gladiator*. Actor Russell Crowe, playing Marcus Aurelius's favorite general, is preparing to smash the last vestige of a Germanic tribe refusing to bend the knee to the Roman Empire. With the Roman Legion ready for battle, the general cries, "On my signal, unleash hell."[70] Hell began in earnest on March 17, 2003, when President Bush delivered an ultimatum: "Saddam Hussein and his sons must leave Iraq within 48 hours. Their refusal to go will result in military conflict commenced at the time of our choosing."[71] Simultaneously, the British ambassador to the United Nations declared that the diplomatic process on Iraq had ended, and with the Security Council's support, all UN weapons inspectors should evacuate Iraq.[72] Three days later, the invasion began.

U.S. military operations in Iraq began with a bombing campaign on March 20, 2003, against Baghdad, targeting key ministries and palaces thought to be potential residences of Saddam Hussein. The Dora Farm, a large complex in southern Baghdad where the CIA suspected Saddam had hidden out, was also hit with bombs and cruise missiles. Though it was unclear if Saddam had been hit directly, reports from the south and west suggested that U.S. invasion forces were experiencing little opposition from the Iraqi army. In fact, the army's 5th Corps, that had crossed the Iraq–Kuwait border at the beginning of the invasion on its way to Baghdad through the desert west of the Euphrates, reported that the Iraqi army was simply melting away, just as Bush strategists had predicted. U.S. Marines on the east side of the Euphrates also faced little opposition. But the British troops who were attacking from the Persian Gulf encountered stiff resistance in and around Basra, a southern Shiite stronghold. Regular Iraqi troops were joined by the Fedayeen, a loyal militia headed up by Saddam's eldest son, Uday. Ali Hassan al-Majid, known as "Chemical Ali" for his gas attacks upon the Kurds in northern Iraq in the late 1980s, was also involved in the fighting near Basra. Ali, a cousin of Saddam Hussein, had fallen out of grace with the dictator because of his illegal grain sales in Iran. Just before the American invasion in March 2003, however, Saddam had ordered him to take command of Iraqi forces in the south. During the battles in and around Basra, British sources claimed that Ali had been killed in an air strike. The reports later proved to be inaccurate. Still, the fighting around Basra was a harbinger of things to come.

The promised "shock and awe" came to Iraq on Saturday, March 22, when intense air strikes hit Baghdad, Tikrit, Mosul, and Kirkuk, severely dismantling the regular Iraqi army's warmaking capabilities. For example, 8,000 of Iraq's 51st Army Division reportedly surrendered or deserted following air attacks in the south. U.S. troops had advanced more than 150 miles inside Iraq and some had crossed the Euphrates River on their way to Baghdad. The U.S. Air Force and Navy flew 1,500 sorties in a two-day period, the most intense bombings by American forces since the Balkans crisis. But on Sunday, March 23, U.S. forces met their first significant opposition. U.S. Marines from Charlie Company of the 1st Battalion, Second Marines were ambushed as they made a wrong turn in the southeastern city of Nasiriya. They were met with light arms resistance and artillery fire in the early morning hours, and by the end of the day eighteen Americans were dead and another six had been captured, including Private First Class Jessica Lynch. Wounded in the firefight, Lynch was taken prisoner and held for over one week before she was rescued by special operations forces. Lynch gained national attention, and the heartwarming story shielded the American public from a war that was already starting to triangulate. New armed groups were emerging just as American forces were putting down the Republican Guard.

On March 30, CENTCOM increased air strikes against Saddam's Republican Guard troops in one of the heaviest days of bombing of the entire campaign. According to the Pentagon, over 800 sorties were launched against military and political installations. Despite the apparently one-sided nature of the war, some foreign reporters in Iraq suggested that the conflict had already created new militias whose loyalties and political ambitions were difficult to discern. One reporter, Peter Arnett, appeared on Iraqi state-run television, arguing that the Pentagon had already begun to change its war plans because it had underestimated Iraqi resistance. Public pressure forced NBC to fire Arnett, a long-time war correspondent. According to NBC News president Neal Shapiro, "It was wrong for Mr. Arnett to grant an interview to state-controlled Iraqi TV, especially at a time of war. . . . And it was wrong for him to discuss his personal observations and opinions in that interview."[73] Against this backdrop, U.S. forces encountered little resistance in the first week of April as they neared Baghdad, even though it was clear that resistance groups were forming.

On April 2, the U.S. Army's 3rd Infantry Division captured the holy city of Karbala, the site of an important battle in Shia history. The largely Sunni army brigades had no local support, as the Shiites in this city 60 kilometers from Baghdad had often stood in opposition to Saddam's rule. The 1st Marines, meanwhile, had captured a major bridge over the Tigris leading to Baghdad. This secured access to the city for American forces and closed off a significant escape route for Saddam's Republican Guard. The international airport was secured on April 5, and the following day U.S.-led coalition forces completely encircled Baghdad, preparing for the last battle of the war against Saddam Hussein. On Monday, April 7, the army's 3rd Infantry seized two of Saddam's Baghdad palaces, and two days later Marines helped local protestors topple a huge statue of the Iraqi leader in Firdos Square. An overjoyed president Bush told the Iraqi people: "You're free! And freedom is beautiful."[74]

In Iraq, the war was experienced in several different ways. Many were pleased that Saddam had been driven from power, but they remained fearful of the future. The long sanctions regime combined with Saddam's brutal rule had depleted the country of even the most basic resources, and few believed that an American-led invasion would do much to fix this problem. Most worried that the bombing raids had taken an enormous toll on ordinary Iraqis. The late Anthony Shadid, then Middle East reporter for the *New York Times*, was perhaps most eloquent when capturing the voices of Iraqis living under the bombs. Shortly after the 2003 invasion began, Shadid wrote:

> The melancholy wail sailed across the city and pierced the walls of the middle-class Baghdad home. The sleepless family listened in silence until the mother, her faced lined with fear and pain, shook her head. "Siren," she whispered. At that, her daughter jumped up and threw open the door. She ran to open the windows next, fearful the blast would shatter them. The son sprinted outside, hoping to spot a low-flying cruise missile that would send the family huddling, yet again, in a hallway.
>
> And they waited for the bombs.

"It's terrible," the mother said, as the minutes passed. "We really suffer, and I don't know why we should live like this." Her daughter nodded. "I get so scared, I shake," she said. "I'm afraid the house is gong to collapse on my head."

While the outside world has grown accustomed to detached images of fire and fury over Baghdad, and the government here boasts of victory over the invaders, this rattled family of five in the middle-class neighborhood of Jihad has watched war turn life upside down. Their world now is isolation, dread, and a bitter sense that they do not deserve their fate.

"We're in a dark, dark tunnel, and we don't see the light at the end of it," the daughter-in-law said.[75]

Shadid's reporting brought the cost of the war in Iraq home for many Americans. Public opinion polls showed that most supported the removal of Saddam Hussein from power and the U.S. troops, but many questioned the war's human cost. In one Gallup poll conducted six months after the invasion began, 40 percent of those Americans polled believed it had been a mistake to send U.S. troops to Iraq.[76] For the remainder of the war, monthly polling usually showed that most Americans did not support sending U.S. armed forces to Iraq.[77]

Despite the public skepticism, the Bush administration was pleased with the war's progress. In just a few short weeks, the president reported, coalition forces had launched an ambitious invasion of Iraq and now controlled most of its major cities. Some hard-core resistance fighters continued to pester American forces in Baghdad during the second week of April, but by April 12 all but the city of Tikrit, Saddam's hometown, appeared to be under allied control. Still, Baghdad's information minister, Saeed Sahhaf, appeared before the international press corps, declaring that "There is not any American presence or troops in the heart of the capital, at all. The soldiers of Saddam Hussein gave them a great lesson that history will not forget." With American troops in full view in downtown Baghdad, Sahhaf claimed that all U.S. soldiers in the city "are going to surrender or be burned in their tanks."[78] It was the last ridiculous stand of a tyrant's regime, or so it seemed at the time.

Although it would take until the end of the year to finally capture Saddam, most in the Bush White House believed that major combat operations were over in Iraq and that now it would simply be a matter of rebuilding the state apparatus to care for the public welfare and supporting the creation of new civil society institutions. Most in the military command, however, understood that only the first phase of the battle for Iraq was over. Most military strategists correctly surmised that Saddam's Republican Guard was no match for U.S. forces during the conventional stage of the war. But they also figured that this first leg was likely to be the easiest and shortest chapter of the war. While Washington celebrated, military planners feared that the second phase of the war was about to begin. This would be "a protracted guerrilla war" against coalition forces.[79] A suicide bombing on April 10 at a Marine checkpoint in Baghdad ushered in the new phase, though few in Washington understood this at the time. Instead, most civilians in the Pentagon were downplaying the looting taking place in Baghdad and talking as if nation-building were a naturally occurring phenomenon. Paul Wolfowitz claimed that "We're not going to need as many people to do peacekeeping as we needed to fight the war."[80] Most in the Bush White House agreed. Skeptics in the Pentagon were quickly silenced and told to watch events unfold from afar.

Notes

1   *The 9/11 Commission Report* (Boston: Bedford/St. Martin's, 2007), 49.
2   Ibid.
3   Ibid., 139.
4   Wolfowitz interview on PBS with Margaret Warner, September 14, 2001.
5   Ron Suskind, *The Price of Loyalty: George W. Bush, The White House, and the Education of Paul O'Neill* (New York: The Free Press, 2004), 73–84.
6   William Kristol and Robert Kagan, *Present Dangers* (San Francisco: Encounter Books, 2000), 20.
7   Richard Pipes, "Team B – The Reality Behind the Myth," *Commentary* (October 1986), 25–40, and Murray Freidman, *The Neoconservative Revolution* (Cambridge: Cambridge University Press, 2005).
8   John Prados, *Hoodwinked: The Documents That Reveal How Bush Sold Us a War* (New York: The New Press, 2004), 6.
9   *Washington Post*, May 31, 2009.
10   Ibid.
11   Richard Haass, *War of Necessity, War of Choice: A Memoir of Two Iraq Wars* (New York: Simon & Schuster, 2009), 192.
12   Quoted in Prados, *Hoodwinked*, 8.
13   President George W. Bush, State of the Union address, January 29, 2002.
14   As reported by BBC News, February 15, 2002.
15   Lloyd Gardner, *The Long Road to Baghdad: A History of U.S. Foreign Policy from the 1970s to the Present* (New York: The New Press, 2008), 131.
16   Michael Isikoff and David Corn, *Hubris: The Inside Story of Spin, Scandal, and the Selling of the Iraq War* (New York: Three Rivers Press, 2007), 104.
17   The White House, http://www.whitehouse.gov.
18   As quoted in Robert K. Brigham, *Iraq, Vietnam, and the Limits of American Power* (New York: PublicAffairs, 2008),14.
19   Ibid.
20   "Declaration of the Shia," July 2002.
21   Unclassified report to Congress on the acquisition of technology relating to weapons of mass destruction and advanced conventional munitions, July 1–December 2002.

22   Samantha Power, *A Problem from Hell: America and the Age of Genocide* (New York: Perennial, 2002), 171–246.
23   As quoted in Prados, *Hoodwinked*, 28.
24   As quoted in Gardner, *The Long Road to Baghdad*, 144.
25   Ibid.
26   Ibid.
27   Ibid., 145.
28   CNN.com, "White House Spells Out Case Against Iraq," September 12, 2002.
29   Ibid.
30   Ibid.
31   Joint Resolution to Authorize the Use of United States Armed Forces in Iraq. White House Press Release, October 2, 2002.
32   Ibid.
33   Brigham, *Iraq, Vietnam, and the Limits of American Power*, 29.
34   CNN.com, "Senate Approves Iraq War Resolution," October 11, 2002.
35   "Memorandum for Daniel J. Bryant, Assistant Attorney General, Office of Legislative Affairs, Authorization for the Use of Military Force Against Iraq Resolution of 2002," John C. Yoo, Office of Legal Counsel, October 21, 2002.
36   State of the Union Address, White House Press Release, January 29, 2003.
37   Brigham, *Iraq, Vietnam, and the Limits of American Power*, 109–148.
38   Ibid.
39   "The Downing Street Memo," reprinted in *Sunday Times*, May 11, 2005.
40   CNN.com, "Transcript of Powell's UN Presentation," February 6, 2003.
41   Ibid.
42   Ibid.
43   Tom Ricks, *Fiasco: The American Military Adventure in Iraq* (New York: Penguin, 2006), 90.
44   *Huffington Post*, November 17, 2005.
45   *Guardian*, March 18, 2003.
46   Ibid.
47   *New York Times*, February 17, 2003.
48   As quoted in Gardner, *The Long Road to Baghdad*, 161.
49   Ibid., 162.
50   U.S. ambassador to the United Nations John Negroponte's letter to Ambassador Mamady Traore, president of the United Nations Security Council, March 20, 2003; the letter is reproduced and discussed in Harold Koh, "On American Exceptionalism," *Stanford Law Review*, 55 (May 2003), 1521.
51   *Washington Post*, March 21, 2003.
52   As quoted in Koh, "American Exceptionalism," 1521.
53   Ibid., 1523.
54   Ibid., 1515.
55   President of the United States, The National Security Strategy of the United States of America 34 (2002), available at http:www.whitehouse.gov/nsc/nss.pdf, accessed January 10, 2013.
56   Koh, "American Exceptionalism," 1519.
57   Michael Gordon and General Bernard E. Trainor, *Cobra II: The Inside Story of the Invasion and Occupation of Iraq* (pbk edn., New York: Vintage, 2007).

58   As quoted in Ricks, *Fiasco*, 87–88.
59   Brigham, *Iraq, Vietnam, and the Limits of American Power*, 50.
60   As quoted in Ricks, *Fiasco*, 83.
61   Ibid., 97.
62   Gordon and Trainor, *Cobra II*, 118.
63   As quoted in Ricks, *Fiasco*, 108.
64   Ibid., 109.
65   *Christian Science Monitor*, January 30, 2003.
66   As quoted in Gardner, *The Long Road to Baghdad*, 165.
67   As quoted in *Slate*, "Meet Mr. Shock and Awe," April 1, 2003.
68   Fred Kaplan, "The Flaw of Shock and Awe," *Slate*, March 26, 2003.
69   As quoted in James Fallows, *Blind into Baghdad: America's War in Iraq* (New York: Vintage, 2006), 100.
70   As described in Gordon and Trainor, *Cobra II*, 188.
71   BBC News, March 18, 2003.
72   Ibid.
73   As quoted in Jack Shafer, "Sacking Arnett for the Wrong Reason," *Slate*, March 31, 2003.
74   As quoted in Gardner, *The Long Road to Baghdad*, 170.
75   *New York Times*, March 24, 2003.
76   Gallup poll, October 2003, at http://www.gallup.com/poll/1633/iraq.aspx, accessed January 10, 2013.
77   Gallup polls, March 2003–December 2011, ibid.
78   As quoted in Ricks, *Fiasco*, 133–134.
79   As quoted ibid., 137.
80   As quoted ibid., 138.

DOCUMENTS

──────────── Document 3-A ────────────

Excerpts from George W. Bush's State of the Union address, January 29, 2002

Thank you very much. Mr. Speaker, Vice President Cheney, members of Congress, distinguished guests, fellow citizens: As we gather tonight, our nation is at war, our economy is in recession, and the civilized world faces unprecedented dangers. Yet the state of our Union has never been stronger.

We last met in an hour of shock and suffering. In four short months, our nation has comforted the victims, begun to rebuild New York and the Pentagon, rallied a great coalition, captured, arrested, and rid the world of thousands of terrorists, destroyed Afghanistan's terrorist training camps, saved a people from starvation, and freed a country from brutal oppression. . . .

... Our second goal is to prevent regimes that sponsor terror from threatening America or our friends and allies with weapons of mass destruction. Some of these regimes have been pretty quiet since September the 11th. But we know their true nature. North Korea is a regime arming with missiles and weapons of mass destruction, while starving its citizens. Iran aggressively pursues these weapons and exports terror, while an unelected few repress the Iranian people's hope for freedom. Iraq continues to flaunt its hostility toward America and to support terror.

The Iraqi regime has plotted to develop anthrax, and nerve gas, and nuclear weapons for over a decade. This is a regime that has already used poison gas to murder thousands of its own citizens – leaving the bodies of mothers huddled over their dead children. This is a regime that agreed to international inspections – then kicked out the inspectors. This is a regime that has something to hide from the civilized world.

States like these, and their terrorist allies, constitute an axis of evil, arming to threaten the peace of the world. By seeking weapons of mass destruction, these regimes pose a grave and growing danger. They could provide these arms to terrorists, giving them the means to match their hatred. They could attack our allies or attempt to blackmail the United States. In any of these cases, the price of indifference would be catastrophic.

We will work closely with our coalition to deny terrorists and their state sponsors the materials, technology, and expertise to make and deliver weapons of mass destruction. We will develop and deploy effective missile defenses to protect America and our allies from sudden attack. And all nations should know: America will do what is necessary to ensure our nation's security.

We'll be deliberate, yet time is not on our side. I will not wait on events, while dangers gather. I will not stand by, as peril draws closer and closer. The United States of America will not permit the world's most dangerous regimes to threaten us with the world's most destructive weapons.

Our war on terror is well begun, but it is only begun. This campaign may not be finished on our watch – yet it must be and it will be waged on our watch. We can't stop short. If we stop now – leaving terror camps intact and terror states unchecked – our sense of security would be false and temporary. History has called America and our allies to action, and it is both our responsibility and our privilege to fight freedom's fight ...

... Time and distance from the events of September the 11th will not make us safer unless we act on its lessons. America is no longer protected by vast oceans. We are protected from attack only by vigorous action abroad, and increased vigilance at home.

During these last few months, I've been humbled and privileged to see the true character of this country in a time of testing. Our enemies believed America was weak and materialistic, that we would splinter in fear and selfishness. They were as wrong as they are evil ...

. . . Steadfast in our purpose, we now press on. We have known freedom's price. We have shown freedom's power. And in this great conflict, my fellow Americans, we will see freedom's victory. Thank you all. May God bless.

QUESTIONS TO CONSIDER

1   What were President Bush's priorities for U.S. foreign policy? How did invading Iraq help the United States achieve these objectives?
2   Did Iraq possess weapons of mass destruction, according to President Bush?
3   Do you agree with the president that the United States is "only protected from attack by vigorous action abroad"?

—————— Document 3-B ——————

Excerpts from "The National Security of the United States of America," September 2002

. . . We must be prepared to stop rogue states and their terrorist clients before they are able to threaten or use weapons of mass destruction against the United States and our allies and friends. Our response must take full advantage of strengthened alliances, the establishment of new partnerships with former adversaries, innovation in the use of military forces, modern technologies, including the development of an effective missile defense system, and increased emphasis on intelligence collection and analysis . . .

. . . Traditional concepts of deterrence will not work against a terrorist enemy whose avowed tactics are wanton destruction and the targeting of innocents: whose so-called soldiers seek martyrdom in death and whose most potent protection is statelessness. The overlap between states that sponsor terror and those that pursue WMD [weapons of mass destruction] compels us to action.

For centuries, international law recognize that nations need not suffer an attack before they can lawfully take action to defend themselves against forces that present an imminent danger of attack. Legal scholars and international jurists often conditioned the legitimacy of preemption on the existence of an imminent threat – most often a visible mobilization of armies, navies, and air forces preparing for attack.

We must adapt the concept of imminent threat to the capabilities and objectives of today's adversaries. Rogue states and terrorists do not seek to attack us using conventional means. They know such attacks would fail. Instead, they rely on acts of terror and, potentially, the use of weapons of mass destruction – weapons that can be easily concealed, delivered covertly, and used without warning ...

...The United States has long maintained the option of preemptive actions to counter sufficient threat to our national security. The greater the threat, the greater the risk of inaction – and the more compelling the case for taking antici-patory action to defend ourselves, even if uncertainty remains as to the time and place of the enemy's attacks. To forestall or prevent such hostile acts by our adversaries, the United States will, if necessary, act preemptively ...

... the purpose of our actions will always be to eliminate a specific threat to the United States or our allies and friends. The reasons for our actions will be clear, the force measured, and the cause just.

QUESTIONS TO CONSIDER

1   What do you think of the legal justification for preemptive strikes? Is it compelling? Should nations be allowed to make preemptive attacks?

Document 3-C

"The Problem of the Shia," July 2002

"Declaration of the Shia of Iraq, July 2002"

Introduction

A series of meetings were held in London during 2001 and 2002 to discuss the sectarian problem in Iraq and its effects on Iraq's present conditions and future. A broad range of personalities were involved in these meetings ranging from intellectuals, politicians, military personnel, writers, tribal chiefs, academics, to businessmen and professionals, drawn from a wide political spectrum, including islamists, nationalists, socialists and liberals. These meetings were not constrained by any particular ideological or organisational considerations, with the partici-pants being motivated primarily by a concern for the national interests of Iraq. The ideas expressed at these meetings were strictly those of the participants in their individual capacities, even though a number of them were attached to specific political groups or ideational currents.

The meetings had the important effect of facilitating the formulation of com-monly accepted parameters regarding the sectarian problem in Iraq, and the methods that should be employed to tackle this issue in any future restructuring of the political order in the country. This document – *Declaration of the Shia of Iraq* – is the result of these discussions and deliberations.

1. *The genesis of the problem* Following the establishment of the constitutional entity that became modern Iraq in 1923, and the organisation of its administrative and political affairs, the sectarian paradigm became a key organising principle of the governing powers. It then quickly evolved into a set of fixed political rules of power and control that has continued into present times.

A number of Iraq's leading political figures were acutely aware of the dangers of pursing a deliberate sectarian policy on the part of the state and its deleterious effects on the country. They introduced a number of political initiatives and programmes that were designed to highlight and reverse the sectarian framework of governmental policies, and to counter the hardening of official sectarian discrimination against the Shia. The most important of these initiatives would include:

- The detailed letter that King Faysal I addressed to his ministers in 1932, and in which he highlighted the injustice that has been afflicted on the Shia and the critical importance of addressing their concerns and sense of betrayal by the state.
- The letter that was addressed to the Iraqi Government by Sheikh Muhammed Hussein Kashif al-Ghita in which he drew attention to the discrimination that has been meted out to the Shia and the necessity of removing its causes and manifestations.
- The initiative of the Shia religious authorities under the guidance of the Imam Sayyid Muhsin al-Hakim in the 1960's that encompassed representations to the authorities on the sectarian issue.
- The 1964 letter of Sheikh Muhammed Ridha al-Shibibi that was addressed to the then Prime Minister of Iraq, Abdul Rahman Al Bazzaz, and which detailed the condition of the Shia and their grievances.

All of these initiatives shared a common concern that rejected the sectarian bases of political power and authority in Iraq, and its decidedly anti-Shia bias. These initiatives called for the abandonment of these sectarian policies, the granting of full political and civil rights to the Shia, and called for their treatment within the framework of sound constitutional principles based on a notion of citizenship that was inherently inclusive and fair.

These initiatives also provided the catalyst for subsequent activities in the fight against sectarianism that was joined by writers, intellectuals and the *ulema*, all of whom called for the dissolution of the sectarian structures of policy-making and the confirmation of the Shia's civil and political rights in line with those of other groups in society.

However, none of these initiatives and activities met with anything but total rejection by the state, which continued in its sectarian biases irrespective of the damage that this caused, and would continue to cause, to the fabric of society and its integrity. The authorities simply ignored the catastrophic consequences of these policies, which were to influence all Iraqis regardless of their sectarian, ethnic or religious affiliations.

The Iraqi Shia problem is now a globally recognised fault line and is no longer restricted to the confines of Iraq's territory. It has ceased to be a local issue, for the international community and its organisations (such as Amnesty International, Human Rights Watch, the UN's Special Rapporteur on Iraq) have now acknowledged openly the existence of a serious sectarian problem in Iraq, and have expressed their sympathy and solidarity with the plight of the Shia of Iraq and the sectarian biases that they daily encounter from the authorities.

The sectarian issue has now emerged into the light of day in spite of the Iraqi authorities' attempts, through their political and media apparatuses, to cover up its reality. The rights of the Shia are now an issue that is central to the present and future conditions of Iraq, and must now be included in any plan or programme that tries to tackle the reconstruction of the Iraqi state. It is for the very reason of its criticality that a calm and reasoned debate is now called for to discuss the rights and demands of the Shia.

This declaration draws on the long line of similar efforts made in the past by the leaders of the Shia in Iraq. It follows closely on their path of calling, responsibly and persistently, for the legitimate rights that are due the Shia, and in a manner that reflects properly the views of the Iraqi Shia as a whole. This is especially relevant today where the Shia in Iraq do not have an authoritative leadership that can tackle the issues and problems that concern them, not least their political, cultural and civil rights.

2. *Who are the Shia?* A dictionary definition of the Shia would be those who claim a historic loyalty to the Household of the Prophet and their school of Islam. In the context of Iraq however, the Shia is any person who belongs to the Jaafari sect of Islam either by birth or choice. The Shia in Iraq are not an ethnic group nor a race nor nation, but rather, can comprise any social combination that believes that its Shia fealty has led it to suffer from persistent sectarian disadvantage over the centuries.

The policies of discrimination against the Shia of Iraq have caused every Shia to believe that he or she is targeted because of their Shiism and for no other reason. The Shia is treated as a second-class citizen almost from birth, and is deliberately distanced from any major position of authority or responsibility. He or she suffers from an in-built preference given to others even though others are less skilled or qualified.

This sectarian pattern has been employed in Iraq over the centuries. The Shia were frequently the objects of the retribution and oppression of the authorities simply because of sectarian considerations, even though the intensity and frequency of the anti-Shia activities of the authorities might have ebbed and flowed. However, the oppression has been ratcheted up drastically over the past twenty years.

The determination of the authorities to implement these policies and their insistence on the continuing isolation of the Shia from any meaningful exercise of power has contributed, in the modern period, to the transformation of the Iraqi Shia into a recognisable social entity with its own peculiarities, far from any specific ideological and religious considerations. In other words the crystallisation of the Shia as a distinct group owes far more to the policies of discrimination and retribution than to any specifically sectarian or religious considerations. This condition now defines the status of the Shia in Iraq irrespective of the individual Shia's doctrinal, religious or political orientations.

3. The Shia and the modern Iraqi state The Shia's disillusioning experience with the circumstances that underpinned the formation of the first Iraqi government in 1920 was the defining historical factor in their political evolution. This statement can be amply justified by any number of impartial historical studies. The Iraqi state was designed within clear sectarian boundaries, with the intention of distancing the Shia and their leadership from the decision-making structures of the nascent state. And even though the sectarian principles of power and authority were not explicitly set out in the original basic law of the country, they became the unwritten code for generations of politicians in both monarchical and republican Iraq.

This is painfully ironic in as much as the Shia played a pivotal role in establishing the conditions for an independent Iraq, being the main actors in the Iraqi Uprising of 1920. The subsequent gross diminution of the position of the Shia in the Iraqi state cannot be reconciled in any way therefore with the importance that their leaders had in the struggle against foreign rule. The connivance of the foreign controlling power in the establishment of sectarian bases of political power set the stage for the evolution of the sectarian system that has continued to the present day.

4. The authorities' objectives in pursuing sectarianism The British occupation of Iraq was met by rejection from a united front between the Shia and Sunni populations of Iraq. Both groups were unanimous in refusing the occupation and insistent on the formation of a national government free of foreign control. This unity was further strengthened by the rejection of the two communities of all the projects and programmes advanced by the occupying administration to reconcile them to their condition, culminating in the common positions adopted by them in their support for the 1920 Uprising. However, Britain succeeded in dividing the two communities when it proposed the formation of an Iraqi government that was based on sectarian principles and advantage, and this became the model, which was followed scrupulously by subsequent governments.

The powers that controlled the Iraqi state strove to convince the Sunnis of Iraq that all the emblems and trappings of power, both civil and military, were the lot of their community by right, and that any serious Shia involvement in the government would be at the expense of their controlling share of power. The authorities, both in monarchical and republican Iraq, succeeded therefore in both the weakening of any potential or real inter-sectarian solidarity as well as in marginalizing the role of the Shia. The raising of any specifically Shia demand for redress became the subject of vitriolic accusations of "sectarianism" by the authorities, even though the Shia were the prime victims of the state's sectarianism. Patriotism and national unity became appropriated by the state as a cover for this sectarian reality.

The famous dictum of Iraq's first prime minister, Abd el-Rahman an-Naqib, addressed to the Shia leadership who were advocating the rejection of the Mandate terms:

"I am the owner (governor) of this land, so what do you (the Shia) have to do with it?"

is an accurate gauge of the political direction that Iraq was to take. The principle of rejecting serious Shia participation in the state became the dominant recurring theme of the governing authorities. Sunnis were to rule by their vigilant control over the main sources of civil, military and social power, while the Shia majority were to be marginalized and isolated. In this way, the Shia's numerical majority in Iraq would be overridden by the deliberate policies of sectarian preference and discrimination, and if need be, oppression.

This has been the basis of Iraq's political life, with the state actively waging war against the Shia's sense of identity, self-confidence and purpose. Violent propaganda campaigns were waged against the Shia and their beliefs, while the state never ceased to remind the Sunnis of the Shia menace and the threat that the Shia posed to their rights and privileges and to their superior social and political status.

The authorities never relented in their discriminatory policies against the Shia. Each new ruler in Iraq found himself confronted with the inchoate anger of the Shia, to which the classic response was to deflect and defuse that threat by a further reduction of the Shia's presence and role. This constant increase in the level and extent of discrimination and state violence against the Shia has made an explosion inevitable.

This relentless increase of sectarian discrimination against the Shia has culminated in the present ruling powers aggressively working towards the elimination of any aspect of Shia public life, within a calculated plan to destroy the institutions of the Shia and thereby weaken and eliminate their communal underpinnings. Shia schools and institutions of higher learning, such as the *Fiqh* (Jurisprudence) College in Najaf and the College of Religious Sciences in Baghdad, were closed as was the cancellation of the Shia-inspired and backed but broadly non-religious University of Kufa. Shia merchants and businessmen were deported in droves, mainly to destroy the economic and commercial vitality of the Shia. The violence perpetrated against the Shia *ulema* and study circles has been unprecedented, driving the Shia specifically, and the country generally, into an extremely dangerous crisis situation.

5. *The nature of the Shia opposition* In spite of the fact that the Shia in Iraq subscribe to numerous political and intellectual groupings, it is the islamist movement that has acted as the main political drive for the Shia at the present moment. The islamist current has been broadly connected, by political commentators and analysts in the region and internationally, with the aspirations of the Shia as a whole. As such, the islamist movement has been seen as reflective of the Shia's views and aims, and in certain respects its proxy. To some extent this is an inappropriate attribution as the islamist parties in Iraq have an explicitly Islamic, rather than sectarian, orientation. Moreover, the condition of the Shia in Iraq is such that they can owe allegiances to a variety of political and cultural currents that are not necessarily islamic in direction.

The Shia's opposition to the state in Iraq is based on political rather than sectarian considerations and has evolved as a consequence of a prolonged process of continuing sectarian discrimination and cruel oppression by the state.

6. *The politics of sectarianism* In spite of the long-standing nature of the policies of sectarian discrimination, Iraq has not witnessed social discrimination in terms of one community, the Sunnis, consciously oppressing another, the Shia. The discrimination with which the Shia have been afflicted is entirely the work of the state. This is a vital point to ponder, as the crises with which Iraq had to contend are a consequence of official rather than communal discrimination. Any programme that hopes to reconstruct the terms of power in Iraq has to start from the point of officially inspired discrimination and not mutual communal hostility.

It is crucial to differentiate between legitimate sectarian differences due to doctrinal and other factors, and a policy of officially sanctioned sectarian advantage and discrimination. Iraq suffers from a sectarian system and not from communal sectarianism per se. There is no overt problem between Iraq's sectarian communities, but rather the opposite is the case, as Iraq has managed to accommodate, at the social level, the differences between its ethnic and sectarian groups. A relatively high degree of harmony has prevailed between the Sunnis and the Shia, in many ways superior to the conditions prevailing in most multi-ethnic and multi-sectarian countries. The struggle for national sovereignty and independence was joined equally by both the Sunnis and the Shia, at the level of their respective leaderships and right down to the community rank and file. Most of the national parties had a broad base of sectarian representation, and sectarian considerations did not dominate the response to key issues and moments that affected the destiny of the country.

The Shia's main driving forces in their struggle for national independence and the building of the modern Iraqi state, were the rejection of foreign hegemony over Iraq and the insistence on sovereign independence. By acceding to the granting of the crown of Iraq to one of Sharif Hussain's sons, Faysal, the Shia clearly indicated their willingness to transcend purely sectarian considerations when dealing with vital national issues, even though it could have been possible for them to demand a Shia king, given their relative weight in Iraq's social and political landscape at that time. It is quite possible that the kingship of Faysal would not have materialised if the Shia religious and political leadership had vigorously opposed to it.

Iraq's political crisis has nothing to do with either social discrimination or a latent Shia sense of inferiority towards the Sunnis, or vice versa. It is entirely due to the conduct of an overtly sectarian authority determined to pursue a policy of discrimination solely for its own interests of control, a policy that has ultimately led to the total absence of political and cultural liberties and the worse forms of dictatorship. It is not possible for Iraq to emerge out of this cul-de-sac without the complete banishment of official sectarianism from any future political construct, and its replacement by a contract premised on a broad and patriotic definition of citizenship that is far removed from sectarian calculations and divisions.

Any policy that calls for the official adoption of the division of powers on the basis of overt sectarian percentages- such as the situation in Lebanon- cannot be workable in the context of Iraq, given its social and historical experience, and will not resolve the current impasse. It is quite probable that such a solution may well result in further problems, dilemmas and crises being laid in store for the country. The only way out of this conundrum is the total rejection of the anti-Shia practices of the state, and the adoption of an inclusive and equitable system of rule that would define the political direction of the future Iraq. This is what the Shia want and not some bogus solution based on the division of the spoils according to demographic formulae, a condition that would very probably result in communal sectarianism becoming a social and political reality rather than a manifestation of an unscrupulous state authority.

The airing in public of the sectarian issues facing Iraq does not subject Iraq's unity to any serious threat. It is intended to confront the problem directly, in order to correctly define its nature and to proffer solutions that would lead to its elimination. Ignoring the problem, or sweeping it under the carpet because of some ill-defined "threat" to national unity only compounds the issue and is an affront to the memory of the untold multitudes that have perished or suffered hardships and indignities because of their sectarian identity and allegiances.

There is the unavoidable reality that there are two sects in Iraq, a fact which it would be foolish to deny or ignore. The imposition of an enforced and artificial homogeneity on this reality only serves to compound the problem and pushes it to the point where an explosion becomes inevitable. The recognition and even celebration of Iraq's sectarian diversity is an important platform in reconstructing the terms of dialogue between the state and the people, and by confirming the civil and religious rights of all the sects and groups in Iraq, the ground is strengthened for enhancing the sense of unity and patriotism in the country.

The sectarian issue in Iraq will not be solved by the imposition of a vengeful Shia sectarianism on the state and society. It can only be tackled by defining its nature and boundaries and formulating a complete national programme for its resolution. At the same time, the imperative of national unity should not be used as a pretext to avoid the necessity of dismantling the sectarian state and its harmful policies.

7. Sectarian differences and sectarian discrimination The distinction between the existence of sectarian differences and sectarian discrimination as such, must be established clearly. The state has masked its exploitation of the existence of sectarian differences in order to pursue its policy of sectarian discrimination.

The sectarian differences within Islam can be traced to the dawn of the Islamic era. Iraq's Muslim population is divided between Sunnis and Shia and there should be no harm or fear about acknowledging this fact. The sects have co-existed by and large for generations with no serious sectarian crises resulting in consequence. Sectarian differences do not constitute a social, intellectual or political issue in the Iraqi context, and sectarian affiliations should be a matter of course.

The real issue is official sectarianism rather than sectarian differences. Or in other words, the exploitation of the differences between the sects for the purpose of discriminating between them in order to promote a specific policy of power and control. It is this deliberate policy of enshrining sectarian differences to promote discriminatory and retrograde policies that has been used to strip the Shia of their political and civil rights and to reduce them to the status of second-class citizens. The label of "Shia" has been sufficient cause to remove the ordinary Shia from any consideration of positions of power and authority irrespective of his qualities and competences, and in spite of his political affiliations. To be a Shia in Iraq is to be condemned to a lifetime of powerlessness, fear, anxiety and discrimination.

The absence of any noticeable Shia representation in the upper reaches of state and power is clearly evident and incontrovertible, as is the manifest discrimination employed against them. The reconstruction of Iraq's state and society requires therefore a deep understanding of what the Shia actually want from their state, starting from the abolition of official discrimination and the return to them of their civil and constitutional rights from which they have been deprived for decades.

Civil and political rights must be guaranteed through the development of a body of laws and institutions that guard against sectarian discrimination. These should also aim to remove all traces of sectarian practices in Iraq and would be empowered with the authority to enforce these new policies. Sectarian loyalties that unite peoples who share a common heritage and history are a natural occurrence and each person should be free to declare his sectarian affinities without fear or anxiety. But this should not result in the enshrining of sectarianism as a policy or as a basis for political action.

8. The Shia of Iraq and national unity The lessons drawn from Iraq's history are clear- the Shia have at no point sought to establish their own state or unique political entity. Rather, whenever the opportunity was afforded to them, they participated enthusiastically in nation-wide political movements and organisations, ever conscious of the need to maintain national unity and probably more so than other groups inside Iraq. This can be abundantly established by examining the Shia's involvement in the struggle to establish the independent Iraqi state within its current recognised borders. The Shia, both in their islamist and non-islamist manifestations, have avoided being dragged into separatist schemes, and have been steadfast in their commitment to the unitary Iraqi state. The vital support that they gave to the claims of the Sharifian candidate to the Iraqi throne, in addition to the general sympathy that was exhibited to the cause of the Sharifs of Mecca after the Great War, was symptomatic of their patriotism.

This historic position of the Shia in favour of the unitary constitutional Iraqi state was not given its due measure, unfortunately, by successive Iraqi governments. In fact, the Shia role in safeguarding the unity of Iraq was constantly belittled and frequently ignored. The earliest political parties and movements in which the Shia were involved, were clear in their platforms and programmes of an absolute commitment to an independent and constitutional state stretching from the Province of Mosul in the north to the Province of Basra in the south. The slogan, *"An Arab Islamic Government"*, that was demanded by the Shia leadership in the referendum of 1919 is the incontrovertible evidence of the commitment of the Shia to an Arab/Muslim form of rule for Iraq, and the rejection of any status not commensurate with full political independence for the country.

This position of the Shia remained firm in spite of their oppression and discrimination at the hands of successive governments. The expulsion of Sheikh Mahdi al-Khalisi to Iran by the government of Muhsin as-Saadoun, in blithe disregard of the role that he played in securing popular approval for the demand for national sovereignty and independence, was one of the first manifestations of the policy of official anti-Shiism in action. But the constant harassments and threats that the Shia leadership were subjected to in the early days of independence did not deflect them from their commitment to the Iraqi state.

Even as we are in the midst of the present explosive situation, where state anti-Shiism has reached unprecedented levels of violence, the Shia have not raised the banner of withdrawal from the body politic of Iraq. The insistence on national unity as a clear starting principle has been the common denominator for all the active Iraqi Shia oppositionists, as has been the recognition that the problems arising from the atrocious misgovernment of the multi-ethnic and multi-sectarian state that is Iraq, could best be resolved in the context of a single Iraqi state.

The Shia of Iraq, in spite of being constantly and maliciously tested as to the depth of their national loyalty, have proven, time and again, their commitment to Iraq even at the expense of their own sectarian interests. Their call for the restitution of their civil and political rights can in no way be seen as a threat to national unity, when they have indisputably proven that they have been its principal protectors in word and in deed.

What do the Shia want?

The demands of the Shia can be succinctly summarised as follows:

1. The abolition of dictatorship and its replacement with democracy.
2. The abolition of ethnic discrimination and its replacement with a federal structure for Kurdistan
3. The abolition of the policy of discrimination against the Shia

The *Declaration of the Shia of Iraq* aims to elaborate on a Shia perspective on the political future of Iraq .Its principal points are as follows:

1. Abolition of ethnic and sectarian discrimination, and the elimination of the effects of these erroneous policies
2. The establishment of a democratic parliamentary constitutional order, that carefully avoids the hegemony of one sect or ethnic group over the others
3. The consolidation of the principles of a single citizenship for all Iraqis, a common citizenship being the basic guarantor of national unity.
4. Full respect for the national, ethnic, religious, and sectarian identities of all Iraqis, and the inculcation of the ideals of true citizenship amongst all of Iraq's communities.
5. Confirmation of the unitary nature of the Iraqi state and people, within the parameters of diversity and pluralism in Iraq's ethnic, religious and sectarian identities.
6. Reconstruction of, and support for, the main elements of a civil society and its community bases.
7. Adoption of the structures of a federal state that would include a high degree of decentralisation and devolution of powers to elected provincial authorities and assemblies.
8. Full respect for the principles of universal human rights.
9. Protection of the Islamic identity of Iraqi society.

Firstly, Democracy: Dictatorship has been one of the main factors that have buttressed the structures of official sectarian and ethnic discrimination, and constitutional democracy, operating through vital and effective institutions, is the necessary cure for this virulent ailment. The Shia do not want to solve their sectarian problems by creating an analogous one for other groups. Rather, they are seeking redress through a system that would guard the rights of all the constituent elements of Iraq's society, whereby all will be treated on an equal footing.

Secondly, Federalism: One of the key elements of the Iraqi conundrum is the near exclusive concentration of powers in the capital, Baghdad, in a manner that has robbed the outlying regions of any opportunity to address their local concerns, needs and special conditions and particularities. The solution has to be in the devolution of powers and authorities to these areas within a framework of broad administrative decentralisation.

Federalism as a system would be designed to negotiate between the need to have a central authority with effective but not hegemonic powers, and regions that enjoy a high order of decentralised powers, all within a framework of careful delineation of rights and responsibilities as between the centre and the regions. Ideally, a federal system would also legislate for the maintenance of Iraq's unitary nature, but recognises the need to fully accommodate Iraq's diversity.

Iraq's federal structure would not be based on a sectarian division but rather on administrative and demographic criteria. This would avoid the formation of sectarian-based entities that could be the prelude for partition or separation.

The proposed federal system would grant considerable powers to the regions, including legislative, fiscal, judicial and executive powers, thereby removing the possibility of the centre falling under the control of a dominant group which would extend its hegemony over the entire country. Iraq's federalist structures would benefit greatly from the experience of countries that have adopted this system of government successfully.

Thirdly, Abolition of the policies of sectarianism: The *Declaration of the Shia of Iraq* envisages the elimination of official sectarianism through the adoption of specific political and civil rights that would eliminate the disadvantage of the Shia.

A/ Political Rights:

In order to eliminate the accumulation of sectarian policies and codes of conduct employed by the authorities over decades, it would be necessary to examine the administrative structures of the Iraqi state and its civil and military institutions. In particular, the employment and promotion policies that have been pursued in the past must be remedied by policies that stress merit, effectiveness and competence as the basis for all employment. A federal authority with a remit to combat sectarianism would be established, which would examine closely the principles employed for filling all senior governmental posts, and which would be charged also with adjudicating all complaints and cases of sectarianism. The federal authority's mandate could be extended to include the combat of all forms of sectarianism in official and private institutions.

A fund would be established to compensate all those who have been harmed as a result of sectarian and ethnic discrimination and policies. Such a fund would be administered by a council that would establish the norms and procedures for evaluating the extent of damages and the restitution due.

A set of laws would be introduced to abolish sectarianism and that would criminalize sectarian conduct.

A new nationality law would be introduced that would be based on a notion of citizenship that would emphasise loyalty to Iraq rather than to any sectarian, national or religious affiliation.

B/Civil Rights:

The key civil rights that have a special resonance for the Shia would include:

1. Their right to practice their own religious rites and rituals and to autonomously administer their own religious shrines and institutions, through legitimate Shia religious authorities.
2. Full freedom to conduct their religious affairs in their own mosques, meeting halls and other institutions.
3. Freedom to teach in their religious universities and institutions with no interference by the central or provincial authorities.
4. Freedom of movement and travel and assembly on the part of the higher Shia religious authorities, *ulema* and speakers, and guarantees afforded to the teaching circles-the *hawzas*- to conduct their affairs in a manner that they see fit.
5. Ensuring that the Shia's religious shrines and cities are entered into UNESCO's World Heritage Sites and are thus protected from arbitrary acts of change and destruction.
6. Full freedoms to publish Shia tracts and books and to establish Shia religious institutions and assemblies.
7. The right to establish independent schools, universities and other teaching establishments and academies, within the framework of a broad and consensual national education policy.
8. Introduction the elements of the *Jafari* creed and rites into the national educational curriculum, in a manner similar to the way in which other schools of Islamic jurisprudence are taught.
9. Revising the elements of the history curriculum to remove all disparagement of the Shia, and the writing of an authentic history that would remove any anti-Shia biases.
10. Freedom to establish Shia mosques, meeting halls and libraries.
11. Respect for the burial grounds of the Shia.
12. Official recognition by the state of the key dates of the Shia calendar.
13. Repatriation of all Iraqis who were forcibly expelled from Iraq, or who felt obliged to leave under duress, and the full restitution of their constitutional and civil rights.

Conclusion

It is essential that all the elements of Iraq's political spectrum, as well as the representatives of Iraq's varied communities, become involved in the process of finding a way out of the terrible situation that Iraq finds itself in now and which threaten its very survival. All these groups must participate in the process of change and the design of a new Iraqi state so that all have a stake in the outcome and could feel themselves true and equal partners in the country.

The Iraqi crisis has to be tackled at all its levels-political, through the elimination of dictatorship; sectarian, through the abolition of sectarian discrimination; and ethnic, through the elimination of ethnic and national preference. Furthermore, it would be necessary to consider policies and programmes that would provide redress to the many aggrieved groups in the country, and to establish a vision of Iraq's future in which all would share. Any shortfall from this objective by adopting one perspective over another on the grounds of a gradualism that postpones the tackling of these issues to some indeterminate date in the future, is a recipe for further suffering and possibly disaster.

Constitutional guarantees and rights must be afforded to all of Iraq's groups and communities, as well as the means to defend or enforce them. This must be the minimum requirement for rebuilding the Iraqi state on a new basis. The order of priorities in this declaration have been ranked in a methodical manner, and the sequential adoption of the policies that underpin needed change are based on the principle of their voluntary adoption through information dissemination and persuasion rather than their imposition by force or fiat.

The adoption of the constituent components of Iraq's society of the elements of this declaration is important, not least for the reason that each should feel that they have accepted the main sources of grievance and redress of the other groups, and that they have all participated equally in the fashioning of a new Iraqi order.

QUESTIONS TO CONSIDER

1 What has been the main political problem facing Iraq since 1923?
2 What are the two best solutions to this political problem, according to this document?
3 Who are the Shia and what do they want?

——————— **Document 3-D** ———————

Unclassified report to Congress on the acquisition of technology relating to weapons of mass destruction and advanced conventional munitions, July 1–December 2002

Key Judgments

Iraq has continued its weapons of mass destruction (WMD) programs in defiance of UN resolutions and restrictions. Baghdad has chemical and biological weapons as well as missiles with ranges in excess of UN restrictions; if left unchecked, it probably will have a nuclear weapon during this decade.

Baghdad hides large portions of Iraq's WMD efforts. Revelations after the Gulf war starkly demonstrate the extensive efforts undertaken by Iraq to deny information.

Since inspections ended in 1998, Iraq has maintained its chemical weapons effort, energized its missile program, and invested more heavily in biological weapons; most analysts assess Iraq is reconstituting its nuclear weapons program.

- Iraq's growing ability to sell oil illicitly increases Baghdad's capabilities to finance WMD programs; annual earnings in cash and goods have more than quadrupled.
- Iraq largely has rebuilt missile and biological weapons facilities damaged during Operation Desert Fox and has expanded its chemical and biological infra-structure under the cover of civilian production.
- Baghdad has exceeded UN range limits of 150 km with its ballistic missiles and is working with unmanned aerial vehicles (UAVs), which allow for a more lethal means to deliver biological and, less likely, chemical warfare agents.
- Although Saddam probably does not yet have nuclear weapons or sufficient material to make any, he remains intent on acquiring them.

How quickly Iraq will obtain its first nuclear weapon depends on when it acquires sufficient weapons-grade fissile material.

- If Baghdad acquires sufficient weapons-grade fissile material from abroad, it could make a nuclear weapon within a year.
- Without such material from abroad, Iraq probably would not be able to make a weapon until the last half of the decade.

Iraq's aggressive attempts to obtain proscribed high-strength aluminum tubes are of significant concern. All intelligence experts agree that Iraq is seeking nuclear weapons and that these tubes could be used in a centrifuge enrichment program. Most intelligence specialists assess this to be the intended use, but some believe that these tubes are probably intended for conventional weapons programs.

- Based on tubes of the size Iraq is trying to acquire, a few tens of thousands of centrifuges would be capable of producing enough highly enriched uranium for a couple of weapons per year.

Baghdad has begun renewed production of chemical warfare agents, probably including mustard, sarin, cyclosarin, and VX. Its capability was reduced during the UNSCOM inspections and is probably more limited now than it was at the time of the Gulf war, although VX production and agent storage life probably have been improved.

- Saddam probably has stocked a few hundred metric tons of CW agents.
- The Iraqis have experience in manufacturing CW bombs, artillery rockets, and projectiles, and probably possess CW bulk fills for SRBM warheads, including for a limited number of covertly stored, extended-range Scuds.

All key aspects – R&D, production, and weaponization – of Iraq's offensive BW program are active and most elements are larger and more advanced than they were before the Gulf war.

- Iraq has some lethal and incapacitating BW agents and is capable of quickly producing and weaponizing a variety of such agents, including anthrax, for delivery by bombs, missiles, aerial sprayers, and covert operatives, including potentially against the US Homeland.
- Baghdad has established a large-scale, redundant, and concealed BW agent production capability, which includes mobile facilities; these facilities can evade detection, are highly survivable, and can exceed the production rates Iraq had prior to the Gulf war.

Iraq maintains a small missile force and several development programs, including for a UAV that most analysts believe probably is intended to deliver biological warfare agents.

- Gaps in Iraqi accounting to UNSCOM suggest that Saddam retains a covert force of up to a few dozen Scud-variant SRBMs with ranges of 650 to 900 km.
- Iraq is deploying its new al-Samoud and Ababil-100 SRBMs, which are capable of flying beyond the UN-authorized 150-km range limit.
- Baghdad's UAVs – especially if used for delivery of chemical and biological warfare (CBW) agents – could threaten Iraq's neighbors, US forces in the Persian Gulf, and the United States if brought close to, or into, the US Homeland.

• Iraq is developing medium-range ballistic missile capabilities, largely through foreign assistance in building specialized facilities.

QUESTIONS TO CONSIDER

1   Does this report offer credible evidence that Iraq possessed weapons of mass destruction? What should the burden of proof be for such serious allegations?
2   How should the United Nations have responded to Saddam Hussein's violations of resolution after resolution?

———————— **Document 3-E** ————————

Excerpts from H.J. 114, Joint Resolution to Authorize the Use of United States Armed Forces Against Iraq, 107th Congress, 2nd session, October 2, 2002

To authorize the use of United States Armed Forces against Iraq.

Whereas in 1990 in response to Iraq's war of aggression against and illegal occupation of Kuwait, the United States forged a coalition of nations to liberate Kuwait and its people in order to defend the national security of the United States and enforce United Nations Security Council resolutions relating to Iraq;

Whereas after the liberation of Kuwait in 1991, Iraq entered into a United Nations sponsored cease-fire agreement pursuant to which Iraq unequivocally agreed, among other things, to eliminate its nuclear, biological, and chemical weapons programs and the means to deliver and develop them, and to end its support for international terrorism;

Whereas the efforts of international weapons inspectors, United States intelligence agencies, and Iraqi defectors led to the discovery that Iraq had large stockpiles of chemical weapons and a large scale biological weapons program, and that Iraq had an advanced nuclear weapons development program that was much closer to producing a nuclear weapon than intelligence reporting had previously indicated;

Whereas Iraq, in direct and flagrant violation of the cease-fire, attempted to thwart the efforts of weapons inspectors to identify and destroy Iraq's weapons of mass destruction stockpiles and development capabilities, which finally resulted in the withdrawal of inspectors from Iraq on October 31, 1998;

Whereas in 1998 Congress concluded that Iraq's continuing weapons of mass destruction programs threatened vital United States interests and international peace and security, declared Iraq to be in "material and unacceptable breach of its international obligations" and urged the President "to take appropriate action, in accordance with the Constitution and relevant laws of the United States, to bring Iraq into compliance with its international obligations" (Public Law 105-235);

Whereas Iraq both poses a continuing threat to the national security of the United States and international peace and security in the Persian Gulf region and remains in material and unacceptable breach of its international obligations by, among other things, continuing to possess and develop a significant chemical and biological weapons capability, actively seeking a nuclear weapons capability, and supporting and harboring terrorist organizations;

Whereas Iraq persists in violating resolutions of the United Nations Security Council by continuing to engage in brutal repression of its civilian population thereby threatening international peace and security in the region, by refusing to release, repatriate, or account for non-Iraqi citizens wrongfully detained by Iraq, including an American serviceman, and by failing to return property wrongfully seized by Iraq from Kuwait;

Whereas the current Iraqi regime has demonstrated its capability and willingness to use weapons of mass destruction against other nations and its own people;

Whereas the current Iraqi regime has demonstrated its continuing hostility toward, and willingness to attack, the United States, including by attempting in 1993 to assassinate former President Bush and by firing on many thousands of occasions on United States and Coalition Armed Forces engaged in enforcing the resolutions of the United Nations Security Council;

Whereas members of al Qaida, an organization bearing responsibility for attacks on the United States, its citizens, and interests, including the attacks that occurred on September 11, 2001, are known to be in Iraq;

Whereas Iraq continues to aid and harbor other international terrorist organizations, including organizations that threaten the lives and safety of American citizens;

Whereas the attacks on the United States of September 11, 2001, underscored the gravity of the threat posed by the acquisition of weapons of mass destruction by international terrorist organizations;

Whereas Iraq's demonstrated capability and willingness to use weapons of mass destruction, the risk that the current Iraqi regime will either employ those weapons to launch a surprise attack against the United States or its Armed Forces or provide them to international terrorists who would do so, and the extreme magnitude of harm that would result to the United States and its citizens from such an attack, combine to justify action by the United States to defend itself;

Whereas United Nations Security Council Resolution 678 authorizes the use of all necessary means to enforce United Nations Security Council Resolution 660 and subsequent relevant resolutions and to compel Iraq to cease certain activities that threaten international peace and security, including the development of weapons of mass destruction and refusal or obstruction of United Nations weapons inspections in violation of United Nations Security Council Resolution 687, repression of its civilian population in violation of United Nations Security Council Resolution 688, and threatening its neighbors or United Nations operations in Iraq in violation of United Nations Security Council Resolution 949;

Whereas Congress in the Authorization for Use of Military Force Against Iraq Resolution (Public Law 102-1) has authorized the President "to use United States Armed Forces pursuant to United Nations Security Council Resolution 678 (1990) in order to achieve implementation of Security Council Resolutions 660, 661, 662, 664, 665, 666, 667, 669, 670, 674, and 677";

Whereas in December 1991, Congress expressed its sense that it "supports the use of all necessary means to achieve the goals of United Nations Security Council Resolution 687 as being consistent with the Authorization of Use of Military Force Against Iraq Resolution (Public Law 102-1)," that Iraq's repression of its civilian population violates United Nations Security Council Resolution 688 and "constitutes a continuing threat to the peace, security, and stability of the Persian Gulf region," and that Congress, "supports the use of all necessary means to achieve the goals of United Nations Security Council Resolution 688";

Whereas the Iraq Liberation Act (Public Law 105-338) expressed the sense of Congress that it should be the policy of the United States to support efforts to remove from power the current Iraqi regime and promote the emergence of a democratic government to replace that regime;

Whereas on September 12, 2002, President Bush committed the United States to "work with the United Nations Security Council to meet our common challenge" posed by Iraq and to "work for the necessary resolutions," while also making clear that "the Security Council resolutions will be enforced, and the just demands of peace and security will be met, or action will be unavoidable";

Whereas the United States is determined to prosecute the war on terrorism and Iraq's ongoing support for international terrorist groups combined with its development of weapons of mass destruction in direct violation of its obligations under the 1991 cease-fire and other United Nations Security Council resolutions make clear that it is in the national security interests of the United States and in furtherance of the war on terrorism that all relevant United Nations Security Council resolutions be enforced, including through the use of force if necessary;

Whereas Congress has taken steps to pursue vigorously the war on terrorism through the provision of authorities and funding requested by the President to take the necessary actions against international terrorists and terrorist organizations, including those nations, organizations or persons who planned, authorized, committed or aided the terrorist attacks that occurred on September 11, 2001, or harbored such persons or organizations;

Whereas the President and Congress are determined to continue to take all appropriate actions against international terrorists and terrorist organizations, including those nations, organizations or persons who planned, authorized, committed or aided the terrorist attacks that occurred on September 11, 2001, or harbored such persons or organizations;

Whereas the President has authority under the Constitution to take action in order to deter and prevent acts of international terrorism against the United States, as Congress recognized in the joint resolution on Authorization for Use of Military Force (Public Law 107-40); and

Whereas it is in the national security of the United States to restore international peace and security to the Persian Gulf region: Now, therefore, be it

Resolved by the Senate and House of Representatives of the United States of America in Congress assembled.

QUESTIONS TO CONSIDER

1 Is this document a declaration of war?
2 Has Congress made a compelling case to use U.S. armed forces against Iraq?
3 Did Congress hold a full and frank debate over the war powers provisions outlined in this document?

Document 3-F

"The Downing Street Memo," from Matthew Rycroft, private secretary to Prime Minister Tony Blair, to David Manning, British ambassador to the United States, July 23, 2002

SECRET AND STRICTLY PERSONAL – UK EYES ONLY
DAVID MANNING
From: Matthew Rycroft
Date: 23 July 2002
S 195 /02

cc: Defence Secretary, Foreign Secretary, Attorney-General, Sir Richard Wilson, John Scarlett, Francis Richards, CDS, C, Jonathan Powell, Sally Morgan, Alastair Campbell

IRAQ: PRIME MINISTER's MEETING, 23 JULY

Copy addressees and you met the Prime Minister on 23 July to discuss Iraq. This record is extremely sensitive. No further copies should be made. It should be shown only to those with a genuine need to know its contents.

John Scarlett summarised the intelligence and latest JIC assessment. Saddam's regime was tough and based on extreme fear. The only way to overthrow it was likely to be by massive military action. Saddam was worried and expected an attack, probably by air and land, but he was not convinced that it would be immediate or overwhelming. His regime expected their neighbours to line up with the US. Saddam knew that regular army morale was poor. Real support for Saddam among the public was probably narrowly based.

C reported on his recent talks in Washington. There was a perceptible shift in attitude. Military action was now seen as inevitable. Bush wanted to remove Saddam, through military action, justified by the conjunction of terrorism and WMD. But the intelligence and facts were being fixed around the policy. The NSC had no patience with the UN route, and no enthusiasm for publishing material on the Iraqi regime's record. There was little discussion in Washington of the aftermath after military action.

CDS said that military planners would brief CENTCOM on 1–2 August, Rumsfeld on 3 August and Bush on 4 August.

The two broad US options were:

(a)   Generated Start. A slow build-up of 250,000 US troops, a short (72 hour) air campaign, then a move up to Baghdad from the south. Lead time of 90 days (30 days preparation plus 60 days deployment to Kuwait).
(b)   Running Start. Use forces already in theatre (3 x 6,000), continuous air campaign, initiated by an Iraqi casus belli. Total lead-time of 60 days with the air campaign beginning even earlier. A hazardous option.

The US saw the UK (and Kuwait) as essential, with basing in Diego Garcia and Cyprus critical for either option. Turkey and other Gulf states were also important, but less vital.

The three main options for UK involvement were:

(i)   Basing in Diego Garcia and Cyprus, plus three SF squadrons.
(ii)   As above, with maritime and air assets in addition.
(iii) As above, plus a land contribution of up to 40,000, perhaps with a discrete role in Northern Iraq entering from Turkey, tying down two Iraqi divisions.

The Defence Secretary said that the US had already begun "spikes of activity" to put pressure on the regime. No decisions had been taken, but he thought the most likely timing in US minds for military action to begin was January, with the timeline beginning 30 days before the US Congressional elections.

The Foreign Secretary said he would discuss this with Colin Powell this week. It seemed clear that Bush had made up his mind to take military action, even if the timing was not yet decided. But the case was thin. Saddam was not threatening his neighbours, and his WMD capability was less than that of Libya, North Korea or Iran. We should work up a plan for an ultimatum to Saddam to allow back in the UN weapons inspectors. This would also help with the legal justification for the use of force.

The Attorney-General said that the desire for regime change was not a legal base for military action. There were three possible legal bases: self-defence, humanitarian intervention, or UNSC authorisation. The first and second could not be the base in this case. Relying on UNSCR 1205 of three years ago would be difficult. The situation might of course change.

The Prime Minister said that it would make a big difference politically and legally if Saddam refused to allow in the UN inspectors. Regime change and WMD were linked in the sense that it was the regime that was producing the WMD. There were different strategies for dealing with Libya and Iran. If the political context were right, people would support regime change. The two key issues were whether the military plan worked and whether we had the political strategy to give the military plan the space to work.

On the first, CDS said that we did not know yet if the US battleplan was workable. The military were continuing to ask lots of questions.

For instance, what were the consequences, if Saddam used WMD on day one, or if Baghdad did not collapse and urban warfighting began? You said that Saddam could also use his WMD on Kuwait. Or on Israel, added the Defence Secretary.

The Foreign Secretary thought the US would not go ahead with a military plan unless convinced that it was a winning strategy. On this, US and UK interests converged. But on the political strategy, there could be US/UK differences. Despite US resistance, we should explore discreetly the ultimatum. Saddam would continue to play hard-ball with the UN.

John Scarlett assessed that Saddam would allow the inspectors back in only when he thought the threat of military action was real.

The Defence Secretary said that if the Prime Minister wanted UK military involvement, he would need to decide this early. He cautioned that many in the US did not think it worth going down the ultimatum route. It would be important for the Prime Minister to set out the political context to Bush.

Conclusions:

(a) We should work on the assumption that the UK would take part in any military action. But we needed a fuller picture of US planning before we could take any firm decisions. CDS should tell the US military that we were considering a range of options.

(b)   The Prime Minister would revert on the question of whether funds could be spent in preparation for this operation.

(c)   CDS would send the Prime Minister full details of the proposed military campaign and possible UK contributions by the end of the week.

(d)   The Foreign Secretary would send the Prime Minister the background on the UN inspectors, and discreetly work up the ultimatum to Saddam.

He would also send the Prime Minister advice on the positions of countries in the region especially Turkey, and of the key EU member states.

(e)   John Scarlett would send the Prime Minister a full intelligence update.

(f)   We must not ignore the legal issues: the Attorney-General would consider legal advice with FCO/MOD legal advisers.

(I have written separately to commission this follow-up work.)

MATTHEW RYCROFT

QUESTIONS TO CONSIDER

1   What position does the British government take on the war in Iraq?
2   What did the prime minister say about Saddam's refusal to allow UN weapon inspectors into Iraq?
3   Did the British attorney general have any doubts about the war's legality?

——————— **Document 3-G** ———————

Excerpts from U.S. Secretary of State Colin Powell's presentation at the United Nations Security Council, February 6, 2003

Thank you, Mr. President.

Mr President, Mr Secretary General, distinguished colleagues, I would like to begin by expressing my thanks for the special effort that each of you made to be here today.

This is important day for us all as we review the situation with respect to Iraq and its disarmament obligations under UN security council resolution 1441.

Last November 8, this council passed resolution 1441 by a unanimous vote. The purpose of that resolution was to disarm Iraq of its weapons of mass destruction. Iraq had already been found guilty of material breach of its obligations, stretching back over 16 previous resolutions and 12 years.

Resolution 1441 was not dealing with an innocent party, but a regime this council has repeatedly convicted over the years. Resolution 1441 gave Iraq one last chance, one last chance to come into compliance or to face serious consequences. No council member present in voting on that day had any illusions about the nature and intent of the resolution or what serious consequences meant if Iraq did not comply.

And to assist in its disarmament, we called on Iraq to cooperate with returning inspectors from Unmovic and IAEA.

We laid down tough standards for Iraq to meet to allow the inspectors to do their job.

This council placed the burden on Iraq to comply and disarm and not on the inspectors to find that which Iraq has gone out of its way to conceal for so long. Inspectors are inspectors; they are not detectives.

I asked for this session today for two purposes: First, to support the core assessments made by Dr Blix and Dr El-Baradei. As Dr Blix reported to this council on January 27: "Iraq appears not to have come to a genuine acceptance, not even today, of the disarmament which was demanded of it."

And as Dr El-Baradei reported, Iraq's declaration of December 7: "Did not provide any new information relevant to certain questions that have been outstanding since 1998."

My second purpose today is to provide you with additional information, to share with you what the United States knows about Iraq's weapons of mass destruction as well as Iraq's involvement in terrorism, which is also the subject of resolution 1441 and other earlier resolutions.

I might add at this point that we are providing all relevant information we can to the inspection teams for them to do their work.

The material I will present to you comes from a variety of sources. Some are U.S. sources. And some are those of other countries.

Some of the sources are technical, such as intercepted telephone conversations and photos taken by satellites. Other sources are people who have risked their lives to let the world know what Saddam Hussein is really up to.

I cannot tell you everything that we know. But what I can share with you, when combined with what all of us have learned over the years, is deeply troubling.

What you will see is an accumulation of facts and disturbing patterns of behavior. The facts on Iraqis' behavior – Iraq's behavior demonstrate that Saddam Hussein and his regime have made no effort – no effort – to disarm as required by the international community. Indeed, the facts and Iraq's behavior show that Saddam Hussein and his regime are concealing their efforts to produce more weapons of mass destruction.

QUESTIONS TO CONSIDER

1   What evidence against Iraq did Colin Powell present at the United Nations?
2   According to Powell, who had the burden of proof when it came to UN weapons inspectors in Iraq?
3   Did Saddam Hussein make any effort to disarm as required by various UN resolutions?

—————————— **Document 3-H** ——————————

U.S. ambassador to the United Nations John Negroponte's letter to Ambassador Mamady Traore, president of the United Nations Security Council, March 20, 2003

To: Mr Mamady Traore President – Security Council United Nations New York, New York

Excellency:

Coalition forces have commenced military operations in Iraq. These operations are necessary in view of Iraq's continued material breaches of its disarmament obligations under relevant Security Council resolutions including 1441 (2002). The operations are substantial and will secure compliance with these obligations. In carrying out these operations, our forces will take all reasonable precautions to avoid civilian casualties.

The actions being taken are authorized under existing Council resolutions: including resolution 678 (1990) and resolution 687 (1991). Resolution 687 imposed a series of obligations on Iraq, including most importantly, extensive disarmament obligations, that were the conditions of the cease-fire established under it. It has been long recognized and understood that a material breach of these obligations removes the basis of the ceasefire and revives the authority to use force under resolution 678. This has been the basis for coalition use of force in the past and has been accepted by the Council, as evidenced, for example, by the Secretary General's public announcement in January 1993 following Iraq's material breach of resolution 687 that coalition forces had received a mandate from the Council to use force according to resolution 678.

Iraq continues to be in material breach of its disarmament obligations under resolution 687, as the Council affirmed in resolution 1441. Acting under the authority of Chapter VII of the UN Charter, the Council unanimously decided that Iraq has been and remained in material breach of its obligations and recalled its repeated warnings to Iraq that it will face serious consequences as a result of its continued violations of its obligations. The resolution then provided Iraq a "final opportunity" to comply, but stated specifically that violations by Iraq of its obligations under resolution 1441 to present a currently accurate, full and complete declaration of all aspects of its weapons of mass destruction programs and to comply with and cooperate fully in the resolution's implementation would constitute a further material breach.

The Government of Iraq decided not to avail itself of its final opportunity under resolution 1441 and has clearly committed additional violations. In view of Iraq's material beaches, the basis for the cease-fire has been removed, and the use of force is authorized under resolution 678.

Iraq repeatedly has refused, over a protracted period of time, to respond to diplomatic overtures, economic sanctions, and other peaceful means designed to help bring about Iraqi compliance with its obligations to disarm and to permit full inspection of its WMD and related programs.

The actions that coalition forces are undertaking are an appropriate response. They are necessary to defend the United States and the international community from the threat posed by Iraq and to restore international peace and security in the area. Further delay would simply allow Iraq to continue its unlawful and threatening conduct.

It is the Government of Iraq that bears full responsibility for the serious consequences of its defiance of the Council's decisions. I would be grateful if you could circulate the text of this letter as a document of the Security Council.

Sincerely, (signed) John D. Negroponte

QUESTIONS TO CONSIDER

1 According to Ambassador Negroponte, why were U.S. military actions taken in Iraq?
2 Was an invasion of Iraq an appropriate response to Saddam Hussein, according to Ambassador Negroponte? What do you think?

4

The Deadliest Fighting, 2003–2006

Chronology

May 2003	President Bush's "Mission Accomplished" speech
May 2003	Creation of the Coalition Provisional Authority
February 2004	General Taguba's report on Abu Ghraib
March 2004	First Battle of Fallujah
June 2004	Ambassador Negroponte replaces Bremer
August 2004	Shiite militia attacks Najaf
November 2004	Second Battle of Fallujah
February 2005	Sunni insurgents bomb Golden Dome in Samarra
May 2006	Nouri al-Maliki elected prime minister

The United States and Iraq Since 1990: A Brief History with Documents,
First Edition. Edited by Robert K. Brigham.
© 2014 Robert K. Brigham. Published 2014 by Blackwell Publishing Ltd.

"My fellow Americans: Major combat operations in Iraq have ended," President George W. Bush declared from the deck of the USS *Abraham Lincoln* in early May 2003, just two months after the U.S. invasion began. "In the battle of Iraq, the United States and our allies have prevailed. And now our coalition is engaged in securing and reconstructing that country."[1] It was a theme Bush would repeat throughout the next year, and it set the tone for his administration. And yet the battle was far from over. The heaviest fighting in the war was yet to come, and the conflict would spread in ways little understood at the time Bush made his now famous declaration. For the next three years, there was a dramatic increase in sectarian violence in Iraq, claiming the lives of thousands of Iraqis and thousands of Americans. But sectarian violence was not the only form the conflict would take. Neighboring states and transnational terrorist networks also joined the fight, complicating the military and political problems facing the Bush White House. Adding to the administration's difficulties were reported human rights abuses by the Baghdad government and U.S. troops. Furthermore, no one in the Bush administration fully appreciated how complicated nation-building would be in a hostile environment. What started in May 2003 as a victory speech, therefore, ended in 2006 with a concession from the president that the war was going badly and that dramatic changes needed to happen if the United States was going to succeed in Iraq.

The road from victory was paved with military difficulties and political nightmares. From the very beginning of the Iraq War, the president and his key national security advisors had grossly underestimated the scope and nature of the conflict. Taking Baghdad had been relatively easy for the U.S. military, but that experience would not define U.S. military operations. Instead, a battle at Fallujah, a small city 35 miles west of Baghdad, would come to symbolize the early years of the war. The Bush administration faced a growing Sunni insurgency, as the Battle of Fallujah clearly showed, as well as a growing radical Shiite movement controlled by various Shiite militias. During the Fallujah battles, there was unmistakable evidence that some of Iraq's Sunnis had received training and weapons from transnational terrorist groups, including al-Qaeda. The insurgency was a complicated mix, however, probably involving a combination of the many Iraqi tribal leaders with former elements of the "old regime acting in alliance with indigenous Islamic radicals and a small number of foreign fighters."[2] To the Bush administration, it now seemed that Sunnis and Shiites were fighting each other in a growing civil war, but that each group was also targeting American soldiers. Roadside bombs and suicide bombers appeared more regularly following the Battle of Fallujah in April 2004, and this development created new terror among ordinary Iraqis and the U.S. troops sent to protect them.

Tensions between Americans and the Baghdad government increased as the U.S. presence grew following Fallujah. The two peoples approached each other with colossal ignorance. The lack of trust and communication between Iraqis and their American allies was monumental. There was little coordination of policies, and this was reflected in day-to-day relations between Americans and Iraqis inside the Green Zone in Baghdad. The Battle of Fallujah also highlighted difficulties in coordination between the White House and the Coalition Provisional Authority (CPA), the group responsible for helping to rebuild Iraq, leading many critics of the Bush administration's Iraq policies to conclude that once again American troops were bogged down in a protracted conflict against well-armed and highly motivated insurgents. Once again U.S. troops were giving their all to defend a national government that could not put its own army in the field at full strength. Once again policymakers in Washington had no clear-cut strategy for dealing with an asymmetrical war that required a political as well as a military program. After Fallujah, Iraq became a state of mind, just like Vietnam three decades earlier. Only one year after the invasion of Iraq and President Bush's declaration that the mission in Iraq had been accomplished, many Americans wondered if this conflict was worth the sacrifice. Fallujah had highlighted all the problems with U.S. policy in Iraq and it was the place where "the security problems and the political problems" in Bush's war policy "had finally converged."[3]

The Battle of Fallujah

The Battle of Fallujah began at the end of March 2004, when U.S. Marines found themselves confronting insurgent activity throughout the city. Anti-government forces had responded negatively to increased Marine patrols following their takeover of the region from the U.S. Army's 82nd Airborne. Insurgents shut down the city with roadblocks and barricades, hoping to disrupt the patrols and increase their own visibility within Iraq's growing crisis. The Marines instead increased their patrols, hoping to "stir them [insurgents] up and get them out in the open."[4] The Marines were joined in Fallujah by a growing number of security experts from Blackwater, a private contracting firm with ties to Vice President Cheney. One week after the transfer of responsibility from the army to the Marines, a small convoy of Blackwater security guards bypassed a Marine checkpoint on the outskirts of Fallujah and drove into danger. Obviously tipped off about the convoy, a small group of insurgents pulled four Blackwater contractors from their cars, dismembered them, dragged them through the streets of Fallujah, burned their bodies, and then hung two badly beaten corpses from a bridge over the Euphrates River. Embedded reporters captured the grisly scene on film and in photographs, helping ignite feelings of U.S. vulnerability and American outrage.

The Bush White House demanded immediate revenge. With echoes of Mogadishu ringing in their ears, civilian leaders in Washington urged a swift and uncompromising response. According to Lt. General Ricardo Sanchez, who held the top U.S. military position in Iraq at the time of the Fallujah battle, the president was apoplectic about the insurgent actions. "Kick ass!" he quoted the president as saying during a videoconference with his national security team. "If somebody tries to stop the march to democracy, we will seek them out and kill them! We must be tougher than hell! Our will is being tested, but we are resolute. We have a better way. Stay strong. Stay the course! Kill them! Be confident! Prevail! We are going to wipe them out! We are not blinking!"[5] Despite pleas from some U.S. military commanders, including Lt. General James Conway, the U.S. Marine Corps general in charge of western Iraq, not to respond with a heavy hand in Fallujah, the Bush administration pushed the Marines to "go in and clobber people."[6] Conway and several other high-ranking U.S. officers believed that "we ought to probably let the situation settle before we appeared to be attacking out of revenge." He feared that an American attack against an already restive city might lead many residents to support the insurgents.[7] In a speech given on the evening of the attacks, an undeterred president Bush warned a friendly audience, "We still face thugs and terrorists in Iraq who would rather go on killing the innocent than accept the advance of liberty. This collection of killers is trying to shake our will. America will never be intimidated by thugs and assassins. We are aggressively striking the terrorists in Iraq."[8] L. Paul Bremer, the head of the CPA, promised that the four Blackwater security officers' deaths would not go unpunished.[9] On April 5, 2004, on orders from Washington, the Marines launched Operation Vigilant Resolve.

For the next week, over 2,500 U.S. Marines from three battalions faced well-armed insurgents in Fallujah. U.S. commanders on the ground were shocked at how well trained the insurgents seemed to be. Insurgents skillfully demonstrated operational freedom of movement by moving men and supplies through the Marines' blockade of the city and then launched ambushes and stand-off attacks against U.S. troops. Some insurgents showed considerable knowledge of anti-tank operations, waiting to attack until the main gun was raised or creating diversions to expose the rear armor. There were other surprises in store for the U.S. command. Marine commanders ordered the Second Battalion of the National Iraqi Army (NIA) – reportedly the best in Iraq – into Fallujah, but nearly a third deserted or refused the order. This was unexpected because so many in the NIA were Kurds and Shiites, not Sunnis. The fear had always been that the NIA would exact revenge on Sunnis if given the chance following years of Sunni brutality under Saddam Hussein. Most American commanders believed that Fallujah was the center of what was known as the Sunni triangle, a stronghold of pro-Saddam sentiment. But Fallujah had also resisted Saddam through the years, even though the city was indeed dominated by Sunnis. Complicating matters for the U.S. Marines was the fact that one year earlier, in April 2003, U.S. soldiers had reportedly killed fifteen Fallujah residents who were demonstrating against the government. Since then, the city had been "bitterly, hatefully anti-American."[10] But, the NIA did not respond. When General James Mattis therefore asked for more U.S. troops, he was turned down because the fighting had spread to Ramadi, Mosul, and Najaf. Not only did the Americans have to put down the insurgents, but they also had to deal with the forces of Mogtada al-Sadr, a radical Shiite cleric who controlled the Mahdi Army and whose followers made up a significant wing of the Baghdad government. Unknown to most American commanders at the time of the Fallujah battle, Iraq's civil war was just beginning to take shape.

As American AC-130 gunships strafed Fallujah to sounds of the rock group ACDC's song, "Hells Bells," the Marines laid siege to the city. They closed off all exit roads, created new roadblocks, shut down many public buildings, and searched for insurgents neighborhood by neighborhood. Fallujah was an early example of what the military calls MOUT (military operations in urban terrain), and it proved to be the most difficult type of warfare for American soldiers in Iraq. Well-armed insurgents had made Fallujah a major center of anti-government activity, blending in with the general population and launching deadly IED (improvised explosive devices) attacks. As in wars past, insurgents also seemed quite capable of rallying public support against the Americans in Fallujah. Angry residents of the city protested against U.S. actions daily, making it more difficult for the Marines to conduct combat operations. Some Iraqi journalists reported that the level of violence in the city center was unprecedented, and others suggested that the U.S. had used napalm and white phosphorous bombs against a largely civilian population.[11] Though these claims are still being debated today, it now seems clear that the Battle of Fallujah was far more complicated than removing Saddam's statue from the center of Baghdad. American military commanders were quick to report that the fighting environment in Fallujah was unlike anything they had experienced before. "The layout of the city is random," they contended. "Zones distinguishing between residential, business, and industrial are nonexistent."[12] Complicating operations in Fallujah was increased anti-American activity in all of south-central Iraq and in Sadr City, the largely Shiite ghetto in eastern Baghdad. Sunnis and Shiites were now targeting American troops and the Baghdad government as well as each other. It was difficult to gauge who was leading the Sunnis, but al-Sadr was clearly in charge of a large group of Shiites who willingly joined his Mahdi Army.

The Shiite cleric and his army directly challenged U.S. authority in Iraq and called on all Iraqis – Kurds, Sunnis, and Shiites – to resist the American occupation by any means necessary. It was the first appeal by al-Sadr for unified attacks against U.S. troops. In a fiery speech at Friday prayers at the Kufa mosque, near Najaf, the spiritual center of Shiite Islam, al-Sadr claimed that Iraq was under attack by Americans and he urged his followers in the Mahdi Army and others to "strike them where you meet them."[13] Within days, radicalized Shiites attacked the U.S. Army's 1st Cavalry Division in Sadr City. Soon, other attacks occurred against U.S. troops and convoys in Karbala, Basra, and Nasiriyah, three strategically important southern Iraqi cities. According to U.S. after-action reports, the Mahdi Army was a formidable enemy. Journalist Tom Ricks reported that U.S. soldiers developed a grudging appreciation for the competence of their foes. "The Mahdi army fought very courageously and demonstrated good tactical patience," concluded one army captain.[14] For two long weeks, American troops were engaged in fierce combat operations in an arch from Fallujah in south-central Iraq to Sadr City in eastern Baghdad and down to Basra in Iraq's southern zone. The war took on a distinctively urban flavor. Insurgents took taxicabs to their target areas and escaped the same way. The car bomb came to symbolize the war in this early stage largely because the road was the war's most significant center of gravity.[15]

Despite al-Sadr's anti-American attacks, Fallujah still presented the most difficult situation for the Bush administration. Sensing the battle's symbolic importance, General John Abizaid, leader of the Central Command, told reporters that the U.S. military would "get Fallujah under control."[16] General Abizaid was a Lebanese American, fluent in Arabic and holder of a Master's degree from Harvard in Middle Eastern Studies. He also had a clear understanding of how difficult urban warfare was. But he worried that al-Sadr was trying to turn the conflict into a holy war. He feared that the NIA and the national police, many of them Shiites, would follow al-Sadr and not the dictates of the Baghdad government. Abizaid told one reporter during the opening days of the attacks in Sadr City that several policemen "did not stay with their post and that in some cases, because we've seen films of policemen with Sadr's militia in particular, that there were some defections."[17] Abizaid saw the major problems at Fallujah in purely operational terms. He needed to work with the Baghdad government to slightly adjust training of Iraqi government troops and policemen. He needed to improve military fundamentals among the Iraqis and better coordinate military activities with the Americans. The problems seemed manageable and Fallujah was as good a place to start making the needed changes. But Abizaid had also been terribly inconsistent in his thinking on the Fallujah attacks. At first, he claimed that the United States had to respond "in a big way"

because "my guys . . . are sitting ducks out there." But just before the decision to attack was made, Abizaid told members of Bush's national security
staff that "maybe we shouldn't assault the place."[18] Even President Bush
had second thoughts, suggesting that the political situation had to develop
more before such large-scale attacks could take place, or the United States
risked alienating many in the Middle East. Eventually, both Abizaid and
Bush signed off on the attacks, but not without considerable concern over
their efficacy.

Reflecting that concern, the entire U.S. military operation in Fallujah was
shut down after just two weeks. Apparently, some Iraqi officials, including
Mohammed al-Shehwani, the director of intelligence, and the U.S. Marine
headquarters in Baghdad believed that a continued attack in urban neighborhoods in Fallujah would destroy the fragile coalition government the
United States was trying to build in Baghdad (see DOCUMENT 4-A, EXCERPTS
FROM COALITION PROVISIONAL AUTHORITY BRIEFING WITH GENERAL JOHN
ABIZAID). Putting this disparate coalition of Sunnis, Kurds, and Shiites
together required a delicate balancing act, and continued fighting in Fallujah
threatened that balance. According to General Sanchez, the United States
agreed to initiate the freeze in Fallujah, "on the request of the Governing
Council," the Iraqi group helping the CPA rebuild the country. He explained
that the U.S. command:

> Suspended our offensive operations initially to allow some discussions to
> occur and for some humanitarian assistance provided by the Iraqi government
> to get into the city of Fallujah, to help the noncombatants. After an initial
> period of discussions, we then implemented a unilateral cease-fire, with coor-
> dination through those Governing Council members. And to this afternoon,
> that appears to be holding. It's tenuous, and we have over the course of the
> last two days – have continued to take some attacks in there, but we have
> responded appropriately.[19]

Under this arrangement, U.S. Marines handed over control of the city to
the Fallujah Brigade, a loosely bound group of former supporters of Saddam
Hussein and insurgents who opposed the Baghdad government. As one U.S
Marine reported, "We turned the city over to the Fallujah Brigade – which
was made up of people we'd been fighting against."[20] President Bush tried
to put widespread fears to rest by claiming that the city was secure enough
for Americans to turn it over to the Fallujah Brigade. But some Middle
Eastern reporters immediately challenged the president, claiming that American tanks were literally in reverse heading out of the city center as residents
cheered their departure.[21]

In his memoir, Paul Bremer, the director of the CPA, reported that he
was shocked by the turn of events in Fallujah.[22] He had no idea, he claimed,
that the Marines would turn the city over to former supporters of Saddam.

He watched in horror as Jassim Mohammed Saleh, one of Saddam's former generals who had apparently participated in the bloody repression of Shiites in Karbala in 1991, proudly marched into Fallujah following the American retreat wearing the green uniform and red berets of Saddam's notorious army. The CPA had been sent to Iraq to oversee the rebuilding of Iraq and the development of new institutions responsible for political, economic, and social change. Even though the CPA supported the coalition government, it did not endorse or understand the decision to hand Fallujah over to the Sunni coalition. Bremer had dismissed the old Iraqi army in hopes of building a new force that better represented the dreams and aspirations of ordinary Iraqis. The new army's performance at Fallujah, coupled with the obvious problems within the ranks of the national police force, meant that Bremer's decision to outsource the training of troops and police officers was a poor one.

But Bremer was not alone in his miscalculations. Secretary of Defense Donald Rumsfeld believed that residents of Fallujah would simply hand over the Blackwater contractors' killers if the United States demonstrated its firepower. Smart bombs and laser-guided missiles would convince the insurgents that they were no match for the United States. Rumsfeld's plan backfired, however, as ordinary citizens seemed to rally to the insurgents' side in the face of increased violence in the city. Some even claimed support for the hated al-Sadr and his Shiite militia because they were causing great harm to the Americans in Shiite neighborhoods throughout Iraq. Watching events unfold in Fallujah, British prime minister Tony Blair phoned the White House on April 7 to register his objections to what seemed like significant attacks against civilians.[23]

One year after the U.S. invasion of Iraq had begun, Fallujah had become a rallying point for all that was wrong in Iraq. Surrounded by angry Iraqis, American troops were forced to retreat from the city to calm fears of an American occupation and to support a fragile coalition government. U.S. firepower had not changed the goals of the insurgency and it may have driven many ordinary Iraqis into the insurgents' arms. Perhaps more important, the Battle of Fallujah had exposed the major weaknesses in the Bush administration's Iraq War policies. A severe lack of coordination between the armed forces and the CPA resulted in decisions on the size and scope of the use of force that appeared heavy-handed to many observers. Compounding the problems on the ground in Fallujah was the decision by the highest-ranking national security officials in the Bush administration to deny that anything was wrong. On April 28, President Bush, with the support of Vice President Cheney and Rumsfeld, reported that "most of Fallujah is returning to normal."[24] Few Americans accepted the president's optimistic reporting, and public support for the war diminished as the credibility gap grew. At the time of the president's remarks, few interested observers could have predicted that events in Iraq would go from bad to worse. That same night, however, reports of human rights abuses of Iraqis held in an American-run prison near Baghdad first surfaced. The Bush administration now had a full-blown crisis on its hands.

Human Rights and Abu Ghraib

"Frankly, I think all of us are disappointed by the actions of a few," General Mark Kimmitt, the deputy director of coalition operations in Iraq, told Dan Rather of CBS News. "Every day, we love our soldiers, but frankly, some days we're not always proud of our soldiers."[25] General Kimmitt was responding to news reports about abuses at Abu Ghraib, an American-run prison on the outskirts of Baghdad. During Saddam's reign of terror, the prison had been home to horrific human rights abuses. Tens of thousands of Iraqis were taken to Abu Ghraib, often without formal charges, and tortured and executed. The prison became a symbol of Saddam's power and his ruthlessness. After the liberation of Baghdad in March 2003, American officials were stunned to see Abu Ghraib in person. "It was the most awful sight I've ever seen," reported the Central Intelligence Agency's top Baghdad official, Bob Baer. "If there's ever a reason to get rid of Saddam Hussein, it's because of Abu Ghraib. There were bodies that were eaten by dogs, torture. You know, electrodes coming out of the walls. It was an awful place."[26] Part of the CPA's responsibility in helping Iraqis rebuild civil society was to make vast improvements in Iraq's prison system, including the establishment of a legal code that protected minority rights and followed standard practices. The U.S. Army assumed command of Abu Ghraib in late spring 2003 and began work on the facility immediately. Vast infrastructure improvements to the prison were seen as the first step in the effort to rehabilitate Abu Ghraib. Reserve Brigadier General Janis Karpinski was put in charge of the prison that would house three categories of prisoners: common criminals; security detainees suspected of crimes against the coalition; and a small number of "high-value" members of the insurgency.[27]

From the start, abuses occurred in the prison. Military police from the 372nd police company of the 320th M.P. Battalion were in charge of prisoners until intelligence officers interrogated the suspects. Apparently, it was common practice for these intelligence officers to tell the guards to "set favorable conditions for subsequent interviews," a euphemism for breaking the prisoners' will to resist hard questioning.[28] Several members of the 372nd told army investigators that they assumed the command to abuse prisoners had come from the very top ranks of the military and that "if they were doing things out of the ordinary or outside the guidelines, someone would have said something."[29] In fact, there were no guidelines. None of the reservists who served as prison guards at Abu Ghraib were trained properly to handle prisoners of war. Unlike enlisted service members in the regular army, the reservists did not go through specialized training in the meaning of the Geneva Convention and how these rules applied to prisoners. Furthermore, the reservists who did complain about the abuses to their commanding officers believed that the "issue was taken care of," even though there is no evidence that anyone took action before the army's own internal investigation uncovered the human rights violations at Abu Ghraib.

In November 2003, just six months after the invasion began, General Ricardo Sanchez, the senior commander in Iraq, ordered a full investigation into rumors that something awful was happening at Abu Ghraib. He appointed Major General Antonio Taguba to handle the sensitive report. Taguba issued his findings in late February 2004, just in time for the U.S. presidential primary season. The report created a sensation inside the army, but much of its findings remained undisclosed until CBS decided to air its special broadcast on Abu Ghraib during a segment of the show *Sixty Minutes II*. The CBS report included photographs of male Iraqi prisoners stripped naked and made to perform sexual acts with each other. Other photographs showed naked prisoners standing on boxes with hoods over their heads and still others captured attack dogs being used against prisoners in Abu Ghraib. Perhaps the two most disturbing photographs were of two dead Iraqi men, obviously beaten to death during interrogation. One of the men was packed on ice because he had been beaten to death before he had even been registered into the prison system. The next day his body was placed on a stretcher and taken from the prison as if a medical condition had led to his death.

Some critics of the Bush administration claimed that the president's own Justice Department had created the conditions that allowed the abuses in Abu Ghraib to occur. Citing what became known as the "Torture Memos," several human rights organizations and legal experts challenged the president's approval of "enhanced interrogation techniques."[30] Beginning in May 2002, the Office of Legal Counsel at the U.S. Department of Justice issued a series of reports that gave approval to the Central Intelligence Agency and the Defense Department to harshly interrogate suspected al-Qaeda members in U.S. custody. The Justice Department approved ten forms of extracting valuable information from suspects, including "stress positions," "sleep deprivation," and "the waterboard."[31] In a post-September 11 climate, the Justice Department reasoned that high-level prisoners did hold important information that could possibly prevent another terrorist attack from occurring. Since time was a factor, it had ruled that extraordinary circumstances demanded extraordinary action, though some Justice Department rulings insisted that there was legal consistency in their findings. In the most infamous of the rulings, John Yoo, a former Berkeley law school professor who served as Bush's deputy assistant attorney general, dismissed several legal impediments to the use of extreme interrogation techniques. In a March 14, 2003 memo, Yoo claimed that the U.S. Constitution was not in play because the Fifth Amendment (which provides for due process of law) and the Eighth Amendment (which prevents the government from employing cruel and unusual punishment) "does not extend to alien enemy combatants held abroad." Furthermore, Yoo found that any government defendant harming an enemy combatant during an interrogation in a manner that might arguably violate a criminal prohibition "would be doing so in order to prevent further attacks on the United States by the al-Qaeda terrorist network. In that case, we believe he could argue that the executive branch's constitutional authority to protect the nation from attack justified his actions."[32] (See DOCUMENT 4-B, "MILITARY INTERROGATION OF ALIEN UNLAWFUL COMBATANTS HELD OUTSIDE THE UNITED STATES.") In short, the Bush administration's Justice Department ruled that some forms of torture were essential to extract valuable information from prisoners. In 2008, however, the Justice Department also released a report stating that the Federal Bureau of Investigation raised serious concerns about the controversial interrogation techniques approved by Yoo and used by the CIA in Iraq, Afghanistan, and Guantánamo Bay.[33] The FBI's concerns went generally unnoticed.

The Abu Ghraib scandal could not have come at a worse time for President Bush. Just one year after claiming victory against Saddam Hussein, the president now faced a growing military and political crisis in Iraq. The Abu Ghraib abuses highlighted the increasing difficulties the administration had coordinating events in Iraq and brought into question the leadership of top Bush administration officials. In an election year, Abu Ghraib was not the story Bush wanted on the front page of newspapers around the country. The administration's initial response only hurt the president. At the Pentagon, Rumsfeld first suggested that the he had not even looked at the pictures because the abuses at the prison were such a minor story. When the president privately rebuked Rumsfeld, the story was leaked to the press. Rumsfeld was outraged; claiming that whoever went to the press was harming the president's Iraq policies and his chances for re-election. The *New York Times* reported that Condoleezza Rice, Bush's national security advisor, favored a Rumsfeld resignation. Rumsfeld, the paper quoted Rice as saying, "appears to have become a liability for the president, and has complicated the mission."[34] In typical Rumsfeld fashion, the defense secretary first offered Bush his resignation and then found subordinates to blame for the debacle at Fallujah and the abuses at Abu Ghraib. Eventually, in testimony before Congress (see DOCUMENT 4-C), he apologized and took full responsibility for the Abu Ghraib affair, claiming that "I feel terrible about what happened to these Iraqi detainees. They are human beings. They were in U.S. custody. Our country had an obligation to treat them right. We didn't do that. That was wrong."[35] The president rejected Rumsfeld's offer to resign, and instead went to the Pentagon on May 10, to proclaim to the press and the defense secretary that "You're doing a superb job. You are a strong secretary of defense, and our nation owes you a debt of gratitude."[36]

It did not take long for Rumsfeld's handling of the war to become a campaign issue. Shortly after receiving his party's nomination for president of the United States, Senator John Kerry (D-Massachusetts) used statements made by Paul Bremer and others to highlight what he perceived as Rumsfeld's mismanagement of the war. In early October 2004, Bremer told a private audience that the United States did not send enough troops to Iraq to establish security following Saddam's ouster. Since Rumsfeld had been a staunch proponent of a limited force in Iraq, he caught Kerry's full political assault. Kerry suggested that Bremer's statement about troop strength was evidence that Rumsfeld and the Bush administration had mismanaged the war.[37] The Bush White House scrambled to defend Rumsfeld yet again, and to rein in Bremer, who had been replaced at the CPA by a full U.S. embassy with John Negroponte at the helm. White House press secretary Scott McClellan insisted that Bremer had never raised any concerns about troop levels to the president. "They met on a regular basis," McClellan told the press, but "I don't remember that Ambassador Bremer ever talked about that. . . ."[38] This was not the first conflict over policy between the CPA and the White House.

The Coalition Provisional Authority

The Bush administration's first attempts to rebuild Iraq were directed by the Office of Reconstruction and Humanitarian Assistance (OHRA), headed up by retired U.S. Army general Jay Garner, who had come to the rescue of thousands of ethnic Kurds following the First Gulf War in what became known as Operation Provide Comfort. Garner had been hand-picked by Rumsfeld for the difficult job of handling the transition from Saddam Hussein to democratic rule in Iraq. Both expected that the American occupation of Iraq, so labeled and recognized by UN Security Council on May 23, 2003, would be short-lived. Though Garner's tenure was short, he had performed a useful function for the Bush administration. Bush's top national security staff at the Pentagon had been highly critical of the "Future of Iraq Project," a group assembled by the U.S. State Department in early 2002 to help plan for a post-Saddam Iraq. The group included Iraqi exiles, experts from the State Department's Middle East Bureau, economists, security specialists, and political consultants. They met in a series of topical workshops designed to give the Bush administration the best thinking on nation-building after the potential overthrow of Saddam Hussein. The project issued a number of specific reports, especially on the social aspects of nation-building. Shortly before the March 2003 invasion began, however, the Pentagon took full control of the project, rejecting much of the already completed work. Garner reported that Rumsfeld had told him to "shelve" the project.[39]

There had been significant debate between the State Department and the Pentagon over the Future of Iraq Project, but on the eve of the invasion the Bush administration made the calculated decision to scrap the project in favor of its own military planners. Instead of focusing on the social and economic aspects of nation-building and reconstruction, ORHA and General Garner focused almost entirely on promoting democracy in post-Saddam Iraq. For some, like Richard Perle, the former chairman of the Defense Policy Board, and Kanan Makiya, an Iraqi intellectual and advisor to the Iraqi National Congress, the ORHA corrected much of the State Department's flawed thinking on nation-building. Makiya confirmed his belief that the State Department was only concerned with meaningless social questions, such as how the United States would collect garbage in the streets the day after Iraqi liberation, or how Americans could recruit healthcare workers.[40] He was particularly critical of Tom Warrick, the senior State Department official in charge of the project, claiming he stood in the way of the promotion of democracy in Iraq. What was needed in post-Saddam Iraq was a full commitment to de-Baathification, the "process of eliminating the ideology of the Baath Party [Saddam's party] and its adherents from Iraq's body politic," and the establishment of a new political system.[41] Before Garner assumed control of ORHA, Doug Feith at the Pentagon helped coordinate the thinking on postwar Iraq. In early January 2003, Garner got the call to come to Washington to head ORHA. He would be on the job only five months.

The transition in May 2003 from ORHA to the Coalition Provisional Authority headed by Paul Bremer did not go smoothly. Bremer was highly critical of the limited political and military work that had already been completed. and he wanted to pick up the pace of change inside Iraq. Bremer's first two mandates as ambassador, the title given to the CPA director, remain controversial. The first was a de-Baathification order (see DOCUMENT 4-D). Drawn up at the Pentagon by Rumsfeld and Feith, but attributed at times to the White House, the de-Baathification order stated that the Baath Party was organized by rank, and that full members of the party, those in the top four ranks, would be "immediately removed from their posts and banned from future government employment."[42] The second order was related to the first; it disbanded the entire Iraqi Defense and

Interior Ministries. Garner advised against instituting both measures. He warned Bremer: "You can get rid of an army in a day, but it takes years to build one."[43] Garner, who had served two tours in Vietnam, had seen what happened when you try to build an army from scratch. After the French decamped from Vietnam, the first action the Americans took there in 1955 was to dismantle completely the Vietnamese National Army, which had had ties to the French colonial government. Nearly half the army inherited from the French was dismissed, and the United States then had to build a new national army from the ground up. Lost in that transfer was years of command and combat experience. Still, American military advisors at the time believed it was better to start with a smaller army composed of U.S.-trained soldiers than it was to use an experienced army that had ties to France.[44] In Iraq, the Bush administration also discarded experienced soldiers and officers when it created the new National Iraqi Army. Fearing that the army was made up of Baathist supporters of Saddam, the Bush administration gambled that it could create a new army with no ties to the old regime.

Almost immediately, problems with Bremer's orders surfaced. For one, the orders had made no provisions for payments to separated soldiers or for their reintegration into civilian society.[45] There had been no systematic program for disarming and demobilizing the army even though the United Nations and other groups had had significant experience in these matters for decades. This sudden dismissal of tens of thousands of troops led to great resentment, especially in Sunni areas, and probably fed the insurgency. The insurgency would take advantage of the years of training and experience of dismissed officers, and it showed during Fallujah. Bremer's dictates also released tens of thousands of civil servants from their jobs, creating a huge problem in managing the country. White House and Pentagon officials had assumed all along that former Baathists would not be allowed to hold political office or civil service jobs, and such thinking had significant support among Kurds and Shiites who had been brutalized by Saddam. Bremer had always assumed that the CPA would initiate a process of rehabilitation and reinstatement in the civil service, but he turned that authority over to the Iraqi governing council, which used the program to punish former enemies.

The creation of a governing council made up of Iraqi émigrés and internal leaders handpicked by Bremer and a handful of area specialists was seen by many as an effort to institutionalize Iraqi oversight of CPA decisions, but it took many months for the council to have much influence. Bremer had only limited experience with the governing council at the time of the Battle of Fallujah, and its fragile coalition was certainly a factor in the decision to stop the U.S. Marine attacks against the city. But Bremer himself put limits on the effectiveness of the council. For example, during his tenure, Bremer continually denied efforts by the council to control some of Iraq's financial resources. According to Ali A. Allawi, a former minister of finance, defense, and trade in Iraq during Bremer's tenure, "Bremer was not going to sign away the main rights and prerogatives of the CPA as the UN-sanctioned occupying authority."[46] The governing council was only a temporary arrangement until the interim government of Prime Minister Ayad Allawi was in place. Apparently, Bremer did not want to surrender too much power to the governing council out of fear that the scheduled January 2005 elections might not move forward or that it might use U.S. funds to entrench its interests. Many critics have suggested that Bremer could have found a way to involve Iraqis more in the decision-making process.[47]

Others were less generous in their criticism of Bremer and the CPA. Rajiv Chandrasekaran, a *Washington Post* journalist stationed in Iraq during Bremer's term as CPA director, wrote a highly influential book critical of the U.S. nation-building program in Iraq. *Imperial Life in the Emerald City* claims that Bremer was just as committed to building free markets and privatizing state-owned enterprises as he was to promoting democracy and securing the population. "It will be a wrenching, painful process," Bremer told Chandrasekaran, "but if we don't get their economy right, no matter how fancy our political transformation, it won't work."[48] The problem, according to Chandrasekaran, was that the CPA had few qualified economists on staff. Instead of experienced technocrats, the CPA often hired people loyal to the Republican Party. "The criterion for sending people over there was that they had to have the right political credentials," explained Frederick Smith, who served as deputy director of the CPA's Washington office. Smith told the story of a young man who had sent his résumé to James O'Beirne, the White House liaison at the Pentagon. O'Beirne looked at the résumé and declared the young man "an ideal candidate" for a job in Iraq with the CPA because he had worked for the Republican Party in Florida during the presidential election in 2000.[49] The result of political patronage, according to Chandrasekaran, was an economic nightmare in Iraq. But other critics of the CPA have argued that it was not the junior appointments that plagued Iraq's development, but the senior appointees. James Dobbins, a former assistant secretary of state under Presidents Bill Clinton and George W. Bush, wrote in *Foreign Affairs* that "Bremer filled nearly all the senior jobs in Iraq with seasoned professionals and only turned to White House patronage machine when the administration proved unable to staff the more junior posts with career professionals." Still, he warned, "it is not the junior but the most senior and influential positions that are filled by individuals chosen primarily for their ideological convictions and personal loyalty," and here is where the CPA ran into severe oversight and management problems.[50]

Indeed, for many years following Saddam's ouster, the CPA's initial privatization efforts did little to revive Iraq's economy. Iraqi unemployment was unusually high during the CPA's administration and Iraq's inflation rate was staggering.[51] Several independent reports during Bremer's tenure and through the end of 2006 claimed that the average Iraqi citizen was only slightly better off economically under the U.S. occupation than they had been under Saddam.[52] In several sectors, the U.S. nation-building effort actually created more problems than it solved. For example, the 2005 per capita income in Iraq was $3,400 per year, just ahead of Cuba's. The 2005 unemployment rate was 25 percent, a figure that would have been significantly higher without jobs in the U.S.-supported armed forces.[53] In 2005, only Zimbabwe had a higher annual inflation rate than Iraq's 40 percent.[54] Bob Herbert of the *New York Times* reported in early 2006 that despite the infusion of $16 billion in American taxpayer money, "virtually every measure of the performance of Iraq's oil, electricity, water and sewage sectors has fallen below prewar levels."[55] Herbert's sources were U.S. government witnesses who had testified before a U.S. Senate committee hearing. Compounding Iraq's economic problems was the fact that there was "a virtual youth explosion," making job creation an essential part of nation-building. Few of the CPA's policies addressed this issue concretely.[56] Even though the CPA was disbanded in June 2004, replaced by a regularized U.S. embassy in Baghdad, its economic policies still influenced Iraq for many years. There was no shortage of critics of the CPA's handling of the Iraqi economy, and there is still considerable controversy surrounding the awarding of private contracts to American firms without competitive bidding for the rebuilding of Iraq.

The CPA was plagued by other problems, some of its own making. When Bremer left for Baghdad he had no agreed-upon plan of action for Iraq, and questions of organizational structure remained unanswered. He would hold the rank of ambassador, but he reported to both the president and the Defense Department. He was the director of the CPA, but also the leader of a foreign, occupying government. Bremer had a vast mandate from Washington, but limited instructions. There was very little oversight on what Bremer did inside Iraq with Iraqi resources, and, at the same time, too many restrictions on what Bremer could do with U.S. funds. As is often the case, the ambassador clashed with the military command over security matters. Even though Bremer believed internal security to be his first priority in Iraq, how to accomplish that goal was a subject of intense debate between Bremer and General Sanchez. Bremer concurred with the findings of a report produced by the RAND Corporation, an independent think-tank from Santa Monica, California, that had concluded the United States needed roughly 500,000 troops in Iraq in 2003 to fulfill its many obligations. In his memoir, Bremer insists that he raised this issue with the president and with Rumsfeld, but neither ever replied.[57] The CPA itself was hopelessly understaffed, leading one Middle East expert and former National Security Council member to conclude that it had "virtually no presence outside of Baghdad," and therefore the entire reconstruction effort was in jeopardy.[58] General James Conway, who was commander of the 1st Marine Expeditionary Force, has suggested that the CPA was unable to meet the Iraqis' expectations for rebuilding their country and that the Marines stationed west of Baghdad were often forced to "become city managers, chiefs of policy and agricultural experts" because Bremer's local governance teams never arrived.[59]

Despite the CPA's chronic difficulties, there was considerable optimism in Washington when the first U.S. ambassador to post-Saddam Iraq, John Negroponte, took over from Bremer in June 2004. Negroponte was sent to Baghdad to supervise the transition of the CPA into a full-fledged embassy and to coordinate policy with the new interim government of Ayad Allawi. Secretary of State Colin Powell suggested that Negroponte had the experience and the wisdom to handle the difficult transition, and that the new interim Allawi government had the full support of the United States. At the time of the transition in June 2004, Powell stated that "complete political transition" in Iraq was just around the corner. The CPA had been a necessary step in the process of Iraq's transition to democracy, Powell concluded, and with the new embassy and Allawi government in place, it was only a matter of time before the partnership between Iraqis and Americans produced the desired results.[60] However, before the Iraqi government could reach its goals, security had to improve dramatically. "As recent events have demonstrated," Powell wrote Lauro L. Baja, Jr., president of the UN Security Council, in June 2004, "continuing attacks by insurgents, including former regime elements, foreign fighters, and illegal militias challenge all those who are working for a better Iraq."[61] Powell had no idea how prophetic his statement would be.

General Casey and the Iraqi Civil War

In July 2004, General George Casey replaced General Sanchez as the commander of the multi-national force in Iraq. Following the dismantling of the CPA, General Casey's appointment was seen by the Bush administration as the next necessary step to improve Iraqi security. The president and Rumsfeld wanted a full general in charge in Iraq, fearing that Sanchez had too little experience to handle the difficulties he faced. Rumsfeld reported that he had not even been aware that a three-star lieutenant general, Sanchez, had been named top commander in Iraq and that he wanted to change the system that had led to such an appointment.⁶² That change began with Casey, who had thirty years of command experience at every level of the army, from platoon to division. General Casey went to Iraq to institute dramatic change in the way the U.S armed forces approached the war. Under General Sanchez, there was a limited campaign plan to deal with the growing insurgency. Some critics of General Sanchez, including retired army colonel Andrew Bacevich, claimed that Sanchez had "misunderstood the nature of the conflict he faced." When Sanchez took command, the insurgency had hardly begun. One year later, when he was replaced by General Casey, "Iraq was all but coming apart at the seams."⁶³ Casey issued a campaign plan within one month of his arrival in Iraq. The plan called for containing insurgent violence, building up Iraqi security forces, and reaching out to the Sunni community to bring some into the government and convince others that the U.S. could not lose in Iraq. Casey was also prepared to work more closely with the interim government of Prime Minister Ayad Allawi.

Casey's plan, supported by Tony Blair and the British government, offered a fresh start in Iraq, and the Bush administration was hopeful that the new campaign plan could keep the U.S. commitment limited while still meeting the administration's ambitious goals. It did not take long, however, for events in Iraq to overrun the plan. In August 2004, al-Sadr and his Mahdi Army were once again engaging American troops in fierce combat, this time near Najaf. The Mahdi Army moved into the holiest of Shiite shrines, the Imam Ali mosque in Najaf, claiming subnational power for their radical movement. The followers of al-Sadr had gambled that they could claim leadership of the Shiite movement in the absence from Iraq of Grand Ayatollah al-Sistani, who was in London for medical treatment. They believed that the United States was unwilling to attack the shrine for fear of dividing an already weak Allawi-led interim government. Allawi, no supporter of al-Sistani or al-Sadr, urged the United States to take a strong stance against the Mahdi forces in Najaf. General Casey moved nearly every sniper team to the mosque, and they inflicted heavy damage on al-Sadr's forces. Still, the American command was in a difficult spot. Most realized that al-Sadr had a significant following, no matter how distasteful he may have been. To alienate his followers would have been the death knell to the entire political process, and Muslim leaders throughout the region warned the Bush White House not to attack the shrine. Eventually, al-Sadr's troops were allowed to leave Najaf under a ceasefire, but the damage had already been done. Radical Shiites had clearly demonstrated to the Bush administration that they could determine the course of battle despite the fact that the United States held preponderant military power. The government in Baghdad simply did not have enough support without al-Sadr and other radical Shiite groups to govern. Like Hezbollah, al-Sadr could dictate terms to the government from this favored position of subnational power.

The experience left Casey extremely frustrated. He had come to Iraq determined to turn major combat responsibilities over to the Iraqis, to secure the cities from incessant insurgent attacks, and to create a security climate in which the democratic process could work itself out in Baghdad. In his first test, he moved the Mahdi Army out of a major urban area, a city with great historical and religious significance to Shiites, but he had done so with very little cooperation from Baghdad and no feeling that Iraq was growing more secure. Casey felt this same frustration with the Sunni insurgency. In November 2004, Casey launched an ambitious military campaign to reclaim Fallujah and drive radical Sunnis from the city. Unlike the previous battle, Casey mounted overwhelming force and coordinated a complete civilian evacuation of the city. Improved resupply lines meant that American troops were not exposed to roadside bombs or exploding IEDs under long U.S. convoys. After ten days of fighting, the Marines captured the city, claiming to have killed nearly 1,000 hardcore Sunni insurgents in the process. Some U.S. commanders went public with claims of a great military victory. "We feel right now that we have . . . broken the back of the insurgency and we have taken away this safe haven," reported Lt. General Statler. "The insurgents are on the run." Others were less sanguine. "The Battle of Fallujah was not a defeat," suggested Marine officer Jonathan Keiler, "but we cannot afford many more victories like that."[64] The fighting had been fierce, with Marines eventually forced to clear every building in the city center. It was a massive undertaking and pointed to the difficulties of urban counterinsurgency efforts.

Following apparent U.S. victories in Najaf and in Fallujah, the violence intensified. In February 2005 a car bomb in Hilla, a city just south of Baghdad, killed 114 people, the worst single incident since the U.S.-led invasion. That spring, following the bombing in Hilla and the election of Jalal Talabani, a Kurd, as president of Iraq and Ibrahim Jaafri, a Shiite, as prime minister, the sectarian violence grew to unprecedented levels. In May 2005, the number of civilian deaths due to car bombs, explosions, and assassinations doubled from the previous month. By July 2005, over 25,000 Iraqi civilians had been killed since the March 2003 invasion. Most of the violence was between Sunni insurgents and Shiites connected to various militia groups. When the Shia-led United Iraqi Alliance emerged as the winner of the December 2005 parliamentary elections, insurgent attacks threatened to destabilize the Baghdad government even more. In February, Sunni insurgents blew up the Golden Dome mosque in Samarra, one of the holiest Shiite shrines in Iraq. Shiite militia groups launched reprisal attacks all over Iraq, killing a number of imams and kidnapping several others. The week following the assault on Sumarra, mobs attacked over thirty Sunni mosques in Baghdad alone. From Lebanon, al-Sadr called on the new Iraqi parliament, which included thirty-two of his followers, to "meet and vote on a request for coalition forces to leave Iraq."[65] Making matters even worse, Shiite leader Abdul Asis al-Hakim, who had supported the U.S. invasion, claimed that the new U.S. ambassador to Iraq, Zalmay Khalizad, was partly responsible for the attack. He suggested that the ambassador's recent comments about Shiite death squads operating freely within the Ministry of the Interior led the Sunnis to take such violent action.[66] Following Samarra, a bloody pattern of violence settled over Iraq – attacks and reprisals – highlighting the inability of the United States to stop the violence and the weaknesses of the Baghdad government.

In May 2006, following months of bloodshed and arguments over the December 2005 election results, Nouri al-Maliki became the new prime minister of Iraq. Al-Maliki was a leader of the Dawa Party, a Shiite political group that for years had led an armed underground resistance to Saddam Hussein. He promised a unity government, but at the height of Iraq's civil war most Sunnis simply refused to believe he was willing or capable of "bringing Sunnis in from the cold."[67] The new government ratified a constitution that also promised to bring all Iraqis together as citizens of a republic (see DOCUMENT 4-E). In May and June 2006, the United Nations reported that at least 100 civilians were being killed each day.[68] Al-Maliki failed to distance himself from some of the more radical elements of the Shiite power structure, including al-Sadr, and the violence raged out of control. A massive refugee problem also plagued the Baghdad government, and its half-hearted response to the crisis led many members of the U.S. Congress to question the efficacy of the Maliki government. An estimated 2,000 Iraqis fled their homes each day in 2005 and 2006, making this exodus of people one of the largest population movements in the region since 1948.[69] Nearly 1.6 million Iraqis became internally displaced people (IDPs), putting tremendous pressure on the Maliki government to care for them.[70]

Some American planners believed that oil revenues would help the Baghdad government reach out to others as it centralized profits and redistributed them evenly to Iraq's social welfare programs and people. When the private oil contracts did not reach the expected bid amounts, this philosophy began to unravel. Sunnis continually reported that Shiites – who dominated the government and the national police – were not interested in a shared past or a common future with Iraq's other religious elements. Pictures of leading Shiites hung in all government buildings and police stations, including posters of Imam Hussein, grandson of the Prophet Mohammed and a Shiite martyr celebrated annually during Muharam. On concrete barriers outside the Baghdad national assembly there was a large mural of Shiite pilgrims marching to Karbala.[71] After Saddam Hussein's trial and eventual execution in late 2006, Sunni reprisal attacks in Shiite neighborhoods were a common occurrence. In November 2006, a car bombing in Sadr City killed 213 and set off a new wave of attacks. All of this contributed to the insurgency and the violence, making General Casey's job very difficult indeed. But Casey pressed on, thinking that the United States could provide security with the forces at hand and believing that the responsibility for Iraqi security ultimately rested with the National Iraqi Army and the national police. Casey favored shifting responsibility to these Iraqi forces as soon as possible. The president was fond of saying, "When they stand up, we will stand down."[72] Both believed that the United States was doing all it could to help stabilize Iraq.

In Congress, however, there was a growing number of war skeptics. Some, like John Murtha, a Vietnam veteran and Democratic congressman from Pennsylvania, called for an immediate troop withdrawal from Iraq. The usually hawkish Murtha set off a firestorm in Washington when he claimed that U.S. troops were the primary target of the insurgency and al-Sadr's forces and that Americans had become a "catalyst for violence." Murtha concluded that it was time to bring the troops home.[73] Others, like John McCain (R-Arizona), another Vietnam veteran, had concluded that there were not enough American "boots on the ground" and that General Casey had no strategy for winning the war.[74] Presidential hopefuls Joseph Biden (D-Delaware) and Hillary Clinton (D-New York) argued that the administration had to push Baghdad officials toward becoming a truly national government of reconciliation by bringing in disaffected Sunnis. They believed that such inclusion would siphon off support for the insurgency and would also provide an effective counter to al-Sadr's radical Shiites. Clinton and Biden favored turning the war over to Iraqi security forces too, but only after a more comprehensive training program had been developed. In effect, what the Democratic senators wanted seemed to the Bush administration what General Casey was already offering.

To make that connection, the Bush White House supported General Casey's reworking of a war campaign document that could be used to quiet domestic critics and show that the administration was making progress in Iraq. The document, the "National Strategy for Victory in Iraq" (see Docu-MENT 4-F), was reworked by the National Security Council, and explained how "all elements of American power were being mobilized" to achieve U.S. goals in Iraq.[75] The document was released to the press and the American public to great fanfare, including several public talks by the president. Had the United States finally found the military leader who understood the difficult problems in Iraq and who was now building a coordinated war campaign to deal with them effectively? Would the "National Strategy for Victory in Iraq" secure bipartisan support for a course of action that combined political and security needs?

Answers to these and other questions about the war came soon enough. In a matter of weeks, the strategy for victory in Iraq had unraveled. Iraqi security forces continued to show an unwillingness to go after the most radicalized Shiite elements in and around Baghdad, and they proved even more inept against Sunnis to the south and west. Though there had been some success with Casey's limited counterinsurgency measures in An Bar province and other Sunni strongholds, the weakness of the Baghdad government continued to plague the Bush administration's efforts to end the civil war. Some skeptics in Washington wondered if the U.S. should simply allow the civil war to run its course and deal with whatever government came to power. Others suggested that the Bush administration should make a stronger effort to include Sunnis in the national government, including allowing some former Baathists to hold political office. Some of General Casey's U.S. Army commanders had tried "turning" Sunni elements in Anbar, and this too seemed to produce some limited, but positive, early results. By early summer 2006, however, most White House officials doubted that Casey's war campaign plan could get the job done and they advocated a full policy review. Following the stunning defeat of many Bush administration supporters in the 2006 mid-term elections, that review became increasingly important to the White House. Throughout the fall, analysts in the National Security Council reviewed the Casey strategy with an "eye to developing a new way forward."[76] What they turned to – now known as "the surge" – was not a dramatic departure from Casey's tactics, but was rather a way to pressure Baghdad to make necessary changes more quickly and to cover its weaknesses. The surge in troops caused insurgents and militias to temporarily freeze their military operations, but it did not succeed in breaking the back of the insurgency and limiting the power of the Shiite militias. Nor did it lead to dramatic reform by the Maliki government.

Notes

1 Text of Bush speech, "President Declares End to Major Combat in Iraq," *CBS News On-line*, May 1, 2003.
2 Toby Dodge, *Iraq's Future: The Aftermath of Regime Change* (London: International Institute for Strategic Studies, 2005), 16.
3 Bob Woodward, *A State of Denial* (New York: Simon & Schuster, 2006), 298.
4 As quoted in Tom Ricks, *Fiasco: The American Military Adventure in Iraq* (New York: Penguin, 2006), 331.
5 *Washington Post*, June 2, 2008.
6 As quoted in Robert K. Brigham, *Iraq, Vietnam, and the Limits of American Power* (New York: PublicAffairs, 2008), 49.
7 *Washington Post*, September 13, 2004.
8 Woodward, *A State of Denial*, 297.
9 L. Paul Bremer, *My Year in Iraq: The Struggle to Build a Future of Hope* (New York: Threshold Editions, 2006), 317.

10 Fred Kaplan, "Iraq Hawks Down: Is Fallujah Iraq's Mogadishu?", *Slate*, April 1, 2004.

11 *New York Times*, July 18, 2007.

12 Ricks, *Fiasco*, 334.

13 For a full description of al-Sadr's speech at Kufa, see Soraya Barhaddi Nelson, "Family Follows Shiite Cleric into Holy Battle for Iraq," *Knight Rider*, 21 April 2004. As quoted in Ricks, *Fiasco*, 337.

14 Ricks, *Fiasco*, 338.

15 Andrew Krepinevich, Jr., "How to Win the Iraq War," *Foreign Affairs*, 84 (September/October 2005), 91–93.

16 As quoted in Ricks, *Fiasco*, 342.

17 Coalition Provisional Authority Briefing with General John Abizaid, Commander, U.S. Central Command, Teleconference between Baghdad, Iraq, and the Pentagon, Arlington, Virginia, 12 April 2004.

18 As quoted in Woodward, *A State of Denial*, 298.

19 Ibid.

20 Ricks, *Fiasco*, 343.

21 "Marines Withdraw from Fallujah," *History Commons*, 30 April 2004.

22 Bremer, *My Year in Iraq*, 344.

23 Rajiv Chandrasekaran, *Imperial Life in the Emerald City* (New York: Bloomsbury, 2006), 307.

24 Ricks, *Fiasco*, 343.

25 CBS News, *Sixty Minutes II*, April 28, 2004.

26 Ibid.

27 Seymour Hersh, "Torture at Abu Ghraib," *The New Yorker*, May 10, 2004.

28 Report by Provost Marshall Donald Ryder as cited in Hersh, "Torture at Abu Ghraib."

29 As quoted in Hersh, "Torture at Abu Ghraib."

30 *New York Times*, April 17, 2009.

31 August 1, 2002, Memorandum for John Rizzo, Acting General Counsel of the Central Intelligence Agency – Interrogation of al-Qaeda Operative, U.S. Department of Justice, Office of Legal Counsel.

32 March 14, 2003, Memorandum for William J. Haynes II, General Counsel of the Department of Defense – Military Interrogation of Alien Unlawful Combatants Held Outside the United States, U.S. Department of Justice, Office of Legal Counsel.

33 *New York Times*, May 4, 2011.

34 *New York Times*, May 8, 2004, as quoted in Woodward, *A State of Denial*, 306.

35 Testimony of Secretary of Defense Donald Rumsfeld before the Senate and House Armed Services Committees, 7 May 2004, Department of Defense.

36 As quoted in Woodward, *A State of Denial*, 306.

37 *New York Times*, October 5, 2004.

38 Ibid.

39 "Turf Wars and The Future of Iraq," *Frontline* online at http://www.pbs.org/wgbh/pages/frontline/shows/truth/fighting/turfwars.html, accessed January 14, 2013.

40   Brigham, *Iraq, Vietnam, and the Limits of American Power*, 73.
41   Ali A. Allawi, *The Occupation of Iraq: Winning the War, Losing the Peace* (New Haven: Yale University Press, 2007), 84.
42   Woodward, *A State of Denial*, 193.
43   Ibid., 195.
44   Robert K. Brigham, *ARVN: Life and Death in the South Vietnamese Army* (Kansas: University Press of Kansas, 2006).
45   James Dobbins, Seth G. Jones, Benjamin Runkle, and Siddharth Mohandas, *Occupying Iraq: A History of the Coalition Provisional Authority* (Santa Monica, CA: RAND Corporation, 2009), xxiii.
46   Allawi, *The Occupation of Iraq*, 166.
47   Peter Galbraith, *The End of Iraq: How American Incompetence Created a War without End* (New York: Simon & Schuster, 2006), 123–127.
48   Chandrasekaran, *Imperial Life*, 68.
49   Ibid., 101.
50   James Dobbins, "Who Lost Iraq?" *Foreign Affairs*, 86 (September/October 2007), 67.
51   Central Intelligence Agency, *World Fact Book on Iraq* (Washington, D.C.: Government Printing Office, 2005).
52   Ibid.
53   Ibid.
54   Ibid.
55   *New York Times*, February 13, 2006.
56   Anthony H. Cordesman, "One Year On: Nation Building in Iraq," Working Paper, Center for Strategic and International Studies, April 16, 2004, 15.
57   Bremer, *My Year in Iraq*, 10.
58   Kenneth Pollack, "After Saddam: Assessing the Reconstruction of Iraq," *Foreign Affairs*, 83 (January/February 2004).
59   Michael Gordon and General Bernard Trainor, *Cobra II: The Inside Story of the Invasion and Occupation of Iraq* (New York: Vintage, 2006), 567.
60   Letter from the Secretary of State of the United States to Lauro Baja, Jr., President of the Security Council, United Nations, 5 June 2004, Annex, United Nations Security Council, Resolution 1546, 8 June 2004.
61   Ibid.
62   Woodward, *A State of Denial*, 298.
63   As quoted in Ricks, *Fiasco*, 392.
64   As quoted ibid., 405.
65   *New York Times*, February 22, 2006.
66   Ibid.
67   Brigham, *Iraq, Vietnam, and the Limits of American Power*, 104.
68   BBC News at http://news.bbc.co.uk/1/hi/world/middle_east/737483.stm, accessed January 14, 2013.
69   "Iraq's Displacement Crisis," *Forced Migration Review*, June 2007.
70   UNCHR, United Nations Refugee Agency-Iraq, Country Operations Profile; UNHCR Iraq Fact Sheet, "Crisis in Iraq," September 1, 2008; and OCHA Iraq Office in Amman, "Humanitarian Crisis in Iraq: Facts and Figures," Representative of the United Nations Assistance Mission in Iraq, November 13, 2007.

71   Nir Rosen, "The Gathering Storm," *The National*, 10 April 2009.
72   Brigham, *Iraq, Vietnam, and the Limits of American Power*, 54.
73   *Washington Post*, November 18, 2005.
74   Brigham, *Iraq, Vietnam, and the Limits of American Power*, 123.
75   Peter Feaver, "Anatomy of the Surge," *Commentary* (April 2008), 25.
76   Ibid., 26.

DOCUMENTS

Document 4-A

Excerpts from Coalition Provisional Authority briefing with General John Abizaid, commander, U.S. Central Command, and Lt. General Ricardo Sanchez, commander, CJTF-7, April 12, 2004

General Sanchez . . . On the request of the Governing Council, we initiated a freeze to offensive operations. We suspended our offensive operations initially to allow some discussions to occur and for humanitarian assistance provided by the Iraqi government to get into the city of Fallujah, to help the noncombatants. After an initial period of discussions, we then implemented a unilateral cease-fire, with coordination through those Governing Council members. And to this afternoon, that appears to be holding. It's tenuous, and we have over the course of the last two day – have continued to take some attacks in there, but we have responded appropriately. Today it seems a little bit better.

General Sanchez . . . The part that is tenuous is that we are continuing to get attacks from the insurgents that are in the city. As I stated, we suspended our offensive operations to allow these discussions to go forward, and I must add that these are just initial discussions. We are not negotiating at this point until we achieve some confidence building and period of stability; then we would consider going into significant negotiations to end this battle. But at this point, we have had continued attacks by the insurgents up until about eight to 12 hours ago.

General Abizaid . . . I would like to add about the Fallujah situation – I was just there talking to the Marines a couple of days ago. The Marines have been doing a great job in conducting military operations. They've been very precise. They have attempted to protect civilians to the best of their ability. The Arab press, in particular Al-Jazeera and Al-Arabiyah, are portraying their actions as purposefully targeting civilians. And we absolutely do not do that, and I think everybody knows that.

It is always interesting to me how Al-Jazeera manages to be at the scene of the crime whenever a hostage shows up or some other problem happens to be there. So they are – they have not been truthful in their reporting, they haven't been accurate, and it is absolutely clear that American forces are doing their very best to protect civilians and at the same time get at the military targets there.

General Abizaid ... I would just like to add on the situation down south, that Muqtada Sadr is isolating himself. This was not by any stretch of imagination a Shi'a uprising. And it's a combination of some military action on our part but, probably much more importantly, very, very important, Shi'a political action that's isolating him and showing people out there that a person such as Muqtada Sadr, who is anti-democratic and attacks the people of Iraq and their institutions, won't be tolerated. And we've had a very good relationship with the Shia population in the south. We aim to continue that. But the Shi'a population down there is working very hard to isolate him.

General Sanchez ... the tactics being used at Fallujah are fairly straightforward. We've been attacking to secure the city of Fallujah, and we're running into active resistance. It is very clear where we're taking fire from, and where we're taking fire from we're applying the appropriate, apportionate combat power to elimi-nate that resistance. We are being very deliberate and precise in the application of that combat power to prevent any wounding or injuring of noncombatants in the area.

QUESTIONS TO CONSIDER

1   Why did U.S. Marines suspend military operations in Fallujah? Who gave the order? What political considerations went into the "freeze"?
2   What military tactics were used in Fallujah?

--------------------- **Document 4-B** ---------------------

Excerpts from memorandum for William J. Haynes II, general counsel of the Department of Defense, "Military Interrogation of Alien Unlawful Combatants Held Outside the United States," March 14, 2003, U.S. Department of Justice, Office of Legal Counsel

[Y]ou have asked our Office to examine the legal standards governing military interrogations of alien unlawful combatants held outside the United States. You have requested that we examine both domestic and international law that might be applicable to the conduct of those interrogations.

In Party I, we conclude that the Fifth and Eighth Amendments, as interpreted by the Supreme Court, do not extend to alien enemy combatants held abroad. In Part II, we examine federal criminal law. We explain that several canons of construction apply here. Those canons of construction indicate that federal criminal laws of general applicability do not apply properly-authorized interrogations of enemy combatants, undertaken by military personnel in the course of an armed conflict. Such criminal statutes, if they were misconstrued to apply to the interrogation of enemy combatants, would conflict with the Constitution's grant of the Commander-in-Chief power solely to the President.

. . . In Part III, we examine international law applicable to the conduct of interrogations. First, we examine the U.N. Convention Against Torture and Other Cruel, Inhuman, or Degrading Treatment or Punishment . . . and conclude that U.S. reservations, understandings, and declarations ensure that our international obligations mirror the standard of 18 U.S.C./2340A. Second, we address the U.S. obligation under CAT to undertake to prevent the commission of "cruel, inhuman, or degrading treatment or punishment." We conclude that based on its reservation, the United States' obligation extends only to conduct that is "cruel and unusual" within the meaning of the Eighth Amendment or otherwise "shocks the conscience" under the Due Process Clauses of the Fifth and Fourteenth Amendments.

Third, we examine the applicability of customary international law. We conclude that as an expression of state practice, customary international law cannot impose a standard that differs from U.S. obligation under CAT, a recent multilateral treaty on the same subject. In any event, our previous opinions make clear that customary international law is not federal law and that the President is free to override it at his discretion.

In Part IV, we discuss defenses to an allegation that an interrogation method might violate any of the various criminal prohibitions discussed in Part II. We believe that necessity or self-defense could provide defenses to a prosecution.

QUESTIONS TO CONSIDER

1   Why did the Justice Department rule that Fifth and Eighth Amendment protections did not apply to enemy combatants? What is an enemy combatant? How are they different from soldiers?

—————————— **Document 4-C** ——————————

Testimony of Secretary of Defense Donald H. Rumsfeld before the Senate and House Armed Services Committees, 7 May 2004

Mr. Chairman, members of the Committee – Thank you for the opportunity to testify today.

In recent days, there has been a good deal of discussion about who bears responsibility for the terrible activities that took place at Abu Ghraib. These events occurred on my watch. As Secretary of Defense, I am accountable for them. I take full responsibility. It is my obligation to evaluate what happened, to make sure those who have committed wrongdoing are brought to justice, and to make changes as needed to see that it doesn't happen again.

I feel terrible about what happened to these Iraqi detainees. They are human beings. They were in U.S. custody. Our country had an obligation to treat them right. We didn't do that. That was wrong.

To those Iraqis who were mistreated by members of U.S. armed forces, I offer my deepest apology. It was un-American. And it was inconsistent with the values of our nation.

Further, I deeply regret the damage that has been done: First, to the reputation of the honorable men and women of our armed forces who are courageously, skillfully and responsibly defending our freedom across the globe. They are truly wonderful human beings, and their families and loved ones can be enormously proud of them. Second, to the President, the Congress and the American people. I wish we had been able to convey to them the gravity of this was before we saw it in the media; third, to the Iraqi people, whose trust in our coalition has been shaken; and finally to the reputation of our country.

The photographic depictions of U.S. military personnel that the public has seen have unquestionably offended and outraged everyone in the Department of Defense.

If you could have seen the anguished expressions on the faces of those of us in the Department upon seeing the photos, you would know how we feel today.

We take this seriously. It should not have happened. Any wrongdoers need to be punished, procedures evaluated, and problems corrected.

It's important for the American people and the world to know that while these terrible acts were perpetrated by a small number of the U.S. military, they were also brought to light by the honorable and responsible actions of other military personnel. There are many who did their duty professionally and we should mention that as well: First the soldier, Specialist Joseph Darby, who alerted the appropriate authorities that abuses of detainees were occurring. My thanks and appreciation to him for his courage and his values. Second, those in the military chain of command who acted promptly upon learning of those activities by initiating a series of investigations – criminal and administrative – to ensure that the abuses were stopped, that the responsible chain of command was relieved and replaced, and that the Uniform Code of Military Justice was followed; third, units singled out for praise in General Taguba's Report for the care they provided detainees in their custody and their intolerance of abuses by others. And finally, the CENTCOM chain of command for taking action and publicly announcing to the world that investigations of abuse were underway.

The American people and members of the committee deserve an accounting of what has happened and what's being done to fix it. Gathered today are the senior military officials with responsibility in the care and treatment of detainees. The responsibility for training falls to the U.S. Army. The responsibility for the actions and conduct of forces in Iraq falls to the combatant commander. And the ultimate responsibility for the department rests with me. Each of us has had a strong interest in getting the facts out to the American people.

We want you to know the facts. I want you to have all the documentation and the data you require. If some material is classified, we will ensure members get an opportunity to see it privately.

Having said that, all the facts that may be of interest are not yet in hand. In addition to the Taguba Report, there are other investigations underway. We will make the results of these investigations available to you. But because all the facts are not in hand, there will be corrections and clarifications to the record as more information is learned. If we have something to add later, we'll do so. If we find something that we've said that needs to be corrected, we'll correct it.

From the other witnesses here, you will be told the sequence of events and investigations that have taken place since these activities first came to light.

What I want to do is to inform you of the measures underway to remedy some of the damage done and to improve our performance in the future.

Before I do that, let me make one further note: As members of this Committee are aware, each of us at this table is either in the chain of command or has senior responsibilities in the Department. This means that anything we say publicly could have an impact on legal proceedings against those accused of wrongdoing in this matter. Our responsibility at this hearing, and in our public comments, is to conduct ourselves consistent with that well known fact. So please understand that if some of our responses are measured, it is to ensure that pending cases are not jeopardized by seeming to exert "command influence" and that the rights of any accused are protected.

Now let me tell you the measures we are taking to deal with this issue. When this incident came to light and was reported within the Chain of Command, we took several immediate actions. These will be discussed in detail by others here today, but let me highlight them.

General Sanchez launched a criminal investigation immediately. He then asked for an administrative review of procedures at the Abu Ghraib facility. That is the so-called Taguba Report. These two investigations have resulted thus far in criminal or administrative actions against at least 12 individuals, including the relief of the prison chain of command and criminal referrals of several soldiers directly involved in abuse.

The Army also launched an Inspector General Review of detainee operations throughout Afghanistan and Iraq. That review continues. The Army has initiated an investigation of Reserve training with respect to military intelligence and police functions.

General Sanchez also asked for an Army Intelligence review of the circumstances discussed in General Taguba's report and that is ongoing. And, I also asked the Navy Inspector General to review procedures at Guantanamo and the Charleston Naval Brig.

As these investigations mature, we will endeavor to keep you informed. But there is more to be done. First, to ensure we have a handle on the scope of this catastrophe, I will be announcing today the appointment of several senior former officials who are being asked to examine the pace, breadth, and thoroughness of the existing investigations, and to determine whether additional investigations need to be initiated. They are being asked to report their findings within 45 days of taking up their duties. I am confident these distinguished individuals will provide a full and fair assessment of what has been done thus far – and recommend whether further steps may be necessary. I will encourage them to meet with members of Congress to keep them apprised of their progress. I look forward to their suggestions and recommendations.

Second, we need to review our habits and procedures. One of the things we've tried to do since September 11th is to get the Department to adjust its habits and procedures at a time of war, and in the information age. For the past three years, we have looked for areas where adjustments were needed, and regrettably, we have now found another one. Let me be clear. I failed to identify the catastrophic damage that the allegations of abuse could do to our operations in the theater, to the safety of our troops in the field, the cause to which we are committed. When these allegations first surfaced, I failed to recognize how important it was to elevate a matter of such gravity to the highest levels, including leaders in Congress. Nor did we anticipate that a classified investigation report that had not yet been delivered to the senior levels of the Department would be given to the media. That was my failing. In the future, we will take whatever steps are necessary to elevate to the appropriate levels charges of this magnitude.

Third, I am seeking a way to provide appropriate compensation to those detainees who suffered grievous and brutal abuse and cruelty at the hands of a few members of the U.S. military. It is the right thing to do. I'm told we have the ability to do so. And so we will – one way or another.

One of the great strengths of our nation is its ability to recognize failures, deal with them, and to strive to make things better. Indeed, the openness with which these problems are being dealt is one of the strengths of our free society. Democracies are imperfect, because they are made up of human beings who are, by our nature, imperfect. Of course, we wish that every person in our government and our Armed Forces would conduct themselves in accordance with the highest standards of ethics. But the reality is some do not.

One mistake we have made during our initial investigation into these charges, for example, was failing to sufficiently call to your attention the information made public in the CENTCOM press release regarding the investigations they had initiated back in January. We also failed to sufficiently call your attention and brief you on the preliminary findings of the criminal investigation announced on March 20 by General Kimmitt. I am advised the Army has had periodic meetings to inform Congressional staffs. There are indications that the information provided was penetrating at some level, however. On January 20th, for example, CNN reported that a CID investigation was being conducted into allegations of detainee abuse at Abu Ghraib, and mentioned the possible existence of photographs taken of detainees. Nonetheless, I know that we did not fully brief you on this subject along the way and we should have done so. I wish we would have known more sooner and been able to tell you more sooner. But we didn't. For that, I apologize.

We need to discuss a better way to keep you informed about matters of such gravity in the future.

The fact that abuses take place – in the military, in law enforcement, and in our society – is not surprising. But the standard by which our country and our government should be judged is not by whether abuses take place, but rather how our nation deals with them. We are dealing with them forthrightly. These incidents are being investigated and any found to have committed crimes or misconduct will receive the appropriate justice. Most of the time, at least, the system works.

None of this is meant to diminish the gravity of the recent situation at Abu Ghraib. To the contrary, that is precisely why these abuses are so damaging – because they can be used by the enemies of our country to undermine our mission and spread the false impression that such conduct is the rule and not the exception – when, in fact, the opposite is true.

Which is why it is so important that we investigate them publicly and openly, and hold people accountable in similar fashion. And that is exactly what we are doing.

QUESTIONS

When we first were told about these activities and saw those photographs, I and everyone at this table was as shocked and stunned as you were. In the period since, a number of questions have been raised – here in the Congress, in the media, and by the public. Let me respond to some of them.

Some have asked: Why weren't those charged with guarding prisoners properly trained?

If one looks at the behavior depicted in those photos, it is fair to ask: what kind of training could one possibly provide that would stop people from doing that?

Either you learn that in life, or you don't. And if someone doesn't know that doing what is shown in those photos is wrong, cruel, brutal, indecent, and against American values, I am at a loss as to what kind of training could be provided to teach them.

The fact is, the vast majority of the people in the United States Armed Forces are decent, honorable individuals who know right from wrong, and conduct themselves in a manner that is in keeping with the spirit and values of our country. And there is only a very small minority who do not.

Some have asked: Hasn't a climate allowing for abuses to occur been created because of a decision to "disregard" the Geneva Convention?

No. Indeed, the U.S. Government recognized that the Geneva Conventions apply in Iraq, and the armed forces are obliged to follow them. DoD personnel are trained in the law of war, including the Geneva Conventions. Doctrine requires that they follow those rules and report, investigate, and take corrective action to remedy violations.

We did conclude that our war against al-Qaeda is not governed precisely by the Conventions, but nevertheless announced that detained individuals would be treated consistent with the principles of the Geneva Conventions.

Some have asked: Can we repair the damage done to our credibility in the region?

I hope so and I believe so. We have to trust that in the course of events the truth will eventually come out. And the truth is that the United States is a liberator, not a conqueror. Our people are devoted to freedom and democracy, not enslavement or oppression. Every day, these men and women risk their lives to protect the Iraqi people and help them build a more hopeful future. They have liberated 25 million people; dismantled two terrorist regimes; and battled an enemy that shows no compassion or respect for innocent human life.

These men and women, and the families who love and support them, deserve better than to have their sacrifices on behalf of our country sullied by the despicable actions of a few. To that vast majority of our soldiers abroad, I extend my support and my appreciation for their truly outstanding service.

One final thought:

Today we'll have a full discussion of this terrible incident and I welcome that. But first, let's take a step back for a moment. Within the constraints imposed on those of us in the chain of command, I want to say a few additional words.

First, beyond abuse of prisoners, we have seen photos that depict incidents of physical violence towards prisoners – acts that may be described as blatantly sadistic, cruel, and inhuman.

Second, the individuals who took the photos took many more. The ramifications of these two facts are far reaching. Congress and the American people and the rest of the world need to know this. In addition, the photos give these incidents a vividness – indeed a horror – in the eyes of the world.

Mr. Chairman, that is why this hearing today is important. And why the actions we take in the days and weeks ahead are so important. Because however terrible the setback, this is also an occasion to demonstrate to the world the difference between those who believe in democracy and human rights and those who believe in rule by the terrorist code.

We value human life; we believe in their right to individual freedom and the rule of law.

For those beliefs we send the men and women in the armed forces abroad – to protect that right for our own people and to give millions of others who aren't Americans the hope of a future of freedom.

Part of that mission – part of what we believe in – is making sure that when wrongdoing or scandal occur that they are not covered up, but exposed, investigated, publicly disclosed – and the guilty brought to justice.

Mr. Chairman, I know you join me today in saying to the world: Judge us by our actions. Watch how Americans, watch how a democracy deals with wrongdoing and scandal and the pain of acknowledging and correcting our own mistakes and weaknesses. And then after they have seen America in action – then ask those who preach resentment and hatred of America if our behavior doesn't give the lie to the falsehood and slander they speak about our people and way of life. Ask them if the resolve of Americans in crisis and difficulty – and, yes, the heartache of acknowledging the evil in our midst – doesn't have meaning far beyond their code of hatred.

Above all, ask them if the willingness of Americans to acknowledge their own failures before humanity doesn't light the world as surely as the great ideas and beliefs that first made this nation a beacon of hope and liberty to all who strive to be free.

We know what the terrorists will do. We know they will try to exploit all that is bad to obscure all that is good. That is the nature of evil. And that is the nature of those who think they can kill innocent men, women and children to gratify their own cruel will to power.

We say to the enemies of humanity and freedom: Do your worst. Because we will strive to do our best I thank you Mr. Chairman.

QUESTIONS TO CONSIDER

1 According to Secretary of Defense Rumsfeld, who is responsible for the scandal at Abu Ghraib?
2 Who alerted the military command that abuses were taking place at Abu Ghraib?
3 What measures did the Defense Department take to ensure that no future prisoner abuse would take place?
4 Does Rumsfeld believe that the United States can overcome the damage done to its credibility in the Middle East? If so, why?
5 Would the abuses have been investigated without the existence of photographic evidence?

———————— **Document 4-D** ————————

Coalition Provisional Authority Order Number One: "De-Baathification of Iraqi Security," Coalition Provisional Authority, Baghdad, Iraq, May 16, 2003

Pursuant to my authority as Administrator of the Coalition Provisional Authority (CPA), relevant U.N. Security Council resolutions, and the laws and usages of war,

Recognizing that the Iraqi people have suffered large scale human rights abuses and depravations over many years at the hands of the Baath Party,

Noting the grave concern of Iraqi society regarding the threat posed by the continuation of Baath Party networks and personnel in the administration of Iraq, and the intimidation of the people of Iraq by Baath Party officials,

Concerned by the continuing threat to the security of the Coalition Forces posed by the Iraqi Baath Party,

I hereby promulgate the following:

Section 1 Disestablishment of the Baath Party

1) On April 16, 2003, the Coalition Provisional Authority disestablished the Baath Party of Iraq. This order implements the declaration by eliminating the party's structures and removing its leadership from positions of authority and responsibility in Iraqi society. By this means, the Coalition Provisional Authority will ensure that representative government in Iraq is not threatened by Baathist elements returning to power and that those in positions of authority in the future are acceptable to the people of Iraq.

2) Full members of the Baath Party holding the ranks of "Udw Qutriyya" (Regional Command Member), "Udw Far" (Branch Member), "Udw Shu'bah" (Section Member), and "Udw Firqah" (Group Member) (together, "Senior Party Members") are hereby removed from their positions and banned from future employment in the public sector. These Senior Party Members shall be evaluated for criminal conduct or threat to the security of the Coalition. Those suspected of criminal conduct shall be investigated and, if deemed a threat to security or a flight risk, detained or placed under house arrest.

3) Individuals holding positions in the top three layers of management in every national government ministry, affiliated corporations and other government institutions (e.g., universities and hospitals) shall be interviewed for possible affiliation with the Baath Party, and subject to investigation for criminal conduct and risk to security. Any such persons detained to be full members of the Baath Party shall be removed from their employment. This includes those and risk to security. Any such persons determined to be full members of the Baath Party shall be removed from their employment. This includes those holding the more junior ranks of "Udw" (Member) and "Udw Amil" (Active Member), as well as those determined to be Senior Party Members.

4) Displays in government buildings or public spaces of the image or likeness of Saddam Hussein or other readily identifiable members of the former regime or of symbols of the Baath Party or the former regime are hereby prohibited.
5) Rewards shall be made available for information leading to the capture of senior members of the Baath Party and individuals complicit in the crimes of the former regime.
6) The Administrator of the Coalition Provisional Authority or his designees may grant exceptions to the above guidance on a case-by-case basis.

Section 2
Entry into Force
This Order shall enter into force on the date of signature.
L. Paul Bremer, Administrator
Coalition Provisional Authority, 16 May 2003.

QUESTIONS TO CONSIDER

1   What did CPA Order Number One demand?
2   Had the United States ever presided over the decommissioning of so many officers before? What happened then? Was the ARVN decommissioning a good lesson for the CPA?
3   What options existed besides the de-Baathification of the armed forces and national security police?

Document 4-E

Excerpts from the Constitution of Iraq, October 2005, Iraqi News Agency

THE PREAMBLE
In the name of God, the most merciful, the most compassionate
We have honored the sons of Adam.
We are the people of the land between two rivers, the homeland of the apostles and prophets, abode of the virtuous imams, pioneers of civilization, crafters of writing and cradle of numeration. Upon our land the first law made by man was passed, the most ancient just pact for homelands policy was inscribed, and upon our soil, companions of the Prophet and saints prayed, philosophers and scientists theorized and writers and poets excelled.
Acknowledging God's right over us, and in fulfillment of the call of our homeland and citizens, and in response to the call of our religious and national

leaderships and the determination of our great (religious) authorities and of our leaders and reformers, and in the midst of an international support from our friends and those who love us, marched for the first time in our history toward the ballot boxes by the millions, men and women, young and old, on the thirtieth of January two thousand and five, invoking the pains of sectarian oppression sufferings inflicted by the autocratic clique and inspired by the tragedies of Iraq's martyrs, Shiite and Sunni, Arabs and Kurds and Turkmen and from all the other components of the people and recollecting the darkness of the ravage of the holy cities and the South in the Sha'abaniyya uprising and burnt by the flames of grief of the mass graves, the marshes, Al-Dujail and others and articulating the sufferings of racial oppression in the massacres of Halabcha, Barzan, Anfal and the Fayli Kurds and inspired by the ordeals of the Turkmen in Basheer and as is the case in the remaining areas of Iraq where the people of the west suffered from the assassinations of their leaders, symbols and elderly and from the displacement of their skilled individuals and from the drying out of their cultural and intellectual wells, so we sought hand in hand and shoulder to shoulder to create our new Iraq, the Iraq of the future free from sectarianism, racism, locality complex, discrimination and exclusion.

Accusations of being infidels, and terrorism did not stop us from marching forward to build a nation of law. Sectarianism and racism have not stopped us from marching together to strengthen our national unity, and to follow the path of peaceful transfer of power and adopt the course of the just distribution of resources and providing equal opportunity for all.

We the people of Iraq who have just risen from our stumble, and who are looking with confidence to the future through a republican, federal, democratic, pluralistic system, have resolved with the determination of our men, women, the elderly and youth, to respect the rules of law, to establish justice and equality to cast aside the politics of aggression, and to tend to the concerns of women and their rights, and to the elderly and their concerns, and to children and their affairs and to spread a culture of diversity and defusing terrorism.

We the people of Iraq of all components and shades have taken upon ourselves to decide freely and with our choice to unite our future and to take lessons from yesterday for tomorrow, to draft, through the values and ideals of the heavenly messages and the findings of science and man's civilization, this lasting constitution. The adherence to this constitution preserves for Iraq its free union, its people, its land and its sovereignty.

SECTION ONE: FUNDAMENTAL PRINCIPLES

Article 1:
(The Republic of Iraq is a single, independent federal state with full sovereignty. Its system of government is republican, representative 61/27Parliamentary63/47 and democratic. This Constitution is the guarantor of its unity)

Article 2:

First: Islam is the official religion of the State and it is a fundamental source of legislation:

A. No law that contradicts the established provisions of Islam may be established.
B. No law that contradicts the principles of democracy may be established.
C. No law that contradicts the rights and basic freedoms stipulated in this constitution may be established.

Second: This Constitution guarantees the Islamic identity of the majority of the Iraqi people and guarantees the full religious rights of all individuals to freedom of religious belief and practice such as Christians, Yazedis, and Mandi Sabeans.

Article 3:

(Iraq is a country of many nationalities, religions and sects and is a founding and active member of the Arab League and is committed to its covenant. Iraq is a part of the Islamic world.)

Article 4:

First: The Arabic language and Kurdish language are the two official languages of Iraq. The right of Iraqis to educate their children in their mother tongue, such as Turkmen, Syriac and Armenian, in government educational institutions in accordance with educational guidelines, or in any other language in private educational institutions, is guaranteed.

Second: The scope of the term official language and the means of applying the provisions of this article shall be defined by law which shall include:

A. Publication of the official gazette, in the two languages;
B. Speech, conversation and expression in official settings, such as the Council of Representatives, the Council of Ministers, courts, and official conferences, in either of the two languages;
C. Recognition and publication of the official documents and correspondences in the two languages;
D. Opening schools that teach the two languages, in accordance with the educational guidelines;
E. Use of both languages in any settings enjoined by the principle of equality such as bank notes, passports and stamps.

(Third: The federal institutions and agencies in the Kurdistan region shall use the Arabic and Kurdish languages.)

Fourth: The Turkmen language and Syriac language are two other official languages in the administrative units in which they represent density of population.

Fifth: Each region or governorate may adopt any other local language as an additional official language if the majority of its population so decide in a general referendum.

Article 5: The law is sovereign. The people are the source of authorities and its legitimacy, which the people shall exercise in a direct general secret ballot and through their constitutional institutions.

Article 6:
Transfer of authority shall be made peacefully through democratic means as stipulated in this Constitution.

Article 7:
First: No entity or program, under any name, may adopt racism, terrorism, the calling of others infidels, ethnic cleansing, or incite, facilitate, glorify, promote, or justify thereto, especially the Saddamist Baath in Iraq and its symbols, regardless of the name that it adopts. This may not be part of the political pluralism in Iraq. This will be organized by law.

Second: The State shall undertake combating terrorism in all its forms, and shall work to protect its territories from being a base or pathway or field for terrorist activities.

Article 8:
Iraq shall observe the principles of a good neighborliness, adhere to the principle of non-interference in the internal affairs of other states, endeavor to settle disputes by peaceful means, establish relations on the basis of mutual interests and reciprocity, and respect its international obligations.

Article 9:
First:

A. The Iraqi Armed Forces and Security Services will be composed of the components of the Iraqi people with due consideration given to its balance and its similarity without discrimination or exclusion and shall be subject to the control of the civilian authority. The Iraqi Armed Forces shall defend Iraq and shall not be used as an instrument of oppression against the Iraqi people, shall not interfere in the political affairs and shall have no role in the transfer of authority.

B. The formation of military militia outside the framework of the armed forces is prohibited.

C. The Iraqi Armed Forces and its personnel, including military personnel working at the Ministry of Defense or any subordinate departments or organizations, may not stand for election to political office, campaign for candidates, or participate in other activities prohibited by the Ministry of Defense regulations. This ban encompasses the activities of the personnel mentioned above acting in their personal or official capacities. Nothing in this Article shall infringe upon the right of these personnel to cast their vote in the elections.

D. The Iraqi National Intelligence Service shall collect information, assess threats to national security, and advise the Iraqi government. This service shall be under civilian control and shall be subject to legislative oversight and shall operate in accordance with the law and pursuant to the recognized principles of human rights.

E.   The Iraqi Government shall respect and implement Iraq's international obligations regarding the non-proliferation, non-development, non-production, and nonuse of nuclear, chemical, and biological weapons, and shall prohibit associated equipment, materiel, technologies, and delivery systems for use in the development, manufacture, production, and use of such weapons.

Second: National service will be stipulated by law.

Article 10:
The holy shrines and religious places in Iraq are religious and cultural entities. The State is committed to confirming and safeguarding their sanctity, and guaranteeing the free practice of rituals in them.

Article 11:
Baghdad is the capital of the Republic of Iraq.

Article 12:
First: The flag, national anthem, and emblem of Iraq shall be fixed by law in a way that represents the components of the Iraqi people.

Second: A law shall regulate the decorations, official holidays, religious and national occasions and the Hijri and Gregorian calendar.

Article 13:
First: This constitution is the sublime and supreme law in Iraq and shall be binding in all parts of Iraq without exception.

Second: No law shall be enacted that contradicts this constitution. Any text in any regional constitutions or any other legal text that contradicts it is deemed void.

QUESTIONS TO CONSIDER

1   What liberties and civil rights does the Constitution of Iraq guarantee? How are they enumerated?
2   What are the most important fundamental principles of the new constitution?
3   Who will make up the armed forces and the security police in the new Iraqi state? How will the make up of these security organizations be monitored?
4   Does the new constitution guarantee freedom of religion? Does it protect religious shrines?

───────────── **Document 4-F** ─────────────

Excerpts from "National Strategy for Victory in Iraq," National Security Council, November 30, 2005

Victory in Iraq is Defined in Stages

Short Term, Iraq is making steady progress in fighting terrorists, meeting political milestones, building democratic institutions, and standing up security forces.

Medium Term, Iraq is in the lead defeating terrorists and providing its own security, with a fully constitutional government in place, and on its way to achieving its economic potential.

Longer Term, Iraq is peaceful, united, stable, and secure, well integrated into the international community, and a full partner in the global war on terror.

Victory in Iraq is a Vital U.S. Interest

Iraq is the central front in the global war on terror. Failure in Iraq will embolden terrorists and expand their reach; success in Iraq will deal them a decisive and crippling blow.

The Fate of the Greater Middle East – which will have a profound and lasting impact on American security – hangs in the balance.

Failure is not an Option

Iraq would become a safe haven from which terrorists could plan attacks against America, American interests abroad, and our allies.

Middle East reformers would never again fully trust American assurances of support for democracy and human rights in the region – a historic opportunity lost.

The resultant tribal and sectarian chaos would have major consequences for American security and interests in the region.

The Enemy is Diffuse and Sophisticated

The enemy is a combination of rejectionists, Saddamists, and terrorists affiliated with or inspired by Al Qaida. Distinct but integrated strategies are required to defeat each element.

Each element shares a common short-term objective – to intimidate, terrorize, and tear down – but has separate and incompatible long-term goals.

Exploiting these differences within the enemy is a key element of our strategy.

Our Strategy for Victory is Clear

We will help the Iraqi people build a new Iraq with a constitutional, representative government that respects civil rights and has security forces sufficient to maintain domestic order and keep Iraq from becoming a safe haven for terrorists. *To achieve this end, we are pursuing an integrated strategy along three broad tracks* [italics in original], which together incorporate the efforts of the Iraqi government, the Coalition, cooperative countries in the region, the international community, and the United Nations.

The Political Track involves working to forge a broadly supported national compact for democratic governance by helping the Iraqi government:

Isolate enemy elements from those who can be won over to the political process by countering false propaganda and demonstrating to all Iraqis that they have a stake in a democratic Iraq;

Engage those outside the political process and invite those willing to turn away from the violence through ever expanding avenues of participation; and

Build stable, pluralistic, and effective national institutions that can protect the interests of all Iraqis, and facilitate Iraq's full integration into the international community.

The Security Track involves carrying out a campaign to defeat the terrorists and neutralize the insurgency, developing Iraqi security forces, and helping the Iraqi government:

Clear areas of enemy control by remaining on the offensive, killing and capturing enemy fighters and denying them safe-have;

Hold areas freed from enemy influence by ensuring that they remain under the control of the Iraqi government with an adequate Iraqi security force presence; and

Build Iraqi Security Forces and the capacity of local institutions to deliver services, advance the rule of law, and nurture civil society.

The Economic Track involves setting the foundation for a sound and self-sustaining economy by helping the Iraqi government:

Restore Iraq's infrastructure to meet increasing demand and the needs of a growing economy;

Reform Iraq's economy, which in the past has been shaped by war, dictatorship, and sanctions, so that it can be self-sustaining in the future; and

Build the capacity of Iraqi institutions to maintain infrastructure, rejoin the international economic community, and improve the general welfare of all Iraqis.

This Strategy is Integrated and its Elements are Mutually Reinforcing

Progress in each of the political, security, and economic tracks reinforces progress in the other tracks. For instance, as the political process has moved forward, terrorists have become more isolated, leading to more intelligence on security threats from Iraqi citizens, which has led to better security in previously violent areas, a more stable infrastructure, the prospect of economic progress, and expanding political participation.

Victory Will Take Time

Our strategy is working: Much has been accomplished in Iraq, including the removal of Saddam's tyranny, negotiation of an interim constitution, restoration of full sovereignty, holding free national elections, formation of elected government, drafting of a permanent constitution, ratification of that constitution, introduction of a sound currency, gradual restoration of neglected infrastructure, the ongoing training and equipping of Iraqi security forces, and the increasing capability of those forces to take on the terrorists and secure their nation.

Yet many challenges remain: Iraq is overcoming decades of a vicious tyranny, where governmental authority stemmed solely from fear, terror, and brutality. It is not realistic to expect a fully functioning democracy, able to defeat its enemies and peacefully reconcile generational grievances, to be in place less than three years after Saddam was finally removed from power.

Our comprehensive strategy will help Iraqis overcome remaining challenges, but defeating the multi-headed enemy in Iraq – and ensuring that it cannot threaten Iraq's democratic gains once we leave – requires persistent effort across many fronts.

Our Victory Strategy Is (and Must Be) Conditions Based

With resolve, victory will be achieved, although not by a date certain.

No war has ever been won on a timetable and neither will this one.

But lack of a timetable does not mean our posture in Iraq (both military and civilian) will remain static over time. As conditions change, our posture will change.

We expect, but cannot guarantee, that our force posture will change over the next year, as the political process advances and Iraqi security forces grow and gain experience.

While our military presence may become less visible, it will remain lethal and decisive, able to confront the enemy wherever it may organize.

Our mission in Iraq is to win the war. Our troops will return home when that mission is complete.

QUESTIONS TO CONSIDER

1 What were the long-term goals of the United States in Iraq? How would the Bush administration achieve them? Did the administration have enough resources to accomplish its goals?

2 How long did the president say a victory in Iraq would take?

3 What were the conditions of the U.S. victory strategy?

5

The Surge, 2006–2008

Chronology

November 2006	U.S. mid-term elections
November 2006	Rumsfeld forced to resign
January 2007	President Bush announces the surge
February 2007	General Casey replaced in Iraq
September 2007	Congressional hearings on Iraq War
April 2008	General Petraeus testifies before Congress

"We're not winning the war in Iraq," President Bush told a reporter in late December 2006, but, he added, "we're not losing."[1] The president was in a quandary over what to do next in Iraq to stop the sectarian violence and let the full impact of U.S. nation-building programs be felt by ordinary Iraqis. The November 2006 U.S. elections clearly showed that the American people no longer supported the president's war and that they demanded a dramatic change in Iraq. The mid-term elections were a sweeping victory

The United States and Iraq Since 1990: A Brief History with Documents,
First Edition. Edited by Robert K. Brigham.
© 2014 Robert K. Brigham. Published 2014 by Blackwell Publishing Ltd.

for the Democrats, who captured the House, the Senate, and a majority of governorships and state legislatures from the Republicans. Bush's approval ratings were at an all-time low, and public opinion polls showed a majority of Americans favored a U.S. withdrawal from Iraq.[2] But throughout his political career Bush had had a penchant for political survival. Just when the hour looked darkest, a previously unbending president changed the public's perception of the war in Iraq completely by embracing what is now known as "the surge."

The surge, a substantial increase in the number of combat brigades in Iraq, was born out of the desperation of a few military and national security experts who refused to accept most of the Iraq Study Group's (ISG) conclusions. In March 2006, Congress had appointed ten foreign policy experts to assess the war in Iraq and to make recommendations for its successful conclusion. Co-authored by former U.S. policymakers James Baker and Lee Hamilton, the bipartisan *Iraq Study Group Report* (see DOCUMENT 5-A) was published in early December 2006, but its contents were known months before publication. The report's main recommendations were to transition security operations to the Iraqi Security Forces (ISF), reach out to Iraq's neighbors for a diplomatic solution to the crisis, and then launch a phased withdrawal of American troops. The ISG favored General Casey's approach of increasing the number of U.S. troops in Iraq temporarily to achieve these objectives. Surge proponents believed that this was not enough to stave off defeat in Iraq. Instead of a temporary increase in the number of U.S. troops in Iraq they argued for a substantial and permanent increase in the overall number, and questioned the wisdom of transitioning security operations to the ISF. Furthermore, they vehemently opposed the notion of a phased withdrawal of U.S. troops. In fact, some surge supporters wanted a more enduring U.S. presence in the Middle East for years to come.

The *Iraq Study Group Report* differed substantially from this view. It concluded:

> The situation in Iraq is grave and deteriorating. There is no path that can guarantee success, but the prospects can be improved. In this report, we make a number of recommendations for actions to be taken in Iraq, the United States, and the region. Our most important recommendations call for new and enhanced diplomatic and political efforts in Iraq and the region, and a change in the primary mission of U.S. forces in Iraq that will enable the United States to begin to move its combat forces out of Iraq responsibly. We believe that these two recommendations are equally important and reinforce one another. If they are effectively implemented, and if the Iraqi government moves forward with national reconciliation, Iraqis will have an opportunity for a better future, terrorism will be dealt a blow, stability will be enhanced in an important part of the world, and America's credibility, interests, and values will be protected.[3]

General Casey supported most of the ISG recommendations and had already implemented several of them on his own. For Casey, providing enough security to transition responsibility to the ISF and then overseeing a phased American withdrawal was how the war would end successfully.

There were subtle distinctions between the surge and General Casey's tactics, but the Bush administration promoted the surge as a dramatic departure from current policy. In fact, General Casey had already increased U.S. troop strength in Iraq in August 2006 to "clear insurgent and militia-infested neighborhoods," and most empirical evidence suggests that the violence was actually on the decline in late 2006 before the surge.[4] Still, the president claimed that the surge was a new and bold strategy that promised to rescue victory from the jaws of defeat. The key to the surge was embedding American soldiers with Iraqi civilians to improve security, even if such a move exposed U.S. troops to greater risk. The surge also required a longer-term U.S. commitment to Iraq, because successful nation-building inside a counterinsurgency program was measured in decades, not months, or even years.

The surge had roots in the colonial counterinsurgency operations of the 1950s. Drawing heavily on the work of Sir Robert Thompson, who had played a significant role in the British campaign in Malaya, and David Galula, a French officer who had trained troops in counterinsurgency during the Algerian War, and who had been a regular participant in counterinsurgency seminars during the Kennedy years, counterinsurgency emphasized the political nature of war and the importance of improving security while building better relationships with the local population. Thompson would become a special advisor on counterinsurgency for three U.S. presidents, but it was Galula's two influential books, *Pacification in Algeria* (1962) and *Counterinsurgency Warfare* (1964), that had the most impact on the application of counterinsurgency theory in Vietnam and beyond.[5] Galula's main ideas on counterinsurgency focused on "winning over the population by a participatory approach, helping local leaders emerge through democratic means."[6] He believed that counterinsurgency conflicts were "20% combat and 80% everything else."[7] The trick was how to quickly build up the non-military aspects of counterinsurgency and to get the military to begin training its people in these "new" techniques. Galula also argued that ordinary people had to become the center of gravity for the conflict. The idea was to remove the enemy from the heart of battle through targeted and limited military strikes at its leadership infrastructure. Then, with the conflict devoid of an enemy at its core, the focus could be on building state programs that tied the population to the government. Like many of his contemporaries, Galula believed that modern insurgencies were a "mass social phenomenon," one in which the enemy "rides and manipulates a social wave consisting of genuine popular grievances."[8] The counterinsurgents were therefore required to effectively deal with "this broader social and political dynamic, while gaining time for targeted reforms to work by applying a series of tailored, full-spectrum security measures."[9] Galula warned, however, that such wars could take years, perhaps even decades, to successfully put down an insurgency.

Counterinsurgency was reborn in late 2006, as the president and others searched desperately for a plan to help the U.S. out of an intractable situation. The Iraqi civil war had turned quite violent in early 2006 and threatened to topple the Baghdad government. More than simply sectarian violence between rival religious groups – Shiites, Kurds, and Sunnis – the civil war was multidimensional and even involved outside influences. There was also a dangerous non-state element involved, al-Qaeda, making strategic and tactical predictions difficult for the U.S. military command and its allies in Baghdad. Worse still, the increasing violence had destroyed all aspects of civil society, leading to massive internal and external displacement of much of Iraq's middle class. Few professionals stayed in Iraq during these bloody years, migrating to neighboring Syria, Jordan, and even Iran. As the blood toll increased, Iraq became one of the most dangerous places on earth. Many policymakers and military leaders supported Casey's position, but the Bush administration equated the transition of security operations to the ISF and a U.S. withdrawal with ignoble surrender. Bush was delighted that a number of national security experts challenged Casey's view of the war, and even more pleased that they offered what appeared to be a dramatic shift in tactics in Iraq. A popular saying among those committed to staying the course in Iraq was "go long or go home," an acknowledgment that success came to those patient enough to see the long process of counterinsurgency unfold.

Among the leaders of this long war group was retired U.S. Army general Jack Keane, who thought a military withdrawal from Iraq was unnecessary. Keane believed that there was still a chance to save the Baghdad government from a shameful defeat. Worried that U.S. operations in Iraq were not "designed to defeat the insurgency and therefore the insurgency thrives, and the violence is growing,"[10] Keane believed that the U.S. armed forces had to use what had been successful in the past against insurgents, "proven counterinsurgency practices – and that is by protecting people and permanently isolating the insurgents from the population."[11] Keane, like David Kilcullen, an Australian expert on counterinsurgency hired by the U.S. government to help transition American forces for the long war, believed that a successful counterinsurgency program "focuses on the population, seeking to protect it from harm by – or interaction with – the insurgent, competing with the insurgent for influence and control at the grassroots level."[12] It combines smaller military operations with political programs that focus on building trust in the national government. Nation-building is an essential part of counterinsurgency, and so Keane was prepared for the long war. He was willing to extend and expand the American commitment in Iraq if the president was willing to change strategic course. Instead of strategic withdrawal, Keane favored an escalation of U.S. troops in key areas of Iraq, such as Anbar province in the west and Baghdad, and a dramatic change in operational tactics. Remembering his years in Vietnam as young army officer, Keane was advocating a pacification program similar to that used by General Abrams in the last years of the war, but different in one fundamental way. At the heart of Keane's ideas on counterinsurgency was the need to have the U.S. place civilian security above all other priorities in Iraq. One of the major problems with pacification in Vietnam had been the use of indiscriminate violence to reduce the communists' political infrastructure. This intensification of the violence countered many of the gains made by pacification under Abrams. For Iraq, Keane thought the United States had to convince ordinary Iraqis that the U.S. and its Baghdad allies were on their side.

Keane was not alone in his initial support for a surge in Iraq. Inside the beltway in Washington a host of others had grown increasingly critical of General Casey's handling of the war and had periodically called on President Bush to challenge Donald Rumsfeld's leadership at the Pentagon. One of the most outspoken critics of how the war was being fought was Fred Kagan, a former West Point history professor, who was now a senior fellow at the American Enterprise Institute, a neoconservative think-tank in Washington. Kagan thought the U.S. was right to have intervened in Iraq and he supported the promotion of democracy throughout the Middle East. He was, however, dismayed at U.S. operational tactics. According to Kagan, Iraq had reached a critical point. In a paper titled "Choosing Victory: A Plan for Success" (see DOCUMENT 5-B) he said: "The strategy of relying on a political process to eliminate the insurgency had failed and rising sectarian violence threatened to break America's will to fight. This violence will destroy the Iraqi government, armed forces, and people if it is not rapidly controlled." He believed that victory was still possible in Iraq if the United States adopted a new approach to the war "quickly and decisively." Specifically, Kagan argued that the United States had to increase its number of soldiers on the ground in Iraq and it must train Iraqi troops to secure the Iraqi population and contain the rising violence. Even though the United States had not had a population-centric approach to the war in its first three years, Kagan concluded it "must become the first priority." Kagan believed that these additional U.S. forces and a new strategy would make all the difference. He called for a "surge of seven Army brigades and Marine regiments to support clear-and-hold operations" immediately.[13] These new U.S. troops would clear Iraqi neighborhoods of insurgents and then stay behind to maintain security. The ultimate goal was to provide enough security for the Baghdad government's political programs to take root.

Kagan and Keane met secretly at the American Enterprise Institute on December 10, 2006, just one day before President Bush had agreed to meet with a handful of national security experts to discuss the war in Iraq. The goal was to give Keane, who was invited to the White House meeting, something concrete to discuss with the president. After several hours, it became clear that the Kagan–Keane group advocated increased counterinsurgency tactics in Iraq and new American military leadership in Baghdad. At the White House meeting on December 11, Keane suggested that the United States not only needed more troops in Iraq, exactly the opposite of what Rumsfeld had been arguing, but that the American military command had to use these new troops differently. Another participant, Eliot Cohen of the Johns Hopkins School for Advanced International Studies, agreed and then added that there needed to be drastic changes in the military leadership in Iraq. He concluded that the normal rotation and promotion policy had not produced the right people for this difficult job. Cohen suggested that U.S. Army general David Petraeus, who had already served two tours in Iraq, be put in charge of the entire American operation there because counterinsurgency tactics would demand a leader who was capable of adapting to the changing face of war, and he was the most promising military leader. The president did not tip his hand during the meeting, but indicated that he would take this advice under consideration.

Meanwhile, three other important actors in the development and implementation of the surge were hard at work convincing their colleagues that drastic changes were needed in Iraq. Peter Feaver, special advisor for strategic planning at the National Security Council, had been instrumental in organizing the December 11 White House meeting. He had also helped coordinate the ongoing discussions inside the White House on how to change course in Iraq, initially called "the bridge." The problem, as Feaver saw it in 2006, was that the president's Iraq War critics in Congress had concluded that the current policies were not working, that the Bush administration needed to push the Iraqi government to come together in national political reconciliation to adequately administer to the country's affairs, and that the U.S. needed to train Iraqi troops to take over the military aspects of the nation-building program from American forces. In Feaver's mind, this was precisely what the White House had been doing and this had not produced the desired results. The *Iraq Study Group Report* urged similar policy changes, which to Feaver's way of thinking were no changes at all. The report did not adequately address the deteriorating situation in Iraq, and Feaver saw no meaningful analysis in the report on the inability of Iraqi Security Forces to handle the escalating civil war. Everyone, including President Bush, had longed for the day when Iraqi forces stepped up and American forces stepped down.[14] By late 2006, it looked to many in Washington as if Baghdad's security forces were not capable of stepping up, and if the United States did not respond dramatically, the conflict would spiral out of control.

At the State Department, Philip Zelikow, counselor to Secretary of State Rice, had also supported a big military push in Iraq to secure the population and expand the political and economic modernization efforts. According to General Casey's plan for Iraq, the goal was to withdraw U.S. troops from Iraq as Sunni insurgents laid down their arms in Anbar province and Baghdad to give the newly elected government a chance to succeed on its own. Casey grew increasingly worried that the United States would be seen as an occupier if it stayed on in Iraq indefinitely. "It has always been my view," Casey reported in early 2006, "that a heavy and sustained American military presence was not going to solve the problems in Iraq over the long term."[15] Accordingly, Casey had planned to decrease the number of American combat brigades from fourteen to twelve by September 2006, and then to ten by December if conditions allowed. If the ISF continued to assume more responsibility for Iraqi security, the U.S could reduce its overall presence to five or six combat brigades by December 2007, Casey claimed. Casey was clear, however, that no transfer of responsibility could happen until the ISF was ready for the increased responsibility, and it was clear to Casey in 2006 that the ISF was not ready to assume this burden. Casey's August increase in U.S. troop strength in Iraq was evidence of his belief that the ISF could not combat sectarian violence effectively. But Zelikow saw several problems with Casey's strategy. For one, the number of ISF troops never reached their promised target levels. Of the six Iraqi battalions promised for security operations in and around Baghdad, only two ever materialized. Furthermore, Zelikow warned, the insurgency had created a "strategic void" in Iraq that had allowed the increased violence to grow unchecked. Something had to be done to improve internal security in Iraq, or all that the administration had worked for would be lost. Casey's incremental increase in U.S. troop strength in Iraq in August 2006 was a welcome change, but it did not go far enough, according to Zelikow, and others in the Bush administration believed that the American public needed to believe dramatic change in Iraq was underway.

This was also the view of U.S. Army general Ray Odierno, who was responsible for the day-to-day U.S. military operations in Iraq. General Odierno had come to believe that the American strategy in Iraq was not addressing the fundamental problems facing ordinary Iraqis in 2006, and that the ISF was not capable of providing enough security for the government's programs to find success. He began to hear of others in Iraq and Washington, like Feaver and Zelikow, who favored the introduction of new American troops to provide this security, coupled with a change in leadership and tactics. Odierno had grown increasingly convinced that General Casey's strategy in Iraq was not working. He feared that Casey had become too associated with incrementalism and retreat from Baghdad, even if that was not Casey's intended plan. The perception was certainly in the public's mind that Casey was, like General Westmoreland in Vietnam, tied to a set of tactics that were not working. By late summer 2006, Odierno had begun to openly criticize Casey and the idea of transitioning military responsibilities to the ISF. He too believed that such a move was premature and that the Iraqi troops were simply overmatched by the level and pace of sectarian and other forms of violence. Unlike many others in the American military, Odierno believed that the ISF was capable of providing security if fully supported by American troops until the violence was stabilized. It was a complicated mixture of strategic and tactical concerns that led Odierno to support the concept of an increased counterinsurgency effort in Iraq underpinned by an increase in American troop levels. Once he went public with his concerns, Odierno was surprised to find that there was considerable support for his views among other military leaders and that the political momentum in Washington might make the surge possible.

A Change in Tactics

In an ironic twist, the 2006 mid-term elections that brought several new congressional seats to the Democratic Party also allowed the president to suggest that the war was not going as well he and several others in his administration had been saying all along. The American public had grown tired of the war long ago, and it seemed that the 2006 election was a mandate for change in Iraq. While most political pundits considered change to mean an American withdrawal, the Bush administration was determined to define change in a different way. Embracing the surge meant that Bush could no longer continue the war with his current defense policy team in place. A dramatic change in tactics, as the surge was billed, required new and bold leadership to be realized. Rumsfeld and Casey had to be replaced by defense experts willing to embrace the surge and all that it promised.

In November 2006, following the mid-term elections, President Bush forced Rumsfeld to resign. Because of his inability to address the major problems in Iraq or make appropriate adjustments in personnel and tactics, Rumsfeld was seen by many in Washington as a major obstacle to success. When reviewing strategic alternatives throughout 2006, the one constant for security experts inside and outside of government was that Rumsfeld had to be replaced. With Rumsfeld gone, Bush could divorce himself from the controversial secretary of defense and claim to be making a dramatic departure from past policies in Iraq. Bush was also concerned about General Casey. The general, fairly or unfairly, had been tarnished by the war's trajectory, and Bush could no longer afford to have him at the helm of U.S.

defense policy in Iraq. During the 2006 review, the two names that continued to surface were General David Petraeus and Robert Gates.

Gates had been in government for forty years, first in the Central Intelligence Agency, where he had climbed the ranks from junior officer to
director, and then as George H.W. Bush's deputy national security advisor.
Gates was vastly different from his predecessor at the Pentagon in some
fundamental ways. For one, he had always had a good working relationship
with Congress. For another, the new secretary of defense was not one to
get bogged down in the minutiae of policy decisions. He was a bold thinker
and his record was one of dramatic action. While Rumsfeld tended to
discipline subordinates routinely for their failings, the soft-spoken Gates
delegated authority to those around him and then supported their decisions
inside the administration. Gates was also known for having a good working
relationship with Democrats, a throwback to the days when foreign policy
was not so polarized. Gates was the perfect choice for the political requirements of the job, Bush thought. Almost everyone knew that General Petraeus
would be given the opportunity to shape the surge, and that he would
ultimately be ordered to go to Baghdad to implement it. General Casey was
pushed upstairs to army chief of staff, paving the way for Petraeus and
Odierno to oversee the next phase of the Iraq War, one promoted by the
Bush White House as vastly different from the transitioning strategy Casey
had been planning.

Petraeus was the obvious choice because of his role in the creation of
the U.S. Army/Marines new counterinsurgency manual (see DOCUMENT
5-C). In early 2006, after two tours in Iraq, Petraeus had been sent to Fort
Leavenworth, to oversee the development of the new manual. From this
vantage point, he was on the front line of discussions favoring staying the
course in Iraq. Although he dismissed the assignment at first, Petraeus grew
to see its importance in changing the geometry in Iraq. In February, he
gathered over one hundred military officers, strategic thinkers, policymakers, academics, and human rights activists under the direction of his West
Point classmate, Conrad Crane. Crane was a retired U.S. Army officer, who
now directed the Military History Institute in Carlisle, Pennsylvania. Like
many others, Crane had feared that U.S. policy in Iraq was focusing on the
wrong problems, but that it might be too late to change course. Focusing
on future wars that all agreed would be irregular conflicts, Crane and those
assembled favored a population-centric counterinsurgency strategy for
potential conflicts. For three days, those at Fort Leavenworth discussed the
value of adopting a counterinsurgency approach to war that put civilian
protection and security first. The new manual, FM 3-24, reflected that
belief. The general strategic concept of FM 3-24 is to "adopt a population
centered approach instead of one focused primarily, if not exclusively, on
the insurgents. The latter approach concentrates on physically destroying

the unseen opponent embedded in the general population,"[16] while the preferred course of action is to secure the civilian population.

While the manual was not written specifically for Iraq, supporters of FM 3-24 nonetheless argued that it was a dramatic departure from the strategies employed by General Casey. They suggested that Casey's command had placed too much emphasis on transitioning responsibility to the ISF and not enough on protecting civilians and building bridges from the Baghdad government to the general population.[17] This latter goal would be accomplished by moving away from General Casey's Forward Operating Bases – where U.S. troops reportedly hunkered down at night behind high cement walls after big-unit patrols in hostile neighborhoods during the day – and toward hundreds of combat outposts and joint security sites (JSS) that placed American soldiers among the population they were now trying to protect. With increased security, the Baghdad government could then show national energy and resolve through a host of modernization projects, ultimately allowing the government to assume full responsibility for the public welfare. Though this description of Casey's tactics in Iraq is incomplete, it was the dominant view of many security experts in Washington.

Bush used the Gates appointment to announce the surge. In a solemn speech to the nation from the White House library on January 10, 2007 (see DOCUMENT 5-E), President Bush accepted full responsibility for the conduct of the war and admitted that too many mistakes had been made in Iraq. He declared, "The situation in Iraq is unacceptable to the American people, and it is unacceptable to me. Our troops in Iraq have fought bravely. They have done everything we have asked them to do. Where mistakes have been made, the responsibility rests with me." Bush then spoke the words that many had been hoping to hear for so long, "It is clear we need to change our strategy in Iraq." The president outlined the comprehensive review that had taken place inside his administration and told the nation that he had also "consulted members of Congress from both parties, allies abroad, and distinguished outside experts." Bush then listed his administration's new priorities in Iraq, and at the top of the list was improved security, especially near Baghdad. The president explained, "eighty percent of Iraq's sectarian violence occurs within 30 miles of the capital. This violence is splitting Baghdad into sectarian enclaves and shaking the confidence of all Iraqis." In the past, U.S. and Iraqi efforts to secure the population had failed, Bush argued, because "there were not enough Iraqi and American troops to secure neighborhoods that had been cleared of terrorists and insurgents, and there were too many restrictions on the troops we did have." To remedy this situation, the Iraqi government was making a renewed commitment to internal security by deploying additional Iraqi brigades across Baghdad's nine districts. But this was not enough. The president argued that for the Iraqis to succeed, they "will need our help." Accordingly, he committed to "increasing American force levels" to more than "20,000 additional American troops to Iraq." Bush concluded his explanation of the surge by stating clearly, "Our troops will have a well-defined mission: to help Iraqis clear and secure neighborhoods, to help them protect the local population, and to help ensure that the Iraqi forces left behind are capable of providing the security that Baghdad needs."[18]

Some listening to the president believed that this was just another empty promise from the man who, only one year earlier, had also assured the American people that he had "a strategy for victory in Iraq." The original plan, championed by General Casey and supported by Rumsfeld, had called for turning over responsibility for security to the ISF, shrinking the number of American bases, and launching the phased withdrawal of American troops, when the ISF and Baghdad were ready. The perceived failure of that plan to stop the sectarian violence in Iraq had led to Casey's removal and Rumsfeld's resignation. Now, one year later, the president was announcing yet another plan to secure victory in Iraq by ending the sectarian violence and shoring up the Baghdad government, but this time through the introduction of new American ground troops. Those not intimately involved in the strategic review of American policy in Iraq that occurred throughout 2006 were dismayed at the president's pessimism on the one hand and unbridled confidence in the surge on the other. But by September 2006 it had become clear to many in Washington that Bush was no longer interested in the Casey and Rumsfeld plan. He regularly dismissed those who called for a "graceful exit" in Iraq, as some suggested the *Iraq Study Group Report* had, and instead urged military leaders at the Pentagon to come up with a plan on "how we're going to win" in Iraq, and "not how we're going to leave."[19] The president had never felt comfortable with the Iraq Study Group findings, which had also called for increased ISF action and a limited American withdrawal from Baghdad and its surrounding areas. The report had also hinted at the need to "increase the number of U.S. military personnel, including combat troops, imbedded in and supporting Iraqi Army units," but only until the Iraqi army increased its size and capabilities.[20] The surge, with its long-term commitment to Baghdad and its enhanced counterinsurgency tactics, appealed far more to the president's sensibilities than any of the previous plans. Bush was now in his element, talking enthusiastically about the surge and its possibilities to all who would listen.

The State Department was also more confident about prospects in Iraq once the surge was launched. On January 11, a day after the president had announced the surge from the White House, Secretary of State Condoleezza Rice spoke of the new political, economic, and diplomatic initiatives in Iraq that would accompany the increased U.S. troops. Rice promised that the United States would show new resolve in trying to build a host of programs in Iraq to aid the Baghdad government in rebuilding its political and economic infrastructure. Hinting that the nation-building efforts had produced little to date, Rice proclaimed the formation of new provincial reconstruction teams (PRTs) to aid in the development of governmental programs aimed at improving the lives of ordinary Iraqis. Sensing correctly that the new counterinsurgency plan was dependent upon the political side of war for success, Rice suggested that the new PRTs would be the backbone of a renewed civil society in Iraq, one based on mutual respect and inclusion. Focusing on the transition from war to civil society would be the responsibility of the newly created coordinator for Iraq transitional assistance. It was clear that Rice had long felt overshadowed in the administration by Rumsfeld and Cheney, but now the surge required as much work from State as from Defense. Counterinsurgency depended upon the ability of the Baghdad government to provide for the public welfare of ordinary Iraqis, and it was civilians in the State Department who were responsible for helping Baghdad adopt measures to that end. Rice, like President Bush, believed that American power could transform entire societies. She had supported the promotion of democracy throughout the Middle East, but by mid-2006 she too had come to the conclusion that the Casey–Rumsfeld plan was not employing that right tactics to achieve that lofty objective in Iraq. By supporting the surge, Rice joined others in the administration seeking to erase the memories of the failed nation-building efforts immediately following the March 2003 American invasion and replace them with the less ambitious goals of the surge. Furthermore, because of the political nature of war inside a counterinsurgency program, the State Department was elevated in importance following years of neglect. As the surge was announced, therefore, all the new pieces of the American strategy in Iraq were coming together. A new military commander, a new secretary of defense, renewed activity at the State Department, joined with the president's fresh optimism about Iraq.

One of the intended benefits of the surge was that it also called on the Iraqi government to increase its commitment to rebuilding the nation through democracy and federalism. The Bush administration had been unable to pressure the Baghdad government to make needed reforms under the old security system, and many thought that an enhanced counterinsurgency program would force the Maliki government to assume more responsibility. The surge required Baghdad to recast its security operations by focusing on the civilian population. Many in the Bush administration hoped that this change in posture would foster better relations between the Maliki government and the Sunni and Kurdish minorities. Interestingly, following its own internal reviews, the Maliki government concluded, in a paper titled "Iraq First" (see DOCUMENT 5-D), that Iraq's current problems were the result of: "The previous regime's policy of minimizing the legitimate roles of government institutions," which:

led to their collapse after the collapse of the Head of the Government. All this resulted in significant difficulties and conditions that permitted the growth of corruption and organized crime, especially as the result of the lack of security that followed the collapse of the previous regime. These difficulties came simultaneously with the rise of people's expectations for immediate improvement in all aspects of life.[21]

The government would redouble its efforts, therefore, to provide for the public welfare by ending corruption in the nation-building program, and at the same time improve relations with Sunnis and Kurds. To achieve these goals, the ISF would embrace the enhanced counterinsurgency tactics as well, with their focus on the civilian population. In the paper's national security assessment, the Maliki government pledged to change the course of the war by making dramatic changes to its security operations:

> The size and composition of Iraq's Security Forces are based on defeating the identified threats within Iraq's strategic environment. As the first priority in the current period, Iraq's Joint Forces will focus on defeat of terrorism and insurgency as their primary mission, with other threats accorded a lesser priority to the extent that available resources permit. In this current period, Iraq's Joint Forces will achieve self reliance such that only minimal external assistance and support are needed for accomplishing the primary mission. As Iraq's security is reestablished and the terrorist and insurgency threats abate, Iraq's Joint Forces will transition to a conventional defensive posture for ensuring the security of the nation and its territory in conjunction with regional and international security arrangements. Likewise, Iraq's Police and Border Enforcement Forces will transition to conventional maintenance of domestic law and order and maintaining the integrity of Iraq's borders. Iraq's police forces will focus on local police self-reliance except in emergency situations that require reinforcement by National Police or the Iraqi Joint Forces. The capabilities of Iraq's Joint Forces will be such that they do not by their size or capabilities appear as threatening to Iraq's neighbors.

It now seems clear that Maliki embraced the surge to continue American support. Problems would remain in the ISF throughout the surge, and without major reform in Baghdad there was little hope of ending the sectarian violence that threatened to tear Iraq apart.

Surging in Iraq

Shortly after the surge began, report after report concluded that security had increased dramatically following the introduction of surge troops and that sectarian violence was down considerably.[22] Toby Dodge, an expert on Iraq, agreed. In a 2007 interview with *Foreign Policy*, Dodge explained,

"General Petraeus had some undoubted successes to sell. There has been a ferocious debate about the metrics and certainly August is an odd month because of the intensity of the heat, so conflict tends to drop off a bit. However, I think violence has undoubtedly dropped off compared to 2006. Iraq, especially Baghdad, was in the midst of a civil war in 2006. In 2007, the surge has stopped or put a pause on that civil war."[23] Many inside the Bush administration believed that the surge showed Iraqis that the United States would see this project through, raising the hopes of even the most skeptical members of the Baghdad government. The additional U.S. troops were all that was needed to increase security in key areas of Iraq such as Anbar province and in and around Baghdad, supporters of the surge claimed, and many wondered why the president had not moved in this direction earlier. According to two popular Iraqi bloggers with a large following in the United States, Mohammed and Omar Fadhil, the surge resembled the old clear-and-hold strategy employed by General Abrams in Vietnam. People in Iraq, they claimed, had been waiting for the United States to commit the resources needed for the "hold" to materialize. The plan to secure Baghdad, according to the Fadhils, was "becoming stricter and gaining momentum by the day as more troops pour[ed] into the city, allowing for better implementation of the clear-and-hold strategy."[24] Others have suggested that the surge's initial victory was psychological. Enemies of the Baghdad government went into hiding, believing additional U.S. troops made it impossible for their militant groups to operate freely. The number of security tips about insurgent operations increased dramatically following the surge.

Other significant evidence of the surge's success was highlighted by the administration throughout the spring and summer of 2007. Perhaps the most important among these was the "turning" of the Sunnis in Anbar province and areas near Baghdad where the level of sectarian violence was highest. Beginning in mid-2006 in Ramadi (actually before the surge), the center of government in Anbar province some 110 kilometers from Baghdad, U.S. commanders made the decision to try to employ Sunni insurgents as irregular militias in battles against al-Qaeda in Iraq (AQI). The feeling among the U.S. leadership was that AQI had gone too far in its program of violence, and as a result had alienated many of its former tribal supporters. Organized first as Awakening Councils, then as Local Citizens Councils, eventually these former Sunni insurgents called themselves the Sons of Iraq. The U.S. command "turned" these insurgents away from direct attacks against U.S. troops and toward helping defeat AQI through the payment of large sums of money. Each new recruit was given upward of $300 per month, a significant sum in rural Iraq, to fight AQI instead of Americans or the Baghdad government.[25] Naturally, it was a great risk to employ and arm those who just weeks before had tried desperately to kill American troops and overthrow the Baghdad government. But, many in the U.S. command thought the risk was well worth it given how violent Iraq had become in 2006. And there is a certain amount of theoretical support for such a move inside a broad-based counterinsurgency program. FM 3-24 moved beyond the "people's war" framework of classic counterinsurgency, where the population naturally sided with the government once the insurgents were removed from the scene, and toward a more sophisticated approach that took the organizational structure of traditional societies into account. Using social scientific thinking, the developers of FM 3-24 recognized the power of local and regional networks of people, understanding correctly that traditional populations were often organized along complex layers of local and regional structures. This was clearly the thinking in Ramadi and the rest of Anbar province when U.S. military leaders went to tribal leaders first to "turn" Sunni insurgents.

Supporters of the surge also thought it was responsible for reducing sectarian violence in Iraq because it convinced key Shiite leaders, such as Muqtada al-Sadr, that it would be foolish to wage war against the Sunni minority and other Shiite factions in the face of increased U.S. troops. In the spring and summer of 2007, various Shiite militias attacked each other throughout southern Iraq and in eastern Baghdad. Some were rogue elements of al-Sadr's Mahdi Army, while others were younger militants who had grown too restless to control. In a surprise move, the Baghdad government moved quickly to stop the violence, even using ISF forces against fellow Shiites to stem the tide of the fighting. Some ISF troops were fighting against their compatriots inside the various Shiite militias. Following this flurry of violence, in August 2007, al-Sadr's forces were involved in a series of attacks against another Shiite group, the Badr Corps, in the holy city of Karbala. Sensing an opportunity and a problem with the Karbala street fighting, al-Sadr decided to announce a "freeze" on the Mahdi Army's military activities. He believed that, by standing down, he could take full control of the subnational Shiite movement with the blessing of the United States and the full support of the Baghdad government. Surge troops would have made his life more difficult if he had decided to continue his attacks against Sunnis, and infighting among Shiite militias could allow the Sunnis back into Baghdad through the back door now held open by the United States. By standing down, al-Sadr elevated his political position among fellow Shiites who wanted revenge against Sunnis for years of brutality, but who also wanted an end to the day-to-day violence propped up by the U.S. counterinsurgency program. By repoliticizing his movement, something even General Petraeus recognized when he called al-Sadr a proud son of Mohammed,[26] al-Sadr moved toward his long-term goal of supreme subnational power. Some in the U.S., most notably the National Security staff, saw al-Sadr's freeze as a clear sign that the surge presented him with too many military problems and that he had thrown his power behind the Baghdad government.

Domestic Critics of the Surge

But escalation also aroused widespread criticism. Several early supporters of the war now questioned the efficacy of the surge and the continued U.S. commitment to the Maliki government. Eugene Robinson of the *Washington Post* called the president's new policy a "fantasy-based escalation . . . which could only make sense in some parallel universe where pigs fly and fish commute on bicycles." Former U.S. ambassador to Croatia, Peter Galbraith, suggested that Bush had embraced a strategy that has "no chance of actually working." *Time Magazine's* Joe Klein called the surge "Bush's futile pipe dream," while *Los Angeles Times* reporter Jonathan Chait warned that he found "something genuinely bizarre" about those who supported the surge. "It is not just that they are wrong . . . It's that they are completely detached from reality."[27] Some even suggested that the surge was too little too late and that the United States had already in fact lost the war. Many intellectuals, who had supported the 2003 invasion of Iraq on human rights grounds, now rejected the president's policies. Michael Ignatieff, a founding member of the Carr Center for Human Rights at Harvard and now deputy leader of Canada's Liberal Party, used the pages of the *New York Times Magazine* to apologize for his earlier convictions in an essay titled "Getting Iraq Wrong: What the War Has Taught Me about Political Judgment." Ignatieff wrote, "The unfolding catastrophe in Iraq had condemned the political judgment of a President. But it has also condemned the judgment of many others, myself included, who as commentators supported the [2003] invasion. Many of us believed, as an Iraqi exile friend told me the night the war started, that it was the only chance members of his generation would have to live in freedom in their own country. How distant a dream that new seems."[28] Echoing Ignatieff's general sentiments, the *New York Times* editorialized that the time had come "for the United States to leave Iraq, without any more delay than the Pentagon needs to organize an orderly exit."[29]

In Congress, key Democrats opposed the surge, calling it a tragic mistake. Exactly one week after the president announced the surge, a formal resolution of opposition to President Bush's build-up of troops in Iraq emerged. The resolution concluded, "it is not in the national interest of the United States to deepen its military involvement in Iraq." It also demanded that an "appropriately expedited timeline" for transfer of internal security duties to the ISF, and it backed the Iraq Study Group's recommendation for regional diplomatic efforts to end the crisis.[30] But even before the resolution could be introduced in Congress, a host of powerful U.S. senators drafted a separate measure that proposed to cut funding for the war and "legislatively thwart Bush's surge of 21,500 additional troops."[31] Several members of the Senate Armed Services Committee and Senate Foreign Relations Committee, including Joseph Biden (D-Delaware), Chuck Hagel (R-Nebraska), and Hillary Clinton (D-New York), joined Olympia Snow (R-Maine) and others in opposition to the surge. "I will do everything I can to stop the president's policy," Hagel claimed, "I think it is dangerous and irresponsible."[32] In the weeks that followed, a host of presidential aspirants in Congress introduced similar measures. Christopher Dodd of Connecticut proposed a bill that would force the president to get congressional authorization before any additional troop deployments could be made to Iraq.[33] Senator Edward Kennedy (D-Massachusetts) proposed a bill that would require congressional authorization before any money could be spent on additional troops. Several members of the House demanded that the president be forced to seek new authorization for funding and troops every six months, and others still called for a new convention to strengthen the War Powers Act.[34]

One of the most powerful voices of protest came from presidential hopeful Barack Obama (D-Illinois), who had grown increasingly critical of the war in Iraq. In remarks before the Chicago Council on Global Affairs on April 23, 2007 (see DOCUMENT 5-E), Obama declared, "the president's escalation of U.S. forces may bring a temporary reduction in the violence in Baghdad, at the price of increased American causalities . . . but it cannot change the political dynamic in Iraq. A phased withdrawal can."[35] Indeed, Obama tied his entire political fortune to his opposition to the war, claiming that he would pressure the warring factions in Iraq toward a political settlement and launch a phased withdrawal of American forces with the goal of removing all combat brigades from Iraq by March 31, 2008. That date coincided with the New Hampshire primary, and Obama clearly had his eye on the political calendar as he made his remarks known to increasing crowds across America.

But perhaps the most damaging blow to the president was John Warner's non-binding resolution expressing the sense of Congress on Iraq and openly opposing the surge. Warner, a Virginia Republican, had served on the Senate Armed Services Committee for years. A navy and Marine veteran, Warner often spoke with authority on military issues, and was known to take independent positions, such as supporting gun control laws, quite frequently. Following the president's January 10 White House address, Warner co-sponsored a concurrent resolution stating strong opposition to the surge. Warner argued that every senior military commander in Iraq thought the surge was a bad idea. He quoted heavily from the testimony of U.S. Central Command commander, General John Abizaid, who testified before Congress in November 2006, "I have met with every divisional commander, General Casey, the Corps Commander, and General Dempsey. We all talked together. And I said, in your professional opinion, if we were to bring in more American troops now, does it add considerably to our ability to achieve success in Iraq? And they all said no."[36] Warner agreed with Iraqi prime minister Nouri al-Maliki, who believed that "the crisis is political, and the ones who can stop the cycle of aggravation and bloodletting of innocents are the politicians."[37] Warner's resolution, like many others, failed to get the majority needed for passage. One month later, in February 2007, Warner continued his outspoken opposition to the surge by crossing the aisle as one of seven Republicans to vote in favor of cloture on a nonbinding resolution opposing the troop surge. The measure failed 56–34.

Warner remained an outspoken critic of the surge throughout the summer of 2007. In July, he joined Senator Richard Lugar (R-Indiana), to introduce an amendment to the 2008 defense budget that would require the Bush administration to give congressional leaders a clear exit strategy from Iraq within three months. Warner saw this latest resolution as a "third path," between House Speaker Nancy Pelosi's efforts to get an immediate troop withdrawal and those who wanted to support the surge through ongoing legislation. The Warner–Lugar amendment gave the administration until the mandated September 2007 report to Congress to show significant progress in Iraq or produce an alternative strategy to the surge. The amendment forced the president to provide Congress with a plan for the redeployment of U.S. forces in Iraq and a change in their mission. The measure also called for a new National Intelligence Estimate focused on the surge and political progress in Iraq. This amendment also failed. Increasingly frustrated by the war and the president's insistence that the surge was working, Warner eventually called on Bush to begin a phased troop withdrawal by the end of 2007. Warner made this announcement shortly after returning from a lengthy trip to the Middle East, where he grew increasingly convinced that U.S. policy was adrift.

Despite high-profile critics like Warner, Congress could not muster the votes necessary for a binding resolution opposing the surge. What it could do, however, was require the Bush administration to include benchmarks for the Iraqi government in congressional legislation needed to authorize the troop increases. President Bush eventually signed this legislation in May 2007. A strict requirement for congressional support for the surge, therefore, was a series of mid-year assessments on Iraq. The first came in July 2007. The White House reported that significant progress had been made on a number of fronts, but that it was too soon after the surge to measure its impact on the political situation inside Iraq, something the new counterinsurgency strategy was designed to change. In September 2007, General Petraeus, now in full command in Iraq, and U.S. ambassador to Iraq Ryan

Crocker, gave their required reports to Congress. General Petraeus presented a slightly positive assessment of the surge during the hearings, despite the appearance of a full-page ad in the *New York Times* the day of his testimony claiming that he had betrayed the American people. Petraeus ignored this criticism, suggesting during his comments that American troops and their Iraqi counterparts had significantly increased security in key areas of Baghdad and Anbar province and had "dealt numerous blows to al-Qaeda in Iraq."[38] He claimed that "the security situation in Iraq is improving, Iraqi elements are slowly taking on more of the responsibility for protecting their citizens." He concluded, "Coalition and Iraqi security forces have made progress toward achieving security. As a result, the United States will be in a position to reduce its forces in Iraq in the months ahead."[39] Ambassador Crocker concurred, suggesting that it was impossible to give a timeline for withdrawal, but that he was generally optimistic that the new strategy had produced some needed changes in Iraq already. Crocker believed "a secure, stable, democratic Iraq at peace with its neighbors is attainable."[40]

Members of Congress could hardly contain themselves. In an atmosphere reminiscent of hearings during the Vietnam War, key members of Congress lined up to criticize Petraeus and Crocker's optimistic reporting on Iraq. Senator Joseph Biden (D-Delaware), chairman of the Foreign Relations Committee, began his panel's session suggesting that the surge had been designed to create the space and time needed in Iraq for a political breakthrough in Baghdad and that this simply had not happened. "It's time to turn the corner, in my view . . . We should stop the surge and start bringing our troops home."[41] House member Tom Lantos (D-California) argued that the Government Accountability Office (GAO), which had been charged with measuring progress on congressional benchmarks, had issued a report in late August, claiming that the Baghdad government failed to meet fifteen of the eighteen U.S. targets. According to the report, "Key legislation has not been passed in Iraq, violence remains high, and it is unclear whether the Iraqi government will spend $10 billion of reconstruction funds as promised."[42] Lantos also pointed to a highly skeptical report issued by retired Marine Corps general James L. Jones, who had been charged by Congress with investigating progress in Iraq. "No amount of charts and statistics will improve its [the administration's Iraq policy] credibility," Lantos declared in the hearings.[43] Other members of Congress pointed to a State Department report claiming that religious freedom in Iraq had deteriorated sharply during the past year. Many members of Congress believed that this was most significant because it tested the Baghdad government's ability and willingness to bring Sunnis and Kurds into national political life. There were other concerns. Some in Congress suggested that human rights abuses seemed to be on the rise in Iraq following the surge, not decreasing as the president and others had predicted. The refugee crisis, long an issue in

Iraq, was still a main obstacle facing the Baghdad government, and for many in Congress it was a key measuring stick of progress in Iraq. Since the surge began, little progress had been made on bringing Iraq's estimated 2.2 million refugees home or improving the lives of the roughly 1.6 million Iraqis who were internally displaced.[44] Since many of the refugees were Sunnis, congressional leaders simply thought of the crisis as further proof that Baghdad had no interest in a government of national reconciliation.

The most heated comments, however, came from Senator Hillary Clinton of New York, a likely Democratic presidential candidate in 2008. Late in the hearings, she cast doubt on all that Petraeus had to say: "you have been made the de facto spokesman for what many of us believe to be a failed policy. I think the reports you provide us really require the willing suspension of disbelief." She went on to make obvious reference to Robert McNamara, Kennedy's and Johnson's secretary of defense, who routinely gave progress reports to Congress during the Vietnam War using charts, graphs, and statistics. "Although the charts tell part of the story, I don't think they tell the whole story," Senator Clinton warned. She said the "bottom-up" political reconciliation in Baghdad was at best "anecdotal," and then correctly pointed out that the turning of Sunnis in Anbar province, the most visible sign of surge success, had started well before the surge began. At the end of her remarks, Senator Clinton suggested that there was a lack of clarity in the general's response to earlier questions about American troop levels and political progress in Baghdad, hinting that Petraeus had been purposefully vague. She pressed, "Don't you think the American people deserve a very specific answer about what is expected from our country in the face of the failure of the Iraqi government and its failure to achieve its political agenda?" General Petraeus looked irritated, but responded calmly. "I don't see quite as big a difference as you do," he said. "I would be very hard pressed at that time to recommend a continuation of our current troop levels" if conditions on the ground were the same in a year as they are now. He added that Senator Clinton's question was "quite a bit hypothetical."[45] There was a tinge of politics in Petraeus' response, for he clearly understood that the next president of the United States would most likely come from the Senate Foreign Relations Committee.

There were other powerful voices casting doubt on the surge's success, some from within the military's own ranks. By the fall of 2007, a small group of army officers with command experience in Iraq began to speak out against the surge and the way the new counterinsurgency manual had influenced strategic decisions. They were also concerned about the lack of political development within Iraq and feared that the surge only masked the real problems in Baghdad. They pointed to what they thought was a major weakness in the strategy, the use of "turned" Sunnis to fight AQI.

Colonel Gian Gentile, a West Point history professor with two tours of command in Iraq, represented this group of skeptics well. He called the deals with the Sunni insurgents "cash for cooperation."[46] He suggested that Sunni tribal leaders could turn support for the U.S. program "off" and "on" as conditions on the ground dictated. He believed that paying off these Awakening groups was bad policy because it was unsustainable and unpredictable. Worse yet, what if the Sunnis were cooperating with the U.S. against AQI only to buy time and support against their Shiite rivals? Had the Sunnis "really sided with us? Or, are they siding with their own side and using us and our money to prepare for a bigger fight down the road they know is coming?"[47] In other words, were all sides standing down during the surge only to begin the real civil war once the United States withdrew from Iraq? Others agreed with Gentile. During one meeting with the president, retired U.S. Army general Barry McCaffrey suggested that the "surge is a fool's errand. Yes, it will have short-term impact. But it isn't sustainable."[48]

The administration moved quickly to counter its critics. The president invited dissident members of Congress and newspaper editors in for hour-long sessions on the surge and its intended benefits. He also launched his own public relations campaign to increase support for the new plan. In June 2007, in a speech at the Naval War College in Newport, Rhode Island, Bush mentioned that coalition forces are going into areas such as Anbar and Ramadi "where they couldn't operate before," and they're driving al-Qaeda out of those areas. On the ground, our forces can see the difference the surge is making." Bush said. He quoted General Petraeus as describing "astonishing signs of normalcy" in Baghdad. Bush concluded that Petraeus was executing a "well-conceived plan," developed by "smart military people."[49] Two months later, during a tour in Asia, Bush met with Australian prime minister John Howard, who assured the president that Australia supported the surge and would continue to keeps its coalition forces in Iraq until the political situation in Baghdad had been turned around completely. Outside of Tony Blair, Howard had been one of the president's most vital supporters. And Bush also had the support of a growing number of security experts who believed counterinsurgency tactics promised the best success in the Iraq War and probably for some time to come, including David Kilcullen, who had replaced David Galula as the modern-day international expert on counterinsurgency.[50] Fred Kagan, one of the initial architects of the surge, repeatedly reported that the increase in American troops and the mission change in Iraq had allowed the United States to win "an important battle in the war on terror."[51] Kagan pointed out that "terrorist operations in and around Baghdad have dropped by 59 percent. Car bomb deaths are down by 81 percent. Casualties from enemy attacks dropped 77 percent."[52]

Kagan was no doubt correct that the violence had subsided, but it had been in a steady decline since late 2006, before the surge began. Even as the violence decreased, Petraeus and his command remained cautious. The general was careful not to make any bold claims: "Nobody says anything about turning a corner, seeing lights at the end of tunnels, any of those phrases," he told journalists in early December 2007. "There's nobody in uniform who is doing victory dances in the end zone."[53] Still, events on the ground, especially the decreasing violence, had had a dramatic impact on public opinion. Almost from the beginning, the public responded positively to the surge. When the surge began in early January 2007, 71 percent of Americans believed the war was going badly. By September 2007, however, a nationwide Pew survey found "a striking rise in public optimism about the situation in Iraq." Nearly 60 percent of those polled now believed that war was going well and the same percentage thought the United States would achieve its objectives in Iraq.[54]

Public perceptions of the surge had also changed the character of politics in Washington. In early 2008, a presidential election year, the White House reported that "the surge is working . . . overall violence is Iraq is down significantly . . . civilian deaths are down . . . sectarian killings are down."[55] Such optimistic statements had been issued every month since the March 2003 invasion, but by early 2008 the American public believed them for the first time, and so did many of their representatives in Washington. When General Petraeus appeared before Congress in April 2008 suggesting that American troops should remain in Iraq "indefinitely," no one questioned his conclusions. In fact, Hillary Clinton, now a presidential hopeful, was photographed with Petraeus in a warm handshake, a far cry from the confrontation they had in September 2007. Whatever the long-term results of the surge, for the immediate future it was clear that the next president would inherit a significant U.S. troop presence in Iraq. It also seemed clear that victory, however defined, was no closer in 2008 than it had been when President Bush had declared "mission accomplished" in 2003.

Notes

1 *Washington Post*, December 20, 2006.
2 Gallup poll, at: http://www.gallup.com/poll/1633/iraq.aspx, accessed January 14, 2013.
3 *Iraq Study Group Report* (Washington, D.C.: United States Institute for Peace Press, 2006), 6.
4 "Measuring Stability in Iraq, March 2008 Report to Congress in Accordance with the Department of Defense Appropriations Act of 2008," (Washington, D.C.: Department of Defense, 2008), 18. For a summary of levels of violence,

see the *New York Times*, August 31, 2008. For deaths in Iraq, see "Iraq Body Count" at: http://www.iraqbodycount.org/, accessed January 14, 2013.

5   For the latest editions of these classics see, David Galula, *Pacification in Algeria, 1956–1986* (1962; Santa Monica, CA: RAND Corporation, 2006) and *Counterinsurgency Warfare: Theory and Practice* (1964; New York: Praeger, 2006).

6   Rufus Phillips, "Meeting Lt. Col. David Galula, April 1962," *Small Wars Journal on-line*, www.smallwarsjournal.com (2008), accessed January 14, 2013. Rufus Phillips became a member of the Saigon Military Mission in 1954, and the following year served as the sole advisor to two Vietnamese army pacification operations, earning the CIA's Intelligence Medal of Merit for his work. He later worked as a CIA civilian case officer in Vietnam and Laos, then joined the U.S. Agency for International Development's Saigon Mission to lead its counterinsurgency efforts. In 1964 he became a consultant for USAID and the State Department and served as an advisor to Vice President Hubert Humphrey.

7   Galula, *Counterinsurgency Warfare*, 89.

8   David Kilcullen, *The Accidental Guerrilla: Fighting Small Wars in the Midst of a Big One* (Oxford: Oxford University Press, 2009), xv.

9   Ibid.

10 As quoted in Tom Ricks, *The Gamble: General David Petraeus and the American Military Adventure in Iraq, 2006–2008* (New York: Penguin, 2009), 88.

11 Ibid., 89.

12 Kilcullen, *The Accidental Guerrilla*, xv.

13 Fred Kagan, "Choosing Victory: A Plan for Success," January 5, 2007, American Enterprise Institute Paper.

14 Peter Feaver, "Anatomy of the Surge," *Commentary* (April 2008).

15 *New York Times*, January 2, 2007.

16 *The U.S. Army/Marine Corps Counterinsurgency Field Manual* (Chicago: University of Chicago Press, 2007), xxiv.

17 Peter Mansoor, *Baghdad at Sunrise: A Brigade Commander's War in Iraq* (New Haven: Yale University Press, 2008).

18 President Bush's White House Address, January 10, 2007, Office of the White House Press Secretary.

19 *New York Times*, January 2, 2007.

20 *Iraq Study Group Report*, 48.

21 "Iraq First: The National Security Strategy of Iraq," Republic of Iraq, the Cabinet.

22 For the most interesting trending, see "Iraq Body Count," at: http://www.iraqbodycount.org/database/, accessed January 14, 2013.

23 *Foreign Policy*, September 26, 2007.

24 *Washington Post*, March 11, 2007.

25 Ricks, *The Gamble*, 209.

26 Ibid., 267.

27 Peter Wehner, "Liberals and the Surge," *Commentary on-line* (November 2008).

28 Ibid.
29 Ibid.
30 John Dickerson, "The Surge Dirge," *Slate,* 9 January 2007, online at: http://www.slate.com/id/2157162/, accessed January 14, 2013.
31 *Washington Post*, January 18, 2007.
32 Ibid.
33 Ibid.
34 Ibid.
35 Barack Obama, Chicago World Affairs Council, April 23, 2007. Online at: http://my.barackobama.com/page/content/fpccga/, accessed January 14, 2013.
36 *Washington Post*, January 28, 2007.
37 Ibid.
38 "General Petraeus Testifies before Congress on the Status of Iraq," *Congressional Quarterly Wire*, September 10, 2007.
39 Ibid.
40 Ibid.
41 Quoted in Ricks, *The Gamble*, 247.
42 *Washington Post*, August 30, 2007.
43 See Robert K. Brigham, *Iraq, Vietnam and the Limits of American Power* (New York: PublicAffairs, 2008), 129.
44 United Nations Commission on Human Rights, United Nations Refugee Agency-Iraq, Country Operations Profile; UNHCR Iraq Fact Sheet, "Crisis in Iraq," September 1, 2008; and OCHA Iraq Office in Amman, "Humanitarian Crisis in Iraq: Facts and Figures," Representative of the United Nations Assistance Mission in Iraq, November 13, 2007.
45 "General Petraeus Testifies before Congress on the Status of Iraq," *Congressional Quarterly Wire*, September 10, 2007.
46 Ricks, *The Gamble*, 209. See also Colonel Gian Gentile, "A Slightly Better War: A Narrative and Its Defects," *World Affairs* (Summer 2008).
47 Colonel Gian Gentile, "Think Again: Counterinsurgency," *Foreign Policy* (January 2009); "Eating Soup with a Spoon," *Armed Forces Journal* (September 2007); "LTC Gian Gentile on War, Strategy, and the Future," *Small Wars Journal* (June 2008); and "A Slightly Better War: A Narrative and its Defects," *World Affairs* (Summer 2008).
48 Quoted in Ricks, *The Gamble*, 100.
49 Office of the White House Press Secretary, June 28, 2007.
50 David Kilcullen, *The Accidental Guerrilla, and Counterinsurgency* (New York: Oxford University Press, 2010).
51 Frederick Kagan, "Winning One Battle, Fighting the Next," *Weekly Standard*, 13(8), November 5, 2007.
52 Ibid.
53 As quoted in Lawrence Freedman, *A Choice of Enemies: America Confronts the Middle East* (New York: PublicAffairs, 2008), 447.
54 As cited in Wehner, "Liberals and the Surge."
55 "Fact Sheet: Five Years Later: New Strategy Improving Security in Iraq," The White House, Office of the Press Secretary, March 19, 2008.

DOCUMENTS

———— **Document 5-A** ————

Excerpts from the *Iraq Study Group Report*, December 6, 2006

Executive Summary

The situation in Iraq is grave and deteriorating. There is no path that can guarantee success, but the prospects can be improved.

In this report, we make a number of recommendations for actions to be taken in Iraq, the United States, and the region. Our most important recommendations call for new and enhanced diplomatic and political efforts in Iraq and the region, and a change in the primary mission of U.S. forces in Iraq that will enable the United States to begin to move its combat forces out of Iraq responsibly. We believe that these two recommendations are equally important and reinforce one another. If they are effectively implemented, and if the Iraqi government moves forward with national reconciliation, Iraqis will have an opportunity for a better future, terrorism will be dealt a blow, stability will be enhanced in an important part of the world, and America's credibility, interests, and values will be protected.

The challenges in Iraq are complex. Violence is increasing in scope and lethality. It is fed by a Sunni Arab insurgency, Shiite militias and death squads, al Qaeda, and widespread criminality. Sectarian conflict is the principal challenge to stability. The Iraqi people have a democratically elected government, yet it is not adequately advancing national reconciliation, providing basic security, or delivering essential services. Pessimism is pervasive.

If the situation continues to deteriorate, the consequences could be severe. A slide toward chaos could trigger the collapse of Iraq's government and a humanitarian catastrophe. Neighboring countries could intervene. Sunni-Shia clashes could spread. Al Qaeda could win a propaganda victory and expand its base of operations. The global standing of the United States could be diminished. Americans could become more polarized.

During the past nine months we have considered a full range of approaches for moving forward. All have flaws. Our recommended course has shortcomings, but we firmly believe that it includes the best strategies and tactics to positively influence the outcome in Iraq and the region.

External Approach

The policies and actions of Iraq's neighbors greatly affect its stability and prosperity. No country in the region will benefit in the long term from a chaotic Iraq.

Yet Iraq's neighbors are not doing enough to help Iraq achieve stability. Some are undercutting stability.

The United States should immediately launch a new diplomatic offensive to build an international consensus for stability in Iraq and the region. This diplomatic effort should include every country that has an interest in avoiding a chaotic Iraq, including all of Iraq's neighbors. Iraq's neighbors and key states in and outside the region should form a support group to reinforce security and national reconciliation within Iraq, neither of which Iraq can achieve on its own.

Given the ability of Iran and Syria to influence events within Iraq and their interest in avoiding chaos in Iraq, the United States should try to engage them constructively. In seeking to influence the behavior of both countries, the United States has disincentives and incentives available. Iran should stem the flow of arms and training to Iraq, respect Iraq's sovereignty and territorial integrity, and use its influence over Iraqi Shia groups to encourage national reconciliation. The issue of Iran's nuclear programs should continue to be dealt with by the five permanent members of the United Nations Security Council plus Germany. Syria should control its border with Iraq to stem the flow of funding, insurgents, and terrorists in and out of Iraq.

The United States cannot achieve its goals in the Middle East unless it deals directly with the Arab-Israeli conflict and regional instability. There must be a renewed and sustained commitment by the United States to a comprehensive Arab-Israeli peace on all fronts: Lebanon, Syria, and President Bush's June 2002 commitment to a two-state solution for Israel and Palestine. This commitment must include direct talks with, by, and between Israel, Lebanon, Palestinians (those who accept Israel's right to exist), and Syria.

As the United States develops its approach toward Iraq and the Middle East, the United States should provide additional political, economic, and military support for Afghanistan, including resources that might become available as combat forces are moved out of Iraq.

Internal Approach

The most important questions about Iraq's future are now the responsibility of Iraqis. The United States must adjust its role in Iraq to encourage the Iraqi people to take control of their own destiny.

The Iraqi government should accelerate assuming responsibility for Iraqi security by increasing the number and quality of Iraqi Army brigades. While this process is under way, and to facilitate it, the United States should significantly increase the number of U.S. military personnel, including combat troops, imbedded in and supporting Iraqi Army units. As these actions proceed, U.S. combat forces could begin to move out of Iraq.

The primary mission of U.S. forces in Iraq should evolve to one of supporting the Iraqi army, which would take over primary responsibility for combat operations.

By the first quarter of 2008, subject to unexpected developments in the security situation on the ground, all combat brigades not necessary for force protection could be out of Iraq. At that time, U.S. combat forces in Iraq could be deployed only in units embedded with Iraqi forces, in rapid-reaction and special operations teams, and in training, equipping, advising, force protection, and search and rescue. Intelligence and support efforts would continue. A vital mission of those rapid reaction and special operations forces would be to undertake strikes against al Qaeda in Iraq.

It is clear that the Iraqi government will need assistance from the United States for some time to come, especially in carrying out security responsibilities. Yet the United States must make it clear to the Iraqi government that the United States could carry out its plans, including planned redeployments, even if the Iraqi government did not implement their planned changes. The United States must not make an open-ended commitment to keep large numbers of American troops deployed in Iraq.

As redeployment proceeds, military leaders should emphasize training and education of forces that have returned to the United States in order to restore the force to full combat capability. As equipment returns to the United States, Congress should appropriate sufficient funds to restore the equipment over the next five years.

The United States should work closely with Iraq's leaders to support the achievement of specific objectives – or milestones – on national reconciliation, security, and governance. Miracles cannot be expected, but the people of Iraq have the right to expect action and progress. The Iraqi government needs to show its own citizens – and the citizens of the United States and other countries – that it deserves continued support.

Prime Minister Nouri al-Maliki, in consultation with the United States, has put forward a set of milestones critical for Iraq. His list is a good start, but it must be expanded to include milestones that can strengthen the government and benefit the Iraqi people. President Bush and his national security team should remain in close and frequent contact with the Iraqi leadership to convey a clear message: there must be prompt action by the Iraqi government to make substantial progress toward the achievement of these milestones.

If the Iraqi government demonstrates political will and makes substantial progress toward the achievement of milestones on national reconciliation, security, and governance, the United States should make clear its willingness to continue training, assistance, and support for Iraq's security forces and to continue political, military, and economic support. If the Iraqi government does not make substantial progress toward the achievement of milestones on national reconciliation, security, and governance, the United States should reduce its political, military, or economic support for the Iraqi government.

Our report makes recommendations in several other areas. They include improvements to the Iraqi criminal justice system, the Iraqi oil sector, the U.S.

reconstruction efforts in Iraq, the U.S. budget process, the training of U.S. government personnel, and U.S. intelligence – capabilities.

Conclusion

It is the unanimous view of the Iraq Study Group that these recommendations offer a new way forward for the United States in Iraq and the region. They are comprehensive and need to be implemented in a coordinated fashion. They should not be separated or carried out in isolation. The dynamics of the region are as important to Iraq as events within Iraq.

The challenges are daunting. There will be difficult days ahead. But by pursuing this new way forward, Iraq, the region, and the United States of America can emerge stronger.

QUESTIONS TO CONSIDER

1   What were the major policy recommendations of the Iraq Study Group Report?
2   What were the major challenges facing the United States in Iraq?
3   How would diplomacy be used to end the violence in Iraq?

Document 5-B

Fred Kagan, "Choosing Victory," January 5, 2007, American Enterprise Institute

Executive Summary

Victory is still an option in Iraq. America, a country of 300 million people with a GDP of $12 trillion and more than 1 million soldiers and Marines, has the resources to stabilize Iraq, a state the size of California with a population of 25 million and a GDP under $100 billion. America must use its resources skillfully and decisively to help build a successful democratically elected, sovereign government in Iraq.

Victory in Iraq is vital to America's security. Defeat will likely lead to regional conflict, humanitarian catastrophe, and increased global terrorism.

Iraq has reached a critical point. The strategy of relying on a political process to eliminate the insurgency has failed. Rising sectarian violence threatens to break America's will to fight. This violence will destroy the Iraqi government, armed forces, and people if it is not rapidly controlled.

Victory in Iraq is still possible at an acceptable level of effort. We must adopt a new approach to the war and implement it quickly and decisively.

We must act now to restore security and stability to Baghdad. We and the enemy have identified it as the decisive point.

There is a way to do this.

- We must balance our focus on training Iraqi soldiers with a determined effort to secure the Iraqi population and contain the rising violence. Securing the population has never been the primary mission of the U.S. military effort in Iraq, and now it must become the first priority.
- We must send more American combat forces into Iraq and especially into Baghdad to support this operation. A surge of seven Army brigades and Marine regiments to support clear-and-hold operations that begin in the spring of 2007 is necessary, possible, and will be sufficient to improve security and set conditions for economic development, political development, reconciliation, and the development of Iraqi Security Forces (ISF) to provide permanent security.
- American forces, partnered with Iraqi units, will clear high-violence Sunni and mixed Sunni-Shia neighborhoods, primarily on the west side of the city.
- After those neighborhoods are cleared, U.S. soldiers and Marines, again partnered with Iraqis, will remain behind to maintain security, reconstitute police forces, and integrate police and Iraqi Army efforts to maintain the population's security.
- As security is established, reconstruction aid will help to reestablish normal life, bolster employment, and, working through Iraqi officials, strengthen Iraqi local government.
- Securing the population strengthens the ability of Iraq's central government to exercise its sovereign powers.

This approach requires a national commitment to victory in Iraq:

- The ground forces must accept longer tours for several years. National Guard units will have to accept increased deployments during this period.
- Equipment shortages must be overcome by transferring equipment from non-deploying active-duty, National Guard, and reserve units to those about to deploy. Military industry must be mobilized to provide replacement equipment sets urgently.
- The president must request a dramatic increase in reconstruction aid for Iraq. Responsibility and accountability for reconstruction must be assigned to established agencies. The president must insist upon the completion of reconstruction projects. The president should also request a dramatic increase in Commander's Emergency Response Program (CERP) funds.

- The president must request a substantial increase in ground forces end strength. This increase is vital to sustaining the morale of the combat forces by ensuring that relief is on the way. The president must issue a personal call for young Americans to volunteer to fight in the decisive conflict of this generation.
- The president and his representatives in Iraq must forge unity of effort with the Iraqi government.

Other courses of action have been proposed. All will fail.

- Withdraw immediately. This approach will lead to immediate defeat. The Iraqi Security Forces (ISF) are entirely dependent upon American support to survive and function. If U.S. forces withdraw now, the Iraqi forces will collapse. Iraq will descend into total civil war that will rapidly spread throughout the Middle East.
- Engage Iraq's neighbors. This approach will fail. The basic causes of violence and sources of manpower and resources for the warring sides come from within Iraq. Iraq's neighbors are encouraging the violence, but they cannot stop it.
- Increase embedded trainers dramatically. This approach cannot succeed rapidly enough to prevent defeat. Removing U.S. forces from patrolling neighborhoods to embed them as trainers will lead to an immediate rise in violence. This rise in violence will destroy America's remaining will to fight and escalate the cycle of sectarian violence in Iraq beyond anything an Iraqi army could bring under control.
- Failure in Iraq today will require far greater sacrifices tomorrow in far more desperate circumstances.

Committing to victory now will demonstrate America's strength to our friends and enemies around the world.

QUESTIONS TO CONSIDER

1 How was victory in Iraq still possible? What would it require?
2 What role would Iraq have in the new path forward?
3 How many new U.S. troops would be required for Iraq? How was their mission going to be different?

--------- **Document 5-C** ---------

Excerpts from *U.S. Army/Marine Corps Counterinsurgency Field Manual*, pp. 51–52

. . . COIN (counterinsurgency) is an extremely complex form of warfare. At its core, COIN is a struggle for the population's support. The protection, welfare, and support of the people are vital to success. Gaining and maintaining that support is a formidable challenge. Achieving these aims requires synchronizing the efforts of many nonmilitary and HN (host nation) agencies in a comprehensive approach.

Designing operations that achieve the desired end state requires counterinsurgents to understand the culture and the problems they face. Both insurgents and counterinsurgents are fighting for the support of the populace. However, insurgents are constrained by neither the law of nor the bounds of human decency as Western nations understand them. In fact, some insurgents are willing to commit suicide and kill innocent civilians carrying out their operations – and deem this a legitimate option. They also will do anything to preserve their greatest advantage, the ability to hide among the people. These amoral and often barbaric enemies survive by their wits, constantly adapting to the situation. Defeating them requires counterinsurgents to develop the ability to learn and adapt rapidly and continuously. This manual emphasizes this "Learn and Adapt" imperative as it discusses ways to gain and maintain the support of the people.

Popular support allows counterinsurgents to develop the intelligence necessary to identify and defeat insurgents. Designing and executing a comprehensive campaign to secure the populace and then gain its support requires carefully coordinating actions along several LLOs (logical line of operations) over time to produce success. One of these LLOs is developing HN security forces that can assume primary responsibility for combating the insurgency. COIN operations also place distinct burdens on leaders and logisticians. All of these aspects of COIN are described and analyzed in the chapters that follow.

QUESTIONS TO CONSIDER

1　What is counterinsurgency? How does it differ from traditional concepts of warfare?
2　Why did insurgents fight? What are their goals?
3　How do you best defeat an insurgency?

—————— **Document 5-D** ——————

Excerpts from "Iraq First: The National Security Strategy of Iraq," Republic of Iraq – the Cabinet

الـعـراق جمهوريـة
الـوزراء مجلـس

Republic of Iraq
The Cabinet

"Iraq First: The Iraqi National Security Strategy, 2007–2010"

...First. Completing the development, missions, and functions of Iraqi Security Forces

The size and composition of Iraq's Security Forces are based on defeating the identified threats within Iraq's strategic environment. As the first priority in the current period, Iraq's Joint Forces will focus on defeat of terrorism and insurgency as their primary mission, with other threats accorded a lesser priority to the extent that available resources permit. In this current period, Iraq's Joint Forces will achieve self reliance such that only minimal external assistance and support are needed for accomplishing the primary mission. As Iraq's security is reestablished and the terrorist and insurgency threats abate, Iraq's Joint Forces will transition to a conventional defensive posture for ensuring the security of the nation and its territory in conjunction with regional and international security arrangements. Likewise, Iraq's Police and Border Enforcement Forces will transition to conventional maintenance of domestic law and order and maintaining the integrity of Iraq's borders. Iraq's police forces will focus on local police self-reliance except in emergency situations that require reinforcement by National Police or the Iraqi Joint Forces. The capabilities of Iraq's Joint Forces will be such that they do not by their size or capabilities appear as threatening to Iraq's neighbors.

Second. Enhancing the constitutional civilian command of the security institutions

Articles (9) and (48) of the first part of the Constitution state that the Security Services and the National Intelligence Service are to be under the command of the civil authority – and should not be a tool for abusing the people and interfering in political affairs or the Government's transfer of authority. The Government is striving to achieve this principle through presenting its draft National Intelligence Law, in addition to continually monitoring the security ministries and directorates through the Security Ministries Reform Committee. The efforts exerted by the security training institutions and academies should be continued to rehabilitate the military and civilian cadres and they should focus on human rights topics, democracy, and constitutional civilian control of the security institutions.

Third. Completing the transition of operational control of the Iraqi army divisions from the Multinational Force, Iraq to the Iraqi Government

The Multinational Force has been assisting the Government of Iraq to create new security forces, police and military forces, so that it may become self-reliant in meeting its security needs. The Multinational Force established the Multinational Security Transition Command, Iraq in 2004 to assist Iraq in organizing, equipping, and training its security forces and transferring their operational control initially to the Multinational Force, Iraq. The Multinational Force and the Iraqi Government established a transition process whereby the Multinational Force would transfer operational control of divisions to the Iraqi Government when the divisions reached a level of readiness as demonstrated in actual operations that was mutually agreed by the Multinational Force and the Iraqi Government. This transition process will continue until all Iraqi Army divisions are under the operational control of the Iraqi Government. When all divisions are solely under Iraqi control, the Iraqi Government will have reached a major milestone in achieving security self-reliance.

Fourth. Completing the development of the command and control system

The Government of Iraq has started building a complete and advanced command and control system to control all government national security facilities through an advanced structure starting with the head of the executive authority (Prime Minister – Commander-in-Chief of the Armed Forces) to all other subordinate national security units of the Government. The next phase requires: (1) Completing a secure and reliable communications network Iraq-wide; and (2) Completing a command and control system that includes security forces in the regions and the provinces.

Fifth. Achieving security self reliance

Iraqi Security Forces, including all services, are growing in numbers, becoming stronger and more experienced. Current conditions confirm the need for more forces to enforce the law, protect Iraqi citizens, and protect Iraqi territory, which requires: (1) Providing and rehabilitating training institutions and academies and adopting a recruiting policy that ensures accurate demographic representation of Iraq. (2) Completing the logistics system of the Armed Forces. (3) Completing the supply stocks, fire support capabilities and the Air Force. (4) Completing intelligence capabilities. (5) Completing counterterrorism capabilities.

Sixth. Developing counterterrorism capabilities and Programs

(1) The Government of Iraq is undertaking increasing and reinforcing its counterterrorism security forces; (2) Establishing and implementing a policy to mobilize all national capabilities towards counterterrorism; and (3) Actively participating in international efforts to counter terrorism through reinforcing

Border Enforcement Forces, border entry and exit points, and security coordination with neighboring countries.

Seventh. Developing a policy to solve the problem of militias and to reintegrate them into the society

Militias originated in Iraq under different circumstances; some of them fought the dictatorial Baathist regime, and some originated after the collapse of Saddam's regime for various reasons. The Government is endeavoring to establish a program to disband these militias and reintegrate them into the society in an effort to solve the security problem. This is accomplished through: **(1)** Reaching a political agreement and a suitable balanced legislative framework to disband the militias in order to control weapons possession. In addition, a series of other procedures is being pursued that lead to building the trust of militia members with Government authority, such as a legislative decision for general amnesty based on transitional justice criteria and national loyalty.

(2) Creating political and economic conditions that contribute to implementation and balance the giving up of weapons with new social status as an encouraging factor for reintegration. **(3)** Adopting – with the assistance of the international community and commitment to the International Compact with Iraq – a general program with suitable balanced funding that leads to disbanding of the militias and reintegrates them into the society taking into account International experience in post-conflict situations. **(4)** Enhancing economic reforms to establish appropriate conditions leading to forming programs related to reintegration of the militias and other illegal armed groups.

Eighth. Reforming, completing, and supporting the Judiciary

Establishing a legal framework compatible with the Constitution and with national and international commitments on human rights requires conducting a general assessment of judicial institutions and their procedures to enforce the rule of law, to reinforce the administration of the judicial system according to international standards and support from the international community and the United Nations, in a way that removes fear from Iraqi people's souls. The Government of Iraq is also updating criminal and civil law to accommodate a civilized democratic society that requires qualified, independent legislators in addition to increasing the number of courts, judges and institutions that prepare law enforcement officials and conduct rehabilitation activities.

Ninth. Developing rehabilitation institutions and their employees

The development of rehabilitation institutions is a national objective and one of the pillars of the criminal justice system. This is accomplished through: **(1)** Establishing care and rehabilitation programs (for inmates and other participants) according to international criteria. **(2)** Assessing rehabilitation employees and increasing their numbers and capabilities in order institutions to be compatible with the nature of their tasks according to international rules of behavior. **(3)** Introducing technologies to assist in running these institutions. **(4)** Cooperating with international humanitarian organizations and utilizing their procedures, expertise, and training. **(5)** Undertaking to enact and implement laws for care of those released from rehabilitation institutions in

---

QUESTIONS TO CONSIDER

1   What were the new priorities for the Iraqi government?
2   What were the Maliki government's greatest security concerns in Iraq?
3   How would the militias be reintegrated into society?
4   What role did the judiciary have in national security?

Document 5-E

Excerpts from President George W. Bush's speech to the nation on the Iraq War, January 10, 2007

Good evening. Tonight in Iraq, the Armed Forces of the United States are engaged in a struggle that will determine the direction of the global war on terror – and our safety here at home. The new strategy I outline tonight will change America's course in Iraq, and help us succeed in the fight against terror.

When I addressed you just over a year ago, nearly 12 million Iraqis had cast their ballots for a unified and democratic nation. The elections of 2005 were a stunning achievement. We thought that these elections would bring the Iraqis together, and that as we trained Iraqi security forces we could accomplish our mission with fewer American troops.

But in 2006, the opposite happened. The violence in Iraq – particularly in Baghdad – overwhelmed the political gains the Iraqis had made. Al Qaeda terrorists and Sunni insurgents recognized the mortal danger that Iraq's elections posed for their cause, and they responded with outrageous acts of murder aimed at innocent Iraqis. They blew up one of the holiest shrines in Shia Islam – the Golden Mosque of Samarra – in a calculated effort to provoke Iraq's Shia population to retaliate. Their strategy worked. Radical Shia elements, some supported by Iran, formed death squads. And the result was a vicious cycle of sectarian violence that continues today.

The situation in Iraq is unacceptable to the American people – and it is unacceptable to me. Our troops in Iraq have fought bravely. They have done everything we have asked them to do. Where mistakes have been made, the responsibility rests with me.

It is clear that we need to change our strategy in Iraq. So my national security team, military commanders, and diplomats conducted a comprehensive review. We consulted members of Congress from both parties, our allies abroad, and distinguished outside experts. We benefitted from the thoughtful recommendations of the Iraq Study Group, a bipartisan panel led by former Secretary of State James Baker and former Congressman Lee Hamilton. In our discussions, we all agreed that there is no magic formula for success in Iraq. And one message came through loud and clear: Failure in Iraq would be a disaster for the United States.

The consequences of failure are clear: Radical Islamic extremists would grow in strength and gain new recruits. They would be in a better position to topple moderate governments, create chaos in the region, and use oil revenues to fund their ambitions. Iran would be emboldened in its pursuit of nuclear weapons. Our enemies would have a safe haven from which to plan and launch attacks on the American people. On September the 11th, 2001, we saw what a refuge for extremists on the other side of the world could bring to the streets of our own cities. For the safety of our people, America must succeed in Iraq.

The most urgent priority for success in Iraq is security, especially in Baghdad. Eighty percent of Iraq's sectarian violence occurs within 30 miles of the capital. This violence is splitting Baghdad into sectarian enclaves, and shaking the confidence of all Iraqis. Only Iraqis can end the sectarian violence and secure their people. And their government has put forward an aggressive plan to do it.

Our past efforts to secure Baghdad failed for two principal reasons: There were not enough Iraqi and American troops to secure neighborhoods that had been cleared of terrorists and insurgents. And there were too many restrictions on the troops we did have. Our military commanders reviewed the new Iraqi plan to ensure that it addressed these mistakes. They report that it does. They also report that this plan can work.

Now let me explain the main elements of this effort: The Iraqi government will appoint a military commander and two deputy commanders for their capital. The Iraqi government will deploy Iraqi Army and National Police brigades across Baghdad's nine districts. When these forces are fully deployed, there will be 18 Iraqi Army and National Police brigades committed to this effort, along with local police. These Iraqi forces will operate from local police stations – conducting patrols and setting up checkpoints, and going door-to-door to gain the trust of Baghdad residents.

This is a strong commitment. But for it to succeed, our commanders say the Iraqis will need our help. So America will change our strategy to help the Iraqis carry out their campaign to put down sectarian violence and bring security to the people of Baghdad. This will require increasing American force levels. So I've committed more than 20,000 additional American troops to Iraq. The vast majority of them – five brigades – will be deployed to Baghdad. These troops will work alongside Iraqi units and be embedded in their formations. Our troops will have a well-defined mission: to help Iraqis clear and secure neighborhoods, to help them protect the local population, and to help ensure that the Iraqi forces left behind are capable of providing the security that Baghdad needs.

Many listening tonight will ask why this effort will succeed when previous operations to secure Baghdad did not. Well, here are the differences: In earlier operations, Iraqi and American forces cleared many neighborhoods of terrorists and insurgents, but when our forces moved on to other targets, the killers returned. This time, we'll have the force levels we need to hold the areas that have been cleared. In earlier operations, political and sectarian interference prevented Iraqi and American forces from going into neighborhoods that are home to those fueling the sectarian violence. This time, Iraqi and American forces will have a green light to enter those neighborhoods – and Prime Minister Maliki has pledged that political or sectarian interference will not be tolerated.

I've made it clear to the Prime Minister and Iraq's other leaders that America's commitment is not open-ended. If the Iraqi government does not follow through on its promises, it will lose the support of the American people – and it will lose the support of the Iraqi people. Now is the time to act. The Prime Minister understands this. Here is what he told his people just last week: "The Baghdad security plan will not provide a safe haven for any outlaws, regardless of [their] sectarian or political affiliation."

This new strategy will not yield an immediate end to suicide bombings, assassinations, or IED attacks. Our enemies in Iraq will make every effort to ensure that our television screens are filled with images of death and suffering. Yet over time, we can expect to see Iraqi troops chasing down murderers, fewer brazen acts of terror, and growing trust and cooperation from Baghdad's residents. When this happens, daily life will improve, Iraqis will gain confidence in their leaders, and the government will have the breathing space it needs to make progress in other critical areas. Most of Iraq's Sunni and Shia want to live together in peace – and reducing the violence in Baghdad will help make reconciliation possible.

A successful strategy for Iraq goes beyond military operations. Ordinary Iraqi citizens must see that military operations are accompanied by visible improvements in their neighborhoods and communities. So America will hold the Iraqi government to the benchmarks it has announced . . .

. . . The changes I have outlined tonight are aimed at ensuring the survival of a young democracy that is fighting for its life in a part of the world of enormous importance to American security. Let me be clear: The terrorists and insurgents in Iraq are without conscience, and they will make the year ahead bloody and violent. Even if our new strategy works exactly as planned, deadly acts of violence will continue – and we must expect more Iraqi and American casualties. The question is whether our new strategy will bring us closer to success. I believe that it will.

Victory will not look like the ones our fathers and grandfathers achieved. There will be no surrender ceremony on the deck of a battleship. But victory in Iraq will bring something new in the Arab world – a functioning democracy that polices its territory, upholds the rule of law, respects fundamental human liberties, and answers to its people. A democratic Iraq will not be perfect. But it will be a country that fights terrorists instead of harboring them – and it will help bring a future of peace and security for our children and our grandchildren ...

... Fellow citizens: The year ahead will demand more patience, sacrifice, and resolve. It can be tempting to think that America can put aside the burdens of freedom. Yet times of testing reveal the character of a nation. And throughout our history, Americans have always defied the pessimists and seen our faith in freedom redeemed. Now America is engaged in a new struggle that will set the course for a new century. We can, and we will, prevail.

We go forward with trust that the Author of Liberty will guide us through these trying hours. Thank you and good night.

QUESTIONS TO CONSIDER

1   What had gone wrong in Iraq in 2006?
2   How would a surge in troops change the nature of the war?
3   What was the most urgent priority in Iraq? How would a surge in troops solve that problem?
4   What will victory look like in Iraq?

Document 5-F

Excerpts from Senator Barack Obama's speech before the Chicago Council on Global Affairs, April 23, 2007

Good morning. We all know that these are not the best of times for America's reputation in the world. We know what the war in Iraq has cost us in lives and treasure, in influence and respect. We have seen the consequences of a foreign policy based on a flawed ideology, and a belief that tough talk can replace real strength and vision.

Many around the world are disappointed with our actions. And many in our own country have come to doubt either our wisdom or our capacity to shape events beyond our borders. Some have even suggested that America's time has passed. But while we know what we have lost as a consequence of this tragic war, I also know what I have found in my travels over the past two years. . . .

. . . The horrific attacks on that clear September day awakened us to this new reality. And after 9/11, millions around the world were ready to stand with us.

They were willing to rally to our cause because it was their cause too – because they knew that if America led the world toward a new era of global cooperation, it would advance the security of people in our nation and all nations.

We now know how badly this Administration squandered that opportunity. In 2002, I stated my opposition to the war in Iraq, not only because it was an unnecessary diversion from the struggle against the terrorists who attacked us on September 11th, but also because it was based on a fundamental misunderstanding of the threats that 9/11 brought to light. I believed then, and believe now, that it was based on old ideologies and outdated strategies – a determination to fight a 21st century struggle with a 20th century mindset.

There is no doubt that the mistakes of the past six years have made our current task more difficult. World opinion has turned against us. And after all the lives lost and the billions of dollars spent, many Americans may find it tempting to turn inward, and cede our claim of leadership in world affairs.

I insist, however, that such an abandonment of our leadership is a mistake we must not make. America cannot meet the threats of this century alone, but the world cannot meet them without America. We must neither retreat from the world nor try to bully it into submission – we must lead the world, by deed and example. . . .

. . . The first way America will lead is by bringing a responsible end to this war in Iraq and refocusing on the critical challenges in the broader region.

In a speech five months ago, I argued that there can be no military solution to what has become a political conflict between Sunni and Shi'a factions. And I laid out a plan that I still believe offers the best chance of pressuring these warring factions toward a political settlement – a phased withdrawal of American forces with the goal of removing all combat brigades from Iraq by March 31st, 2008.

I acknowledged at the time that there are risks involved in such an approach. That is why my plan provides for an over-the-horizon force that could prevent chaos in the wider region, and allows for a limited number of troops to remain in Iraq to fight al Qaeda and other terrorists.

But my plan also makes clear that continued U.S. commitment to Iraq depends on the Iraqi government meeting a series of well-defined benchmarks necessary to reach a political settlement. Thus far, the Iraqi government has made very little progress in meeting any of the benchmarks, in part because the President has refused time and again to tell the Iraqi government that we will not be there forever. The President's escalation of U.S. forces may bring a temporary reduction in the violence in Baghdad, at the price of increased U.S. casualties – though the experience so far is not encouraging. But it cannot change the political dynamic in Iraq. A phased withdrawal can.

Moreover, until we change our approach in Iraq, it will be increasingly difficult to refocus our efforts on the challenges in the wider region – on the conflict in the Middle East, where Hamas and Hezbollah feel emboldened and Israel's prospects for a secure peace seem uncertain; on Iran, which has been strengthened by the war in Iraq; and on Afghanistan, where more American forces are needed to battle al Qaeda, track down Osama bin Laden, and stop that country from backsliding toward instability.

Burdened by Iraq, our lackluster diplomatic efforts leave a huge void. Our interests are best served when people and governments from Jerusalem and Amman to Damascus and Tehran understand that America will stand with our friends, work hard to build a peaceful Middle East, and refuse to cede the future of the region to those who seek perpetual conflict and instability. Such effective diplomacy cannot be done on the cheap, nor can it be warped by an ongoing occupation of Iraq. Instead, it will require patient, sustained effort, and the personal commitment of the President of the United States. That is a commitment I intend to make . . .

QUESTIONS TO CONSIDER

1   Why was Senator Obama opposed to the war in Iraq?
2   How will America lead again? What must it do to regain the trust of its allies?
3   What was Obama's plan to end the war? Was it viable?

6

Obama's War, 2009–2011

Chronology

November 2008	Status of Forces Agreement signed
November 2008	Barack Obama elected U.S. president
February 2009	Obama announces U.S. phased troop withdrawal
March 2010	National elections in Iraq
December 2010	Power-sharing Agreement signed in Baghdad
December 2011	U.S. troop withdrawal completed

"We are going to have to make the Iraqi government start taking more responsibility, withdraw our troops in a responsible way over time, because we are going to have to put additional troops into Afghanistan," declared presidential candidate Barack Obama during a 2008 debate against his rival John McCain.[1] Obama's position on Iraq had evolved considerably since he first spoke on the subject in 2002. At that time, Obama had called Iraq "a dumb war," and suggested that he was opposed to the coming conflict

The United States and Iraq Since 1990: A Brief History with Documents,
First Edition. Edited by Robert K. Brigham.
© 2014 Robert K. Brigham. Published 2014 by Blackwell Publishing Ltd.

in Iraq because it lacked "a clear rationale" and was "without strong inter-national support."[2] Obama modified his position in part because the surge had indeed created a new dynamic inside Iraq, at least temporarily. Yet he remained committed to reorienting American power in the region by placing a stronger emphasis on finding Osama bin Laden and striking out at insur-gents inside Afghanistan and along the frontier region of Pakistan. He believed that the State Department could replace Defense in Iraq, tying Iraq's trade and financial institutions to neighboring Sunni states, a modify-ing influence on the predominantly Shiite government in Baghdad. He hoped that these newer and stronger relationships would cement Iraq inside a regional association of states that moderated extreme actions and estab-lished acceptable rules for behavior. He had campaigned as an idealist out to change the tone and details of American foreign policy. Instead, Obama extended much of the Bush administration's policies in Iraq and embraced many of the old recommendations in the *Iraq Study Group Report*, recom-mendations that were bound by a strong sense of realism and pragmatism.

For Obama, Iraq had always been problematic. He was hostile to the idea of armed nation-building in general, but thought it was especially troubling in Iraq. He did not subscribe to long-term nation-building and modernization as outlined in FM 3-24, and he was doubtful that U.S. power could transform the entire region into prospering democracies.[3] Instead, he believed that the U.S. military presence in Iraq had created a climate that allowed Baghdad to move forward with its own agenda, as long it was within acceptable norms. Obama had campaigned on a pledge to end U.S. military involvement in Iraq, but this was not a retreat from responsibility in the region. Of course, Obama also had domestic pressures forcing him to rethink America's long-term military commitment to Iraq. A weak domestic economy and other security priorities convinced the president that the time had come to end America's military involvement in Iraq. All these considerations led President Obama to push for a phased American troop withdrawal that left Baghdad in charge of its own security. This was not, however, a radical departure from the Bush administration's long-range planning.

In the final months of 2008, the Bush administration declared that the surge had produced enough military stability in Iraq to talk about a phased U.S. withdrawal. The Bush administration had made such optimistic predic-tions before, but in 2008 the president signed a Status of Forces Agreement (SoFA – see DOCUMENT 6-A) with the Maliki government in Baghdad that committed the United States to a troop withdrawal by December 31, 2011. Some critics of the Bush administration have argued that this was an "October surprise," a desperate move by the Republican Party to rescue the struggling presidential campaign of pro-war John McCain. They sug-gested that Bush could sign the agreement for its campaign value, only to have McCain alter it later if necessary, should he be elected. But, SoFA was always open for negotiation and many policymakers in Washington, including then Senator Obama, favored the document's terms, given America's changing economic and security priorities. Once elected, Obama made SoFA the centerpiece of his Iraq policy, asking his senior national security staff to explore options in Afghanistan and Iraq for a redeployment of regional forces.

Reportedly, Obama wanted "three options . . . I want to do a thorough review in Iraq and I want to figure out how we're going to get to where we want to be."[4] For Obama, the real goal was to disrupt the Taliban and destroy much of the capacity of al-Qaeda to do harm in the world, and this meant increasing America's presence in Afghanistan and intelligence in Pakistan. Obama and his secretary of defense, Robert Gates, a holdover from the Bush administration, believed that Iraq was no longer America's security priority in the region. Early in his administration, Obama announced that "al-Qaeda and its allies – the terrorists who planned and supported the 9/11 attacks – are in Pakistan and Afghanistan," and therefore he would focus his efforts on these two countries. "We have a clear and focused goal" in Afghanistan and Pakistan, the president concluded, "to disrupt, dismantle and defeat al-Qaeda in Pakistan and Afghanistan, and to prevent their return to either country in the future."[5] Secretary Gates concurred, noting that the real problem in the war on terror was the safe havens inside Pakistan and the terrorist camps in Afghanistan. "I think as long as they have safe havens to operate there [Pakistan], it is going to be a problem for us in Afghanistan."[6] In his 2010 National Security Strategy report, Obama declared that "our military has been called upon to renew our focus on Afghanistan," and to help defeat al-Qaeda in Pakistan.[7] Neither one of these goals depended upon a strong U.S. contingent force in Iraq. In fact, Iraq had drawn too many resources, the president concluded, and it was time to change America's security priorities.

Obama's national security staff, aided by a report from the RAND Corporation – a private think-tank subcontracted to the government – established several different scenarios dealing with SoFA and the December 31, 2011, withdrawal deadline. The first envisioned all combat forces leaving Iraq within twelve months of the drawdown start date of May 1, 2009. The plan left a residual force of about 44,000 in Iraq until the final months of the drawdown, allowing these forces to continue to provide security and train Iraqi security forces. The second alternative matched the first, but allowed the president more flexibility in the mission of troops left in Iraq until the December 2011 deadline. All U.S. combat forces would leave Iraq by August 2010, ending the combat phase of American operations in Iraq. The remaining 35,000–50,000 troops would be used only to provide training and advice during the transition period. The final option gave a longer time frame for the withdrawal of combat forces, keeping them in Iraq until the very last day outlined in SoFA, requiring them to leave on December 31, 2011. It also gave the president the opportunity to continue security operations until the final withdrawal.[8]

Ultimately, Obama decided on the second option. He unveiled his administration's choice in a speech from Camp Lejeune in North Carolina on February 27, 2009 (see DOCUMENT 6-B). The president suggested that, "To understand where we need to go in Iraq, it is important for the American people to understand where we now stand . . . Violence has been reduced substantially from the horrific sectarian killing of 2006–2007. Al-Qaeda in Iraq has been dealt a serious blow by our troops and Iraq's Security Forces . . . the capacity of Iraq's Security Forces has improved, and Iraq's leaders have taken steps toward political accommodation."[9] Obama warned that "violence will continue to be a part of life in Iraq," but that the time had come for the United States to "pursue a new strategy to end the war in Iraq through a transition to full Iraqi responsibility."[10] The main focus of Obama's speech was the transition. He declared that the United States could not sustain "indefinitely a commitment that has put a strain on our military, and will cost the American people nearly a trillion dollars. America's men and women in uniform have fought block by block, province by province, year after year, to give Iraqis this chance to choose a better future. Now, we must ask the Iraqi people to seize it."[11] Obama had certainly struck a chord with these remarks, understanding fully that many Americans believed that Iraq now bore the burden for its own security and future.

Obama then announced a series of important deadlines that would dramatically alter America's policies and presence in Iraq. He pledged that by "August 31, 2010, our combat mission in Iraq will come to an end."[12] There would be a dramatic drawdown of American forces in Iraq, until they were fewer than 50,000 U.S. servicemen and women stationed inside the country. Furthermore, the president stated that America's new role in Iraq would be an advisory one; Iraq would now be responsible for all security operations and for containing the insurgency. The president promised to aid Iraq in the transition and to train Iraq's security forces, as long as they remained committed to a non-sectarian future. Obama confirmed the goal first outlined by President Bush during the 2008 presidential campaign, the complete American military withdrawal from Iraq by December 31, 2011.

The Planned Withdrawal

The response to Obama's withdrawal plan was mostly positive, with some notable exceptions. Obama's campaign rival, Senator McCain, supported the president's decisions and timeline. "It is encouraging that the dramatic success of the surge strategy has enabled us to move from a discussion about whether the United States could bear the catastrophic consequences of failure in Iraq, to planning the way in which we consolidate success," McCain argued shortly after Obama's Camp Lejeune speech. McCain concluded, "I believe the President's plan is a reasonable one."[13] Several Republican members of Congress concurred, noting in a bill introduced in the House that the Iraqi government controlled thirteen of eighteen provinces and that non-sectarian violence had "diminished significantly."[14] They also believed that "al-Qaeda in Iraq has been defeated as a military force" and that the surge had brought security and stability to Baghdad.[15] Iraq had just gone through a successful provincial election in January 2009, they declared, and therefore the time had come to think about an American withdrawal. Even former vice president Dick Cheney supported the president's timetable, largely because it reflected so much of the Bush administration's thinking on Iraq.

The Democratic leadership in Congress questioned the high number of residual forces left in Iraq, projected to be between 35,000 and 50,000, following the end of the U.S. combat mission. House Speaker Nancy Pelosi declared that this number was "higher . . . than I anticipated." Senate majority leader Harry Reid concurred, stating that he believed that number was too high. "I have long been for a significant drawback of troops in Iraq," Reid reported.[16] Obama convinced his fellow Democrats that he had no intention of renegotiating SoFA and that all American troops would leave Iraq by the target date of December 31, 2011. "The path is not toward the Korea model," explained one senior Obama official.[17] The idea, according to the White House, was to leave the 50,000 U.S. troops in Iraq right up to the December 31, 2011, deadline for withdrawal to aid with training and advising. If this effort increased the capacity of Iraq's security forces, Obama would not hesitate to accelerate the U.S. withdrawal. This seemed to satisfy the Democratic leadership, and in spite of some mild protests they went along with Obama's plan.

Retired general Jack Keane, an architect of the surge, thought the withdrawal plan was "an absolute disaster."[18] Keane argued that "We won the war in Iraq, and we're now losing the peace."[19] In words dripping with irony, Keane proclaimed, "We should be staying there to strengthen that democracy, to let them get the kind of political gains they need to get and keep the Iranians away from strangling that country. That should be our objective, and we are walking away from that objective."[20] Retired brigadier general Mark Kimmitt, who had served as former deputy operations chief in Baghdad, agreed with General Keane's basic assessment. "At the operational level," he reported, "it's going to make a significant change because for years the Iraqi security forces have depended on us for coun-

terterrorism support, for counterintelligence support, for logistical support
. . . We are now pulling all that out, and they will have to go it alone."[21]
Both Keane and Kimmitt feared that a timetable established an unreason-
able goal, and that Iraqi security forces were not yet ready to assume the
full burden of security and counterterrorism. Even Iraq's top military officer,
Lt. General Babaker Zebari, had argued that Iraqi security forces could not
do the job alone for another eight to ten years. He believed that American
forces should stay in Iraq until at least 2020.[22]

General Ray Odierno, U.S. Army chief of staff and former commander
in Iraq, shared General Zebari's concerns. Though Baghdad had requested
eighteen F-16 fighter jets (at a cost of $2.3 billion) as the Americans with-
drew, the U.S. command agreed that replacing U.S. troops with U.S.
equipment was a poor substitute. For General Odierno, the problem was
twofold. First, Iraq wanted fighter jets and other sophisticated weaponry,
but it had no skilled personnel to use it. Training to fly and care for the
F-16s could take as long as fifteen years, the general reported, and this was
simply too long a time frame to do Iraq much good. He had other serious
questions about the Iraqi use of American military hardware. "Will they be
able to depend on radar? Is that enough? Will they ask for support? Can
they get aircraft from some other country?"[23] Second, General Odierno was
also concerned that Iraqi security forces were not yet ready to take over all
peacekeeping functions inside Iraq. Unlike the Balkans conflict of the 1990s
when NATO forces withdrew from the region slowly and a little at a time,
the withdrawal from Iraq was going to be all at once for nearly 50,000
desperately needed U.S. troops. Could Iraqi security forces do the job? As
Americans withdrew, however, Odierno became cautiously optimistic, "I
always tell everybody we have to put it in perspective and I think the military has made incredible strides working with the Iraqi military and the
Iraqi government to provide a level of security that will be sustainable by
the Iraqi Security Forces as we leave," Odierno said. "There's still violence
in Iraq, but the level of violence is significantly less than it has been for a
long time. We believe they have the capacity to sustain peace within Iraq."[24]

The Obama administration shared the general's optimism, but nonetheless the White House tried to renegotiate a longer timetable for withdrawal
in 2011. Obama now wanted to leave a contingent U.S. force in Iraq for
years. Negotiations with Baghdad went on throughout the summer of 2011,
but a deal was never made. Unfortunately for Obama, talks were driven by
domestic political considerations in Baghdad, despite Maliki's assurances
that this was not the case. The major stumbling block to extending the
timetable and for keeping a residual U.S. force in Iraq was Baghdad's refusal
to grant blanket immunity to U.S. troops who stayed in Iraq past the deadline. Maliki believed he could not agree to such a measure because there
was considerable opposition to it inside Iraq. Popular sentiment just would

not allow Americans to be free from judicial deterrence and escape any potential war crimes with impunity. An insulted and frustrated Obama insisted that the White House had not initiated the negotiations and that he had always supported the Status of Forces Agreement and the December 31, 2011, deadline. Senate Foreign Relations Committee chairman John Kerry (D-Massachusetts) backed the administration's argument, stating that a U.S. withdrawal was in the best interests of Iraq and the United States. "The United States is fulfilling our agreement with an Iraqi government that wants to shape its own future," he said. "The President is also following through on his commitment to end both the conflict in Iraq and our military presence . . . These moves appropriately reflect the changes on the ground. American troops in Iraq will be coming home, having served with honor and enormous skill."[25]

Still, Obama must have sensed that the Iraqi security forces were not ready to handle all security and peacekeeping operations themselves, or he would have never broached the subject with Maliki. During his 2008 presidential campaign, Obama was careful to always qualify his comments about withdrawing U.S. troops from Iraq. He clearly stated that as commander in chief he would have to reserve the right to renegotiate SoFA if circumstances in Iraq changed dramatically. As the withdrawal deadline drew near in the fall of 2011, Obama sensed that renewed militia attacks inside Iraq pointed to trouble. Furthermore, he realized that his own political fortunes were tied to Bush's SoFA, and the prospect of a failing Iraqi nation-building project would not bode well for his 2012 U.S. presidential re-election. Despite these concerns, Obama clung stubbornly to SoFA, hoping that Iraq could indeed stand on its own. He did this in the face of growing economic troubles at home, increased violence and human rights abuses against Sunnis inside Iraq, and fears that an aggressive Iran would take advantage of an American military withdrawal from neighboring Iraq. But Obama also favored a dramatic shift in U.S. security thinking in the region, hoping to build up U.S. forces in Afghanistan as he withdrew American troops from Iraq.[26] (See DOCUMENT 6-C, EXCERPTS FROM THE OBAMA ADMINISTRATION'S NATIONAL SECURITY STRATEGY.) It was a combination of these factors that kept the Obama administration focused on the August 2010 change in mission and the December 2011 troop withdrawal deadline.

Economic considerations weighed most heavily on the president as the deadlines drew near. Obama argued that Iraq could no longer draw on American resources to do what Iraqis needed to do for themselves. The Iraq War had been a tremendous drain on the American economy, and the economic crisis now facing the country made a longer-term commitment to ground troops in Iraq unsustainable. Congress had passed seventeen separate emergency funding bills, totaling $822.1 billion for the wars in Iraq and Afghanistan by April 2009, and, according to the president, "after seven years of war, the American people deserve an honest accounting of the cost of our involvement in our ongoing military operations."[27] Even the *New York Times* speculated that one of the major factors in Obama's decision to withdraw U.S. forces from Iraq was economic: "The troop withdrawal could also help ease the budget pressure the White House is facing as Obama seeks to make good on a promise to cut the federal deficit in half by 2013. . . . ."[28] Obama told Congress that his economic recovery plan, some $787 billion of government spending combined with tax incentives and other programs, was also dependent on bringing the costs of the war in Iraq under control. In a prime-time television address from the White House announcing the troop withdrawal, Obama declared that restoring the U.S. economy "must be our central mission as a people and my central responsibility as President." He acknowledged that more than 23 million Americans were either unemployed or underemployed, according to official statistics, and that he did not want the recent slowdown in the economic recovery to lead to a double-dip recession. "And so at this moment, as we wind down the war in Iraq, we must tackle those challenges at home with as much energy, and grit, and sense of common purpose as our men and women in uniform who have served abroad."[29] After spending nearly $1 trillion in Iraq by the end of 2011, it was time to bring the troops home.

Iraq's poor economic recovery since the 2003 invasion had also put more financial pressure on the United States. Bush administration officials had long hoped that oil revenues would help Iraqi leaders rebuild their country after Saddam's disastrous reign. But oil prices dropped worldwide, and the lack of security in some areas kept private investment away. The result was some backsliding for Iraq on some key economic and social indicators. For example, Iraq's shortfall in revenues from oil reduced the government's budget by almost 50 percent at a time when its population was growing tremendously.[30] This put enormous stress, along with the war, on Iraq's social services. Life expectancy in Iraq had dropped from 65 in 1981 to just 58 in 2011, and Iraq's reported infant mortality rate was a region-high 84 deaths per 100,000 live births.[31] Government corruption meant that the little money that was available to support social services in Iraq was being siphoned off into the pockets of some policymakers. According to the United Nations, Iraq had one of the most corrupt governments in the world in 2009, ranking just 176 out of 180 countries on the United Nations international corruption index.[32] Iraq was not prepared to pay more for its own security and protection, but Maliki also understood that Baghdad had to take over the cost of these measures or risk the perception of illegitimacy.

Obama agreed, but he also thought that sectarian violence had unnecessarily drained Iraq's resources. The administration was deeply concerned that Maliki had not done all that he could to bring Sunnis into national political life to alleviate the enormous cost of security and peace-building.

Without national reconciliation, the civil war threatened to destroy all that the United States and Iraq had accomplished. Obama believed that the new Iraqi government was working toward the goal of national reconciliation, but that a deadline for an American withdrawal might force the Maliki government to compromise with its rivals in order to bring Sunnis into national political life. Obama worried that a continued American security presence would not move the Iraqis toward the goal of national reconciliation quickly enough. Indeed, the lack of political compromise in Iraq had created enormous problems for the Bush and Obama administrations for years. There had been a host of human rights abuses under the Maliki government, and government corruption in the humanitarian aid program had cast a long shadow over political affairs in Baghdad.

Human Rights Concerns in Iraq

The most significant problem for the Maliki government, one that had deeply concerned the Bush and Obama administrations, however, was the treatment of Iraq's war refugees. Refugees have always been a product of war, but the Iraqi refugee crisis is one of the largest forced population movements in the region since 1948.[33] According to António Guterres, the former United Nations High Commissioner for Refugees, no other political issue posed a greater threat to Baghdad's ability to govern.[34] Indeed, from 2006 to 2007 an estimated 2,000 Iraqis were forced to leave their homes against their will each day. At the height of sectarian violence, Iraq had 1.6 million internally displaced persons (IDPs).[35] Adding to those numbers were the estimated 2.2 million who had left Iraq altogether for sanctuary in Syria, Jordan, and other neighboring countries. According to Human Rights First, a non-governmental organization working to secure safe passage for Iraqi refugees to the United States, "most refugees cannot obtain work authorization and many refugees lack legal residence rights."[36] As international funds for support of Iraqi refugees declined, host countries experienced frustration and fatigue, leading to anti-refugee feelings and policies. For example, the leading U.S. ally in the region, Saudi Arabia, constructed a $7 billion high-tech barrier on its borders to keep unwanted refugees out. Kuwait and Egypt embraced restrictive clauses in their immigration laws to limit Iraqi refugees. While many Iraqi refugees had temporary permission to remain in Jordan and Syria, by 2007 their visas had expired. They lived in constant fear of being returned to Iraq against their will because neither Jordan nor Syria is a party to the Refugee Convention. One of the most important principles in the 1951 Geneva Convention is that of non-refoulement – a refugee's right not to be returned to a country where they are in danger of persecution.

There were two disturbing trends that dominated the first five years of the Iraq war that highlight the difficulties still facing the U.S. counterinsurgency program. One was the number of IDPs forced to leave their homes for the neighborhoods of like ethnic and religious groups surrounded by protective walls and barriers. Baghdad was once a city of mixed ethnicity and religion, but the hardening of Sunni communities to the west of the Tigris in the Dora and Huriya neighborhoods has created a sectarian city. This may have led to a short-term decrease in violence, but these hardened communities might also be the source of future violence. According to Elizabeth Ferris, an expert on refugees and national security, IDPs represent both "a consequence and contributing factor to sectarian polarization."[37] IDPs are not merely a product of sectarian violence, but rather a key strategy of insurgents and militias seeking to control national and humanitarian geographic space. Johanna Grombach Wagner, adviser to the director general of the International Committee of the Red Cross, explains that the term "espace humanitaire" was coined by former Médecins Sans Frontières (MSF) president Rony Brauman, who described it in the mid-1990s as "a space of freedom in which we are free to evaluate needs, free to monitor the distribution and use of relief goods, and free to have a dialogue with the people."[38] Under international humanitarian law (under the 1949 Geneva Conventions and their Additional Protocols), the primary responsibility for the survival of the population lies with the authorities or, in the case of occupation, with the occupying power. If the responsible authorities do not provide the supplies the civilian population needs for survival, they are obliged to permit the free passage of relief consignments. While the United States had cooperated with several different international agencies – the United Nations and the International Red Cross to name just two – it also insisted as part of its larger counterinsurgency program that Baghdad bear the brunt of the responsibility for the care of IDPs.

But Baghdad was slow to respond, and that created several problems for Bush and then Obama. The Iraqi government delayed incorporating the "Guiding Principles on Internal Displacement" into any national legislation, and it did not guarantee the basic human rights of IDPs, including freedom of movement and non-discrimination. There were also vast shortages of food in some neighborhoods, calling into question the Baghdad government's distribution system.[39] These shortages were so acute in the Sunni areas of Baghdad that many observers concluded that the lack of food was a purposeful policy.[40] Many U.S. policymakers supported the relocation of Sunnis into hardened communities because such action decreased the violence and created an opportunity for the Baghdad government to illustrate its resolve and commitment to national political reconciliation.[41] By removing international organizations – such as the United Nations and the Red Cross – as the caretakers of the public welfare and replacing them with the national government, many in Washington believed that relocated Sunnis would be dependent on the government for their very survival, and that this dependence would then foster political compromise.[42] It took several years for the Maliki government to understand the political importance of such issues, but eventually in 2009 there were signs of progress. Obama's expert on human rights and national security, Samantha Power, monitored events in Baghdad full-time, hoping to illustrate how sensitive this issue was to the White House. Obama made it clear that the American people were putting pressure on him to see a dramatic change in Baghdad. It was now time to see if the Maliki government was ready to step up to the demands of national leadership, some administration officials believed, and a U.S. withdrawal would foster that development. Although Obama remained generally positive about the strides Maliki had made in office, there were others in the administration who were still concerned about democracy and human rights inside Iraq.

Despite the Obama administration's initial diplomatic efforts, there remained the perception that Sunnis were still marginalized inside Iraq. The continued disqualification of political candidates, including the candidacy of Saleh al-Mutlaq, a prominent Sunni, in the March 2010 election, was a source of great discomfort in Sunni neighborhoods all over Iraq. More disturbing still were reports that the Baghdad government substantially increased death sentences against Sunnis in custody in the run-up to the March 2010 elections. According to Amnesty International, forced confessions had led to numerous death sentences in months prior to the U.S. withdrawal in an effort to intimidate Sunnis.[43] A 2009 United Nations report on human rights abuses in Iraq suggested that violations against Sunnis in prisons and on Iraqi streets were on the rise, and that "security in Iraq may not be sustainable unless significant steps are taken to uphold the rule of law and human rights. . . ."[44]

Many Sunnis had long complained about their treatment by Maliki's government. Human rights abuses at a secret prison in the old Muthanna airport in west Baghdad and in Baghdad's al-Rusafa detention facility were commonplace. Researchers at Human Rights Watch often told of beatings, whippings, and torture by electric shock and teeth-pulling in the government's prisons.[45] Many Sunnis had seen the March 2010 elections as the moment of their return to national politics only to find that they had been excluded by the Maliki government once again. Ayad Allawi, a secular Shiite who had once been Iraq's interim prime minister, became the standard bearer in the 2010 election for deposed Sunnis. Born in 1946, Allawi had belonged to the Baathist Party before fleeing Iraq in 1976. A long-time critic of Saddam Hussein, Allawi had survived several assassination attempts while living in exile in London. He returned to Iraq in 2003 following the American intervention, a policy he supported wholeheartedly by claiming,

"There are no words that can express the debt of gratitude that future generations of Iraqis will owe to Americans."[46]Although he initially won the national election in March by two seats, it took nearly ten months to sort out a power-sharing arrangement after Maliki challenged the election results. The power-sharing agreement of December 2010 created a shared governance structure that allowed Allawi to name the Defense Minister, a position important for Sunnis who felt they had been subject to constant harassment by the government's security forces. Maliki refused to approve Allawi's selections, however, and instead appointed himself "as the minister of both interior and defense, claiming that because of the country's tenuous security environment he needed more time to vet the candidates."[47] This left the government in the awkward position of having two prominent leaders and no clear policy agreements.

On the eve of the American withdrawal in December 2011 came another alarming report about the Maliki government. On December 12, 2011, Maliki moved swiftly to consolidate his political power in advance of the U.S. withdrawal by rounding up hundreds of former Baathist Party members and evicting Western companies from the Green Zone, the physical center of the government. The Maliki government explained its actions as a deliberate response to a "tip from Libya's government that revealed Col. Muammar el-Qaddafi was working with insurgents to stage a coup."[48] While some arrested did have ties to Saddam's government, most were "laborers, political adversaries of the government, the elderly. . . ."[49] One Western analyst believed that Maliki routinely used threats of a coup to attack his political rivals. "Baathism here is a symbol that Maliki uses as his bogyman. It gives them the leeway to go around arresting people. It's about a climate of fear."[50] The Obama White House responded to the raids with conspicuous silence.

The administration's refusal to draw attention to Baghdad's attacks on Sunnis in 2011 intensified the climate of fear inside Iraq. As American forces withdrew, many Sunnis believed that American intervention in Iraq had simply provided a tipping point. Instead of creating a national government of goodwill and concord, the United States, some Sunnis believed, had simply provided enough firepower for the Shiites to seize control of the country. Many Sunnis who had sided with the United States during the surge worried that no one would protect them after the American withdrawal. They feared that all Sunnis would be associated with Saddam's brutal rule, and that Shiites and Kurds would seek retribution under the passive eye of the Maliki government. Some of these fears were realized in the fall of 2011, shortly before the American troop withdrawal. In October 2011, Baghdad's security forces arrested over 600 Sunnis in Salahuddin Province, claiming that they were planning a coup. That same month, more than a hundred professors at Tikrit University, in Saddam's hometown, were fired for alleged Baathist connections.[51] In the week before the American withdrawal, Baghdad insisted that the former Sunni Awakening Councils disband and decommission their arms. Sheik Ahmed Abu Risha, one of America's staunchest Sunni allies and a leader of one militia group, estimated at 80,000 members, suggested that Sunnis would not turn in their weapons. "They want to defend themselves," he reported.[52] Some skeptics of the American withdrawal suggested at the time that the United States needed to stay in Iraq beyond the deadline because the political quarrels of the nascent Baghdad government had not yet been worked out, as could be expected in any new democracy. It was unrealistic to assume that Shiites and Sunnis could simply trust each other after years of animosity. Many Sunnis also feared that without American troops on the ground in Iraq, it would be too easy for neighboring Iran to make mischief.

Iran's role inside Iraq had always been problematic, but at the time of the American withdrawal there was indeed new reason for concern. Iranian leaders had strong ties to radical Shiites in Iraq, including Muqtada al-Sadr, and had used this influence to sway politics in Baghdad. Some U.S. officials feared that leaving no American troops behind meant that Iran had won. "We have said one of the reasons for keeping American forces in Iraq was to continue a very strong signal to Iran to draw a line between Persian Iran and the rest of the region," reported General Kimmitt, who supported an extension of the deadline and keeping a residual American force in Iraq.[53] According to Kimmitt, Iran had been providing weapons to Hezbollah in Lebanon and Hamas in the Gaza Strip, as well as to radical Shiite groups inside Iraq, and this was reason enough for the United States to stay.[54] The Obama administration countered, arguing that it would not allow Iran to interfere with Iraq. "Iraq's sovereignty must be respected," the president said during a White House meeting with Maliki in December 2011.[55] It was a thinly veiled warning for Iran to leave Iraq alone. Yet Iran had openly defied the international community on a host of issues in the fall of 2011, so many foreign policy experts speculated that there was little that strong words would do.

In November 2011, the United Nations reported that Iran had continued to develop its nuclear weapons capabilities despite public assurances by Tehran to the contrary.[56] The Obama administration immediately asked Congress to freeze all Iranian assets in the United States and placed sanctions on Tehran. Iran responded by publicly stating that it would let world oil prices climb to $250 per barrel.[57] Tensions only increased when Iran, somehow, was able to secure a U.S. drone missile that had strayed off course. Tehran refused to return the drone to the United States, and many speculated that this was the first salvo in a new fight between old enemies. Some policy experts were also concerned that Iran was taking credit for pushing the United States out of the region. "The Iranians succeeded in their goal of seeing the American military presence [in Iraq] come to an end, and that shouldn't be underestimated," argued Fred Kagan of the American Enterprise Institute. "At the end of the day, Iran's ability to influence Iraqi power politics is growing."[58]

Indeed, Kagan, who had presided over the birth of the surge, believed that Iran was the big winner in Iraq. In a *Los Angeles Times* op-ed essay in October 2011, Kagan declared that the United States had not achieved any of its objectives under the Obama administration, but that Iran was "well on its way to achieving its strategic objectives." Kagan traced Iran's efforts in Iraq since 2004, suggesting that Tehran "sought to drive all American forces out of the country, to promote a weak, Shiite-led government in Baghdad, to develop Hezbollah-like political-militia organizations in Iraq through which to exert influence and intimidate pro-Western Iraqi leaders, and to insinuate its theocratic ideology into Iraq's Shiite clerical establishment." He concluded that Tehran had "largely succeeded in achieving each of those goals."[59] Kagan believed that preventing an extension of SoFA had been Iran's primary goal since 2008, and that Tehran had accomplished this task by working closely with its supporters inside Iraq and by bribing some Baghdad officials. Iran had also supervised renewed Shiite attacks against U.S. forces in southern Iraq and around Baghdad in October 2011, further proof for Kagan that Iran was behind the effort to keep the U.S. to its withdrawal deadline. Comments by Muqtada al-Sadr in November 2011 confirmed these fears, according to Kagan. Al-Sadr, a long-time friend of Iran and leader of one Shiite faction inside Iraq, claimed that, "We do not accept any kind of U.S. presence in Iraq, whether it is military or not. If they stay in Iraq," al-Sadr told Al-Arabiya News, "through a military or non-military (presence) . . . we will consider them an occupation and we will resist them whatever the price will be. Even a civilian presence, we reject it."[60]

Though it took the Iranian threat seriously, the Obama administration believed that the Iraqi leadership had no desire to be a pawn of its Iranian neighbors. The White House reasoned that Iraq had spent enormous energy and had sacrificed a great deal to create new national institutions that bore a decidedly post-Saddam Iraqi imprint. Iran may have been able to direct and support Shiite militias during the bloodiest years of sectarian violence, but once on their own, Obama believed, most Iraqis would strike an independent path forward. Of course, Obama was convinced that the United States would still have influence on Baghdad's thinking, even after the American troop withdrawal. The Obama White House believed it could moderate Iran's influence on Iraq through increased efforts by the U.S. State Department. The White House had always hoped that Baghdad – despite its obvious problems – would rise up against extremism of any kind while tempering its own treatment of Sunnis. In the summer of 2008, the Maliki government ordered attacks on Shiite militias, largely supported by Iran, near the city of Basra, defying those who believed it was a pawn of Tehran. Maliki had come to realize, Obama concluded, that radical Iraqi Shiites backed by Iran were a threat to his leadership as well as to Iraqi Sunnis.

Sunnis remained uneasy, however, and events in early 2012 reflected that fear. Following the American troop withdrawal, several radical Sunni groups launched raids against key Shia shrines and civilians. On July 23, 2012, al-Qaeda in Iraq, a Sunni-led terrorist group, launched coordinated attacks on over a dozen cities, killing over a hundred innocent people. The attacks, Iraq's deadliest since the U.S. withdrawal, came only days after al-Qaeda in Iraq threatened to resume its offensive against the Baghdad government. The new campaign was called "Breaking the Walls," a reference to the walls that surrounded Sunni communities in their "hardened state." One radical Sunni leader, Abu Bakr al-Baghdadi, claimed that the "majority of Sunnis support al-Qaeda and are waiting for its return."[61] To calm Sunni fears, the Maliki government announced in late July 2012 that it would allow some former Sunni officers to return to their posts in the armed services. Following Saddam's overthrow, all officers with connections to the Baathist Party had been dismissed, causing tremendous turmoil and animosity. Most Sunnis saw the government's gesture as too little and too late. Ayad Allawi described Iraq in the summer of 2012 this way: "Things are not good. Things are bad. The society is split and we don't have a real democracy – we have a mockery."[62]

The U.S. State Department seemed to agree. In its official 2011 Human Rights Report for Iraq (see DOCUMENT 6-D), the Bureau of Democracy, Human Rights, and Labor reported that:

During the year the following significant human rights problems were reported: arbitrary or unlawful deprivation of life; extremist and terrorist bombings and executions; disappearances; torture and other cruel, inhuman, or degrading treatment or punishment; poor conditions in pretrial detention and prison facilities; arbitrary arrest and detention; impunity; denial of fair public trials; delays in resolving property restitution claims; insufficient judicial institutional capacity; arbitrary interference with privacy and home; limits on freedoms of speech, press, and assembly and extremist threats and violence; limits on religious freedom due to extremist threats and violence; restrictions on freedom of movement; large numbers of internally displaced persons (IDPs) and refugees; lack of transparency and significant, widespread corruption at all levels of government; constraints on international organizations and nongovernmental organizations' (NGOs) investigations of alleged violations of human rights; discrimination against and societal abuses of women and ethnic, religious, and racial minorities; human trafficking; societal discrimination and violence against individuals based on sexual orientation; and limited exercise of labor rights.[63]

Furthermore, the State Department concluded that "continuing violence, corruption, and organizational dysfunction undermined the government's ability to protect human rights."[64] There had been significant reforms made since Saddam's rule, but still basic human rights violations occurred in Iraq with frequency, and many in the government were complicit. Billions of U.S. dollars and thousands of lives lost had not changed the fundamental political problems in Iraq, and this was most frustrating to the Obama administration. Obama believed all along that Iraq was not the place to go to war, but he could not find the answer to the puzzle either. Despite America's enormous investment in Iraq, there was little Washington policymakers could do to influence their allies in Baghdad. Because counterinsurgency depends so heavily on the host government to deliver the social, economic, and political goods to its people, a foreign power loses initiative and leverage. Baghdad officials knew quite well that the United States was completely dependent on them for success beyond operational tactics, and this decreased America's ability to dictate terms to its allies. When Washington demanded needed reforms, those reforms were slow to materialize or never came at all. This is the nature of counterinsurgency and nation-building in the modern world. This was the American frustration in Iraq.

Obama hid his obvious disappointment over events in Iraq during a White House ceremony in December 2011, celebrating the "end of the war." The president said of Iraq and Maliki:

> Today, I'm proud to welcome Prime Minister Maliki – the elected leader of a sovereign, self-reliant and democratic Iraq. We're here to mark the end of this war; to honor the sacrifices of all those who made this day possible; and to turn the page – begin a new chapter in the history between our countries – a normal relationship between sovereign nations, an equal partnership based on mutual interests and mutual respect.
>
> Iraq faces great challenges, but today reflects the impressive progress that Iraqis have made. Millions have cast their ballots – some risking or giving their lives – to vote in free elections. The Prime Minister leads Iraq's most inclusive government yet. Iraqis are working to build institutions that are efficient and independent and transparent.[65]

It was the prime minister, however, who got the last word on the wars for Iraq in his own speech at this ceremony (see DOCUMENT 6-E). Determined to lead Iraq in a new direction, but one that acknowledged its sovereignty and history, Maliki claimed that "Iraq now has become – reliant completely on its own security apparatus and internal security as a result of the expertise that it gained during the confrontations and the training and the equipping. But it remains in need of cooperation with the United States of America in security issues and information and combating terrorism, and in the area of training and the area of equipping, which is needed by the Iraqi army. And we have started that. And we want to complete the process of equipping the Iraqi army in order to protect our sovereignty, and does not violate the rights of anybody – or do not take any missions from the sovereignty of others" After eight years of war, these were hopeful, if not elusive, goals.

Notes

1   Transcript of Obama–McCain debate, October 7, 2008.
2   Transcript of Senator Obama's speech in Chicago, October 2, 2002.
3   Bob Woodward, *Obama's Wars* (New York: Simon & Schuster, 2010), 258.
4   As quoted ibid., 76.
5   Remarks by the President on a New Strategy for Afghanistan and Pakistan, March 27, 2009, Office of the White House Press Secretary.
6   Interview with Secretary Robert Gates, MSNBC.com, March 1, 2009.
7   U.S. National Security Strategy, May 2010, White House.
8   "Withdrawing from Iraq: Alternative Schedules, Associated Risks, and Mitigating Strategies," RAND Corporation, 2009.
9   Transcript of President Obama's remarks, Camp Lejeune, North Carolina, Friday, February 27, 2009, 12:42 p.m..
10   Ibid.
11   Ibid.
12   Ibid.
13   "Iraq Troop Withdrawal," Congressional Record On-Line, page S2578, http://www.gpo.gov/fdsys/granule/CREC-2009-02-27/CREC-2009-02-27-pt1-PgS2578-4/content-detail.html, accessed January 15, 2013.
14   Transcript of House Resolution 208, March 4, 2009, U.S. House of Representatives, 111th Congress, 1st session.
15   Ibid.
16   David S. Cloud, "Inside Obama's Iraq Decision," *Politico* (February 27, 2009).
17   Ibid.
18   *New York Times*, October 23, 2011.
19   Ibid.
20   Ibid.
21   Ibid.
22   BBC News, August 12, 2010.
23   *New York Times*, July 29, 2009.
24   "Odierno Discusses Iraq Drawdown," III Corps, Fort Hood Public Affairs Office, U.S. Army, December 6, 2011.
25   *Boston Globe*, October 21, 2011.
26   Transcript of President Obama's remarks, Camp Lejeune, North Carolina, Friday, February 27, 2009, 12:42 p.m.
27   Text of a letter from the President to the Speaker of the House of Representatives, April 9, 2009, Office of the White House Press Secretary.

28 *New York Times*, February 25, 2009.
29 Text of President Barack Obama's remarks, the White House, September 1, 2010, Office of the White House Press Secretary.
30 United Nations, "Development Assistance Framework for Iraq, 2011–2014," February 24, 2010.
31 Ibid.
32 Ibid.
33 *Forced Migration Review*, June 2007.
34 Ibid.
35 United Nations Commission on Human Rights, United Nations Refugee Agency-Iraq, Country Operations Profile; UNHCR Iraq Fact Sheet, "Crisis in Iraq," September 1, 2008; and OCHA Iraq Office in Amman, "Humanitarian Crisis in Iraq: Facts and Figures," Representative of the United Nations Assistance Mission in Iraq, November 13, 2007.
36 Human Rights First, "Iraqi Refugee Crisis," http://www.humanrightsfirst.org/our-work/refugee-protection/iraqi-refugee-crisis/, accessed January 15, 2013.
37 Elizabeth Ferris, "The Looming Crisis: Displacement and Security in Iraq," Brookings Institute press release, August 5, 2008.
38 Johanna Grombach Wagner, "An IHL/CRC Perspective on Humanitarian Space," *Humanitarian Exchange Magazine*, 32 (December 2005).
39 United Nations Office for the Coordination of Human Affairs, "Acute Shortages in Clash-Hit Baghdad Suburbs," April 10, 2008.
40 "Humanitarian Situation Report on Baghdad, Basrah, Wassit and Babylon Humanitarian Coordinator on behalf of Humanitarian Agencies and Organisations," United Nations, Sunday, March 30, 2008.
41 Ken Pollack, "The Battle for Baghdad," *National Interest Online* (August 25, 2009). http://nationalinterest.org/article/the-battle-for-baghdad-3216, accessed January 15, 2013.
42 Marc Lynch, "What Does Political Science Literature on Civil Wars Really Say about Iraq?" *Foreign Policy* (September 7, 2009); *Los Angeles Times*, August 4, 2009.
43 Amnesty International, "Iraq Must Halt Spiralling Death Sentences," January 18, 2010, http://www.amnesty.org/en/news-and-updates/iraq-must-halt-spiralling-death-sentences-20100118, accessed January 15, 2013.
44 United Nations, Assistance Mission for Iraq, Human Rights Report, 1 January–30 June 2009, 4.
45 *New York Times*, May 5, 2010.
46 As quoted in Peter Hahn, *Mission Accomplished? The United States and Iraq since World War I* (New York: Oxford University Press, 2012), 178.
47 *New York Times*, June 25, 2011.
48 *New York Times*, December 12, 2011.
49 Ibid.
50 Ibid.
51 *Pittsburgh Post Gazette*, December 13, 2011.
52 *New York Times*, December 13, 2011.
53 *Washington Times*, October 23, 2011.
54 Ibid.

55   *New York Times*, December 11, 2011.
56   International Atomic Energy Association, Report of the Director General, "Implementation of the NPT Safeguards Agreement and Relevant Provisions of Security Council Resolutions in the Islamic Republic of Iran, November 8, 2011," United Nations.
57   *New York Times*, December 5, 2011.
58   *Christian Science Monitor*, December 12, 2011.
59   *Los Angeles Times*, October 17, 2011.
60   Al-Arabiya News, November 4, 2011.
61   Associated Press, July 23, 2012.
62   Ibid.
63   U.S. State Department, Bureau of Democracy, Human Rights and Labor, Country Report 2011, Iraq.
64   Ibid.
65   Remarks by President Obama and Prime Minister al-Maliki of Iraq in a Joint Press Conference, December 12, 2011, Office of the White House Press Secretary.

DOCUMENTS

Document 6-A

Status of Forces Agreement, 2008

Agreement Between the United States of America and the Republic of Iraq On the Withdrawal of United States Forces from Iraq and the Organization of Their Activities during Their Temporary Presence in Iraq

Preamble

The United States of America and the Republic of Iraq, referred to hereafter as "the Parties":

Recognizing the importance of: strengthening their joint security, contributing to world peace and stability, combating terrorism in Iraq, and cooperating in the security and defense spheres, thereby deterring aggression and threats against the sovereignty, security, and territorial integrity of Iraq and against its democratic, federal, and constitutional system;

Affirming that such cooperation is based on full respect for the sovereignty of each of them in accordance with the purposes and principles of the United Nations Charter;

Out of a desire to reach a common understanding that strengthens cooperation between them;

Without prejudice to Iraqi sovereignty over its territory, waters, and airspace; and Pursuant to joint undertakings as two sovereign, independent, and coequal countries;

Have agreed to the following:

Article 1
Scope and Purpose

This Agreement shall determine the principal provisions and requirements that regulate the temporary presence, activities, and withdrawal of the United States Forces from Iraq.

Article 2
Definition of Terms

1. "Agreed facilities and areas" are those Iraqi facilities and areas owned by the Government of Iraq that are in use by the United States Forces during the period in which this Agreement is in force.
2. "United States Forces" means the entity comprising the members of the United States Armed Forces, their associated civilian component, and all property, equipment, and materiel of the United States Armed Forces present in the territory of Iraq.
3. "Member of the United States Forces" means any individual who is a member of the United States Army, Navy, Air Force, Marine Corps, or Coast Guard.
4. "Member of the civilian component" means any civilian employed by the United States Department of Defense. This term does not include individuals normally resident in Iraq.
5. "United States contractors" and "United States contractor employees" mean non-Iraqi persons or legal entities, and their employees, who are citizens of the United States or a third country and who are in Iraq to supply goods, services, and security in Iraq to or on behalf of the United States Forces under a contract or subcontract with or for the United States Forces. However, the terms do not include persons or legal entities normally resident in the territory of Iraq.
6. "Official vehicles" means commercial vehicles that may be modified for security purposes and are basically designed for movement on various roads and designated for transportation of personnel.
7. "Military vehicles" means all types of vehicles used by the United States Forces, which were originally designated for use in combat operations and display special distinguishing numbers and symbols according to applicable United States Forces instructions and regulations.
8. "Defense equipment" means systems, weapons, supplies, equipment, munitions, and materials exclusively used in conventional warfare that are

required by the United States Forces in connection with agreed activities under this Agreement and are not related, either directly or indirectly, to systems of weapons of mass destruction (chemical weapons, nuclear weapons, radiological weapons, biological weapons, and related waste of such weapons).

9. "Storage" means the keeping of defense equipment required by the United States Forces in connection with agreed activities under this Agreement.

10. "Taxes and duties" means all taxes, duties (including customs duties), fees, of whatever kind, imposed by the Government of Iraq, or its agencies, or governorates under Iraqi laws and regulations. However, the term does not include charges by the Government of Iraq, its agencies, or governorates for services requested and received by the United States Forces.

Article 3
Laws

1. While conducting military operations pursuant to this Agreement, it is the duty of members of the United States Forces and of the civilian component to respect Iraqi laws, customs, traditions, and conventions and to refrain from any activities that are inconsistent with the letter and spirit of this Agreement. It is the duty of the United States to take all necessary measures for this purpose.

2. With the exception of members of the United States Forces and of the civilian component, the United States Forces may not transfer any person into or out of Iraq on vehicles, vessels, or aircraft covered by this Agreement, unless in accordance with applicable Iraqi laws and regulations, including implementing arrangements as may be agreed to by the Government of Iraq.

Article 4
Missions

1. The Government of Iraq requests the temporary assistance of the United States Forces for the purposes of supporting Iraq in its efforts to maintain security and stability in Iraq, including cooperation in the conduct of operations against al-Qaeda and other terrorist groups, outlaw groups, and remnants of the former regime.

2. All such military operations that are carried out pursuant to this Agreement shall be conducted with the agreement of the Government of Iraq. Such operations shall be fully coordinated with Iraqi authorities. The coordination of all such military operations shall be overseen by a Joint Military Operations Coordination Committee (JMOCC) to be established pursuant to this Agreement. Issues regarding proposed military operations that cannot be resolved by the JMOCC shall be forwarded to the Joint Ministerial Committee.

3. All such operations shall be conducted with full respect for the Iraqi Constitution and the laws of Iraq. Execution of such operations shall not infringe upon the sovereignty of Iraq and its national interests, as defined by the Government of Iraq. It is the duty of the United States Forces to respect the laws, customs, and traditions of Iraq and applicable international law.
4. The Parties shall continue their efforts to cooperate to strengthen Iraq's security capabilities including, as may be mutually agreed, on training, equipping, supporting, supplying, and establishing and upgrading logistical systems, including transportation, housing, and supplies for Iraqi Security Forces.
5. The Parties retain the right to legitimate self defense within Iraq, as defined in applicable international law.

Article 5
Property Ownership

1. Iraq owns all buildings, non-relocatable structures, and assemblies connected to the soil that exist on agreed facilities and areas, including those that are used, constructed, altered, or improved by the United States Forces.
2. Upon their withdrawal, the United States Forces shall return to the Government of Iraq all the facilities and areas provided for the use of the combat forces of the United States, based on two lists. The first list of agreed facilities and areas shall take effect upon the entry into force of the Agreement. The second list shall take effect no later than June 30, 2009, the date for the withdrawal of combat forces from the cities, villages, and localities. The Government of Iraq may agree to allow the United States Forces the use of some necessary facilities for the purposes of this Agreement on withdrawal.
3. The United States shall bear all costs for construction, alterations, or improvements in the agreed facilities and areas provided for its exclusive use. The United States Forces shall consult with the Government of Iraq regarding such construction, alterations, and improvements, and must seek approval of the Government of Iraq for major construction and alteration projects. In the event that the use of agreed facilities and areas is shared, the two Parties shall bear the costs of construction, alterations, or improvements proportionately.
4. The United States shall be responsible for paying the costs for services requested and received in the agreed facilities and areas exclusively used by it, and both Parties shall be proportionally responsible for paying the costs for services requested and received in joint agreed facilities and areas.
5. Upon the discovery of any historical or cultural site or finding any strategic resource in agreed facilities and areas, all works of construction, upgrading, or modification shall cease immediately and the Iraqi representatives at the Joint Committee shall be notified to determine appropriate steps in that regard.

6. The United States shall return agreed facilities and areas and any non-relocatable structures and assemblies on them that it had built, installed, or established during the term of this Agreement, according to mechanisms and priorities set forth by the Joint Committee. Such facilities and areas shall be handed over to the Government of Iraq free of any debts and financial burdens.

7. The United States Forces shall return to the Government of Iraq the agreed facilities and areas that have heritage, moral, and political significance and any non-relocatable structures and assemblies on them that it had built, installed, or established, according to mechanisms, priorities, and a time period as mutually agreed by the Joint Committee, free of any debts or financial burdens.

8. The United States Forces shall return the agreed facilities and areas to the Government of Iraq upon the expiration or termination of this Agreement, or earlier as mutually agreed by the Parties, or when such facilities are no longer required as determined by the JMOCC, free of any debts or financial burdens.

9. The United States Forces and United States contractors shall retain title to all equipment, materials, supplies, relocatable structures, and other movable property that was legitimately imported into or legitimately acquired within the territory of Iraq in connection with this Agreement.

Article 6
Use of Agreed Facilities and Areas

1. With full respect for the sovereignty of Iraq, and as part of exchanging views between the Parties pursuant to this Agreement, Iraq grants access and use of agreed facilities and areas to the United States Forces, United States contractors, United States contractor employees, and other individuals or entities as agreed upon by the Parties.

2. In accordance with this Agreement, Iraq authorizes the United States Forces to exercise within the agreed facilities and areas all rights and powers that may be necessary to establish, use, maintain, and secure such agreed facilities and areas. The Parties shall coordinate and cooperate regarding exercising these rights and powers in the agreed facilities and areas of joint use.

3. The United States Forces shall assume control of entry to agreed facilities and areas that have been provided for its exclusive use. The Parties shall coordinate the control of entry into agreed facilities and areas for joint use and in accordance with mechanisms set forth by the JMOCC. The Parties shall coordinate guard duties in areas adjacent to agreed facilities and areas through the JMOCC.

Article 7
Positioning and Storage of Defense Equipment

The United States Forces may place within agreed facilities and areas and in other temporary locations agreed upon by the Parties defense equipment, supplies, and materials that are required by the United States Forces in connection with agreed activities under this Agreement. The use and storage of such equipment shall be proportionate to the temporary missions of the United States Forces in Iraq pursuant to Article 4 of this Agreement and shall not be related, either directly or indirectly, to systems of weapons of mass destruction (chemical weapons, nuclear weapons, radiological weapons, biological weapons, and related waste of such weapons). The United States Forces shall control the use and relocation of defense equipment that they own and are stored in Iraq. The United States Forces shall ensure that no storage depots for explosives or munitions are near residential areas, and they shall remove such materials stored therein. The United States shall provide the Government of Iraq with essential information on the numbers and types of such stocks.

Article 8
Protecting the Environment
Both Parties shall implement this Agreement in a manner consistent with protecting the natural environment and human health and safety. The United States reaffirms its commitment to respecting applicable Iraqi environmental laws, regulations, and standards in the course of executing its policies for the purposes of implementing this Agreement.

Article 9
Movement of Vehicles, Vessels, and Aircraft

1. With full respect for the relevant rules of land and maritime safety and movement, vessels and vehicles operated by or at the time exclusively for the United States Forces may enter, exit, and move within the territory of Iraq for the purposes of implementing this Agreement. The JMOCC shall develop appropriate procedures and rules to facilitate and regulate the movement of vehicles.
2. With full respect for relevant rules of safety in aviation and air navigation, United States Government aircraft and civil aircraft that are at the time operating exclusively under a contract with the United States Department of Defense are authorized to over-fly, conduct airborne refueling exclusively for the purposes of implementing this Agreement over, and land and take off within, the territory of Iraq for the purposes of implementing this Agreement. The Iraqi authorities shall grant the aforementioned aircraft permission every year to land in and take off from Iraqi territory exclusively for the purposes of implementing this Agreement. United States Government aircraft and civil aircraft that are at the time operating exclusively under a contract with the United States Department of Defense, vessels, and vehicles

shall not have any party boarding them without the consent of the authorities of the United States Forces. The Joint Sub-Committee concerned with this matter shall take appropriate action to facilitate the regulation of such traffic.

3. Surveillance and control over Iraqi airspace shall transfer to Iraqi authority immediately upon entry into force of this Agreement.

4. Iraq may request from the United States Forces temporary support for the Iraqi authorities in the mission of surveillance and control of Iraqi air space.

5. United States Government aircraft and civil aircraft that are at the time operating exclusively under contract to the United States Department of Defense shall not be subject to payment of any taxes, duties, fees, or similar charges, including overflight or navigation fees, landing, and parking fees at government airfields. Vehicles and vessels owned or operated by or at the time exclusively for the United States Forces shall not be subject to payment of any taxes, duties, fees, or similar charges, including for vessels at government ports. Such vehicles, vessels, and aircraft shall be free from registration requirements within Iraq.

6. The United States Forces shall pay fees for services requested and received.

7. Each Party shall provide the other with maps and other available information on the location of mine fields and other obstacles that can hamper or jeopardize movement within the territory and waters of Iraq.

Article 10
Contracting Procedures

The United States Forces may select contractors and enter into contracts in accordance with United States law for the purchase of materials and services in Iraq, including services of construction and building. The United States Forces shall contract with Iraqi suppliers of materials and services to the extent feasible when their bids are competitive and constitute best value. The United States Forces shall respect Iraqi law when contracting with Iraqi suppliers and contractors and shall provide Iraqi authorities with the names of Iraqi suppliers and contractors, and the amounts of relevant contracts.

Article 11
Services and Communications

1. The United States Forces may produce and provide water, electricity, and other services to agreed facilities and areas in coordination with the Iraqi authorities through the Joint Sub-Committee concerned with this matter.

2. The Government of Iraq owns all frequencies. Pertinent Iraqi authorities shall allocate to the United States Forces such frequencies as coordinated by both Parties through the JMOCC. The United States Forces shall return

frequencies allocated to them at the end of their use not later than the termination of this Agreement.

3. The United States Forces shall operate their own telecommunications systems in a manner that fully respects the Constitution and laws of Iraq and in accordance with the definition of the term "telecommunications" contained in the Constitution of the International Union of Telecommunications of 1992, including the right to use necessary means and services of their own systems to ensure the full capability to operate systems of telecommunications.

4. For the purposes of this Agreement, the United States Forces are exempt from the payment of fees to use transmission airwaves and existing and future frequencies, including any administrative fees or any other related charges.

5. The United States Forces must obtain the consent of the Government of Iraq regarding any projects of infrastructure for communications that are made outside agreed facilities and areas exclusively for the purposes of this Agreement in accordance with Article 4, except in the case of actual combat operations conducted pursuant to Article 4.

6. The United States Forces shall use telecommunications systems exclusively for the purposes of this Agreement.

Article 12
Jurisdiction

Recognizing Iraq's sovereign right to determine and enforce the rules of criminal and civil law in its territory, in light of Iraq's request for temporary assistance from the United States Forces set forth in Article 4, and consistent with the duty of the members of the United States Forces and the civilian component to respect Iraqi laws, customs, traditions, and conventions, the Parties have agreed as follows:

Iraq shall have the primary right to exercise jurisdiction over members of the United States Forces and of the civilian component for the grave premeditated felonies enumerated pursuant to paragraph 8, when such crimes are committed outside agreed facilities and areas and outside duty status. Iraq shall have the primary right to exercise jurisdiction over United States contractors and United States contractor employees.

The United States shall have the primary right to exercise jurisdiction over members of the United States Forces and of the civilian component for matters arising inside agreed facilities and areas; during duty status outside agreed facilities and areas; and in circumstances not covered by paragraph 1.

7. At the request of either Party, the Parties shall assist each other in the investigation of incidents and the collection and exchange of evidence to ensure the due course of justice. Members of the United States Forces and

of the civilian component arrested or detained by Iraqi authorities shall be notified immediately to United States Forces authorities and handed over to them within 24 hours from the time of detention or arrest. Where Iraq exercises jurisdiction pursuant to paragraph I of this Article, custody of an accused member of the United States Forces or of the civilian component shall reside with United States Forces authorities. United States Forces authorities shall make such accused persons available to the Iraqi authorities for purposes of investigation and trial.

The authorities of either Party may request the authorities of the other Party to waive its primary right to jurisdiction in a particular case. The Government of Iraq agrees to exercise jurisdiction under paragraph I above, only after it has determined and notifies the United States in writing within 21 days of the discovery of an alleged offense, that it is of particular importance that such jurisdiction be exercised. Where the United States exercises jurisdiction pursuant to paragraph 3 of this Article, members of the United States Forces and of the civilian component shall be entitled to due process standards and protections pursuant to the Constitution and laws of the United States. Where the offense arising under paragraph 3 of this Article may involve a victim who is not a member of the United States Forces or of the civilian component, the Parties shall establish procedures through the Joint Committee to keep such persons informed as appropriate of: the status of the investigation of the crime; the bringing of charges against a suspected offender; the scheduling of court proceedings and the results of plea negotiations; opportunity to be heard at public sentencing proceedings, and to confer with the attorney for the prosecution in the case; and, assistance with filing a claim under Article 21 of this Agreement. As mutually agreed by the Parties, United States Forces authorities shall seek to hold the trials of such cases inside Iraq. If the trial of such cases is to be conducted in the United States, efforts will be undertaken to facilitate the personal attendance of the victim at the trial.

8. Where Iraq exercises jurisdiction pursuant to paragraph I of this Article, members of the United States Forces and of the civilian component shall be entitled to due process standards and protections consistent with those available under United States and Iraqi law. The Joint Committee shall establish procedures and mechanisms for implementing this Article, including an enumeration of the grave premeditated felonies that are subject to paragraph I and procedures that meet such due process standards and protections. Any exercise of jurisdiction pursuant to paragraph I of this Article may proceed only in accordance with these procedures and mechanisms.

9. Pursuant to paragraphs I and 3 of this Article, United States Forces authorities shall certify whether an alleged offense arose during duty status. In those cases where Iraqi authorities believe the circumstances require a

review of this determination, the Parties shall consult immediately through the Joint Committee, and United States Forces authorities shall take full account of the facts and circumstances and any information Iraqi authorities may present bearing on the determination by United States Forces authorities.

10. The Parties shall review the provisions of this Article every 6 months including by considering any proposed amendments to this Article taking into account the security situation in Iraq, the extent to which the United States Forces in Iraq are engaged in military operations, the growth and development of the Iraqi judicial system, and changes in United States and Iraqi law.

Article 13
Carrying Weapons and Apparel

Members of the United States Forces and of the civilian component may possess and carry weapons that are owned by the United States while in Iraq according to the authority granted to them under orders and according to their requirements and duties.

Members of the United States Forces may also wear uniforms during duty in Iraq.

Article 14
Entry and Exit

1. For purposes of this Agreement, members of the United States Forces and of the civilian component may enter and leave Iraq through official places of embarkation and debarkation requiring only identification cards and travel orders issued for them by the United States. The Joint Committee shall assume the task of setting up a mechanism and a process of verification to be carried out by pertinent Iraqi authorities.

2. Iraqi authorities shall have the right to inspect and verify the lists of names of members of the United States Forces and of the civilian component entering and leaving Iraq directly through the agreed facilities and areas. Said lists shall be submitted to Iraqi authorities by the United States Forces. For purposes of this Agreement, members of the United States Forces and of the civilian component may enter and leave Iraq through agreed facilities and areas requiring only identification cards issued for them by the United States. The Joint Committee shall assume the task of setting up a mechanism and a process for inspecting and verifying the validity of these documents.

Article 15
Import and Export

1. For the exclusive purposes of implementing this Agreement, the United States Forces and United States contractors may import, export (items

bought in Iraq), re-export, transport, and use in Iraq any equipment, supplies, materials, and technology, provided that the materials imported or brought in by them are not banned in Iraq as of the date this Agreement enters into force. The importation, re-exportation, transportation, and use of such items shall not be subject to any inspections, licenses, or other restrictions, taxes, customs duties, or any other charges imposed in Iraq, as defined in Article 2, paragraph 10. United States Forces authorities shall provide to relevant Iraqi authorities an appropriate certification that such items are being imported by the United States Forces or United States contractors for use by the United States Forces exclusively for the purposes of this Agreement. Based on security information that becomes available, Iraqi authorities have the right to request the United States Forces to open in their presence any container in which such items are being imported in order to verify its contents. In making such a request, Iraqi authorities shall honor the security requirements of the United States Forces and, if requested to do so by the United States Forces, shall make such verifications in facilities used by the United States Forces. The exportation of Iraqi goods by the United States Forces and United States contractors shall not be subject to inspections or any restrictions other than licensing requirements. The Joint Committee shall work with the Iraqi Ministry of Trade to expedite license requirements consistent with Iraqi law for the export of goods purchased in Iraq by the United States Forces for the purposes of this Agreement. Iraq has the right to demand review of any issues arising out of this paragraph. The Parties shall consult immediately in such cases through the Joint Committee or, if necessary, the Joint Ministerial Committee.

2.   Members of the United States Forces and of the civilian component may import into Iraq, re-export, and use personal effect materials and equipment for consumption or personal use. The import into, re-export from, transfer from, and use of such imported items in Iraq shall not be subjected to licenses, other restrictions, taxes, custom duties, or any other charges imposed in Iraq, as defined in Article 2, paragraph 10. The imported quantities shall be reasonable and proportionate to personal use. United States Forces authorities will take measures to ensure that no items or material of cultural or historic significance to Iraq are being exported.

3.   Any inspections of materials pursuant to paragraph 2 by Iraqi authorities must be done urgently in an agreed upon place and according to procedures established by the Joint Committee.

4.   Any material imported free of customs and fees in accordance with this Agreement shall be subjected to taxes and customs and fees as defined in Article 2, paragraph 10, or any other fees valued at the time of sale in Iraq, upon sale to individuals and entities not covered by tax exemption or special import privileges. Such taxes and fees (including custom duties) shall be paid by the transferee for the items sold.

5. Materials referred to in the paragraphs of this Article must not be imported or used for commercial purposes.

Article 16
Taxes

1. Any taxes, duties, or fees as defined in Article 2, paragraph 10, with their value determined and imposed in the territory of Iraq, shall not be imposed on goods and services purchased by or on behalf of the United States Forces in Iraq for official use or on goods and services that have been purchased in Iraq on behalf of the United States Forces.
2. Members of the United States Forces and of the civilian component shall not be responsible for payment of any tax, duty, or fee that has its value determined and imposed in the territory of Iraq, unless in return for services requested and received.

Article 17
Licenses or Permits

1. Valid driver's licenses issued by United States authorities to members of the United States Forces and of the civilian component, and to United States contractor employees, shall be deemed acceptable to Iraqi authorities. Such license holders shall not be subject to a test or fee for operating the vehicles, vessels, and aircraft belonging to the United States Forces in Iraq.
2. Valid driver's licenses issued by United States authorities to members of the United States Forces and of the civilian component, and to United States contractor employees, to operate personal cars within the territory of Iraq shall be deemed acceptable to Iraqi authorities. License holders shall not be subject to a test or fee.
3. All professional licenses issued by United States authorities to members of the United States Forces and of the civilian component, and to United States contractor employees shall be deemed valid by Iraqi authorities, provided such licenses are related to the services they provide within the framework of performing their official duties for or contracts in support of the United States Forces, members of the civilian component, United States contractors, and United States contractor employees, according to terms agreed upon by the Parties.

Article 18
Official and Military Vehicles

1. Official vehicles shall display official Iraqi license plates to be agreed upon between the Parties. Iraqi authorities shall, at the request of the authorities

of the United States Forces, issue registration plates for official vehicles of the United States Forces without fees, according to procedures used for the Iraqi Armed Forces. The authorities of the United States Forces shall pay to Iraqi authorities the cost of such plates.

2. Valid registration and licenses issued by United States authorities for official vehicles of the United States Forces shall be deemed acceptable by Iraqi authorities.

3. Military vehicles exclusively used by the United States Forces will be exempted from the requirements of registration and licenses, and they shall be clearly marked with numbers on such vehicles.

Article 19
Support Activities Services

1. The United States Forces, or others acting on behalf of the United States Forces, may assume the duties of establishing and administering activities and entities inside agreed facilities and areas, through which they can provide services for members of the United States Forces, the civilian component, United States contractors, and United States contractor employees. These entities and activities include military post offices; financial services; shops selling food items, medicine, and other commodities and services; and various areas to provide entertainment and telecommunications services, including radio broadcasts. The establishment of such services does not require permits.

2. Broadcasting, media, and entertainment services that reach beyond the scope of the agreed facilities and areas shall be subject to Iraqi laws.

3. Access to the Support Activities Services shall be limited to members of the United States Forces and of the civilian component, United States contractors, United States contractor employees, and other persons and entities that are agreed upon. The authorities of the United States Forces shall take appropriate actions to prevent misuse of the services provided by the mentioned activities, and prevent the sale or resale of aforementioned goods and services to persons not authorized access to these entities or to benefit from their services. The United States Forces will determine broadcasting and television programs to authorized recipients.

4. The service support entities and activities referred to in this Article shall be granted the same financial and customs exemptions granted to the United States Forces, including exemptions guaranteed in Articles 15 and 16 of this Agreement. These entities and activities that offer services shall be operated and managed in accordance with United States regulations; these entities and activities shall not be obligated to collect nor pay taxes or other fees related to the activities in connection with their operations.

5. The mail sent through the military post service shall be certified by United States Forces authorities and shall be exempt from inspection, search, and seizure by Iraqi authorities, except for non-official mail that may be subject to electronic observation. Questions arising in the course of implementation of this paragraph shall be addressed by the concerned Joint Sub-Committee and resolved by mutual agreement. The concerned Joint Sub-Committee shall periodically inspect the mechanisms by which the United States Forces authorities certify military mail.

Article 20
Currency and foreign exchange

1. The United States Forces shall have the right to use any amount of cash in United States currency or financial instruments with a designated value in United States currency exclusively for the purposes of this Agreement. Use of Iraqi currency and special banks by the United States Forces shall be in accordance with Iraqi laws.
2. The United States Forces may not export Iraqi currency from Iraq, and shall take measures to ensure that members of the United States Forces, of the civilian component, and United States contractors and United States contractor employees do not export Iraqi currency from Iraq.

Article 21
Claims

1. With the exception of claims arising from contracts, each Party shall waive the right to claim compensation against the other Party for any damage, loss, or destruction of property, or compensation for injuries or deaths that could happen to members of the force or civilian component of either Party arising out of the performance of their official duties in Iraq.
2. United States Forces authorities shall pay just and reasonable compensation in settlement of meritorious third party claims arising out of acts, omissions, or negligence of members of the United States Forces and of the civilian component done in the performance of their official duties and incident to the non-combat activities of the United States Forces. United States Forces authorities may also settle meritorious claims not arising from the performance of official duties. All claims in this paragraph shall be settled expeditiously in accordance with the laws and regulations of the United States. In settling claims, United States Forces authorities shall take into account any report of investigation or opinion regarding liability or amount of damages issued by Iraqi authorities.

3. Upon the request of either Party, the Parties shall consult immediately through the Joint Committee or, if necessary, the Joint Ministerial Committee, where issues referred to in paragraphs 1 and 2 above require review.

Article 22
Detention

1. No detention or arrest may be carried out by the United States Forces (except with respect to detention or arrest of members of the United States Forces and of the civilian component) except through an Iraqi decision issued in accordance with Iraqi law and pursuant to Article 4.
2. In the event the United States Forces detain or arrest persons as authorized by this Agreement or Iraqi law, such persons must be handed over to competent Iraqi authorities within 24 hours from the time of their detention or arrest.
3. The Iraqi authorities may request assistance from the United States Forces in detaining or arresting wanted individuals.
4. Upon entry into force of this Agreement, the United States Forces shall provide to the Government of Iraq available information on all detainees who are being held by them. Competent Iraqi authorities shall issue arrest warrants for persons who are wanted by them. The United States Forces shall act in full and effective coordination with the Government of Iraq to turn over custody of such wanted detainees to Iraqi authorities pursuant to a valid Iraqi arrest warrant and shall release all the remaining detainees in a safe and orderly manner, unless otherwise requested by the Government of Iraq and in accordance with Article 4 of this Agreement.
5. The United States Forces may not search houses or other real estate properties except by order of an Iraqi judicial warrant and in full coordination with the Government of Iraq, except in the case of actual combat operations conducted pursuant to Article 4.

Article 23
Implementation

Implementation of this Agreement and the settlement of disputes arising from the interpretation and application thereof shall be vested in the following bodies:

1. A Joint Ministerial Committee shall be established with participation at the Ministerial level determined by both Parties. The Joint Ministerial Committee shall deal with issues that are fundamental to the interpretation and implementation of this Agreement.
2. The Joint Ministerial Committee shall establish a JMOCC consisting of representatives from both Parties. The JMOCC shall be co-chaired by representatives of each Party.

3. The Joint Ministerial Committee shall also establish a Joint Committee consisting of representatives to be determined by both Parties. The Joint Committee shall be cochaired by representatives of each Party, and shall deal with all issues related to this Agreement outside the exclusive competence of the JMOCC.
4. In accordance with paragraph 3 of this Article, the Joint Committee shall establish Joint Sub-Committees in different areas to consider the issues arising under this Agreement according to their competencies.

Article 24
Withdrawal of the United States Forces from Iraq
Recognizing the performance and increasing capacity of the Iraqi Security Forces, the assumption of full security responsibility by those Forces, and based upon the strong relationship between the Parties, an agreement on the following has been reached:

1. All the United States Forces shall withdraw from all Iraqi territory no later than December 31, 2011.
2. All United States combat forces shall withdraw from Iraqi cities, villages, and localities no later than the time at which Iraqi Security Forces assume full responsibility for security in an Iraqi province, provided that such withdrawal is completed no later than June 30, 2009.
3. United States combat forces withdrawn pursuant to paragraph 2 above shall be stationed in the agreed facilities and areas outside cities, villages, and localities to be designated by the JMOCC before the date established in paragraph 2 above.
4. The United States recognizes the sovereign right of the Government of Iraq to request the departure of the United States Forces from Iraq at any time. The Government of Iraq recognizes the sovereign right of the United States to withdraw the United States Forces from Iraq at any time.
5. The Parties agree to establish mechanisms and arrangements to reduce the number of the United States Forces during the periods of time that have been determined, and they shall agree on the locations where the United States Forces will be present.

Article 25
Measures to Terminate the Application of Chapter VII to Iraq
Acknowledging the right of the Government of Iraq not to request renewal of the Chapter VII authorization for and mandate of the multinational forces contained in United Nations Security Council Resolution 1790 (2007) that ends on December 31, 2008; Taking note of the letters to the UN Security Council from the Prime Minister of Iraq and the Secretary of State of the United States

dated December 7 and December 10, 2007, respectively, which are annexed to Resolution 1790;

Taking note of section 3 of the Declaration of Principles for a Long-Term Relationship of Cooperation and Friendship, signed by the President of the United States and the Prime Minister of Iraq on November 26, 2007, which memorialized Iraq's call for extension of the above-mentioned mandate for a final period, to end not later than December 31, 2008:

Recognizing also the dramatic and positive developments in Iraq, and noting that the situation in Iraq is fundamentally different than that which existed when the UN Security Council adopted Resolution 661 in 1990, and in particular that the threat to international peace and security posed by the Government of Iraq no longer exists, the Parties affirm in this regard that with the termination on December 31, 2008 of the Chapter VII mandate and authorization for the multinational force contained in Resolution 1790, Iraq should return to the legal and international standing that it enjoyed prior to the adoption of UN Security Council Resolution 661 (1990), and that the United States shall use its best efforts to help Iraq take the steps necessary to achieve this by December 31, 2008.

Article 26
Iraqi Assets

1. To enable Iraq to continue to develop its national economy through the rehabilitation of its economic infrastructure, as well as providing necessary essential services to the Iraqi people, and to continue to safeguard Iraq's revenues from oil and gas and other Iraqi resources and its financial and economic assets located abroad, including the Development Fund for Iraq, the United States shall ensure maximum efforts to:
    a. Support Iraq to obtain forgiveness of international debt resulting from the policies of the former regime.
    b. Support Iraq to achieve a comprehensive and final resolution of outstanding reparation claims inherited from the previous regime, including compensation requirements imposed by the UN Security Council on Iraq.
2. Recognizing and understanding Iraq's concern with claims based on actions perpetrated by the former regime, the President of the United States has exercised his authority to protect from United States judicial process the Development Fund for Iraq and certain other property in which Iraq has an interest. The United States shall remain fully and actively engaged with the Government of Iraq with respect to continuation of such protections and with respect to such claims.
3. Consistent with a letter from the President of the United States to be sent to the Prime Minister of Iraq, the United States remains committed to assist Iraq in connection with its request that the UN Security Council extend the

protections and other arrangements established in Resolution 1483 (2003) and Resolution 1546 (2003) for petroleum, petroleum products, and natural gas originating in Iraq, proceeds and obligations from sale thereof, and the Development Fund for Iraq.

Article 27
Deterrence of Security Threats

In order to strengthen security and stability in Iraq and to contribute to the maintenance of international peace and stability, the Parties shall work actively to strengthen the political and military capabilities of the Republic of Iraq to deter threats against its sovereignty, political independence, territorial integrity, and its constitutional federal democratic system. To that end, the Parties agree as follows:

In the event of any external or internal threat or aggression against Iraq that would violate its sovereignty, political independence, or territorial integrity, waters, airspace, its democratic system or its elected institutions, and upon request by the Government of Iraq, the Parties shall immediately initiate strategic deliberations and, as may be mutually agreed, the United States shall take appropriate measures, including diplomatic, economic, or military measures, or any other measure, to deter such a threat.

The Parties agree to continue close cooperation in strengthening and maintaining military and security institutions and democratic political institutions in Iraq, including, as may be mutually agreed, cooperation in training, equipping, and arming the Iraqi Security Forces, in order to combat domestic and international terrorism and outlaw groups, upon request by the Government of Iraq.

Iraqi land, sea, and air shall not be used as a launching or transit point for attacks against other countries.

Article 28
The Green Zone

Upon entry into force of this Agreement the Government of Iraq shall have full responsibility for the Green Zone. The Government of Iraq may request from the United States Forces limited and temporary support for the Iraqi authorities in the mission of security for the Green Zone. Upon such request, relevant Iraqi authorities shall work jointly with the United States Forces authorities on security for the Green Zone during the period determined by the Government of Iraq.

Article 29
Implementing Mechanisms

Whenever the need arises, the Parties shall establish appropriate mechanisms for implementation of Articles of this Agreement, including those that do not contain specific implementation mechanisms.

Article 30
The Period for which the Agreement is Effective

1. This Agreement shall be effective for a period of three years, unless terminated sooner by either Party pursuant to paragraph 3 of this Article.
2. This Agreement shall be amended only with the official agreement of the Parties in writing and in accordance with the constitutional procedures in effect in both countries.
3. This Agreement shall terminate one year after a Party provides written notification to the other Party to that effect.
4. This Agreement shall enter into force on January 1, 2009, following an exchange of diplomatic notes confirming that the actions by the Parties necessary to bring the Agreement into force in accordance with each Party's respective constitutional procedures have been completed.

Signed in duplicate in Baghdad on this 17th day of November, 2008, in the English and Arabic languages, each text being equally authentic.

FOR THE UNITED   FOR THE
STATES OF AMERICA: REPUBLIC OF IRAQ:

QUESTIONS TO CONSIDER

1   What was the timeline established for the U.S. troop withdrawal?
2   Who had to agree to all U.S. military operations in Iraq besides the U.S. Department of Defense?
3   Who had jurisdiction over members of the U.S. armed services for crimes committed in Iraq? Was this unusual?
4   What environmental factors were considered by the U.S. troop presence in Iraq?

──────────── **Document 6-B** ────────────

Transcript of President Obama's remarks, Camp Lejeune, North Carolina, February 27, 2009

Good morning Marines. Good morning Camp Lejeune. Good morning Jacksonville. Thank you for that outstanding welcome. I want to thank Lieutenant General Hejlik for hosting me here today.

I also want to acknowledge all of our soldiers, sailors, airmen and Marines serving in Iraq and Afghanistan. That includes the Camp Lejeune Marines now serving with – or soon joining – the Second Marine Expeditionary Force in Iraq; those with Special Purpose Marine Air Ground Task Force in Afghanistan; and those among the 8,000 Marines who are preparing to deploy to Afghanistan. We have you in our prayers. We pay tribute to your service. We thank you and your families for all that you do for America. And I want all of you to know that there is no higher honor or greater responsibility than serving as your Commander-in-Chief.

I also want to take this opportunity to acknowledge Ryan Crocker, who recently completed his service as our Ambassador to Iraq. Throughout his career, Ryan always took on the toughest assignments. He is an example of the very best that this nation has to offer, and we owe him a great debt of gratitude. He carried on his work with an extraordinary degree of cooperation with two of our finest Generals – General David Petraeus, and General Ray Odierno – who will be critical in carrying forward the strategy that I will outline today.

Next month will mark the sixth anniversary of the war in Iraq. By any measure, this has already been a long war. For the men and women of America's armed forces – and for your families – this war has been one of the most extraordinary chapters of service in the history of our nation. You have endured tour after tour after tour of duty. You have known the dangers of combat and the lonely distance of loved ones. You have fought against tyranny and disorder. You have bled for your best friends and for unknown Iraqis. And you have borne an enormous burden for your fellow citizens, while extending a precious opportunity to the people of Iraq. Under tough circumstances, the men and women of the United States military have served with honor, and succeeded beyond any expectation.

Today, I have come to speak to you about how the war in Iraq will end.

To understand where we need to go in Iraq, it is important for the American people to understand where we now stand. Thanks in great measure to your service, the situation in Iraq has improved. Violence has been reduced substantially from the horrific sectarian killing of 2006 and 2007. Al Qaeda in Iraq has been dealt a serious blow by our troops and Iraq's Security Forces, and through our partnership with Sunni Arabs. The capacity of Iraq's Security Forces has improved, and Iraq's leaders have taken steps toward political accommodation. The relative peace and strong participation in January's provincial elections sent a powerful message to the world about how far Iraqis have come in pursuing their aspirations through a peaceful political process.

But let there be no doubt: Iraq is not yet secure, and there will be difficult days ahead. Violence will continue to be a part of life in Iraq. Too many fundamental political questions about Iraq's future remain unresolved. Too many Iraqis are still displaced or destitute. Declining oil revenues will put an added strain on a government that has had difficulty delivering basic services. Not all of Iraq's neighbors are contributing to its security. Some are working at times to under-mine it. And even as Iraq's government is on a surer footing, it is not yet a full partner – politically and economically – in the region, or with the international community. In short, today there is a renewed cause for hope in Iraq, but that hope rests upon an emerging foundation.

On my first full day in office, I directed my national security team to undertake a comprehensive review of our strategy in Iraq to determine the best way to strengthen that foundation, while strengthening American national security. I have listened to my Secretary of Defense, the Joint Chiefs of Staff, and commanders on the ground. We have acted with careful consideration of events on the ground; with respect for the security agreements between the United States and Iraq; and with a critical recognition that the long-term solution in Iraq must be politi-cal – not military. Because the most important decisions that have to be made about Iraq's future must now be made by Iraqis.

We have also taken into account the simple reality that America can no longer afford to see Iraq in isolation from other priorities: we face the challenge of refocusing on Afghanistan and Pakistan; of relieving the burden on our military; and of rebuilding our struggling economy – and these are challenges that we will meet.

Today, I can announce that our review is complete, and that the United States will pursue a new strategy to end the war in Iraq through a transition to full Iraqi responsibility.

This strategy is grounded in a clear and achievable goal shared by the Iraqi people and the American people: an Iraq that is sovereign, stable, and self-reliant. To achieve that goal, we will work to promote an Iraqi government that is just, representative, and accountable, and that provides neither support nor safe-haven to terrorists. We will help Iraq build new ties of trade and commerce with the world. And we will forge a partnership with the people and government of Iraq that contributes to the peace and security of the region.

What we will not do is let the pursuit of the perfect stand in the way of achievable goals. We cannot rid Iraq of all who oppose America or sympathize with our adversaries. We cannot police Iraq's streets until they are completely safe, nor stay until Iraq's union is perfected. We cannot sustain indefinitely a commitment that has put a strain on our military, and will cost the American people nearly a trillion dollars. America's men and women in uniform have fought block by block, province by province, year after year, to give the Iraqis this chance to choose a better future. Now, we must ask the Iraqi people to seize it.

The first part of this strategy is therefore the responsible removal of our combat brigades from Iraq.

As a candidate for President, I made clear my support for a timeline of 16 months to carry out this drawdown, while pledging to consult closely with our military commanders upon taking office to ensure that we preserve the gains we've made and protect our troops. Those consultations are now complete, and

I have chosen a timeline that will remove our combat brigades over the next 18 months.

Let me say this as plainly as I can: by August 31, 2010, our combat mission in Iraq will end.

As we carry out this drawdown, my highest priority will be the safety and security of our troops and civilians in Iraq. We will proceed carefully, and I will consult closely with my military commanders on the ground and with the Iraqi government. There will surely be difficult periods and tactical adjustments. But our enemies should be left with no doubt: this plan gives our military the forces and the flexibility they need to support our Iraqi partners, and to succeed.

After we remove our combat brigades, our mission will change from combat to supporting the Iraqi government and its Security Forces as they take the absolute lead in securing their country. As I have long said, we will retain a transitional force to carry out three distinct functions: training, equipping, and advising Iraqi Security Forces as long as they remain non-sectarian; conducting targeted counter-terrorism missions; and protecting our ongoing civilian and military efforts within Iraq. Initially, this force will likely be made up of 35-50,000 U.S. troops.

Through this period of transition, we will carry out further redeployments. And under the Status of Forces Agreement with the Iraqi government, I intend to remove all U.S. troops from Iraq by the end of 2011. We will complete this transition to Iraqi responsibility, and we will bring our troops home with the honor that they have earned.

As we responsibly remove our combat brigades, we will pursue the second part of our strategy: sustained diplomacy on behalf of a more peaceful and prosperous Iraq.

The drawdown of our military should send a clear signal that Iraq's future is now its own responsibility. The long-term success of the Iraqi nation will depend upon decisions made by Iraq's leaders and the fortitude of the Iraqi people. Iraq is a sovereign country with legitimate institutions; America cannot – and should not – take their place. However, a strong political, diplomatic, and civilian effort on our part can advance progress and help lay a foundation for lasting peace and security.

This effort will be led by our new Ambassador to Iraq – Chris Hill. From his time in the Peace Corps, to his work in Kosovo and Korea, Ambassador Hill has been tested, and he has shown the pragmatism and skill that we need right now. He will be supported by the courageous and capable work of so many American diplomats and aid workers who are serving in Iraq.

Going forward, we can make a difference on several fronts. We will work with the United Nations to support national elections, while helping Iraqis improve local government. We can serve as an honest broker in pursuit of fair and durable agreements on issues that have divided Iraq's leaders. And just as we will support Iraq's Security Forces, we will help Iraqi institutions strengthen their capacity to protect the rule of law, confront corruption, and deliver basic services.

Diplomacy and assistance is also required to help the millions of displaced Iraqis. These men, women and children are a living consequence of this war and a challenge to stability in the region, and they must become a part of Iraq's reconciliation and recovery. America has a strategic interest – and a moral responsibility – to act. In the coming months, my administration will provide more assistance and take steps to increase international support for countries already hosting refugees; we'll cooperate with others to resettle Iraqis facing great personal risk; and we will work with the Iraqi government over time to resettle refugees and displaced Iraqis within Iraq – because there are few more powerful indicators of lasting peace than displaced citizens returning home.

Now, before I go any further, I want to take a moment to speak directly to the people of Iraq.

You are a great nation, rooted in the cradle of civilization. You are joined together by enduring accomplishments, and a history that connects you as surely as the two rivers carved into your land. In years past, you have persevered through tyranny and terror; through personal insecurity and sectarian violence. And instead of giving in to the forces of disunion, you stepped back from a descent into civil war, and showed a proud resilience that deserves respect.

Our nations have known difficult times together. But ours is a bond forged by shared bloodshed, and countless friendships among our people. We Americans have offered our most precious resource – our young men and women – to work with you to rebuild what was destroyed by despotism; to root out our common enemies; and to seek peace and prosperity for our children and grand-children, and for yours.

There are those who will try to prevent that future for Iraq – who will insist that Iraq's differences cannot be reconciled without more killing. They represent the forces that destroy nations and lead only to despair, and they will test our will in the months and years to come. America, too, has known these forces. We endured the pain of Civil War, and bitter divisions of region and race. But hostility and hatred are no match for justice; they offer no pathway to peace; and they must not stand between the people of Iraq and a future of reconciliation and hope.

So to the Iraqi people, let me be clear about America's intentions. The United States pursues no claim on your territory or your resources. We respect your sovereignty and the tremendous sacrifices you have made for your country. We seek a full transition to Iraqi responsibility for the security of your country. And going forward, we can build a lasting relationship founded upon mutual interests and mutual respect as Iraq takes its rightful place in the community of nations.

That leads me to the third part of our strategy – comprehensive American engagement across the region.

The future of Iraq is inseparable from the future of the broader Middle East, so we must work with our friends and partners to establish a new framework that advances Iraq's security and the region's. It is time for Iraq to be a full partner in a regional dialogue, and for Iraq's neighbors to establish productive and normalized relations with Iraq. And going forward, the United States will pursue principled and sustained engagement with all of the nations in the region, and that will include Iran and Syria.

This reflects a fundamental truth: we can no longer deal with regional challenges in isolation – we need a smarter, more sustainable and comprehensive approach. That is why we are renewing our diplomacy, while relieving the burden on our military. That is why we are refocusing on al Qaeda in Afghanistan and Pakistan; developing a strategy to use all elements of American power to prevent Iran from developing a nuclear weapon; and actively seeking a lasting peace between Israel and the Arab world. And that is why we have named three of America's most accomplished diplomats – George Mitchell, Dennis Ross and Richard Holbrooke – to support Secretary Clinton and me as we carry forward this agenda.

Every nation and every group must know – whether you wish America good or ill – that the end of the war in Iraq will enable a new era of American leadership and engagement in the Middle East. And that era has just begun.

Finally, I want to be very clear that my strategy for ending the war in Iraq does not end with military plans or diplomatic agendas – it endures through our commitment to uphold our sacred trust with every man and woman who has served in Iraq.

You make up a fraction of the American population, but in an age when so many people and institutions have acted irresponsibly, you did the opposite – you volunteered to bear the heaviest burden. And for you and for your families, the war does not end when you come home. It lives on in memories of your fellow soldiers, sailors, airmen and Marines who gave their lives. It endures in the wound that is slow to heal, the disability that isn't going away, the dream that wakes you at night, or the stiffening in your spine when a car backfires down the street.

You and your families have done your duty – now a grateful nation must do ours. That is why I am increasing the number of soldiers and Marines, so that we lessen the burden on those who are serving. And that is why I have committed to expanding our system of veterans health care to serve more patients, and to provide better care in more places. We will continue building new wounded warrior facilities across America, and invest in new ways of identifying and treating the signature wounds of this war: Post-Traumatic Stress Disorder and Traumatic Brain Injury, as well as other combat injuries.

We also know that service does not end with the person wearing the uniform. In her visits with military families across the country, my wife Michelle has learned firsthand about the unique burden that your families endure every day. I want you to know this: military families are a top priority for Michelle and me, and they will be a top priority for my administration. We'll raise military pay, and continue providing quality child-care, job-training for spouses, and expanded counseling and outreach to families that have known the separation and stress of war. We will also heed the lesson of history – that those who fight in battle can form the backbone of our middle class – by implementing a 21st century GI Bill to help our veterans live their dreams.

As a nation, we have had our share of debates about the war in Iraq. It has, at times, divided us as a people. To this very day, there are some Americans who want to stay in Iraq longer, and some who want to leave faster. But there should be no disagreement on what the men and women of our military have achieved.

And so I want to be very clear: We sent our troops to Iraq to do away with Saddam Hussein's regime – and you got the job done. We kept our troops in Iraq to help establish a sovereign government – and you got the job done. And we will leave the Iraqi people with a hard-earned opportunity to live a better life – that is your achievement; that is the prospect that you have made possible.

There are many lessons to be learned from what we've experienced. We have learned that America must go to war with clearly defined goals, which is why I've ordered a review of our policy in Afghanistan. We have learned that we must always weigh the costs of action, and communicate those costs candidly to the American people, which is why I've put Iraq and Afghanistan into my budget. We have learned that in the 21st century, we must use all elements of American power to achieve our objectives, which is why I am committed to building our civilian national security capacity so that the burden is not continually pushed on to our military. We have learned that our political leaders must pursue the broad and bipartisan support that our national security policies depend upon, which is why I will consult with Congress and in carrying out my plans. And we have learned the importance of working closely with friends and allies, which is why we are launching a new era of engagement in the world.

The starting point for our policies must always be the safety of the American people. I know that you – the men and women of the finest fighting force in the history of the world – can meet any challenge, and defeat any foe. And as long as I am your Commander-in-Chief, I promise you that I will only send you into harm's way when it is absolutely necessary, and provide you with the equipment and support you need to get the job done. That is the most important lesson of all – for the consequences of war are dire, the sacrifices immeasurable.

You know because you have seen those sacrifices. You have lived them. And we all honor them.

"Semper Fidelis" – it means always being faithful to Corps, and to country, and to the memory of fallen comrades like Corporal Jonathan Yale and Lance Corporal Jordan Haerter. These young men enlisted in a time of war, knowing they would face great danger. They came here, to Camp Lejeune, as they trained for their mission. And last April, they were standing guard in Anbar. In an age when suicide is a weapon, they were suddenly faced with an oncoming truck filled with explosives. These two Marines stood their ground. These two Marines opened fire. And these two Marines stopped that truck. When the thousands of pounds of explosives detonated, they had saved fifty Marines and Iraqi police who would have been in the truck's path, but Corporal Yale and Lance Corporal Haerter lost their own lives. Jonathan was 21. Jordan was 19. In the town where Jordan Haerter was from, a bridge was dedicated in his name. One Marine who traveled to the ceremony said: "We flew here from all over the country to pay tribute to our friend Jordan, who risked his life to save us. We wouldn't be here without him."

America's time in Iraq is filled with stories of men and women like this. Their names are written into bridges and town squares. They are etched into stones at Arlington, and in quiet places of rest across our land. They are spoken in schools and on city blocks. They live on in the memories of those who wear your uniform, in the hearts of those they loved, and in the freedom of the nation they served.

Each American who has served in Iraq has their own story. Each of you has your own story. And that story is now a part of the history of the United States of America – a nation that exists only because free men and women have bled for it from the beaches of Normandy to the deserts of Anbar; from the mountains of Korea to the streets of Kandahar. You teach us that the price of freedom is great. Your sacrifice should challenge all of us – every single American – to ask what we can do to be better citizens.

There will be more danger in the months ahead. We will face new tests and unforeseen trials. But thanks to the sacrifices of those who have served, we have forged hard-earned progress, we are leaving Iraq to its people, and we have begun the work of ending this war.

Thank you, God Bless you, and God Bless the United States of America. Semper Fi.

QUESTIONS TO CONSIDER

1 What was the major topic of President Obama's remarks at Camp Lejeune?
2 What were the remaining U.S. goals in Iraq? How would they be accomplished?
3 Who was now responsible for Iraq's future?
4 When did the U.S. combat mission in Iraq end?
5 Why were U.S. troops sent to Iraq? Why did they stay for eight years?

———————— **Document 6-C** ————————

Excerpts from the Obama administration's National Security Strategy, May 2010

Time and again in our Nation's history, Americans have risen to meet – and to shape – moments of transition. This must be one of those moments. We live in a time of sweeping change. The success of free nations, open markets, and social progress in recent decades has accelerated globalization on an unprecedented scale. This had opened the doors for opportunity around the globe, extended democracy to hundreds of millions of people, and made peace possible among the major powers. Yet globalization has also intensified the dangers we face – from international terrorism and the spread of deadly technologies, to economic upheaval and a changing climate.

For nearly a decade, our Nation has been at war with a far-reaching network of violence and hatred. Even as we end one war in Iraq, our military has been called upon to renew our focus on Afghanistan as part of a commitment to disrupt, dismantle, and defeat al-Qa'ida and its affiliates. This is part of a broad, multinational effort that is right and just, we will be unwavering in our commitment to the security of our people, allies, and partners. Moreover, as we face multiple threats – from nations, nonstate actors, and failed states – we will maintain the military superiority that has secured our country, and underpinned global security, for decades.

. . . As we secure the world's most dangerous weapons, we are fighting a war against a far-reaching network of hatred and violence. We will disrupt, dismantle, and defeat al-Qa'ida and its affiliates through a comprehensive strategy that denies them safe haven, strengthens front-line partners, secures our homeland, pursues justice through durable legal approaches, and counters a bankrupt agenda of extremism and murder with an agenda of hope and opportunity. The frontline of this fight is Afghanistan and Pakistan, where we are applying relentless pressure on al-Qa'ida, breaking the Taliban's momentum, and strengthening the security and capacity of our partners. In this effort, our troops are again demonstrating their extraordinary service, making great sacrifices in a time of danger, and they have our full support . . .

. . . Afghanistan and Pakistan: This is the epicenter of the violent extremism practiced by al Qa'ida. The danger from this region will only grow if its security slides backward, the Taliban controls large swaths of Afghanistan, and al-Qa'ida is allowed to operate with impunity. To prevent future attacks on the United States, our allies, and partners, we must work with others to keep the pressure on al-Qa'ida and increase the security and capacity of our partners in this region. In Afghanistan, we must deny al-Qa'ida a safe haven, deny the Taliban the ability to overthrow the government, and strengthen the capacity of Afghanistan's security forces and government so that they can take lead responsibility for Afghanistan's future. Within Pakistan, we are working with the government to address the local, regional, and global threat from violent extremists . . .

QUESTIONS TO CONSIDER

1 What was the source of threats faced by the United States in its global war on terror?
2 How would the U.S. defeat al-Qaeda? How would the Obama administration prevent future attacks on the United States?
3 What were U.S. goals in Afghanistan?

Document 6-D

U.S. State Department, Bureau of Democracy, Human Rights, and Labor, excerpts from Annual Human Rights Report, Iraq–2011

EXECUTIVE SUMMARY

Iraq is a constitutional parliamentary republic. Prime Minister Nouri Kamal al-Maliki was sworn in following free and fair elections in March 2010, once the major political parties reached a power-sharing agreement that allowed the government to be seated in December 2010. While the government is inclusive of all major political parties, significant unresolved issues continued to hamper its operation as permanent ministers of defense and interior had yet to be appointed at year's end.

However, during the year, the role of the Council of Representatives (COR) and provincial governments increased. Iraqi Security Forces (ISF) reported to civilian authorities, but continuing violence, corruption, and organizational dysfunction undermined the government's protection of human rights.

During the year the most significant human rights developments were continuing abuses by sectarian and ethnic armed groups and violations by government affiliated forces. Divisions between Shia and Sunni and between Arab and Kurd empowered sectarian militant organizations. These militants, purporting to defend one group through acts of intimidation and revenge against another, influenced political outcomes. Terrorist attacks designed to weaken the government and deepen societal divisions occurred during the year.

The three most important human rights problems in the country were governmental and societal violence reflecting a precarious security situation, a fractionalized population mirroring deep divisions exacerbated by Saddam Hussein's legacy, and rampant corruption at all levels of government and society. During the year the following significant human rights problems were also reported: arbitrary or unlawful deprivation of life; extremist and terrorist bombings and executions; disappearances; torture and other cruel, inhuman, or degrading treatment or punishment; poor conditions in pretrial detention and prison facilities; arbitrary arrest and detention; denial of fair public trials; delays in resolving property restitution claims; insufficient judicial institutional capacity; arbitrary interference with privacy and home; limits on freedoms of speech, press, and assembly; extremist threats and violence; limits on religious freedom due to extremist threats and violence; restrictions on freedom of movement; large numbers of internally displaced persons (IDPs) and refugees; lack of transparency and significant constraints on international organizations and nongovernmental organizations' (NGOs) investigations of alleged violations of human rights; discrimination against and societal abuses of women and ethnic, religious, and racial minorities; trafficking in persons; societal discrimination and violence against individuals based on sexual orientation and gender identity; and limited exercise of labor rights.

A culture of impunity has largely protected members of the security services, as well as those elsewhere in the government, from investigation and successful prosecution of human rights violations.

Terrorist groups such as al-Qaida in Iraq committed attacks against a wide swath of society, including Sunnis, Shia, and members of other sects or ethnicities, security forces, places of worship, religious pilgrims, economic infrastructure, and government officials. Their means were suicide bombings, attacks with improvised explosive devices, drive-by shootings, and other acts of violence aimed at weakening the government and deepening ethno-sectarian divisions. Certain militant organizations, such as those influenced by Iran, also committed numerous terrorist attacks, primarily against foreign embassies and foreign military forces.

QUESTIONS TO CONSIDER

1   Why were there continued human rights problems in Iraq following the March 2010 elections?
2   What were the continuing human rights abuses?
3   What are the three most pressing human rights problems in Iraq? How will these problems be solved?
4   Why has a culture of impunity developed around Iraqi security forces and some in the government?

─────────── **Document 6-E** ───────────

Speech at the White House by Prime Minister al-Maliki, December 21, 2011, Radio Free Iraq

A positive atmosphere that prevailed among us, and for the obligations, the common obligations, of ending the war, and the commitment to which the American forces will withdraw from Iraq, which is a withdrawal that affects – that indicates success, and not like others have said that it was negative, but the goals that we established were achieved.

Iraq had a political process established, a democratic process, and adoption of the principles of elections and the transfer – peaceful transfer of authority. Iraq is following a policy, a foreign policy, which does not intervene in the affairs of others and does not allow the others to intervene in its own affairs. Iraq is looking for common grounds with the others, and establishes its interest at the forefront and the interest of the others, which it is concerned about, like from any confusion.

Your Excellency, today we meet in Washington after we have completed the first page of a constructive cooperation in which we also thank you and appreciate you for your commitment to everything that you have committed yourself to. And anyone who observes the nature of the relationship between the two countries will say that the relationship will not end with the departure of the last American soldier. It only started when we signed in 2008, in addition to the withdrawal treaty, the Strategic Framework Agreement for the relationship between our two countries.

And because we have proven success in the first mission, a very unique success – nobody imagined that we would succeed in defeating terrorism and the al Qaeda – we must also establish the necessary steps in order to succeed in our second stage, which is the dual relationship under the Strategic Framework Agreement, in the economic sphere, as well as in educational and commercial and cultural and judicial and security cooperation fields.

Iraq now has become – reliant completely on its own security apparatus and internal security as a result of the expertise that it gained during the confrontations and the training and the equipping. But it remains in need of cooperation with the United States of America in security issues and information and combating terrorism, and in the area of training and the area of equipping, which is needed by the Iraqi army. And we have started that. And we want to complete the process of equipping the Iraqi army in order to protect our sovereignty, and does not violate the rights of anybody – or do not take any missions that sovereignty of others.

Today, the joint mission is to establish the mechanisms and the commitments that will expedite our – we have reached an agreement, and we have held a meeting for the higher joint committee under the chairmanship of Mr. Biden, the Vice President, and myself in Baghdad, and we spoke about all the details that would put the framework agreement into implementation.

And here we talked about it and its activation. And there will be other discussions and other meetings with the higher committee here in Washington in order to put the final touches regarding the necessary mechanisms for cooperation and achieving the common vision that we followed, which was based on our common wills and political independent decision, and the desire to respect the sovereignty of each other.

And we feel that we need political cooperation as well, in addition to cooperating in the security and economic and commercial fields. We need a political cooperation, particularly with regard to the matters that are common and are of concern for us as two parties that want to cooperate.

The common vision that we used as a point of departure we have confirmed today. And I am very happy, every time we meet with the American side, I find determination and a strong will to activate the Strategic Framework Agreement. And I will say, frankly, this is necessary and it serves the interests of Iraq, as it is necessary and serves the interests of the United States of America.

This makes us feel that we will succeed with the same commitment, common commitment that we had in combating terrorism and accomplishing the missions, the basis of which Iraq was independent. Iraq today has a lot of wealth and it needs experience and expertise, and American and foreign expertise to help Iraq exploiting its own wealth in an ideal way. Iraq is still suffering from a shortage of resources, and we have established a strategy to increase the Iraqi wealth. And we hope that the American companies will have the largest role in increasing our wealth in the area of oil and other aspects as well.

Iraq wants to rebuild all these sectors that were harmed because of the war and because of the adventurous policies that were used by the former regime, and we need a wide range of reform in the area of education.

We have succeeded in signing several agreements through the educational initiative, which put hundreds of our college graduates to continue their graduate studies and specialized subject in American universities. And I am putting it before everyone who is watching the relationship between the U.S. and Iraq. It is a very – it has very high aspirations.

And I would like to renew my thanks for His Excellency the President for giving me this opportunity, and I wish him more success, God willing. Thank you very much.

QUESTIONS TO CONSIDER

1   What did Prime Minister al-Maliki say about Iraq's relationship with the United States? How would that relationship change following the American troop withdrawal?
2   What must Iraq do to have a peaceful future? Where would most of the burden fall to ensure this outcome?
3   How would Iraq's economy be developed? Who would help develop it? What industries were most promising?
4   How will Iraq conduct its foreign affairs in the future?

Epilogue: The Future

The Obama administration's long-term goals in Iraq were to align the country with other Arab states in a region-wide diplomatic and economic framework that downplayed sectarianism and increased Iraq's membership in a regional order. With State Department advice, the Maliki government increased new foreign investment, especially from Kuwait, Qatar, and the United Arab Emirates, Saudi Arabia, Europe, and, of course, the United States. While most investments went into the oil industry, there was also significant investment in Iraq's infrastructure, including a $13 billion new port for the southern city of Basra. "This is an extraordinarily undercapitalized society," said Todd Schwartz, an economic advisor at the U.S. embassy in Baghdad.[1] Housing demands also created investment opportunities, and Baghdad moved quickly to capture investment for projects. When Maliki attacked the Shiite militias in the spring of 2008 and again in 2011, there was considerable optimism in the Obama administration that economic diplomacy had worked. Iraq's new relationship with its predominantly Sunni neighbors defied Iran's goals of seeing theocratic states develop in the region, and this was precisely why the Obama administration embraced this philosophy.

Secretary of State Hillary Clinton spearheaded the effort to reorient American power in Iraq. She supervised a decided shift in U.S. priorities that began in August 2010 when the Obama administration ended the combat phase of American operations in Iraq. The administration, in an effort to emphasize the change, replaced Operation Iraqi Freedom with Operation New Dawn. Clinton made clear that the United States was not

The United States and Iraq Since 1990: A Brief History with Documents,
First Edition. Edited by Robert K. Brigham.
© 2014 Robert K. Brigham. Published 2014 by Blackwell Publishing Ltd.

going to abandon Iraq. She welcomed the State Department's new role and she vowed that the United States remained committed to Iraq. "As we open this new chapter in a relationship with a sovereign Iraq, to the Iraqis we say: America is with you as you take your next steps in your journey to secure your democracy," Clinton told reporters in Dushanbe, Tajikistan. "And to the countries in the region, especially Iraq's neighbors, we want to emphasize that America will stand with our allies and friends, including Iraq, in defense of our security and interests."[2]

Indeed, the State Department's presence in Iraq increased dramatically following the troop withdrawal. Congress approved funding for an expanded State Department role in Iraq, including hundreds more employees and a stepped-up diplomatic presence outside of Baghdad. The State Department established two permanent consulates and three temporary "provincial development teams" (PDTs) to help improve relations between the central government and the Kurds in the north. Included in the creation of the PDTs were funds to provide for their security. In fact, security remained a primary concern in Iraq, and the State Department took on new responsibilities in this area too.

In an unprecedented experiment, the State Department contracted with non-governmental experts to carry out several functions usually beyond its purview. Used to negotiations and diplomatic maneuvers, Clinton's State Department became more active in Iraq. It supervised its own air operations, security missions, and military training of Iraqi personnel. As one commentator put it at the time, "This is no longer just the foreign service officer standing in the canapé line, and the military out in the field."[3] Indeed, the State Department moved quickly to establish its own air operations, dubbed Embassy Air Iraq, which "has 19 aircraft based in Baghdad, will be expanded to as many as 46 aircraft, including helicopters and fixed-wing planes." [4] The State Department claimed that it needed the aircraft for "quick reaction force movement, search and rescue, medical and casualty evacuation, and route reconnaissance and convoy escort," functions usually served by the military.[5] State Department contractors, some 5,000 of them, helped fly aircraft, and provided security and operated surveillance systems. They helped train Iraqi Security Forces and the national police. For more specific needs, the Iraqi military received training from U.S. armed services personnel out of the country.

Some members of Congress balked at the new State Department role in Iraq. "The fact that we are transitioning from one poorly managed contracting effort to another part of the federal government that has not excelled at this function either is not particularly comforting," complained Senator Claire McCaskill (D-Missouri).[6] It made no sense to have contracted civilians performing military functions inside Iraq, McCaskill concluded; that was a job for the U.S. military. There were other problems with the State

Department's expanded responsibilities in Iraq, including its failed attempts in Congress to increase its budget. When originally planning the transition, the State Department had counted on two additional consulates in Kirkuk and Mosul in the north to aid the PDTs. Funding for these never material-ized. Funding problems also plagued a massive State Department program for training Iraq's national police. The State Department never carried its case to Congress, and as a result its efforts in Iraq during the important transition period remained understaffed and underfunded.

The withdrawal of American troops and the State Department's new security role in Iraq led many ordinary Iraqis to wonder if the Obama administration was merely creating a decent interval between the U.S. departure and the return of civil war. "It is the end for the Americans only," suggested an Iraqi reporter watching U.S. troops leave Iraq forever in December 2011. "Nobody knows if the war will end for Iraqis, too."[7]

Frustrated Americans matched frustrated Iraqis. For eight long years the United States went to war in Iraq hoping that a uniquely American story would emerge. The United States would liberate a country that had been dominated by a tyrant as it also spread democracy throughout the Middle East. Iraq was to be the first of many democratic governments established by the transformative power of American foreign policy. U.S. nation-building experts would use the modernization techniques that had helped the United States prevail in the Cold War, Washington officials believed, and this would lead Iraq to a happy future. The belief in science, technology, and expertise to solve complicated social, cultural, and political problems in Iraq was part of the creed of U.S. policymakers from Eisenhower to Obama. Despite overwhelming odds against success in a land that U.S. policymakers knew little about, successive presidential administrations tried desperately to influence events in Iraq. What is truly remarkable about the wars for Iraq is that the apparent failure to alter Iraqi outlook and policies never stopped U.S. policymakers from believing that they could transform Iraq. U.S. officials continued to overstate American potential influence in Iraq, even after the U.S. troop withdrawal. U.S. policymakers have been slow to realize that there are incredible limits on American power.

Nevertheless, Americans celebrated the end of the war in official ceremo-nies in Iraq and in the United States. In Baghdad, General Lloyd J. Austin III, the sixth and last of the U.S. generals to command American forces in Iraq, declared that "the Iraqi people have unprecedented opportunities." Thanks to the sacrifice of so many American troops, "they have the oppor-tunity to make their voices heard through a democratically elected government, the opportunity to live in a peaceful environment."[8] At the Baghdad airport, Obama's new defense secretary, Leon Panetta, declared the official end to the Iraq War, stating, "After a lot of blood spilled by Iraqis and Americans, the mission of an Iraq that could govern itself has become real. To be sure, the cost was high – in blood and treasure for the United States and the Iraqi people. Those lives were not lost in vain."[9] President Obama greeted returning U.S. troops at a ceremony at Fort Bragg, North Carolina, marking the fulfillment of a campaign promise and President Bush's Status of Force Agreement to bring all U.S. forces home from Iraq after nearly nine years of conflict. "So as your commander in chief, on behalf of a grateful nation, I'm proud to finally say these two words – and I know your families agree, Welcome home. Welcome home. Welcome home."[10]

Notes

1   *USA Today*, September 10, 2008.
2   *Commentary*, October 23, 2011.
3   McClatchy Newspapers, November 24, 2010.
4   *Washington Post*, June 3, 2011.
5   Ibid.
6   McClatchy Newspapers, November 24, 2010.
7   *New York Times*, December 15, 2011.
8   *Washington Post*, December 15, 2011.
9   Ibid.
10 *Los Angeles Times*, December 14, 2011.

List of Documents

The United States and Iraq Since 1990: A Brief History with Documents, First Edition. Edited by Robert K. Brigham.
© 2014 Robert K. Brigham. Published 2014 by Blackwell Publishing Ltd.

Baghdad, Iraq, May 16, 2003, at: http://www.unhcr.org/refworld/docid/468d097d2.html, accessed January 7, 2013.

Document 4-E, Excerpts from the Constitution of Iraq, October 2005, Iraqi News Agency, as translated by the United Nations Human Rights Commission, at: http://www.unhcr.org/refworld/type,LEGISLATION,,IRQ, 454f50804,0.html, accessed January 7, 2013.

Document 4-F, Excerpts from "National Strategy for Victory in Iraq," National Security Council, November 30, 2005, the White House, Washington, D.C.

Document 5-A, Excerpts from the *Iraq Study Group Report*, December 6, 2006, as presented online by the United States Institute of Peace, a government co-sponsor (with the U.S. Congress) of the report, at: http://www.usip.org/iraq-study-group/the-isg-report, accessed January 14, 2013.

Document 5-B, Fred Kagan, "Choosing Victory," January 5, 2007, as presented by the American Enterprise Institute, a non-profit think tank in Washington, D.C., at: http://www.aei.org/papers/foreign-and-defense-policy/regional/middle-east-and-north-africa/choosing-victory-a-plan-for-success-in-iraq-paper/, accessed January 7, 2013.

Document 5-C, Excerpts from U.S. *Army/Marine Corps Counterinsurgency Field Manual*, U.S. Department of Defense (Washington, D.C.: Government Printing Office, 2006), pp. 51–52, at: http://www.fas.org/irp/doddir/army/fm3-24.pdf, accessed January 7, 2013.

Document 5-D, Excerpts from "Iraq First: The National Security Strategy of Iraq," October 25, 2007, Republic of Iraq – the Cabinet, as translated and printed by the U.S. Department of State, Washington, D.C. (Washington, D.C.: Government Printing Office, 2007).

Document 5-E, Excerpts from President George W. Bush's speech to the nation on the Iraq War, January 10, 2007, the White House, Washington, D.C., at: http://www.presidentialrhetoric.com/speeches/01.10.07.html, accessed January 7, 2013.

Document 5-F, Excerpts from Senator Barack Obama's speech before the Chicago Council on Global Affairs, April 23, 2007, Chicago, Illinois, at: https://my.barackobama.com/page/content/fpccga/, accessed January 7, 2013.

Document 6-A, Status of Forces Agreement, 2008, the White House, Washington, D.C., at: http://georgewbush-whitehouse.archives.gov/news/releases/2008/12/20081214-2.html, accessed January 7, 2013.

Document 6-B, Transcript of President Obama's remarks, Camp Lejeune, North Carolina, February 27, 2009, the White House, Washington, D.C., at: http://www.whitehouse.gov/the_press_office/Remarks-of-President-Barack-Obama-Responsibly-Ending-the-War-in-Iraq, accessed January 7, 2013.

Suggestions for
Additional Reading

For Iraq's rich history, please see: Thabit Abdullah, *A Short History of Iraq* (London: Pearson Longman, 2003); Toby Dodge, *Inventing Iraq: The Failure of Nation Building and a History Denied* (New York: Columbia University Press, 2003); Hanna Batatu, *The Old Social Classes and Revolutionary Movements of Iraq: A Study of Iraq's Old Landed and Commercial Classes and of its Communists, Ba'athists, and Free Officers* (Princeton: Princeton University Press, 1978); Robert Fernea and Wm. Roger Louis, eds., *The Iraqi Revolution of 1958* (London: I.B. Tauris, 1991); David Fromkin, *A Peace to End All Peace* (New York: Penguin, 1991); Jane Hathaway, *The Arab Lands under Ottoman Rule* (Harlow: Pearson, 2008); Majid Khadduri, *Republican Iraq* (Oxford: Oxford University Press, 1969); Phebe Marr, *The Modern History of Iraq* (Boulder, CO: Westview Press, 1985); Helmut Mejcher, *Imperial Quest for Oil* (London: Ithaca Press, 1976); Geoff Simons, *Iraq: From Sumer to Saddam* (New York: St. Martin's, 1994); and Adeed Dawisha, *Iraq: A Political History from Independence to Occupation* (Princeton: Princeton University Press, 2009.)

For general histories on U.S. relations with Iraq and the region, please see: Lawrence Freedman, *A Choice of Enemies: America Confronts the Middle East* (New York: PublicAffairs, 2008); Peter Hahn, *Mission Accomplished? The United States and Iraq since World War I* (New York: Oxford University Press, 2012); Burton Kaufman, *The Arab Middle East and the United States* (New York: Twayne, 1996); Douglas Little, *American Orientalism* (Chapel Hill: University of North Carolina Press, 2004); David Malone, *The International Struggle over Iraq* (Oxford: Oxford University

The United States and Iraq Since 1990: A Brief History with Documents, First Edition. Edited by Robert K. Brigham.
© 2014 Robert K. Brigham. Published 2014 by Blackwell Publishing Ltd.

Press, 2006); Michael Oren, *Faith and Fantasy: America is the Middle East* (New York: Norton, 2007); and Michael Palmer, *Guardians of the Gulf: A History of America's Expanding Role in the Persian Gulf, 1883–1992* (New York: Free Press, 1992).

There are several noteworthy histories of U.S. diplomatic relations with Iraq before the First Gulf War, including Peter Hahn, *Crisis and Crossfire* (Washington, D.C.: Potomac Books, 2005); Bruce Jentleson, *With Friends Like These: Reagan, Bush, and Saddam, 1982–1990* (New York: Norton, 1994); and Salim Yaqub, *Containing Arab Nationalism* (Chapel Hill: University of North Carolina Press, 2004).

The best analysis of the First Gulf War remains Lawrence Freedman and Efraim Karsh, *The Gulf Conflict, 1990–1991: Diplomacy and War in the New World Order* (Princeton: Princeton University Press, 1993). Other useful studies include: Anthony Cordesman and Abraham Wagner, *The Lessons of Modern War: The Gulf War* (Boulder, CO: Westview Press, 1996); Michael Gordon and General Bernard Trainor, *The Generals' War: The Inside Story of the Conflict in the Gulf* (Boston: Back Bay Books, 1995); and David Halberstam, *Bush, Clinton, and the Generals* (New York: Scribner, 2001).

On public opinion and the wars for Iraq, please see Ole Holsti, *American Public Opinion on the Iraq War* (Ann Arbor: University of Michigan Press, 2011).

The best single volume on the search for weapons of mass destruction in Iraq remains Hans Blix, *Disarming Iraq: The Search for Weapons of Mass Destruction* (London: Bloomsbury, 2004). Another useful study is Richard Butler, *Saddam Defiant: The Threat of Mass Destruction and the Crisis of Global Security* (London: Weidenfeld & Nicolson, 2000). Avigdor Haselkorn's *The Continuing Storm: Iraq, Poisonous Weapons, and Deterrence* (New Haven: Yale University Press, 1999) is a fascinating study.

An indispensable guide for the economic cost of the wars against Iraq is Joseph Stiglitz and Linda Bilmes, *The Three Trillion Dollar War* (New York: Norton, 2008). For the human costs, please see Joy Gordon, *Invisible War: The United States and the Iraq Sanctions* (Cambridge, MA: Harvard University Press, 2010), and Anthony Shadid, *Night Draws Near: Iraq's People in the Shadows of America's War* (New York: Henry Holt, 2005).

For the Bush administration and its decision to launch preemptive strikes against Iraq, please consult: James Fallows, *Blind into Baghdad: America's War in Iraq* (New York: Vintage, 2006); Peter Galbraith, *The End of Iraq: How American Incompetence Created a War without End* (New York: Simon & Schuster, 2006); Lloyd Gardner, *The Long Road to Baghdad: A History of U.S. Foreign Policy from the 1970s to the Present* (New York: The New Press, 2008); Richard Haass, *War of Necessity, War of Choice: A Memoir of Two Iraq Wars* (New York: Simon & Schuster, 2009); Robert

Kaufman, *In Defense of the Bush Doctrine* (Lexington: University of Kentucky Press, 2007); James Mann, *Rise of the Vulcans: The History of Bush's War Cabinet* (New York: Viking, 2004); George Packer, *The Assassin's Gate: America in Iraq* (New York: Farrar, Straus, & Giroux, 2005); John Prados, *Hoodwinked: The Documents That Reveal How Bush Sold Us a War* (New York: The New Press, 2004); and Bob Woodward's trilogy, *Bush at War* (New York: Simon & Schuster, 2002); *Plan of Attack* (New York: Simon & Schuster, 2004); and *A State of Denial* (New York: Simon & Schuster, 2006).

For comparisons between Iraq and Vietnam, please see Robert K. Brigham, *Iraq, Vietnam, and the Limits of American Power* (New York: PublicAffairs, 2008); John Dumbrell and David Ryan, *Vietnam in Iraq* (London: Routledge, 2007); and Lloyd Gardner and Marilyn Young, eds., *Iraq and the Lessons of Vietnam* (New York: The New Press, 2007).

Tom Ricks has written several useful military histories of the wars for Iraq, including *Fiasco: The American Military Adventure in Iraq* (New York: Penguin, 2006) and *The Gamble: General David Petraeus and the American Military Adventure in Iraq, 2006–2008* (New York: Penguin, 2009). Michael Gordon and General Bernard Trainor's *Cobra II: The Inside Story of the Invasion and Occupation of Iraq* (New York: Vintage, 2006) is also of great interest.

Paul Bremer's *My Year in Iraq: The Struggle to Build a Future of Hope* (New York: Threshold Editions, 2006) and Richard Clarke's *Against All Enemies: Inside America's War on Terror* (New York: Free Press, 2004) are limited but useful memoirs.

The difficulties of nation-building in Iraq have been the subject of several interesting studies, including Ali Allawi, *The Occupation of Iraq: Winning the War, Losing the Peace* (New Haven: Yale University Press, 2007) and Rajiv Chandrasekaran, *Imperial Life in the Emerald City* (New York: Alfred A. Knopf, 2006).

Bob Woodward's *Obama's Wars* (New York: Simon & Schuster, 2010) is a good overview of the Obama administration's Iraq War policies.

Index

Arabic names are listed under the last name (e.g. Bakr, Ahmad Hasan al-); military operations are listed by name (Desert Fox *not* Operation Desert Fox).

The United States and Iraq Since 1990: A Brief History with Documents, First Edition. Edited by Robert K. Brigham.
© 2014 Robert K. Brigham. Published 2014 by Blackwell Publishing Ltd.

WILEY

Packing

For Customer Service Call: (800) 225-5945

ISBN		Description
1405198990	9781405198998	UNITED STATES AND IRAQ SINCE 1990

Total Quantity Shipped:

Carrier: UPS Ground
 PRO#:

Freight ter

slip

LIBERAL ARTS
T
MA   01247-4124

CAL SCI/PUBLIC POLICY

Purchase Order Number	
R BENCE	

Invoice #	Shipment #	Date
7111091	11404307111091	04/30/2014

Send Product Returns to:
  WILEY RETURNS
  380 FREIGHT STREET
  CAMP HILL, PA   17011

Qty	List Price	Disc.	Net Price	Ext Net Price
1	.00		.00	.00

1   .00

: PREPAID

# of Cartons: 1
Total Weight: 1.14

30952	005	0W2	286842	**002**	ATT 2802	